Knowledge-Based Systems
Analysis and Design

BCS Practitioner Series

Series editor: Ray Welland

Knowledge-Based Systems Analysis and Design

A KADS Developer's Handbook

D.S.W. Tansley
and C.C. Hayball
Software & Systems Engineering,
Advanced Technology Centre,
BNR Europe Limited

Prentice Hall

New York   London   Toronto   Sydney   Tokyo   Singapore

First published in 1993 by
Prentice Hall International (UK) Limited
Campus 400, Maylands Avenue
Hemel Hempstead
Hertfordshire, HP2 7EZ
A division of
Simon & Schuster International Group

Typeset in 10/13 pt Times
by Columns Design and Production Services Ltd, Reading

Printed and bound in Great Britain by
Redwood Books, Trowbridge, Wiltshire

Library of Congress Cataloging-in-Publication Data is available from the publisher

British Library Cataloguing in Publication Data

A catalogue record for this book is available from
the British Library

ISBN 0–13–515479–0

1 2 3 4 5   97 96 95 94 93

Contents

Editorial preface

The aim of the BCS Practitioner Series is to produce books which are relevant for practising computer professionals across the whole spectrum of Information Technology activities. We want to encourage practitioners to share their practical experience of methods and applications with fellow professionals. We also seek to disseminate information in a form which is suitable for the practitioner who often has only limited time to read widely within a new subject area or to assimilate research findings.

The role of the BCS is to provide advice on the suitability of books for the Series, via the Editorial Panel, and to provide a pool of potential authors upon which we can draw. Our objective is that this Series will reinforce the drive within the BCS to increase professional standards in IT. The other partners in this venture, Prentice Hall, provide the publishing expertise and international marketing capabilities of a leading publisher in the computing field.

The response when we set up the Series was extremely encouraging. However, the success of the Series depends on there being practitioners who want to learn as well as those who feel they have something to offer! The Series is under continual development and we are always looking for ideas for new topics and feedback on how to further improve the usefulness of the Series. If you are interested in writing for the Series then please contact us.

Knowledge-based systems have now moved out of the research environment to become part of mainstream software development. As the discipline has 'come of age' the need for sound development methods has become apparent. This is a comprehensive book describing the KADS methodology for the practitioner who needs a structured way of developing knowledge-based systems. It provides both a tutorial and a reference manual, together with comprehensive guidance for the system developer.

Ray Welland
Computing Science Department, University of Glasgow

Editorial Panel Members
Frank Bott (UCW, Aberystwyth), Dermot Browne (KPMG), Nic Holt (ICL), Trevor King (Praxis Systems Plc), Tom Lake (GLOSSA), Kathy Spurr (Analysis and Design Consultants), Mario Wolczko (University of Manchester)

Preface

KADS in context

At the time of writing, in the early 1990s, the heady days of extraordinary interest and investment in the branch of Artificial Intelligence known as Knowledge-Based (or expert) Systems (KBSs) seem long gone. However, after the fog of hyperbole has dispersed, we are now seeing knowledge-based technology steadily become an accepted part of the software developer's technology toolkit.

Unfortunately, to date, the development of KBSs has been characterized by ill-structured techniques, usually based on evolutionary prototyping. Such an approach has caused difficulties for project control and management during development, and longer-term problems in the maintenance or enhancement phase once in use.

Today, software developers in commercial and industrial environments (outside the luxury of research environments, where, perhaps, evolutionary system development fortunately merely provides interesting diversions for research grants!) are called to build increasingly advanced computer systems. In particular, they are finding that systems with knowledge-based *components* – conventional systems with sub-systems that are knowledge-based – can have highly desirable but down-to-earth 'intelligence' in their functionality. Such 'intelligence' is nothing more than a higher level of data processing, of course, but it can increase the utility and usability of the system in question, even to the extent of making a system solution practical where before it seemed infeasible.

However, because more systematic approaches to system development have already proved their worth for building conventional software, in our harsh, profit-conscious world there is just as much need to apply engineering principles to the development of such KBS systems or components as to the conventional applications built every day. KADS provides such a systematic method in a proven, practical way.

As it has been gradually adopted, KADS has steadily become the European *de facto* standard methodology for building KBSs, either in its original ESPRIT research project form or as adapted by a number of diverse organizations. Use of the structured KADS methods enables KBSs to be developed more systematically, within a conventional or commercial-standard project management framework. KADS can also be used alongside conventional structured development methods. KBSs and knowledge-based components can therefore be engineered just like and alongside conventional systems, with all the same benefits this brings to project management and post-implementation system development.

However, despite the attractions of KADS, there has been no truly practical handbook for the methods available. This book has been written to address this need.

This book

This book is an introduction to, a full explanation of and a practical guide to the use of the KADS methods. The methods have been developed to support systematic, controllable requirements analysis ('analysis') and system design ('design') phases in the engineering of Knowledge-Based Systems (KBSs) – including conventional systems with knowledge-based components. Thus, in this book, 'KADS' stands for KBS Analysis and Design Support (although there are so many different expansions of the acronym in circulation that 'KADS' is best treated as a proper name).

This book has been written for software engineers who are working, or who may work, on projects developing KBSs using the methods. This is a practical book. It is not for IT or DP managers but for IT and DP *practitioners* – commercial and industrial developers who build real systems. We also hope it will be read by students, in all contexts, who intend moving on to find employment in this profession.

We include full explanations of the methods, but we also stress how they can be put into practice. *We want you to use KADS!* We have tried to make much of the book readable and usable by those with relatively little knowledge of KBSs but, inevitably, KBS experience will prove necessary in some sections (particularly 'expertise modelling' and KBS sub-system design). None the less, we believe that many of the KADS activities needed to be performed in a development project do not require any special KBS skills at all. To facilitate this, we have endeavoured to make KADS readily intelligible to those with an existing knowledge of conventional software development concepts and techniques by using familiar terminology and notations wherever possible.

Acknowledgements

People

While the authors have produced and structured the bulk of the material presented in this book, it would have been much less useful without the hard work of the following past contributors throughout the four internal draft versions produced at BNR Europe Limited over the last two years: Brendan Ward (primarily, generic task model library editor and contributor, but also many helpful diverse comments and suggestions), Nichole Simpson (knowledge-acquisition techniques), Véronique Farrell (problem-solving methods library), Kevin Lewis (generic task model editor), and Andrew Minter and Paul Hamblett (implementation environments). Philip Hesketh and Toby Barrett were heavily involved in the first drafts and are also not forgotten.

The authors would also like to thank Alan Wilkinson and Marco de Alberdi for their help in the early structuring of the book and getting the original internal project off the ground.

We are also grateful for the comments received from the many who have suffered reading the various drafts over the years, especially the students attending the training courses which were supported by the book. Finally, we thank the reviewers and the Prentice Hall team for their help in making this book available to all at long last.

References

Because this is a practical book and not an academic text, we have generally tried to avoid individual references and citations unless particularly important. However, the book's contents are inevitably based on a rich set of existing source material – especially the many ESPRIT project public deliverables, produced by a collaboration of European companies and academic institutions (see below). A comprehensive bibliography at the end of the book contains pointers to useful sources of more detailed information, including those of original material where these have been paraphrased in this book.

The origins of KADS

KADS is not our invention (although both authors were contributing members of the original ESPRIT project). But the particular way it is described in this book is our own, as are some of the details we have added to make KADS usable. The bulk of KADS, though, is the product of the hard work and skills of a remarkable collection of people from many organizations.

The central theme in the KADS methods is modelling: the construction and refinement of models of the future system, its user(s) and its surroundings. The model-driven approach, the methods and their associated models and other objects have all been refined for this book from those in the original 'KADS methodology', as produced by the European Community collaborative ESPRIT research project number 1098: 'A methodology for the development of knowledge-based systems.' This book describes a commercially practical version of this 'ESPRIT KADS', or KADS-I, as it is sometimes called. ESPRIT Project 1098 was conducted in two phases:

- The first phase of the project, starting in March 1985, included the following: University of Amsterdam (Netherlands), Cap Sogeti Innovation (France), SCS Organisationbertung und Informationstechnik GmbH (Germany), Scicon Ltd (UK), KBSC at the Polytechnic of the South Bank (UK), and STC IDEC Ltd (UK).
- The second and final phase of the project, ending in March 1990, included: University of Amsterdam (Netherlands), Cap SESA Innovation (France), NTE Neutech GmbH (Germany), SD-Europe Ltd (UK), KBSC of Touche Ross Management Consultants (UK), and STC Technology Ltd (UK).

STC Technology Ltd is now part of BNR Europe Limited.

Trademarks

Apple Macintosh™
AT&T Unix™
Cadre Technologies TeamWork™ and RqT™
CCTA PRINCE™ and SSADM™
Claris MacDraw™ and Hypercard™
Creative Logic Leonardo™
Gold Hill Computers Goldworks™

IBM PC^{TM}
ICL DecisionPower^{TM}
IDE Software through Pictures^{TM}
Inference Corporation ART^{TM}
Intellicorp KEE^{TM} and Kappa^{TM}
Intelligent Environments Crystal^{TM}
Intelligent Systems International Egeria^{TM}
Marconi Systems Technology RTM^{TM}
MIT X Window System^{TM}
Neuron Data Nexpert Object^{TM}
Quintus Prolog^{TM}
SQL Systems International PCMS^{TM}
Sun Workstation^{TM}, Sun OpenWindows^{TM}, SunOS^{TM}, Sun-4^{TM} and Sun SparcStation^{TM}
Symantec MORE^{TM}
Xerox LOOPS^{TM} and Smalltalk^{TM}

Stewart Tansley and Clive Hayball
BNR Europe Limited, UK
October 1992

Part I
Introductions

This part introduces the reader to the book itself and describes how to get the best out of it. It also introduces KADS, describing what KADS is in simple terms, showing where KADS fits into the software development lifecycle and listing some reasons why someone would want to use KADS.

Chapter 1's objectives

- To define what this book is.
- To provide guidance as to how to use the book efficiently and effectively.
- To define what we mean by the term 'Knowledge-Based System' (KBS).
- To categorize KBSs in various ways.

Chapter 2's objectives

- To say what KADS is, in simple terms.
- To show KADS in the context of a general-purpose software development lifecycle – the 'V' model.
- To introduce the modelling theme in KADS and the seven Analysis and Design models.
- To introduce terms for the levels within the hierarchical structure of the activities in KADS.
- To list all the activities and results in KADS.
- To introduce the 'road map' diagrams.
- To state some of the benefits of using KADS.

1 Introduction to this book

The KADS methods represent a structured, systematic approach to key areas of the development of Knowledge-Based Systems. In particular, they concentrate on the *Analysis* and *Design* phases of development – equivalent to requirements capture and analysis, and system and module-level design in conventional systems. As with conventional structured methods, these phases are split into a set of interrelated *activities* to perform and definitions of the *results* that they should produce.

The use of KADS will provide benefits which include better project control and standardization of the development process, and result in final systems that are more easily maintainable and enhanceable. It will also help in addressing problem domains traditionally seen as difficult in KBS work, and produce results which may be generalized and re-used in subsequent developments. KADS has been proven through its use on numerous commercial developments in Europe and, increasingly, further afield.

Note that KADS *supports* a system's development – it does not prescribe a recipe to follow; also, KADS is a *superset* of *suggested* methods and techniques, to be tailored and adapted for the reader's own needs – it is not a fixed, dogmatic discipline. At its simplest and most direct, it offers an established and popular way to document the development of KBSs. When used to the full, though, KADS also offers a thorough, methodical approach where little more than a sophisticated type of trial and error was previously available.

This first chapter addresses two issues: first, it presents advice and guidance as to how to get the best from this book; second, it describes the sorts of systems whose development KADS is designed to support. (If these topics are not important to you, then skip to Chapter 2, which introduces KADS itself.)

1.1   How do I use this book?

This handbook has been carefully structured in order to present the KADS methods to readers coming from diverse technical backgrounds – but primarily, it is for those who want to put KADS into *practice*. Four main features of the book reflect this:

- *Structure*
- *Examples*
- *Road maps*
- *Pointers*

Considering *structure*, at the first level, the book is divided into four major parts:

> **Part I** – An introduction to the book and to KADS itself.
>
> **Part II** – An in-depth explanation of KADS Analysis and Design, plus special techniques and tools used to support them, all illustrated by a consistent case study example.
>
> **Part III** – A presentation of KADS in a fashion suitable for day-to-day use ('guided tours'), plus libraries and other regularly used reference material which will be useful when KADS is put into practice.
>
> **Part IV** – Supplementary information included to widen the perspective of KADS and place it in context.

After Part I, for the average reader, Parts II and III are probably the most important of the book, but they have been written for different audiences. Part II is designed to be read from start to finish. Part III is a collection of reference material for 'live' use of KADS, to be 'dipped into' as needed. The use of Parts II and III is discussed in more detail in Sections 1.1.1 and 1.1.2 respectively.

After Part IV, at the end of the book is a summary of suggested notations for documenting KADS deliverables, a comprehensive glossary, a bibliography and an index. The *glossary* is especially important – we have endeavoured to greatly simplify the terminology used in contrast to other descriptions of KADS, but the reader should be careful to use this frequently to check any doubtful usage of terms. Also, definitions of terms are generally not placed within the body of the book, to reduce clutter – the reader should default to the glossary for such definitions.

Examples in the book are of two main sorts: case study and *ad hoc*. The *case study* example is particularly important. It is used in Chapters 4 and 7 in Part II, which explain KADS Analysis and Design in full detail. These are tightly structured chapters, describing each part of Analysis and Design, with a consistent case study example provided for every part.

Ad hoc examples, from various domains, are used throughout the book as required.

The '*road maps*' are ways of presenting KADS Analysis and Design as separate compact diagrams, highlighted to show a 'you are here' type of indication. They are based on a simple Gantt chart project schedule format and are used primarily to aid navigation in the in-depth explanatory chapters in Part II, Chapters 4 and 7. A consistent ordering is used in this book to describe the components of KADS, and can be seen by reading the road map diagrams from top to bottom. For their derivation, see Section 2.2.

By *pointers* we simply mean cross-references. But the book has been carefully structured to relocate generally applicable information away from specific descriptions of KADS activities and results. This applies especially to the libraries and other chapters that form the bulk of Part III.

In summary, here is some more specific guidance as to what chapters to read:

- **Different levels of description of KADS:**
  Section 2.1 (The concept of 'models' and general principles only)

  Chapter 3 (Top-level overviews of Analysis activities and results)
  Chapter 6 (Top-level overviews of Design activities and results)

  Chapter 5 (Analysis — how it all fits together)
  Chapter 8 (Design — how it all fits together)

  Chapter 15 (Analysis guided tour)
  Chapter 16 (Design guided tour)

  Chapter 4 (In-depth explanation of Analysis activities and results)
  Chapter 7 (In-depth explanation of Design activities and results)

- **To get an in-depth understanding of KADS:**
  Study chapters 4 (Analysis) and 7 (Design) — in-depth explanations
  Study chapters 5 (Analysis) and 8 (Design) — 'big picture' overviews

- **To put KADS into practice on a project:**
  Read parts I, II, and scan part III in detail, at least once
  Use chapter 9 to help plan and embark on managing your project
  Use chapters 15 (Analysis) and 16 (Design) as checklists to follow when actually following KADS activities

Use the rest of part III (the libraries, etc.) as required per activity
Use part II and the rest of the book where further explanation is needed

Finally, these four different marks are used in the margins of this book to highlight certain special items:

    Case Study example, one per KADS activity in chapters 4 and 7.

KAT   Knowledge acquisition technique in chapter 10.

GTM   Generic Task Model in chapter 12.

    Checklist, one per KADS activity in chapters 15 and 16.

1.2   What types of system is KADS useful for?

KADS is specially designed to aid the development of KBSs, and we must therefore answer the question 'what is a KBS?' The term 'knowledge-based system' (and related ones such as 'expert system', as well as the broader area of 'artificial intelligence') has been surrounded by confusion and ambiguity. One reason for this is that the subject is an evolving and complex one. The complexity derives partly from the definition of 'knowledge' as well as from the breadth of coverage of such systems. However, this book is fundamentally pragmatic in approach. Thus we define:

> **KBS** – any computer system or sub-system which processes 'knowledge', where the knowledge is *represented explicitly* within the system.
>
> **Knowledge** – is a rich form of information, such as that stored by humans as expertise in some restricted domain (e.g. problem-solving skills like medical diagnosis or resource scheduling). It is often expressed as facts, rules, concepts, relationships, assumptions, tasks, etc.

Because this definition covers a broad area it is helpful to refine it. However, we have a number of options as to how to do this. For example, three ways we can classify types of KBS are by:

- *General type of system* – How they will be used and in what context.
- *Task of system* – Main problem-solving task performed.

- *Role of system* – Main interactive role compared with the user or other systems.

We illustrate below some of the various types of KBS, classified in these three ways. Be careful, though, as they are not mutually exclusive!

1.2.1 General types of KBS

This is a very straightforward way of classifying KBSs. Using KADS in their construction gives rise to different advantages per type. Six general types of KBS are (there are many more):

- *Generic systems* – Systems which are designed so that they can be tailored to a specific client's requirements, in terms of both the problem-solving functionality and the appropriate domain knowledge – KADS's system development documentation has well-defined levels of abstraction.
- *General-purpose systems* – Systems that operate in a domain common to many potential customers' requirements – KADS helps in producing systems that have exactly the right degree of flexibility in the task they perform and how they perform it.
- *Bespoke systems* – Systems for specific users that are developed for specific clients requiring specific problem solving in specific domains – KADS can help to reduce costs by facilitating the potential re-use of work done on previous developments, even for these systems.
- *Embedded systems* – The KADS methods can be combined with other software development methodologies to produce 'embedded' systems, (i.e. those in which an expert problem-solving component is nested within a larger application), since KADS clearly separates the different types of system components.
- *Adaptable systems* – The KADS methods provide an analysis and design framework that allows a high degree of adaptability to be built into a KBS, so that the same system can be used by different people (for example) and/or for different purposes at different times.
- *Hybrid systems* – There are many hybrid configurations imaginable, e.g. KBS plus relational or object-oriented database, KBS with neural network components, different types of KBS working together, etc. KADS is very useful for building such systems because it helps to identify and separate the concerns and needs of different areas of a system.

The above classification is quite loose. The next two sub-sections describe more precise classifications and serve to illustrate key parts of the KADS approach.

1.2.2   Types of KBS by problem-solving task

A second way of classifying KBSs is by the main problem-solving task that they are designed to perform, i.e. the function (set) that requires the knowledge explicitly represented in the system. (This idea of problem-solving tasks, and their classification, is very important in KADS, as will be seen later.) A small selection of types of KBSs classified by task is as follows (in fact, there are many more possible types – see Chapter 12 for more ideas):

- *Diagnostic systems* – Systems which are designed to locate the cause of a difference in the observed state of another system, compared to the expected state.
- *Classification systems* – Systems that take objects and produce a result describing the class of those objects.
- *Configuration systems* – Systems that take a set of elements in a structure and a set of requirements on that structure, then map the requirements onto the spatial relationships of the elements to form a final structure which meets the requirements.
- *Scheduling systems* – Systems that take an existing set of activities (a plan) and determine the temporal ordering of those activities according to a set of constraints.

KADS distinguishes over thirty other types of task.

1.2.3   Types of KBS by role

A third way of classifying KBSs is by the role that they are designed to perform, i.e. the way in which the system cooperates with the user or other systems. (This idea of cooperative behaviour between the system and the outside world is also very important in KADS, as will be seen later.) A small selection of types of KBSs classified by role are as follows (in fact, there are many more possible types – see Section 4.2.1 for more ideas):

- *Tutoring systems* – Systems which present problems to the user; solve (or recall) the solutions to these problems; compare the solutions to those produced by the user; and guide the user to become more proficient at solving the problems.
- *Mixed-initiative systems* – Systems that can dynamically change whether they control the steps of a dialogue with a user or other system ('take the initiative') or allow the user or other system to drive the dialogue.

- *Learning systems* – Systems that are able to generate new concepts which are generalizations of existing concepts.

KADS does not specifically label different types of role, but the concept is important to the method none the less.

2 Introduction to KADS

This chapter introduces KADS by describing the methods in very simple terms and shows where KADS fits into the software development lifecycle. The central modelling theme of KADS is introduced, together with the models themselves. The terminology used for the hierarchy of activities in KADS is introduced. A table is presented which contains all the KADS activities, their hierarchical placement and their corresponding results. The derivation of the 'road map' diagrams is described – these are used extensively later in the book. Finally, the benefits of using KADS are summarized. After reading this chapter, the reader will be ready to face the in-depth descriptions of KADS in Part II.

2.1 What is KADS?

KADS is composed of the following:

- Structured activities for requirements Analysis, and Design down to the module-level, for a KBS.
- Definitions of the results, or deliverables, to be produced by those activities – some in the form of templates or frameworks.
- Advice and guidance on the techniques to use to perform the activities.
- Advice and guidance on the tools, software or otherwise, including special libraries, that can be used to support those techniques.
- Support for quality assessment and control (QAC) in producing the results.
- Identified opportunities for prototyping.

The central theme in KADS is **modelling** – the descriptions produced of the future system and its domain are models. Models are representations of some non-trivial concept, designed to exhibit some behaviour which matches that of the real-world manifestation of the concept. In Analysis, one models the required behaviour of the system – specifying *what* the system will do. In Design, one models how the system is going to meet those requirements in terms of modules of program code – specifying the overall system architecture and *how* the KBS components of the system will work. (KADS does not support the design of non-KBS components, as these are already well-served by conventional methods.)

As well as modelling the behaviour of the system and the context within which it will work, KADS also provides a document framework for recording more general requirements and constraints. This ensures that any non KBS-specific areas which may still impact on the development are covered. It also recognizes that requirements of the future system may arise from very diverse sources, and that requirements capture during the Analysis phase cannot just rely on the model-building activities to provide a comprehensive coverage.

Figure 2.1 shows a form of the familiar software development lifecycle, with the degree of support offered by KADS highlighted. The 'V' model is just one of the simple representations one can use – it is not special to KADS.[1] It shows the development of any sort of software system broken down into phases (the boxes).

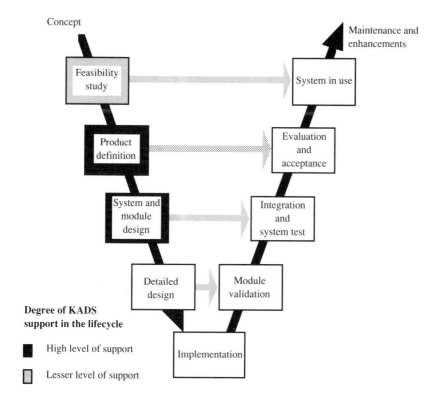

Figure 2.1 Where KADS fits into the software development lifecycle

KADS is therefore primarily concerned with two phases – **Analysis** (Product Definition) and **Design** (System- and Module-level Design). KADS supports these phases where the system to be developed is a Knowledge-Based System, or the embedded knowledge-based component of a larger, conventional system.[2]

To be clear on what these two phases do in system development, and to lead into our description of the KADS Analysis and Design phases and models, see Figure 2.2. This shows schematically the development of a software system through a process of modelling. The goal of the process

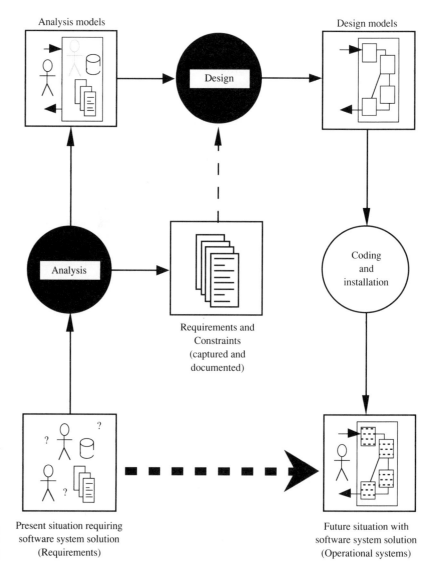

Analysis models

Design

Design models

Analysis

Requirements and
Constraints
(captured and
documented)

Coding
and
installation

Figure 2.2 Software
development by
modelling

Present situation requiring
software system solution
(Requirements)

Future situation with
software system solution
(Operational systems)

is indicated by the large arrow at the bottom of the figure. Of course, unfortunately we cannot traverse this arrow *directly* in real life. It indicates moving from the present situation of a problem statement and a chosen solution option (such as would be contained in the results of a feasibility study) to a future situation with a new or updated system. The main parts of Figure 2.2 show *Analysis* as the phase which contains modelling activities that describe the software *in terms of the original domain*; it also captures and records the functional and non-functional requirements and constraints on the design of the system. *Design* is the phase which models the software *in terms of how the system is to be implemented in code* – the requirements and constraints are shown connected by a dashed line because they serve to *control* the way design is carried out and are therefore not direct inputs in the same way as are the Analysis models. The Analysis and Design bubbles are shown black because they map directly onto KADS Analysis and Design respectively (cf. Figure 2.1).

2.1.1   The KADS models

KADS includes the development activities required to build **seven models** over the Analysis and Design phases. The KADS modelling process involves translating the real-world problem of producing a new system (or new functionality within an existing system) into an abstract form and mapping this abstraction onto a system design in terms of modules of program code. Each model concentrates on one particular aspect of this transformation. They are not produced sequentially, but there are some interdependencies between them. There are also other results to produce apart from the models.

- The three Analysis models:

  1. *Process model* – Models the overall organizational process without the system in place (current view) and with the system in place (future view); models in terms of the tasks that must be performed, and who performs those tasks – the system, the user, or other such 'agents'.
  2. *Cooperation model* – Models in detail the way the future system will interact, or cooperate, with the user or other agents; and also the way the KBS components of the system will cooperate with other components internal to the system.
  3. *Expertise model* – Models the required problem-solving or expert behaviour of the future system's knowledge-based component(s).

- The four Design models:

    4. *Global system architecture* – An overall system structure. It breaks the complete system down into sub-systems, some or all of which will be knowledge-based. (The other KADS design models are solely concerned with refining the design of these KBS sub-systems.)
    5. *Functional design model* – Represents the required problem-solving functionality of the system as a set of functional blocks of four different types.
    6. *Behavioural design model* – Defines what design methods will be used to realize the functions, including which algorithms and data or knowledge structures ('design elements') and knowledge representations to use.
    7. *Physical design model* – Takes the design elements needed by the Behavioural Design and forms them into a physical architecture for the KBS sub-system(s), consisting of specifications for modules of code.

As well as these seven models, KADS requires certain other results to be produced to produce a comprehensive Analysis and Design. An overview of the full set of KADS results, and their associated activities, is shown in Table 2.1.

2.1.2   *Terminology in the KADS lifecycle*

The activities in KADS are part of a hierarchical decomposition of the Analysis and Design phases. There is a need to have terms for each level in the decomposition. In general, we just use the term 'activity' for the things you do within phases. Any level within this hierarchy can have a deliverable – something you produce by performing the activity, stage or phase. These deliverables are all called 'results'. A more precise breakdown of the hierarchy is as follows:

- A lifecycle consists of: **Phases**
- A Phase consists of: **Stages**
- A Stage consists of: **Activities**
- An Activity may consist of: **Sub-Activities**

- Any of the above may produce: **Result(s)**

Table 2.1 All phases, stages, activities and results for Analysis and Design

Phase	Stage	Activity	Result(s)
Analysis			Analysis documentation
	Process analysis		Process model
		Analyze and Decompose Process	Process Decomposition + Process Glossary
		Assign Tasks and Data Stores	Process Distribution + Process Glossary
	Cooperation analysis		Cooperation model
		Analyze User Tasks(s)	User Task Model + [User Model]
		Analyze System Task(s)	System Task Model
		Define User Interface	User Interface Specification
	Expertise analysis		Expertise model
		Analyze Static Knowledge	Domain Structures
		Select Generic Task Model	Generic Task Model
		Construct Expertise Model	Domain Layer + Inference Layer + Task Layer + Strategy Layer
	Constraints analysis		Constraints Document
		Analyze Constraints	Environmental + Technical + Policy
	System overview		System Overview Document
		Produce/Update System Overview	System Objectives + System Functions + System Structure + Information Requirements
Design			Design documentation
	Global design		Global system architecture
		Specify Sub-systems	Sub-system definitions
		Specify Sub-system Interfaces	Sub-system interface definitions
	KBS design		KBS sub-system
		Define KBS Design Framework	KBS Design Framework
		Decompose KBS Functions	Function Blocks + Domain/Data Model
		Assign Design Methods	Problem-solving Methods + Knowledge Representations
		Assemble Design Elements	Module specifications + Module interfaces

2.1.3   Aside: separation of Analysis and Design

As the reader will have started to see already, the description of KADS presented in this book is fundamentally split into 'Analysis' and 'Design'. However, be careful to note that this split is solely for reasons of simplification and clarification of *describing* KADS – *not* of how to put it into practice. When developing software for real, the boundaries between when Analysis and Design activities are fuzzier than is implied by the style of their description in this book.

The reader should not be unduly concerned about this. It is a conventional simplification. It should just be recognized that a small amount of revisiting Analysis activities during Design is perfectly normal, and it is proper to document preliminary design-type decisions during Analysis – as long as neither or both do not get out of hand. It is a project management problem to control the balance (see Chapter 9). We merely mention this here lest the reader has the mistaken impression that KADS assumes that one can cleanly split the Analysis and Design phases, which is normally not the case.

2.1.4   Towards a detailed KADS lifecycle – the road maps

We have mentioned previously a format for describing the Analysis and Design activities of KADS in a compact form, based on the idea of a Gantt chart. These are used extensively in Part II. This section describes how they are derived.

Referring to the 'V' model lifecycle shown in Figure 2.1, if we take the Product Definition and System- and Module-level Design phases as KADS Analysis and Design, respectively, we can break them down into their constituent KADS activities. That is, we can take the boxes representing those phases and show the KADS activities making up those phases *within* the same boxes. If the contents are shown as horizontal parallel bars, with a time axis along the bottom, we obtain a notation like a Gantt chart project plan. The diagrams so produced are used as the basis for the 'road maps'. Figure 2.3 shows the principle.

In this figure each phase has its own local time axis, so that although overlapping activities are correctly shown in each phase, the *apparent overlap* of the Analysis and Design phases should be *ignored*. Also, the time axis within each phase (i.e. within each Gantt chart) is not to be taken too literally – it could be described as 'pseudo-linear'. It is a rough guide for the general case.

The road map diagrams themselves are first shown in Figures 3.3 (Analysis) and 6.1 (Design).

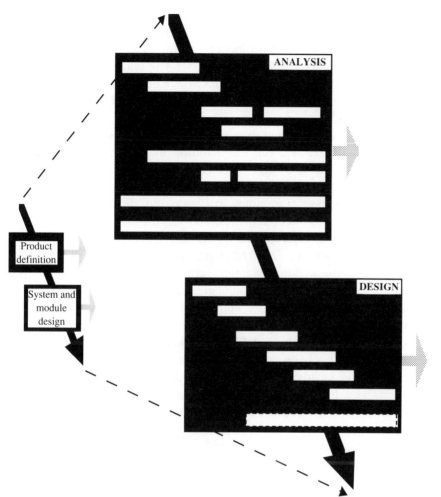

Figure 2.3 Principle of the 'road map' figures used later

2.2   Why use KADS?

To date, the development of KBSs has normally been undertaken using non-structured approaches such as evolutionary prototyping. The success of such systems has been mixed. Two major general problems with such an approach are that it is hard to manage the development, and the resulting implementations are difficult to maintain or enhance – their inadequately structured architectures reflect the lack of structure in their development. By using KADS, however, the developer and client can gain the following advantages over unstructured approaches:

Structuring and systematizing KBS development – The benefits of a more systematic approach are primarily to make project management, control and monitoring easier – commercial KBS development is thus easier to justify and make successful. Further, structured methods are much more compatible with modern quality management techniques, such as those encouraged by ISO 9000. The adoption and use of a disciplined, consistent process of development also facilitates progress up the scale of software process maturity, as defined in the Capability Maturity Model.[3]

Decoupling technical from management activities – As well as making projects easier to control and monitor by simply structuring the development, KADS also decouples the technical development activities from the management activities required in a commercial project. Thus, one can employ existing corporate standard lifecycles for project management activities, and still use KADS.

Maintenance and enhancements – Another benefit is in the areas of maintenance and enhancement of the system. By basing these future activities on the well-documented and well-structured design resulting from a KADS-based development, costs and risks are reduced. Additionally, the structured approach facilitates the traceability of Analysis and Design decisions.

A standard approach to KBS development – The way KADS is described in this book, re-using conventional techniques as much as possible and clearly defining the separation of KBS and non-KBS aspects of a future system, facilitates the integration of KADS with conventional software development methods. In addition, the standard structured system documentation, plus the fact that KADS has become a *de facto* European standard for developing KBSs, means that a common understanding of the system is more easily achieved between present and future staff. Training costs may also be reduced, as a single, standard method is in use.

Difficult domains of expertise – One of the more technical benefits is that the rich support for knowledge acquisition and analysis in KADS enables domains of expertise that are traditionally seen as difficult to be tackled with more confidence. For example:

– Domains with many, disagreeing experts.
– Systems which are not confined to a clear-cut area of expertise, where there may be no single human expert who covers the whole of the domain.
– Domains which are poorly defined or described in ambiguous terms.

Re-usable components – Finally, the structure of certain models in KADS enables their re-use in other systems developed in the future. For example, there is a library of models representing generic problem-solving tasks – new KBS developments may be usefully generalized to add to this library for future use. Again, this may help to reduce costs and the risks of developing KBSs.

These are just some of the benefits of using KADS to develop knowledge-based systems in a more systematic way. The bottom line is that KADS is an approach which finally makes practical the commercial development of advanced knowledge-based technology – at the very least, by being a proven effective development documentation framework.

Notes

1. Further information on the 'V' model lifecycle is presented in Appendix 2. Note that it is *not* proposed as 'the KADS lifecycle'. It is purely illustrative. This book concentrates on what goes on *inside* the lifecycle, not the lifecycle itself. Lifecycles are really project management issues, which are discussed in Chapter 9.
2. This book follows the convention that a new development is assumed. However, the reality is that most software development is done in the context of maintenance and enhancements. These can, though, be considered as special types of new software development – see Appendix 2, section 2.1.4.
   KADS also offers some support to the Feasibility Study – see Appendix 1.
3. A new way of helping organizations to improve their software development process by modelling how well the organization develops software on a scale of five levels of 'maturity'. See Paulk *et al.* (1991) in the Bibliography ('Documents about conventional software engineering').

Part II
KADS explained in detail

This is the major explanatory part of the book, including full descriptions of the KADS Analysis and Design development activities, together with the results they produce. An example of the result of each activity is shown, based on a single real-life case study system. Some background information on the case study system is presented on p. 22 – *it is important to read this in order to fully understand the examples*.

Chapter 3's objectives

- To present an overview of KADS Analysis, in words and diagrams.

Chapter 4's objectives

- To explain in detail each KADS Analysis activity and associated results.
- To present an illustrative example of the result of each activity, based on a consistent case study system.
- To group related Analysis activities into 'stages', and show a 'road map' diagram per stage.

Chapter 5's objectives

- To restate all the pieces that make up KADS Analysis.
- To describe why they are needed.
- To show how they fit together.

Chapter 6's objectives

- To present an overview of KADS Design, in words and diagrams.

Chapter 7's objectives

- To explain in detail each KADS Design activity and associated results.
- To present an illustrative example of the result of each activity, based on a consistent case study system.
- To group related Design activities into 'stages', and show a 'road map' diagram per stage.

Chapter 8's objectives

- To restate all the pieces that make up KADS Design.
- To describe why they are needed.
- To show how they fit together.

Background information on the case study system used in the examples in Chapters 4 and 7 is presented immediately before Chapter 4.

Case study – background information

The aim of the following sections is to introduce the case study example system – the Response Point Expert System (RPES). This KBS, which we actually built using KADS, is used to illustrate each of the KADS activities in Chapters 4 and 7, and the examples are therefore consistent and interrelated. The following should help the reader to understand these examples by providing some important background material which is not described elsewhere in the book. (Other, more detailed, background information for RPES is provided alongside the relevant examples.)

The Response Point domain

The Response Point (RP) domain lies within the Information Services (IS) division of a large international company. IS are responsible for

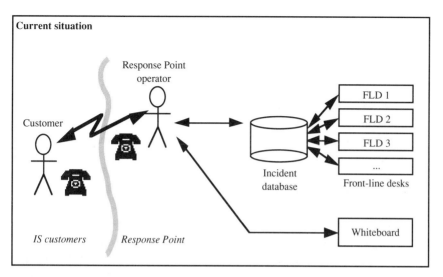

Figure CS 1 Schematic representation of the Response Point domain before RPES

providing and supporting all the internal computer and communications services that the company needs. Response Point is a kind of help-desk facility.

The objective of Response Point is to provide a gateway into IS for customer problems and requests for information – it is the first point of call for their customers. Within Response Point about a dozen trained operators are available to answer calls from customers who are experiencing problems with the services provided by IS. Each operator is trained to answer a customer call, to attempt to determine the type of problem that is being reported, and to route the call on to an appropriate specialist who can carry out detailed diagnosis and resolution. The specialists are grouped into areas of expertise which are known as Front Line Desks (FLDs). An incident database is used to provide the data interface between Response Point and the FLDs – effectively, like an electronic mail facility between the RP operators and the FLDs.

Figure CS 1 illustrates the situation before developing RPES. The RPES development was instigated following the realization that the Response Point operation was suffering from a number of problems:

- Each operator had a limited knowledge which had to be recalled rapidly to ensure quick response to the customer at the end of the telephone line. If more knowledge and information were available then many calls could be cleared without the need to raise an incident report and the administrative overheads would be reduced for the FLDs.

- At the time, a number of calls were being misrouted due to a lack of information or knowledge. This was in part due to the requirement to ask the customer the right questions in order to assess the nature of the problem.
- When calls were cleared immediately via discussion with the customer, these were not logged onto the incident database. This applied to approximately 35–40 per cent of all calls. While there was no requirement to log such calls it would have been useful to hold details of these for purposes of statistics and in order to update the collective experience of Response Point.
- Status information on known problems and network status information was not readily available to a Response Point operator. Although a whiteboard was provided in the room, which all the operators could read, the information was limited in nature and content.
- Several incidents were often recorded against the same fault, because many different manifestations are observed across the large computer network of IS. The Response Point operators had neither the information nor the expertise to identify and flag repeat incident reports.
- At the time there was no easy way to determine the identity of the equipment associated with a particular customer. Ideally, there should be a way to find out information such as the network address of a particular computer or terminal without having to ask the customer.
- There was a lack of communication and feedback between the Response Point and the FLDs. This meant that the routing and problem-solving knowledge at the Response Point was not being updated.
- There was often a lack of feedback from the FLDs to the customer, which led to more calls being received at the Response Point.
- The requirement and effort needed to train the Response point operators was a major concern. A six-month learning curve to proficiency was quoted.

The Response Point Expert System (RPES)

RPES was conceived as a solution to many (but not all) of the above problems. It supports an operator in answering a telephone call from an IS customer, ascertaining the customer's problem, and routing the enquiry to an appropriate specialist (i.e. FLD). The system offers questions to ask the customer in the search for relevant problem details, but can accept other problem aspects as they emerge during the telephone conversation (which may not necessarily be answers to the questions). There are also facilities for making use of network status information and details of previously reported problems to assist in clearing a call.

The ability of RPES to perform the above tasks successfully depends on several critical upgrades to the surrounding environment within Response Point:

- RPES must be coupled with the incident database, so that enquiries and updates of incidents can be performed from within RPES.
- The record formats on the incident database must be upgraded so that a single incident report may be associated with several customer problem reports.
- The whiteboard must be replaced by a computer-based network management/information system which can provide RPES with up-to-date information about the status of the IS network.

Figure CS 2 illustrates the situation after implementing RPES.

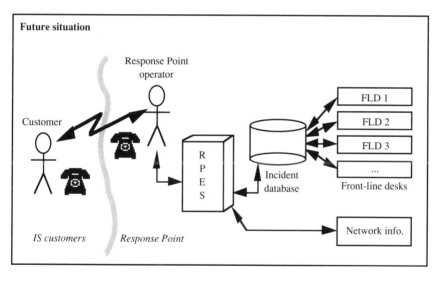

Figure CS 2 Schematic representation of the Response Point domain with RPES

3 Overview of Analysis

This chapter presents a quick overview of the KADS Analysis phase. KADS Analysis can be used to support the 'Product Definition' phase of a KBS product, equivalent to requirements capture and analysis for conventional systems. For a more 'theoretical' description of how all the pieces of Analysis fit together, see Chapter 5.

3.1 Introduction

Analysis takes as input the feasibility and preliminary system concept analysis material produced during a feasibility study or other pre-analysis stage.[1] It produces results which represent a detailed understanding of the problem domain and does this by identifying exactly what the future system will do and what are the constraints on how it must operate. (In addition, the results are suitable for transformation into a design for the KBS in a subsequent phase.) It is split into five 'stages':

Process Analysis – Analyzes the tasks performed by agents (e.g. systems, people) and the information flowing between them.

Cooperation Analysis – Analyzes the interaction between the system and external agents, the interaction between the internal agents of the system, and produces a specification for the user interface.

Expertise Analysis – Analyzes the problem-solving or 'expert' behaviour required of the system.

Constraints Analysis – Captures and maintains the (mostly non-functional) requirements on the system.

System Overview – Produces and maintains an overall view of the system, including the key functional requirements.

The major KADS Analysis results are the *Process Model*, the *Cooperation Model*, the *Expertise Model*, an updated list of *Constraints* on the system, and an up-to-date *System Overview*, which all correspond to their respective stages above.

3.2   Analysis stages

The first stage in KADS Analysis is **Process Analysis**. This starts by identifying the overall organizational process that the system will support. It then decomposes and describes this process using the conventional and well-known technique of drawing Data Flow Diagrams (DFDs). This breaks down the process into high-level ('global') tasks which either the system or some other agent will perform. The stage is completed by assigning ('distributing') such agents to tasks and data stores, specifying 'who does what' and 'who owns what'. In particular, the knowledge-based tasks are identified. A Process Glossary complements the decomposition and distribution by acting as a data dictionary to the DFDs.

Cooperation Analysis takes the results from Process Analysis and analyzes the system boundaries in more detail, especially the user–system interface(s). It is supported by:

- Producing a detailed User Task Model, describing the system's operation in terms of the user's task(s) and the required interactions with the system in terms of events (typically modelled by a State Transition Diagram (STD)).
- Producing a detailed System Task Model, describing the system's internal state-changes and cooperation between internal system agents, in response to the external event triggers defined in the User Task Model (typically modelled by augmenting the STD).
- Producing a specification of the user–system interface itself (typically a prototype supplemented by a description of the final interface).

An optional component of Cooperation Analysis is the User Model, which is a model of the particular characteristics of the 'user' agent. Also, by analogy with the user agent, where a system must cooperate with external agents other than or in addition to the archetypal 'user', Cooperation Analysis would be extended with activities analogous to those above to produce models for other agents and their tasks.

From the Process Model showing which tasks are knowledge-based, plus the input–output characteristics of those tasks from the System Task Model, **Expertise Analysis** investigates and describes the problem-solving details of the knowledge-based tasks. It produces the Expertise Model by building up the four layers of the model, which are:

- *Domain* – defines the static 'factual' knowledge about the domain.
- *Inference* – defines the basic inference steps that the KBS can take.
- *Task* – defines the basic problem-solving tasks.
- *Strategy* – defines how tasks are constructed, modified or chosen dynamically.

These layers can be built in any order, are constructed by a process of iteration and refinement and are validated in conjunction with domain experts (if available). The goal of Expertise Analysis is to produce a model which most closely represents the required problem-solving behaviour of the future system. The iteration stops when the model is sufficiently complete and detailed to allow design to commence.

The Expertise Model is not usually built from scratch. The first step of Expertise Analysis is to gather information in an attempt to select or construct a *Generic Task Model* which matches the new problem domain as closely as possible. There is a library of such models in Chapter 12. Generic Task Models are like previously built Expertise Models with their domain layer details removed. (The domain layer contains the domain-specific knowledge; the other layers are only task-specific.)

Assuming a relevant Generic Task Model is found, its form and content are used to drive knowledge acquisition in a structured and efficient way. A Generic Task Model represents the 'first guess' at the layers of the Expertise Model. If the analyst cannot find a Generic Task Model which is a good match to the problem domain, the Expertise Model must be built from scratch, with perhaps at least suitable *parts* of Generic Task Models selected from the library. If the envisaged system requires other functionality apart from the KBS (for example, conventional data processing) then other parallel streams of activity, such as database and transaction analysis, must also be carried out.

KADS Analysis keeps an up-to-date overall picture of the future system in the form of the **System Overview**. Similarly, it builds and maintains a record of all the **Constraints** on the system, including those arising from environmental and organizational, technical and policy factors. The System Overview includes a place-holder for the functional requirements of the future system. The Constraints are mostly non-functional requirements. Constraints Analysis is just like conventional requirements engineering, and is complementary to the model-building activities in KADS. Both activities generally build upon the work of earlier phases. They are present here as insurance against changing requirements and different amounts (per project) of such analysis work being carried out before KADS Analysis is started. In general, these are not particularly KBS-specific activities.

At the end of KADS Analysis, the various models and results are consolidated to provide a coherent and consistent definition of requirements ready for the system's design. This consolidation usually results in the construction of a single 'Analysis document'.

3.3   Analysis activities and results

Figures 3.1 and 3.2 show *consists-of* hierarchies summarizing the basic Analysis activities and results respectively. They form a useful 'one-page' summary of Analysis.

- **ANALYSIS ACTIVITIES**
  - **Process Analysis**
    - Analyze and Decompose Process
    - Assign Tasks and Data Stores to Agents
  - **Cooperation Analysis**
    - Analyze User Task(s)
    - Analyze System Tasks
    - Define User Interface
  - **Expertise Analysis**
    - Analyze Static Knowledge
    - Select Generic Task Model(s)
    - Construct Expertise Model
  - **Constraints Analysis**
    - Analyze Constraints
  - **System Overview**
    - Produce/Update System Overview

Figure 3.1 Analysis activities, summary

- **ANALYSIS RESULTS**
  - **Process Model**
    - Process Decomposition (e.g. DFDs)
    - Process Distribution (e.g. augmented DFDs with agents)
    - Process Glossary
  - **Cooperation Model**
    - User Task Model(s) (e.g. STDs)
    - System Task Model (e.g. augmented STDs with event details)
    - User Interface Specification
    - [User Model] (optional)
  - **Expertise Model**
    - [Generic Task Model] (Intermediary result)
    - Domain Layer
    - Inference Layer
    - Task Layer
    - Strategy Layer
  - **Constraints Document**
    - Environmental Constraints
    - Technical Constraints
    - Policy Constraints
  - **System Overview Document**

Figure 3.2 Analysis results, summary

3.4   Analysis road map

Figure 3.3 illustrates the Analysis road map. It shows all the basic

Analysis activities in their hierarchical relationships, together with some indication of the potential parallelism between the activities, in a Gantt chart-like project plan format. (See Section 2.2 to see how it has been derived.)

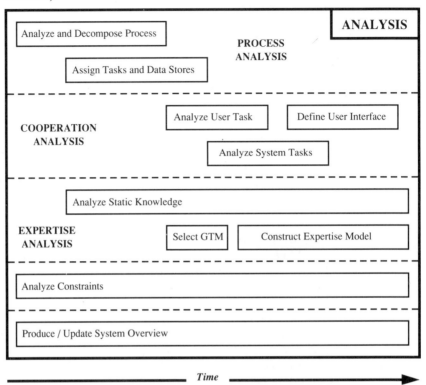

Figure 3.3 The basic KADS Analysis 'road map' diagram

The road map gives only a very rough guide as to the overlap of the various Analysis activities. It should *not* be taken as a literal statement of the optimum scheduling of the activities. (See Chapter 9.) It may be helpful to know that the order of describing the Analysis activities in this book is always the same, and is reflected in reading the road map from top to bottom.

3.5   Analysis process

Figure 3.4 shows the Analysis process and illustrates the flow of development between Analysis activities and results, together with information sources and techniques to support performing the stages. It is an idealistic view, though, and is just one way of illustrating the relationships between the activities and results, based on a dataflow diagram. Like other dataflow diagrams, it does not show *when* things are done but only input–output dependencies. In particular, iteration is not shown, although some would be normal when performing the activities. Refinements of this diagram in the form of 'exploded' views of the

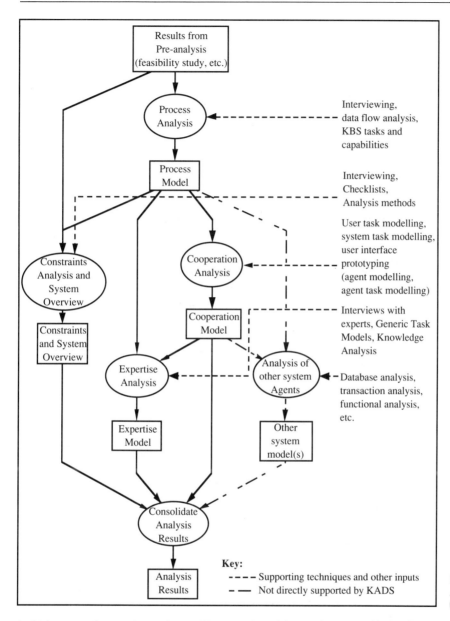

Figure 3.4 The Analysis process (idealized)

bubbles are shown throughout Chapter 4 and have the same limitations. There is one such process diagram per modelling stage, i.e. Process Analysis (Figure 4.2), Cooperation Analysis (Figure 4.11) and Expertise Analysis (Figure 4.24).

Note

1. Appendix 1 shows how KADS can help in this phase preceding Analysis.

4 Analysis activities and results

4.1 Process Analysis

The activities within Process Analysis are normally the first to be undertaken within KADS Analysis. They examine and model the organizational process the system is to fit into and the process to be carried out by it. Figure 4.1 shows the temporal relationship of Process Analysis relative to the other Analysis stages.

The aim of Process Analysis in KADS is to develop an understanding of the immediate environment within which a KBS is to be delivered.

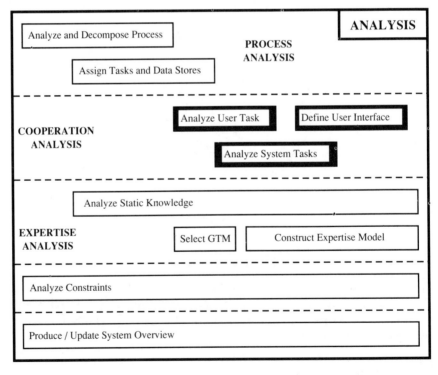

Figure 4.1 The Process Analysis stage

This stage normally starts with a scoped organizational context (i.e. a well-defined part of the client's organization that the system is to work within) plus an identified opportunity for KBS development. However, there is no reason, in principle, why the techniques of Process Analysis should not be applied to an earlier pre-analysis scoping activity and feasibility study.

There are two activities within Process Analysis:

- Analyze and Decompose Process
- Assign Tasks and Data Stores to Agents

These activities may be applied to both the current scoped organizational context without the system in place ('existing environment') and the future context ('future environment') with the prospective system in place.

'Analyze and Decompose Process' explores the process(es) in the relevant part of the client organization in terms of the constituent tasks, data stores and data flows. This activity results in the Process Decomposition and the Process Glossary. Both are interim deliverables within Process Analysis and they will be augmented later. The Process Decomposition is usually provided as a set of Data Flow Diagrams. The Process Glossary describes the data in more detail using either plain English or Backus-Naur Form (BNF).

'Assign Tasks and Data Stores to Agents' assigns the tasks and data stores from the Process Decomposition to system or external agents, describing who performs which tasks and who owns which stores. Thus, it gives a breakdown of the total system environment into a set of discrete areas of concern. This allows the 'cooperating agents' in the environment to be further analyzed in a relatively independent manner by applying techniques appropriate to each kind of agent, e.g. knowledge acquisition for expert tasks and knowledge; user task modelling for user tasks, etc. This activity results in the Process Distribution, which is an augmentation of the Process Decomposition. The Process Glossary may also require updating during this activity.

The Process Decomposition, the Process Distribution and the Process Glossary together make up the Process Model, which is the consolidated output from Process Analysis. As a major side effect, Process Analysis can provide much of the input required for the 'Environmental Constraints' part of Constraints Analysis (see Section 4.4.2).

Process Analysis employs Data Flow Analysis as its primary technique. It draws upon written information about the client environment plus the results of interviews with client personnel. A major objective of Process Analysis is to break up the overall problem into pieces which can be further analyzed in a fairly independent manner, so the activity is supported by an understanding of the nature and capabilities of the various types of agent involved, whether human (user, expert, etc.) or software (database, KBS, etc.). Figure 4.2 illustrates the relationships between the activities and results within Process Analysis, which are then described in further detail in the following sections.

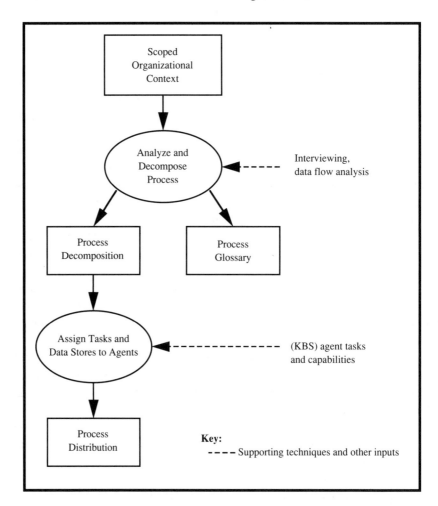

Figure 4.2 Process Analysis activities and results

4.1.1   *Analyze and Decompose Process*

During this activity the processes within the existing and/or the prospective system environment are analyzed and described using Data Flow Analysis. This is a well-known and conventional systems analysis technique which supports both an understanding of the problem area by the systems analyst(s) and the subsequent feedback of that understanding to the client for checking and discussion. At this stage all analysis should be computer-independent – i.e. equal attention is paid to tasks regardless of whether the system or user will carry them out. Although the rationale for undertaking such analysis is that a computer system should perform some of the tasks within the overall process, the analyst does not need to state explicitly which these are (this is done in the next stage of Process Analysis).

Initially, the problem area should be decomposed to the level at which the analyst and client together can agree on the operational objectives and problems and the actions which need to be taken to support a system solution. Later, the scoped problem area can be decomposed in order to be able to identify which problem aspects can be supported by what kind of system functionality – database, KBS, conventional software, etc.

There are no specific inputs required to start the analysis of the overall process, but some understanding of the domain is desirable. The description of the 'Existing Environment' (p. 107), the System Overview (Section 4.5) and any pre-analysis work giving background knowledge may help with this. Some of the forms of knowledge-acquisition technique best suited to gathering this data are the 'Focused Interview' (see Section 10.5.1) and 'Self-report' (see Section 10.6.1).

The initial analysis of the problem is terminated by the production of the Process Decomposition and the Process Glossary. These are described below.

The Process Decomposition

The Process Decomposition is a model of the tasks, data stores and data flows within the client organization's process(es). It can be used to represent the existing or the new situation once the proposed system has been incorporated. At this stage there is no consideration of the division of labour between system, user(s) or other agents.

The Process Decomposition is usually represented as a set of DFDs. The SSADM[1] DFD convention used in this book is rectangular boxes for tasks, open boxes for data stores and arrowed lines to depict data flows; external entities are described within bubbles. (But one could use any alternative DFD notation.)

Data flow diagraming allows the problem to be decomposed through several levels. However, dependencies may hold between Tasks or Data Stores at different levels in the decomposition. The two-dimensional nature of a DFD makes this kind of dependency difficult to express without the use of copious cross-references. An alternative solution is to give two complementary views of the Process Decomposition: first, the hierarchical decomposition of Process elements, and second, a set of input/output dependencies holding between them.

Figures 4.3 and 4.4 illustrate these two alternative notations for describing the hierarchical decomposition. In these examples, tasks are labelled numerically, data flows with lower-case letters and external entities with upper-case letters; data stores are labelled D1 and D2.

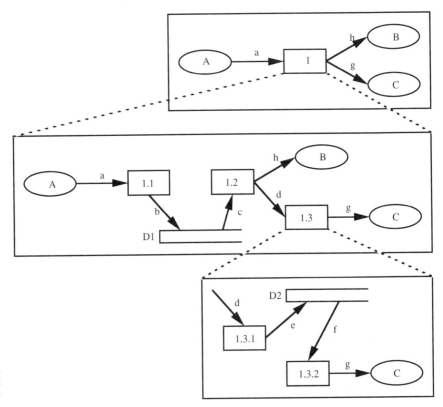

Figure 4.3 Process Decomposition using Data flow Diagrams

Process Decomposition tools and techniques

The basic tools for drawing Data Flow Diagrams are pencil and paper. This is a serious comment – the analyst should avoid making the Process Decomposition diagrams look too formal or 'pretty' early in the Analysis phase. The same applies to all the models produced in liaison with the customer, users and experts (which basically means all the Analysis models). One of the major reasons for drafting these diagrams is for the analyst to check and agree understanding with the client. The analyst must be prepared to refine the diagrams on the basis of feedback from the

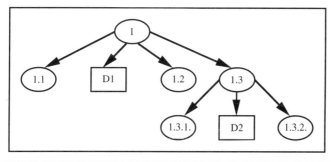

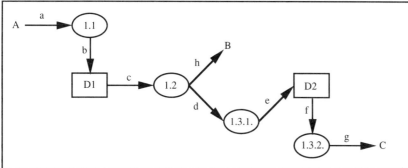

Figure 4.4 Process Decomposition using hierarchies and input–output relations

client and, if the initial drawings look too polished, the client may feel that they are a *fait accompli* and misunderstandings can result.

Final versions of the diagrams can be produced using standard drawing tools such as MacDraw on the Apple Macintosh and similar PC-based packages. Several CASE tools provide support for the production of Data Flow Diagrams and bring benefits beyond general-purpose drawing tools; some even provide a facility for 'animating' the DFDs and may therefore be used to support prototyping or help to verify the proposed Process Decomposition.

The Process Glossary

The Process Decomposition diagrams should be accompanied by a Process Glossary. This is a semi-formal description of the data items encountered during Process Analysis. Thus it is called the Process Glossary because it is a list of terms and their definitions as used in the Process Model. The data items may be described in plain English, or by using a more structured notation such as Backus–Naur Form (BNF) or Entity-Relationship Diagrams (ERDs) from conventional structured analysis.

For conventional parts of the prospective system the Process Glossary forms the basis for any subsequent data analysis/modelling; for knowledge-based system components it provides an important input into Expertise Analysis (see Section 4.3), especially in the construction of the Domain Layer of the Expertise Model.

Example

Analyze and Decompose Process

(Note: This and subsequent case study examples are based on the Response Point Expert System (RPES) development, described on p. 24)

The following procedure is generally adopted by the Response Point operators when actioning a customer enquiry:

1. A customer phones Response Point with a problem or query. The Response Point operator records the basic customer details such as name, location and telephone number.
2. If the customer has a problem then the operator attempts to classify this. Trivial problems may involve an immediate response, in which case the call is concluded and considered resolved. Some information about the status of the network and known problems is available on a whiteboard. This may be used in the classification process. The problem is generally classified via dialogue with the customer.
3. If the problem cannot be resolved immediately then it must be logged on the Incident Database. The information logged consists of:
    *   Customer information (name, location, telephone number)
    *   Problem statement (with as much information as possible on the first line)
    *   Problem area (machine type, machine name, application name)
    *   Priority and classification
    *   Routing information (which Front Line Desk (FLD) will investigate)

    When the incident has been logged on the Incident Database the customer is advised of the enquiry number (from the database application) and told that the appropriate Front Line Desk will phone back within 30 minutes. The call is then cleared.
4. If the customer was phoning up to enquire about a previous incident then the enquiry identity is used to look up the appropriate incident report from the Incident Database. If the customer cannot provide the enquiry identity then facilities are available for searching on customer name, etc. The customer is advised of the current status of the incident report (progress in resolving, who is taking responsibility for handling it, etc.).

5. If the customer is requesting information rather than reporting a problem then the Response Point operator may be able to provide limited information (e.g. from the whiteboard) or advise as to the person to contact.

Figure 4.5 shows the existing Response Point incident classification process decomposed into its constituent tasks and data stores. (Note that the Data Flow Diagrams in this section are described using the SSADM-like notation mentioned earlier, but alternative DFD notations could be employed.)

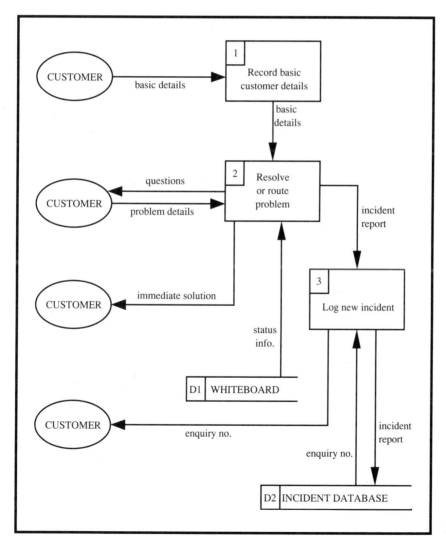

Figure 4.5 DFD for Response Point

The following are two quoted entries from the Process Glossary. This supports understanding of the concepts within the Response Point incident classification process:

'Incident database

The database which is currently used to hold details of all incidents recorded by Response Point. It provides facilities for logging incidents, allocating incidents to engineers for action, clearing solved incidents and general-purpose browsing of incidents.'

'Whiteboard

When new information is detected by an operator and it is of importance in the way calls are handled, then details are written up on a whiteboard in the Response Point office. This is a practical way of circumventing the problems of periodically needing to check the monitor screens. However, during busy periods, operators may not have the time to check them and therefore important information relevant to incoming calls may not be available.'

Figure 4.6 shows the context of the envisaged system. The whiteboard is replaced with direct computer access to network status information (see case study background information). The new system has the capability of using status information plus data on existing incidents to clear a call immediately or to identify the appropriate place to route it. A new task (Provide Solution) provides details of calls cleared immediately and of calls routed, plus optional explanations of how these decisions were reached. Additionally, 'clever' comparison of a new incident against existing incidents in the database is supported. By this means, related incidents can be grouped together, thus providing more evidence for diagnosticians and less duplication of diagnostic effort. Browsing of incidents stored in the database is also supported by the system.

The following is a further Process Glossary extract providing the structural definitions of most of the data elements found in Figure 4.6 in a BNF-type notation:

```
KEY:
A ::= B means 'A is defined in terms of B'
A + B means 'A and B'
A | B means 'A or B'
A* means 'one or more repetitions of A'
CAPITALS means 'a label or other constant'
```

Basic Details	::=	Customer-Name + Customer-Location + Customer-Telephone-Number + Date/Time + Problem-Statement;
Incident_Report	::=	Enquiry_Number + Incident_Status + Problem_Description + Basic_Details* + Priority + Routing_Information + Supporting_Evidence + Resolution;
Network_Element	::=	Hardware_Item | Software_Item;
Problem_Data	::=	Hardware_Involved | Software_Involved | Problem_Type;
Problem_Description	::=	Hardware_Involved + Software_Involved + Problem_Type;
Question	::=	Question-Text + Possible_Answer*;
Routing_Information	::=	Front_Line_Desk + FLD-Specialist;
Solution	::=	(REPEAT-PROBLEM + Enquiry_Number) | (KNOWN-PROBLEM + Resolution + Action) | (PROBLEM-FIXED + Resolution);
Status_Info	::=	(Network_Element + Element_Status)*;

4.1.2 *Assign Tasks and Data Stores to Agents*

This activity basically follows on from 'Analyze and Decompose Process', but can also be partly interleaved with it. Because it augments the Process Decomposition (and, indirectly, the Process Glossary), this activity can be started as soon as reasonably complete versions of it are available.

As KADS is concerned with the analysis and design of potentially complex systems which embed KBS, it is important early in the Analysis phase to identify areas of concern which require specialist skills and techniques to be applied. The KBS system component is one such area since knowledge acquisition requires particular elicitation and analysis skills, and is aided by special techniques. Other potential specialist areas include database analysis and user interface specification. This activity

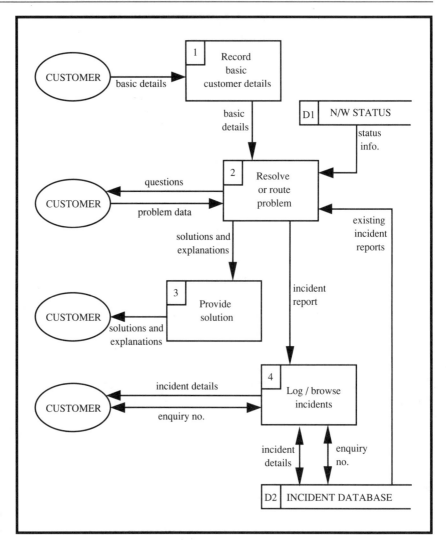

Figure 4.6 DFD for
the envisaged system

seeks to split the total problem area into a set of 'cooperating agents', each of which demands a particular specialist analysis skill. This allows analysis of the agents to proceed in parallel in a relatively independent manner.

Early versions of the Process Decomposition may be insufficiently detailed to support unique agent assignment in this activity. There may be ambiguity about which agent should own a task or data store. In this case the analyst should either seek more information from the client or make a decision and document the reasons for doing so. Alternatively, it may be clear that more than one agent is involved, in which case the task or data store must be decomposed further until assignment to a unique agent is possible.

In addition to the essential Process Decomposition, there will be other inputs to this activity. There will be a large number of ways in which the tasks and data stores may be split up between agents. Hence, there will need to be input from Constraints Analysis and the System Overview (particularly 'Objectives Of Prospective System' and 'Provisional System Structure' – see Section 4.5), as well as general knowledge about what task(s) the KBS component(s) may reasonably be expected to achieve. This will ensure that the assignments generated will be ones which broadly fit in with the objectives of the project and are technically feasible.

Thus, the assignment of tasks and data stores to agents should be guided by the stated objectives of the system. The results of early Constraints Analysis (such as 'the finished system must be able to perform task X unaided') will limit the choices that can be made.

The KADS Generic Task Library (Chapter 12), together with the guidelines for potential KBS support (Appendix 1), may prove useful in deciding which system aspects should be assigned to KBS agents. When assigning tasks and data stores to agents, any deficiencies in the Process Decomposition are likely to become apparent – especially in terms of the level of decomposition. If more than one agent (e.g. both user and KBS) is involved in a task then further decomposition is almost certainly required. In rare cases, joint tasks will never become exclusive, regardless of the level of decomposition specified. The solution then is to assign the user and system to *copies* of the same task. This technique is used where 'critiquing' or 'coaching'-type tasks are present.

The Process Distribution produced by this activity may also be complicated if the number of tasks leads to large and unwieldy distributions. This can, in some circumstances, be alleviated by rethinking the structure of the original Process Decomposition.

Sometimes, depending on the variety of the tasks, it may be necessary to produce different assignments for different classes of agent – for lay user and expert user, for instance. This could be documented using different diagrams for each agent. If this activity requires any changes to the original Process Decomposition the Process Glossary should be updated to reflect this.

The Process Distribution

The end product of the 'Assign Tasks and Data Stores to Agents' activity is the Process Distribution. This is basically the Process

Decomposition with its tasks and data stores assigned to agents. The Process Distribution identifies which tasks are (or will be) performed by which agents. It also defines the ownership of data stores by these agents. These agent assignments split the analysis phase into a set of concerns which can be explored relatively independently by analysts with specialist skills and techniques. The Process Distribution is documented using the same diagrams that were employed for the Process Decomposition (data flow diagrams or hierarchies plus input–output relations), but these are supplemented with agents assigned to the tasks and data stores (e.g. indicated by annotations on the original DFD).

The completed Process Distribution (implicitly including the Process Decomposition) and Process Glossary comprise the final output of Process Analysis. Collectively, these results are called the Process Model. This forms the basis for the construction of the Expertise Model and the Cooperation Model.

Figure 4.7 illustrates two methods for marking the DFD with agent assignments. A third variant can be found in the case study example which follows. The same methods can be used with the hierarchies and input–output relations if these are used instead.

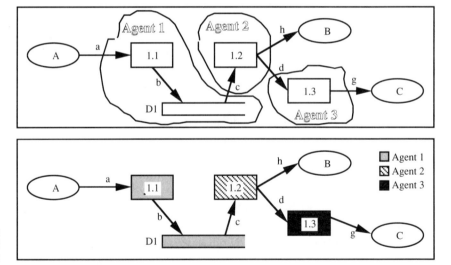

Figure 4.7 Two ways to document agent assignments on DFDs

Process Distribution tools

Since the Process Distribution is an augmentation of the Process Decomposition, the same tools should be used. Where these do not provide direct support for annotating agent assignments they can be added as comments or mark-ups to printed copies.

Assign Tasks and Data Stores to Agents

Figure 4.8 shows the augmented form of the Process Decomposition with tasks and data stores assigned to agents, i.e. a first attempt at the Process Distribution. Since the user of the expert system must act as a 'go-between' in transferring information between customer and system, the customer bubbles have been replaced with user bubbles. The other agents involved in assignments are the KBS (K) and the conventional part of the system (S). (No other agents were involved in this system but this

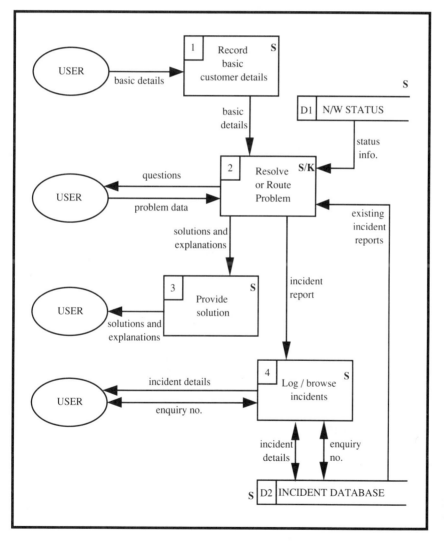

Figure 4.8 Agent assignments for the envisaged system

annotation scheme is easily extended when others are present – the set used here is typical, though.)

Task 2 ('Resolve or Route Problem') involves KBS because expertise is needed both to route problems and to support 'intelligent' requests for further information. Task 3 incorporates provision of explanation but it is assumed that this is generated by task 2.

All tasks require some conventional software to support the user interface and/or data access. Task 2 has not been uniquely assigned and so must be further decomposed and distributed, shown in Figure 4.9.

Four knowledge-based tasks have been identified in Figure 4.9, together with two supporting knowledge stores. The shaded area in the figure can be seen to provide scope for the detailed analysis of the knowledge-based problem-solving capability within RPES.

As for the top-level DFD, Figure 4.9 should be supported by Process Glossary definitions. The additional data definitions include the following (using the same notation as before – see Section 4.1.1 for a key to the notation and definitions of some of the data entities used below):

Incident_Comparison_Result	INCIDENT_COMPARISON + Comparison_Result;
Network_Comparison_Result	NW_STATUS_COMPARISON + Comparison_Result;
Comparison_Result	SUCCESS | FAILURE | INSUFFICIENT_DATA + Problem_ Data*;
Problem_Database	Basic_Details + Problem_Data* + Problem_Description + (Incident_Comparison_Result | Network_Comparison_Result | Routing_Result) + Problem_Hierarchies;
Problem_Hierarchies	Hardware_Type_Hierarchy + Software_Type_Hierarchy + Problem_Type_Hierarchy;
Routing_Knowledge	(Problem_Description + Front_Line_ Desk)*;
Routing_Result	ROUTING_ATTEMPT + Comparison_Result.

In Figure 4.9 the Incident_Comparison_Result is included in the output of the tasks 'Attempt to Route Incident' (2.3) and 'Compare Against

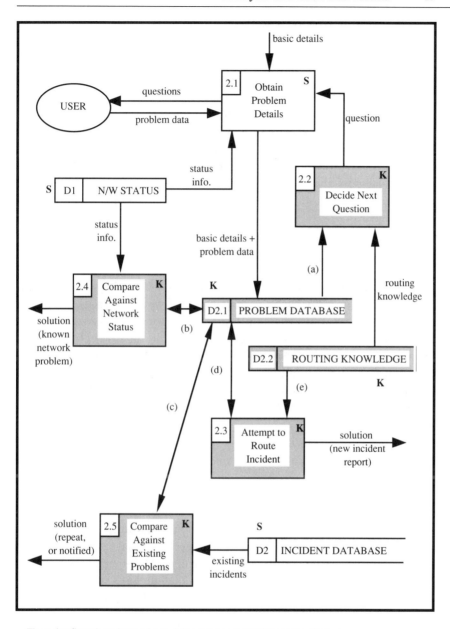

These dataflows have been relocated due to space constraints on the diagram:

(a) problem data (extracted from a comparison result)
(b) problem description and hierarchies   — right to left
    network comparison result   — left to right
(c) problem description and hierarchies   — top to bottom
    incident comparison result   — bottom to top
(d) problem description and hierarchies   — top to bottom
    routing result   — bottom to top
(e) routing knowledge

Figure 4.9 Agent assignments for 'Resolve or Route Problem' (with KBS tasks and stores highlighted)

Existing Problems' (2.5) – in the latter, an 'existing problem' is either just a normal incident that has previously been captured by the system ('repeat') or it is a problem of which Response Point has received prior notification ('notified'). Network_Comparison_Result is the output of 'Compare Against Network Status' (2.4).

The Problem_Database provides a data interface between the conventional and knowledge-based system components, as well as containing support knowledge for the 'route' and 'compare' tasks. The problem hierarchies and routing knowledge, together with any additional knowledge to support the 'K' tasks, will be the subject of further analysis within the Expertise Modelling activity – especially within 'Analyze Static Knowledge'.

4.2   Cooperation Analysis

The Cooperation Analysis stage within KADS Analysis is a logical extension of Process Analysis, although it need not necessarily be carried out as the very next step in Analysis. Process Analysis includes decomposing the prospective system environment into a set of 'cooperating agents'. Cooperation Analysis is concerned with a closer inspection of the relationships between these agents in terms of the role(s) the agents will play when cooperating with each other. Figure 4.10 shows the temporal relationship of Cooperation Analysis relative to the other Analysis stages.

The aim of Cooperation Analysis is to explore the system's external and internal interfaces in more detail than that provided within Process Analysis. Two basic types of agent can be distinguished from the results of Process Analysis – agents which are *external* to the system, such as the user(s) and agents which are *internal* to the system, such as the KBS subsystem(s). The Cooperation Analysis activities incorporate techniques to analyze and specify the interfaces between external agents and the system, and between the internal system agents. These techniques are, in principle, very general, although in KADS the emphasis is placed on the user as far as external agents are concerned. (The principles can be extended to other external agents.)

The three (main) activities within Cooperation Analysis are:

- Analyze User Task(s).
- Analyse System Task(s).
- Define User-System Interface(s).

'Analyze User Task(s)' explores the relationship between the system and its interfaces to external agents. In KADS, the most important external

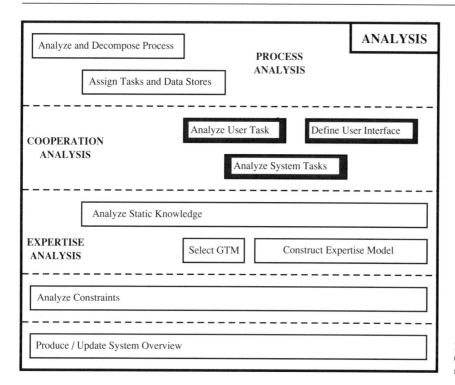

Figure 4.10 The Cooperation Analysis stage

agent is considered to be the human user(s), so the emphasis is placed on modelling the user–system relationship. The activity produces a User Task Model which describes the logic of each user task in terms of a set of user states, the user events which can occur within each state, and the state transitions which are a result of each event. Optionally, the activity may also produce a 'User Model' which would describe the characteristics of each class of user of the system.

'Analyze System Tasks' is, in essence, a refinement of the work carried out in 'Analyze User Task(s)'. While user task analysis provides an understanding of the user–system relationship, system task analysis provides an understanding of the way in which the various system agents must cooperate in response to user actions. The result of this activity is a System Task Model which describes the logic of the processing that must take place by each system agent in response to each user event. The System Task Model can be viewed as a high-level specification of the required control structure of the prospective system.

'Define User–System Interface(s)' also follows on from the work carried out in 'Analyze User Task(s)'. It explores the user's characteristics and specifies the user–system interface requirements in detail. This results in the User Interface Specification, which defines the medium and format(s) that will be used to support information transfer between user(s) and system. It can also be viewed as a refinement of the abstract view of the user–system relationship presented in the User Task Model.

The User Task Model, the System Task Model, the User Interface Specification (and the optional User Model) together make up the Cooperation Model, which is the consolidated output from Cooperation Analysis.

A variety of techniques are available to support Cooperation Analysis. User analysis techniques include interviews with users, user–expert dialogues, the 'Wizard-of-Oz' technique (where the system is simulated in some way) and user interface prototyping. Figure 4.11 illustrates the relationships between the activities and results within Cooperation Analysis, which are then described in further detail in the following sections.

4.2.1   Analyze User Task(s)

Any computer system, KBS or otherwise, must be readily usable if it is to be successful. It must support the functions that the user wants in an accessible way, appropriate for the type of user and the task supported by the system. This activity addresses the user–system relationship with respect to the user tasks which the system is to support, i.e. the style of their interaction. An understanding of the user task(s) and how these relate to the functions which the system must provide is vital to the achievement of an accurate system specification.

User task analysis in KADS is concerned with identifying and analyzing what activities the user carries out, how these are related logically and temporally, what information needs to flow between user and system in support of these activities, and who controls the flow of information. The result is a User Task Model, with cross-references to the elements of the Process Model.

The main input to user task analysis is the Process Model. The Process Decomposition must be complete before user task analysis can begin, as it will form the basis for this further analysis by identifying the major logical data flows between user and system. The work on the Process Distribution should have at least progressed to the stage where user and system functions can be distinguished, even if agent assignments have not yet been made for all the internal system agents.

The importance of user task analysis is highlighted by the following examples of User Task Models for archetypal types of KBS:[2] a consultative system, a tutoring system and a learning system. These examples are simplistic, but serve to demonstrate that the user–system relationship can vary considerably, depending on the role of the system envisaged.

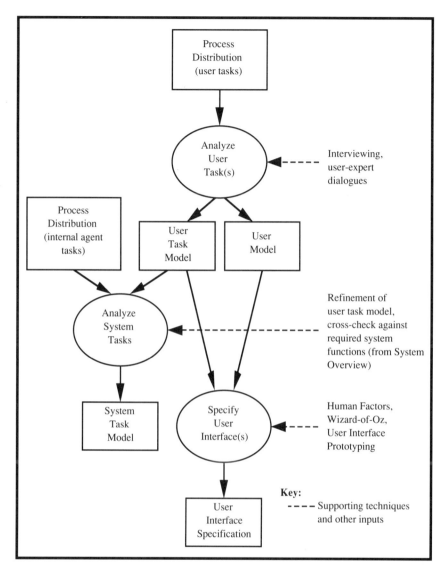

Figure 4.11
Cooperation Analysis
activities and results
(simple form, with no
other external agents
apart from the user)

Figure 4.12 illustrates the user–system relationship for a simple consultative KBS, using pseudo-code notation. Figure 4.13 uses the same notation to illustrate the user–system relationship for a tutoring system, where the aim of the system is to teach the user to solve problems. Figure 4.14 illustrates the user–system logic for a learning system, where the user helps the system to improve by indicating whether or not the solutions provided by the system are correct.

```
WHILE       NOT  exit     DO
     CASE   USER event
            exit:
            request help:
                 SYSTEM     provide help
            specify problem:
                 UNTIL     solved    DO
                     SYSTEM     provide question
                     USER           provide answer
                 LOOP
                 SYSTEM     provide solution
     LOOP
```

Figure 4.12 User Task Model for a consultative system

```
WHILE       NOT  exit     DO
     CASE   USER event
            exit:
            request help:
                 SYSTEM     provide help
            request problem:
                 SYSTEM     provide problem
                 UNTIL  solved OR user abort      DO
                     CASE     USER      event
                         abort:
                         ask question:
                              SYSTEM  provide  answer
                         specify solution:
                              IF    correct
                              THEN
                                   SYSTEM     acknowledge
                              ELSE
                                   SYSTEM     explain solution
                     LOOP
     LOOP
```

Figure 4.13 User Task Model for a tutoring system

User Task Analysis techniques and tools

If the major role of the prospective system is to support an existing expert task then, ideally, the desired behaviour of the system should be derived from observation of the user in action. One way of doing this is through the use of 'user–expert' dialogues, where the 'expert' and 'user' are both observed interacting with the analyst playing a fairly passive role, merely recording the interaction for later analysis. The analyst needs to ensure that the subjects do not stray from performing tasks that the system will be required to support, i.e. those in the Process Decomposition. Within

```
WHILE          NOT    exit         DO
     CASE      USER   event
               exit:
               request help:
                    SYSTEM       provide      help
               specify problem:
                    UNTIL    solved      DO
                         SYSTEM   provide   question
                         USER     provide   answer
                    LOOP
                    SYSTEM       provide      solution
                    IF   solution     is    wrong
                    THEN
                         USER     provide   correction
                         SYSTEM   update    knowledge   base
LOOP
```

Figure 4.14 User Task Model for a learning system

this basic approach, techniques such as mock-ups, the Wizard-of-Oz simulation technique and exploratory prototypes can be employed.

Exploratory prototyping can be used during the main part of this activity, where mock-ups of the tasks to be supported can be constructed and used during dialogue analysis (see Section 10.6.3). However, it may also be employed towards the end of User Task Analysis, where it will be experimental. There it will be used to assess the correctness of the user task logic. Problems detected at this stage will lead to a reworking of the model.

Of particular importance during User Task Analysis is the identification of data flows between user and system. To support their identification, KADS provides a *categorization of data* as follows:

Information – The data which are being used in the context of a specific session:
– Problem descriptions
– Support information
– Solution descriptions
This is the category which is most likely to be the subject of transfer between user and system.

Knowledge – The data that are not situation-specific (in this usage of the term). Knowledge owned by the system is represented in a model of the domain. However, for some systems, knowledge will need to be transferred to and from the user – especially if a knowledge-acquisition tool is incorporated into the system.

Skill – Procedural data. Where this is required for a task, the transfer will be realized as a set of instructions.

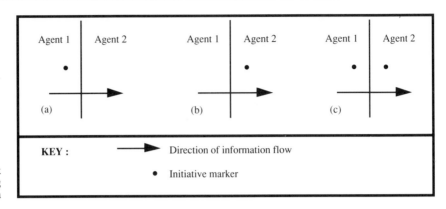

Figure 4.13 User Task
Model for a tutoring
system

It is also important to identify who takes the *initiative* for each flow of
information. Figure 4.15 illustrates the three possibilities when assigning
initiatives to agents in information flow. In case (a) the sender of the
information is the owner of the initiative; in (b) the recipient of the
information is the owner of the initiative; case (c) is a mixed initiative,
where both agents may trigger the information flow.

The User Task Model

'Analyze User Task(s)' results in the production of the User Task Model.
This comprises a specification of the logic of the user task with details of
information flows between user and system and how these are controlled.
Associated system tasks are identified and cross-referenced to the Process
Model.

The User Task Model can be presented in many different formats,
depending on the characteristics of the user task(s). State Transition
Diagrams, Statecharts,[3] pseudo-code or Jackson Structured Design (JSD)
representations may be used to describe tasks which are predominantly
sequential in nature. Special representation techniques, such as Role
Activity Diagrams, may be employed if the user task is unstructured.
(These are all non-KADS-specific notations borrowed from conventional
software analysis.)

Whichever representation style is adopted, it should specify the
following components:

- User states.
- User actions which trigger system activity (user events).
- Flow of information between user and system with an indication of
  who controls it.

- System actions which trigger or are triggered by user actions.
- User state changes in response to user or system actions.
- Cross-references back to the elements of the Process Model.

Figures 4.16–4.18 illustrate some of the acceptable representation formats, all based around the consultative system example provided in Figure 4.12.

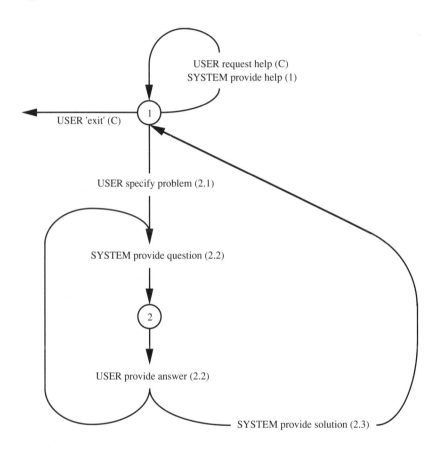

USER request help (C)
SYSTEM provide help (1)

USER 'exit' (C)   1

USER specify problem (2.1)

SYSTEM provide question (2.2)

2

USER provide answer (2.2)

SYSTEM provide solution (2.3)

Figure 4.16 User Task Model using State Transition Diagram

In Figure 4.16 the numbers in parentheses illustrate how cross-references are made back to the Process Model tasks. Agents responsible for initiating data flows prefix each action (event). The letter 'C' in parentheses indicates a flow of control, as opposed to a flow of data.

User Task modelling tools
General-purpose drawing tools such as MacDraw on the Apple Macintosh or similar PC-based packages may be used to construct User Task Model diagrams. Alternatively, support for drawing State Transition

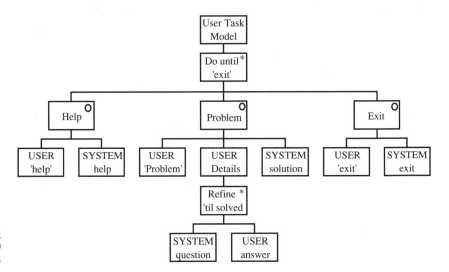

Figure 4.17 User Task
Model using JSD
notation

Diagrams may be found within several conventional CASE tools, which have benefits beyond those provided by general-purpose tools.

Note on other external Agent Task Modelling
If other external agents apart from the user were identified in Process Analysis, analogous 'Agent Task Modelling' to User Task Modelling will be required if the cooperation of these agents with the system is non-trivial. The result will be one or more (External) Agent Task Models using a notation from the same selection that was used for the User Task Model.

The User Model (optional)

The User Model is an optional output from User Task Analysis. Its aim is to present a model of the types of user the system will encounter. If the system is straightforward (has only one type of well-understood user) this document will not be necessary. On the other hand, some systems may have to interact with a variety of users: experts, knowledge engineers, and lay people. It may be an intelligent tutoring system or a KBS with machine-learning capabilities, where the system's expectations of the user alters as the user becomes more familiar with the system. In these cases a User Model becomes desirable. The model itself contains information concerning the capabilities of users; what they know, how they may use this knowledge and how they will interact with the system.

The User Model should be a structured document, but in KADS there

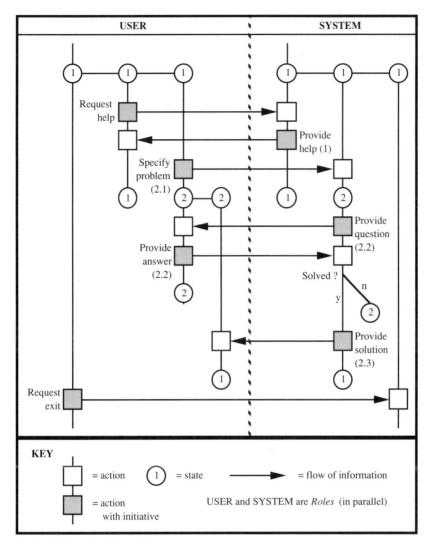

Figure 4.18 Role activity diagram for the User Task Model

is no formalism laid down for representing it. The following list of suggested contents is provided as a guide (others may be found in the human–computer interaction literature):

- User Characteristics – intellectual, physical, emotional.
- Task Content – duties, activities, messages, products, materials, tools.
- Task Context – workstation, workplace, job, organisation, society.

All users represented in the model should be checked with their real-life counterparts to ensure its accuracy.

Note on other External Agent Modelling

If other external agents apart from the user were identified in Process Analysis, analogous 'Agent Modelling' to User Modelling will be required if the cooperation of these agents with the system is non-trivial. The result will be one or more (External) Agent Models.

Example

Analyze User Task(s)

Interviews with Response Point operators identified a set of detailed user requirements refining those documented in the Process Model. These included:

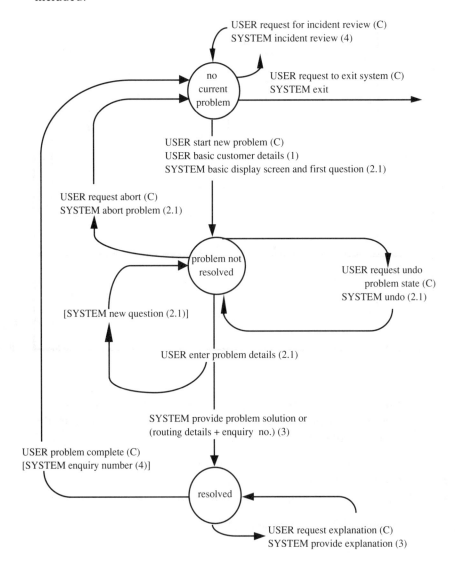

Figure 4.19 The state transition logic of the user task

- An 'undo' facility to retract previously supplied problem details.
- The ability to abort problems before completing their action.

The State Transition Diagram in Figure 14.9 describes the user task. Each state transition is triggered by an information (data) flow and may lead to further information flows. Each information flow is prefaced by the agent responsible for initiating the flow and is suffixed by the system task which manages the information. Some information flows are described as control flows (suffixed by 'C'). These are important to the User Task Model but are outside of the scope of the Process Model. Some flows are in square brackets, indicating that they are optional.

User task analysis may be used to cross-reference the Process Model. However, such analysis often unearths discrepancies in or omissions from the Process Model. The analyst always has the option, if applicable, to go back and enhance the Process Model to bring it in line with the findings of User Task Analysis. Hence, such analysis provides a useful cross-check for the earlier stages of system specification.

4.2.2   *Analyze System Task(s)*

Given the user–system relationship defined from the 'outside' view – the user's (or, in the general case, the external agent's) perspective – this activity addresses the internal view – the relationships between the agents internal to the system, i.e. the different components within the system. More precisely, system task analysis takes the User Task Model and expands the basic system actions into actions by and between the different types of internal system agents.

The main inputs to system task analysis are:

- The User Task Model – to identify the user events and user–system information flows.
- The Process Model – to help identify the agent actions and data flows which occur in reaction to each user event, and to be used as a cross-reference to assist in the traceability of requirements.
- The System Overview – to act as a cross-check, to ensure that all pertinent system functions have been considered.

System task analysis techniques
The basic technique is to take the User Task Model and to expand each system action, using the Process Model (Decomposition plus Distribution) as a guide. Decisions will need to be made during this activity about

the detail of the task distributions, i.e. exactly which actions occur within which tasks. If necessary, the analyst should be prepared to go back and amend the Process Model as needed.

The System Task Model

'Analyze System Task(s)' results in the production of the System Task Model – showing the same information as for the User Task Model but now refined to the level of internal system agent interaction. This model will be a primary input into Global Design (see Section 7.1).

The same basic representations can be used as for the User Task Model, such as State Transition Diagrams, Statecharts, pseudo-code, etc. (see p. 54). One way is to simply expand the prefixes on events from USER and SYSTEM, to include USER plus each internal system AGENT. Figure 4.20 illustrates how to extend the State Transition Diagram to involve internal system agents by being the System Task Model corresponding to the User Task Model shown in this figure. An alternative notation for describing the System Task Model can be found in the case study example below.

System task modelling tools
The System Task Model can be produced using the same tools as for the User Task Model.

Example

Analyze System Tasks

This example expands the trigger events in the User Task Model for the Response Point Expert System and defines the actions taken as a result of each trigger. References are made in each statement to the controlling agent and the corresponding task in the Process Model.

```
STATE no current problem
    EVENT USER request for incident review        (C)
        SYSTEM provide incident review            (4.1)
    EVENT USER request to exit system             (C)
        SYSTEM exit                               (C)
    EVENT USER request to start new problem       (C)
        USER provide basic customer details       (1)
        SYSTEM provide basic display screen       (2.1)
        KBS decide first question                 (2.2)
        SYSTEM display first question             (2.1)
        NEWSTATE problem not resolved
STATE problem not resolved
```

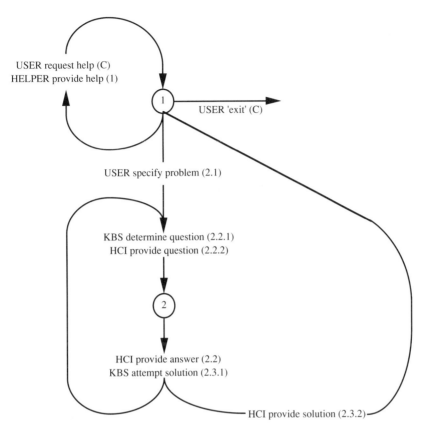

USER request help (C)
HELPER provide help (1)

1

USER 'exit' (C)

USER specify problem (2.1)

KBS determine question (2.2.1)
HCI provide question (2.2.2)

2

HCI provide answer (2.2)
KBS attempt solution (2.3.1)

HCI provide solution (2.3.2)

Figure 4.20 System Task Model using State Transition Diagram

EVENT USER request to abort problem	(C)
SYSTEM clear current problem	(2.1)
NEWSTATE no current problem	
EVENT USER request to 'undo' problem state	(C)
SYSTEM 'undo' problem state	(2.1)
EVENT USER enter problem detail	(2.1)
KBS compare against existing problems	(2.5)
IF solution found	
THEN	
SYSTEM display problem solution	(3)
NEWSTATE resolved	
KBS compare against network status	(2.4)
IF solution found	
THEN	
SYSTEM display problem solution	(3)
NEWSTATE resolved	
KBS attempt to route incident	(2.3)

```
IF solution found
THEN
    SYSTEM display routing decision                    (3.1)
    NEWSTATE resolved
ELSE
    KBS decide next question                           (2.2)
    SYSTEM display next question                       (2.1)
```

```
STATE resolved
    EVENT USER request explanation                     (C)
    KBS construct explanation                          (3.2)
    SYSTEM provide explanation                         (3.3)
    EVENT USER finish problem                          (C)
    IF need to log incident
    THEN
        SYSTEM log incident                            (4.2)
        SYSTEM provide enquiry number                  (4.3)
    NEWSTATE no current problem
```

4.2.3 Define User Interface(s)

User interface specification is an inexact science. There are no reliable methods for specifying or determining what constitutes a good user interface. This section should therefore be treated with caution and viewed as providing a set of guidelines only. The ultimate evaluation of a user interface rests with the user.

The main input to 'Define User Interface(s)' is the User Task Model. This should be backed up with the User Model (if produced), together with any Technical Constraints on the user interface implementation environment (Section 4.4.3) and Policy Constraints on user interface style (Section 4.4.4).

The major output from this activity is the User Interface Specification. User interface mock-ups or prototypes are often used to support this activity, and may even be employed to complement the User Interface Specification as a deliverable.

The User Task Model specifies the logic of the user task together with the information and control facilities which should be provided within the user interface. These details can be used to control User Interface Specification. The following guidelines provide one way to progress this specification activity:

- Choose a basic interaction style for the user interface. The most commonly used styles are:

- Text-based (command line format)
- Forms-based
- Menu-based (hierarchical navigation is usual)
- Graphics-based (views, browsers, pop-ups, pull-downs, etc.)
- Direct manipulation (graphics with real-world analogies).

The choice of interaction style should be moderated by the following considerations:

- The task characteristics – especially with respect to information flow. Simple applications can afford to be text based. If the information to be transferred is complex, then graphics are likely to be essential. Tasks which have static control structures may be well supported by a menu-based approach. A mixture of the above approaches is, of course, always possible.
- The user characteristics – especially with respect to past experience and linguistic capability. A direct manipulation interface is difficult and expensive to implement, but may be well suited to users with little computer experience or with language difficulties (e.g. non-native English speakers).
- The Technical and Policy Constraints. These may dictate the user interface style or specify a development environment which limits the possible choice of style.

- Analyze each control or information flow within the User Task Model and map them onto a user interface component. Initially it will be necessary to make educated guesses as to the best way to represent some information or control, e.g. by choosing a button rather than a menu item. Any doubts about the choice of user interface components should be resolved by prototyping and user trials (see below).
- Group the user interface components into logically related sets, e.g. all controls within a single user state could be mapped onto either a menu or a dialog box.
- Decide how to lay out the user interface components on the screen. Describe how the state of the user interface changes in response to each user or system trigger event.
- Refine the User Interface Specification by user evaluation. This is where user interface prototyping is invaluable (see below).
- Once the basic details of the user interface have been agreed, construct guidelines for user interface implementation later in the development.

User interface prototyping

User interface prototyping is probably the most valuable technique in

User Interface Specification. The form of the prototype can range from a simple paper diagram, through computer-based mock-ups, to a full-blown user interface implementation. The last of these is inadvisable because of the time that will be spent on prototype development. However, many tools are now available that facilitate the rapid development of a user interface façade. Such tools can be used with simple code stubs to provide an early but relatively realistic mock-up of the proposed user interface 'look and feel'. The choice of tool may be constrained by the selected user interface style and implementation environment.

User interface evaluation can be either *subjective* or *objective* (or both). Subjective evaluation by the user(s) is important because, if the user is unhappy with the interface, then the application is likely not to be used. Objective evaluation requires special equipment (to measure response times, etc.), but can provide vital information about the match between user interface and user task.

Finally, user interface prototypes can be either exploratory (helping to define the specification) or experimental (checking that the specification is satisfactory).

The User Interface Specification

The User Interface Specification document should consist of the following sections:

- An overview of the user requirements with references to relevant Constraints documents.
- A description of the chosen interaction style for the user interface.
- A list of descriptions of the user-interface components which will be needed to support the user interface, plus diagrams as required.
- A *consists-of* hierarchy of user interface components, backed up by a schematic view of the user-interface layout.
- Descriptions of the user and system actions which effect changes to the user interface.
- Guidelines for user-interface implementation, including any results of prototyping and advice concerning suitable toolkits.

The exact form of representation will depend largely on the chosen interface style. However, *consists-of* hierarchies help to show how the user interface breaks down into its constituent parts. For complex interfaces, state transition fragments may be associated with individual interface components. In the extreme, this leads the interface style away from direct task support towards a kind of support which is based around the user-interface components. Such interfaces are liable to exhibit a high

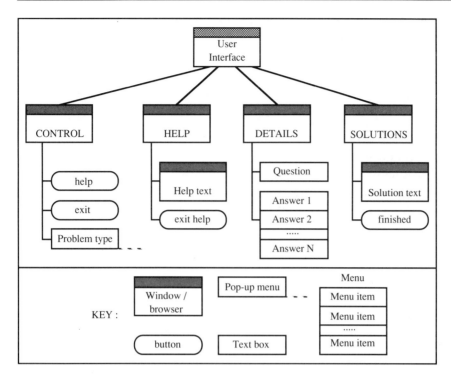

Figure 4.21 Example user interface structure as a *consists-of* hierarchy

degree of parallelism and are well suited to the support of so-called 'professional' tasks (tasks generally performed by professional people, such as managers), where context switches are many and frequent.[4] Figure 4.21 illustrates a *consists-of* hierarchy for an example user interface:

User interface specification tools

General-purpose drawing tools, such as MacDraw on the Apple Macintosh or similar PC-based packages may be used to construct the hierarchy of interface components, and also to illustrate screen layout schematically. An outliner may be found useful for drawing the hierarchy. Conventional CASE tools may also contain editors that can be useful here. The rest of the User Interface Specification can be documented with plain text.

User-interface prototyping is perhaps most easily done using a special-purpose user interface building tool. Many such tools are available for a wide range of hardware platforms, too numerous to mention here. More general, easily programmable tools, such as Hypercard on the Apple Macintosh, have also been found to be effective in this role. The prototypes so built can be used as part of the User Interface Specification, with suitable additional documentation to state where the final interface will differ from the prototype.

Example	**Define User Interfaces**

The User Task Analysis for the Response Point Expert System identified a variety of User Interface requirements. These are:

1. The need to support control information, such as requests to start problem investigation, exit system, abort, undo, etc.
2. A method for the provision of basic customer details (name, location, phone number, etc.).
3. An area for the system to offer questions and elicit answers.
4. An area for the user to offer problem details independently of the question/answer dialogue.
5. Support for the 'undo' facility, by providing the user with a list of current problem details.
6. Support for the display of the problem resolution, as an immediate solution or a routing decision.
7. A way to provide explanations of problem resolutions.
8. Display of the incident enquiry number.
9. Support for browsing previously reported incidents.

Since by this stage of analysis the decision had been taken to use a Graphical User Interface (GUI) to support the expert system, there was good support for all the above requirements. It was decided to map the above requirements onto the following GUI elements:

1. Buttons.
2. Dialog box, only visible at problem start.
3. Fixed menu with directly selectable items.
4. Sensitive boxes for each category of problem detail; attached pop-up menus for further levels of detail.
5. An 'audit trail' of problem details, each detail sensitive to user selection to allow retraction of that problem detail.
6. Dialog box with button for explanation request.
7. Dialog box, visible only when explanation provided.
8. Dialog box, visible only when user has completed a problem which requires incident logging.
9. Dialog box plus Browser, visible only when the user has selected 'browse incidents'.

Figure 4.22 provides a schematic illustration of the proposed interface layout.

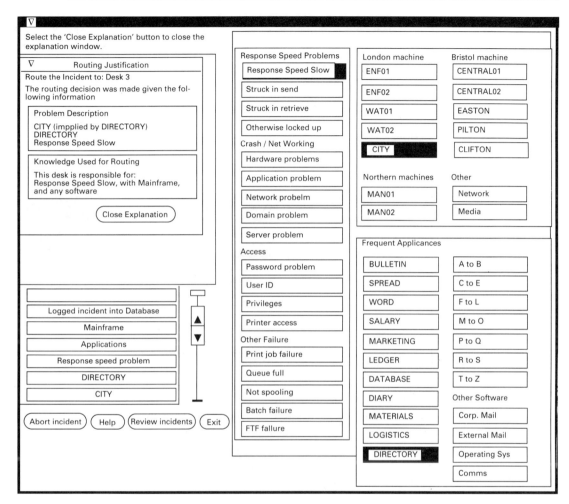

Figure 4.22 The user interface layout

4.3   Expertise Analysis

Expertise Analysis is that stage of KADS Analysis concerned with building a model of the knowledge-based activities that the system must perform. It follows on naturally from Process Analysis and Cooperation Analysis in that Process Analysis will have identified the system tasks and data stores which will be knowledge-based, together with their associated data flows; and Cooperation Analysis (especially system task analysis) will have identified the overall system processing context within which these tasks are invoked. Figure 4.23 shows the temporal relationship of Expertise Analysis relative to the other Analysis stages.

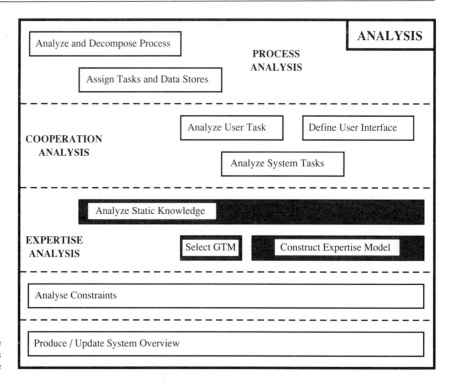

Figure 4.23 The
Expertise Analysis
stage

The main aim of Expertise Analysis is to describe an implementation-independent representation of the problem-solving capability of the prospective system. The resultant model, known as the Expertise Model, is perhaps the key feature of the KADS methodology. It represents problem-solving knowledge in four layers: Domain, Inference, Task and Strategy. The Expertise Model is described in detail in Section 4.3.1.

The primary inputs needed for this stage of Analysis are the Process Model and various Constraints documents. The System Task Model will be needed to complete the activity.

To support the activities of constructing an Expertise Model, and to enable a high degree of re-use of these models, KADS provides a library of so-called Generic Task Models (see Chapter 12). A Generic Task Model (GTM) is basically a domain-independent representation of a problem-solving task, such as classification, planning or monitoring, and is produced by stripping away the domain-specific knowledge from an Expertise Model and generalizing the task-related elements of the other layers. A GTM provides a template which can be used to drive knowledge acquisition and modelling in a structured and efficient manner.

The activities within Expertise Analysis are concerned with the construction of a four-layer Expertise Model, and involve the selection or construction of a Generic Task Model as the primary means to achieve this. There are three activities within Expertise Analysis:

- Analyze Static Knowledge.
- Select/Construct Initial Generic Task Model.
- Construct Expertise Model.

'Analyze Static Knowledge' builds up the Domain Layer of the Expertise Model by identifying and describing the static knowledge which supports problem solving. This knowledge can take many forms, depending on the characteristics of the individual domain and task involved. It is described in terms of structures of concepts and relationships between concepts, known in KADS as Domain Structures.

'Select/Construct Initial Generic Task Model' provides a template for further, task-related knowledge acquisition. The KADS Generic Task Model Library (GTML) supports the selection or construction of an appropriate model. The resultant Generic Task Model identifies the individual problem-solving steps (inferences) and their potential sequences which will be needed to support the knowledge-based system task(s). It guides the analyst during subsequent knowledge acquisition by indicating the types of domain knowledge and control structures which will be needed to achieve problem solving using these inference steps.

'Construct Expertise Model' completes the Expertise Analysis by filling out the details of the Inference, Task and Strategy layers and putting them together with the Domain Layer (from 'Analyze Static Knowledge') to form the final four-layer Expertise Model.

Apart from the selection/construction and use of Generic Task Models, Expertise Analysis is supported in KADS by a variety of knowledge-acquisition techniques. Details of these may be found in Chapter 10, and Section 10.4 in particular. Prototyping may also be used to validate the choice of Generic Task Model or Domain Structure representation. Early prototyping of the entire problem-solving process (i.e. the entire four-layer Expertise Model) can prove useful for complex domains or tasks, but the effort involved should be taken into account when planning such a project.

Figure 4.24 illustrates the relationships between the activities and results within Expertise Analysis. This is followed by a detailed explanation of the structure of the Expertise Model and the individual activities which support its construction.

4.3.1   *The KADS four-layer model of Expertise*

The KADS Expertise Model provides a way of describing a knowledge-

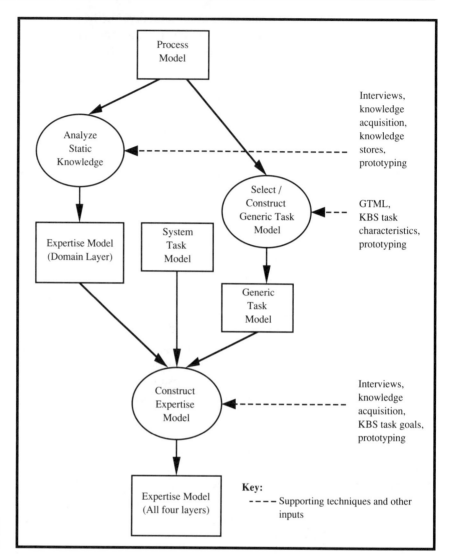

Figure 4.24 Expertise Analysis activities and results

based, problem-solving capability in an implementation-independent manner. The construction of an Expertise Model provides several benefits over the traditional approach of building a KBS by evolutionary prototyping:

- The problem-solving knowledge can be represented in a way that is suited to knowledge acquisition, rather than one that is forced by the chosen implementation tool.
- The knowledge represented within the model can be validated independently of the need to write and execute code.

- Rare or unavailable knowledge can be archived without having to write a system to do this.
- Design decisions can be made without affecting the knowledge-acquisition process.
- The Expertise Model, in whole or in part, can be re-used in future enhancements or re-implementations.
- Parts of the Expertise Model can be re-used to support other tasks in the same domain or the same task in other domains.

The Expertise Model distinguishes four categories of knowledge which mesh together in a layered structure. Figure 4.25 presents a simple schematic view.

Expertise Models are constructed by a process of refinement and filling-out of a template called a 'Generic Task Model' – essentially an Expertise Model with its Domain Layer removed. These are described on p. 78. First, though, each layer of the Expertise Model is described in turn.

The Domain Layer

The first knowledge category in the Expertise Model, the **Domain Layer**, is concerned with a definition of static domain knowledge, consisting of structures of domain concepts and relationships between concepts. This knowledge is static in the sense that it presents a description of the facts

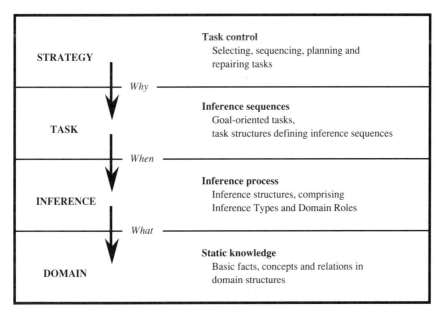

Figure 4.25 The four layers of the Expertise Model

about the domain of interest without any concept of how this knowledge might be used in problem solving. In this sense the domain knowledge is task neutral and can potentially be put to a variety of uses (e.g. diagnosis, prediction, teaching, etc.). The structures of domain concepts and relations are known in KADS as **Domain Structures**. Frames, *is-a* hierarchies, rule sets and algebraic formulae are examples of potential Domain Structures in KADS.[5]

KADS does not prescribe a fixed formalism for describing these Domain Structures. It recognizes that different domains and tasks will place very different requirements upon the way in which the knowledge must be structured and represented, e.g. temporal logic for real-time domains, modal logic for legal domains, linear constraints and heuristic rules for manufacturing logistics domains, etc. The choice of an appropriate representation formalism is left to the knowledge engineer. However, KADS does provide a default – the Domain Modelling Language (DML). This is described in Section 4.3.2.

A non-exhaustive description of Domain Structures is that they may comprise:

- *Concepts* – simple definitions of things of interest.
- *Structures* (or frames) – ways of relating concepts or attributes of concepts.
- *Relations* – ways of associating concepts or structures.
- *'Models'* – ways of grouping relations around problem-solving themes.

Figure 4.26 shows some examples of these types of static knowledge.

The Inference Layer

The second knowledge category in the Expertise Model, the **Inference Layer**, describes a basic inference capability in terms of inference types and domain roles. It identifies what inferences (deductions) are supported over the knowledge in the Domain Layer within the selected task(s), but does not dictate when or in what order the inferences actually happen. Inference types and domain roles are arranged in one or more Inference Structures.

Inference types

Inference types are descriptions of the way domain concepts, relations or structures can be used to make inferences. For instance, the 'classify' inference type takes an object plus its attributes and determines the type of the object. Domain knowledge is static and may be used in a number of ways; an inference type directs the ways in which domain knowledge may be used. Other examples of inference types are 'generalize' and

CONCEPT

    Change_Request   : A structured representation of a request to make
                                               changes to the computer infrastructure

STRUCTURE

    Change_Request

        Type   : form
        Originator   : name
        Location   : place_name
        Items affected   : list_of (item)
        Approved   : boolean
        Approver   : name

RELATIONS

    temperature ***affects*** sound_speed
    change_request ***is_a*** form

MODEL
(Arrows show 'effects' — may actually be modelled as mathematical equations)

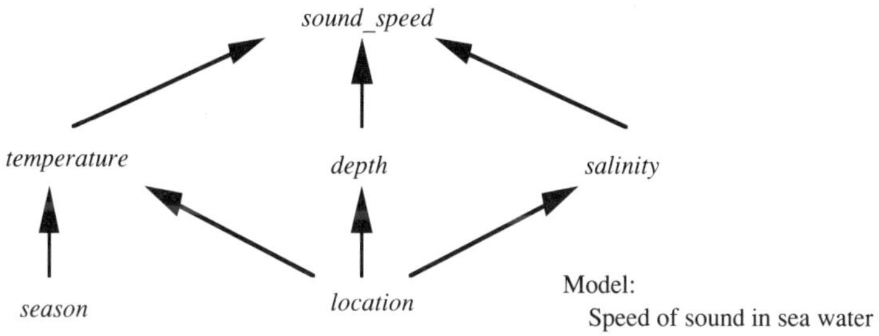

Model:
Speed of sound in sea water

Figure 4.26 Examples of Domain Structure components

'compare' – for a more complete set of definitions of these, refer to Section 11.2.

It is important to note that inference types do not fix a strategy, or sequencing, for problem-solving processes. Rather, they are 'handles' for the control of inference described at the next layer, the Task Layer.

    Domain roles
Domain roles describe the jobs that the packets of domain knowledge may perform. For example, in a medical diagnosis system a particular infection (the domain knowledge: e.g. '*E. coli* bacteria') may be either a hypothesis to be verified or a solution from an earlier reasoning process.

These are *two different roles* for a *single* domain concept. Similarly, a 'fever' may be either a symptom or a manifestation, depending on the roles it plays in different contexts. Thus, an individual domain concept may be associated with more than one domain role and vice versa. Essentially, then, domain roles are a more precise means of speaking about domain concepts within problem-solving processes.

Domain roles are sometimes classified according to the way they are used in problem solving. For example, they can be part of the problem description, general input data, intermediary values, support knowledge ('background' knowledge for an inference type; sometimes private, sometimes not), or the solution (result) of problem solving.

The Inference Structure

The **Inference Structure** is a network of inference types and domain roles. It *explicitly describes* which inferences can be made and *implicitly describes* which cannot. It puts constraints on the reasoning process. There is *no ordering* of inferences at this level, so there is no specification of how and when to perform the inferences. There may be more than one Inference Structure in the Inference Layer.

Ultimately, the Task Layer constrains the reasoning process to define which inferences are *actually made* as opposed to which are *possible to make*.

The **diagrammatic conventions** for Inference Structures are as follows:

- Domain roles are represented as rectangles with their name inside (usually a noun).
- Inference types are ellipses with their name inside (usually a verb).
- Possible directions of inference steps are marked by one-way arrows.
- An inference type is a transformation of one or more domain roles into one or more new domain roles. The constraints on inputs to, and outputs from, inference types are defined in Section 11.2.
- No domain role may be directly connected to another domain role.
- No inference type may be directly connected to another inference type.
- Support knowledge domain roles are optional (they can clutter diagrams).
- Ellipses with emboldened lines and/or the 'inference type' name in italics, are used to indicate sub-tasks used in the guise of inference types, where another entire inference structure may be considered to be embedded within the current one.

Figure 4.27 illustrates the basic diagrammatic elements of an inference structure. The 'Inference Steps' marked would be replaced by valid

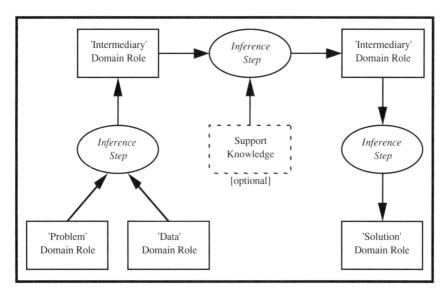

Figure 4.27 Abstract Inference Structure illustrating types of Domain Role

Inference Types in a real Inference Structure. Steps of inference are the run-time manifestations of inference types, and are used here to illustrate the processing of general types of Domain Roles. Many examples of Inference Structures conforming to these rules can be found in the KADS Generic Task Model Library, in Chapter 12; see also the libraries of Domain Roles and Inference Types in Chapter 11.

The Task Layer

The third knowledge category in the Expertise Model is the **Task Layer**. This describes how the individual inferences within the Inference Layer may be sequenced in order to satisfy each of the required problem-solving goals. The knowledge in this category is composed into one or more Task Structures, each of which may be defined statically (with a fixed control structure) or dynamically (e.g. as the result of a planning process within the Strategy Layer – see p. 77).

Task Structures are typically simple sequences of inferences wrapped in some conventional procedural control structures, such as selection (IF . . . THEN . . . ELSE) and repetition (e.g. FOR, WHILE and REPEAT). However, they may also incorporate more complex notions such as parallelism between inferences or groups of inferences, pipelining (in a sequence of inferences, the next sequence may be started before the current sequence is complete) and recursion (the task calls itself).

Task Structures are normally depicted using pseudo-code, although

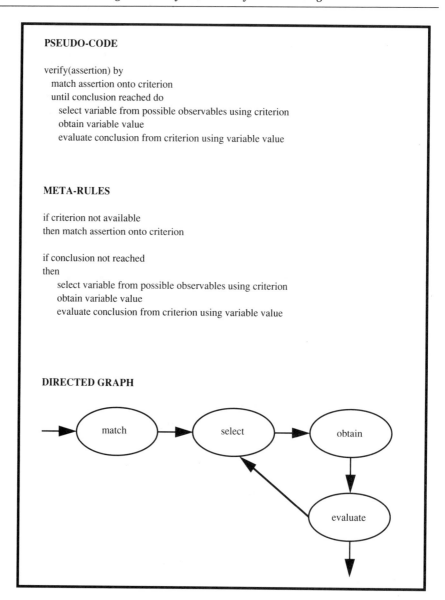

PSEUDO-CODE

verify(assertion) by
  match assertion onto criterion
  until conclusion reached do
    select variable from possible observables using criterion
    obtain variable value
    evaluate conclusion from criterion using variable value

META-RULES

if criterion not available
then match assertion onto criterion

if conclusion not reached
then
    select variable from possible observables using criterion
    obtain variable value
    evaluate conclusion from criterion using variable value

DIRECTED GRAPH

Figure 4.28 Three alternative Task Structure representations

('meta'-)rules and directed graphs (also called 'dependency graphs') are also valid representations. Figure 4.28 illustrates how these three representation techniques may be applied to the same example. (See Section 12.4.2 for a proper description of the 'verification' task.) Further examples of Task Structures can be found in the KADS Generic Task Model Library in Chapter 12, where a slightly more formal form of procedural pseudo-code is used than that shown in Figure 4.28.

The Strategy Layer

The final knowledge category in the Expertise Model is the **Strategy Layer**. This provides strategic knowledge to select, sequence, plan or repair (when a task fails) the necessary Task Structures. Strategic level knowledge provides for a very flexible form of problem solving, for example by rescheduling the set of goals dynamically on detection of impasses due to unavailability of information or conflicts within the reasoning process.[6]

The Strategy Layer may be used to describe the following types of strategic knowledge:

Goal selection – On receipt of some trigger from the user or another agent the KBS agent may need to determine the most appropriate goal(s) to satisfy. For example, if a user supplies the information 'Computer screen showing ERROR 23', does the KBS offer interpretation of the error message or attempt diagnosis (or both)?

Task structure selection – Once a goal to be satisfied has been determined it may be possible to satisfy this in several ways using different task structures. Some aspect of the problem or its input data may be used to select the appropriate task structure to execute. An example of this is provided within the Generic Task Model for Heuristic Classification (see p. 305) where the cost of obtaining data is used to choose between forward or backward chaining.

Goal sequencing – The strategic knowledge may help to determine the best way to sequence problem-solving goals. If not all the relevant information is available to perform a task, for example, the strategy layer may need to add in an extra goal before the main one.

Task structure configuration – This is a more complex form of goal sequencing, where the strategy must first plan the necessary sequence of inferences or goals before execution. This kind of strategy is found only in advanced systems which offer a very general problem-solving capability which must be refined and configured for every new eventuality.

Mode of KBS operation – The way in which a task structure is executed/interpreted may depend on the problem-solving context. For example, in tutoring systems a task may be executed standalone, in teaching mode or in critique mode, with corresponding implications for the way in which the inferences are executed and recorded.

Inference control and repair – A system which supports very flexible problem solving may be able to monitor task execution, detect failures, repair them and continue. For example, a system might start by looking for simple heuristics to effect problem solving, but on failure resort to deeper reasoning – perhaps based on qualitative or causal models.

Having introduced and described the elements of the four-layer Expertise Model, the following section describes the Generic Task Model, which is a modified form of Expertise Model.

Generic Task Models

Generic Task Models are used to provide a bootstrap mechanism for driving the construction of Expertise Models. The idea is that they are a better starting point for building Expertise Models than starting each Expertise Model from scratch. Further, Generic Task Models can be produced from newly built (tested, and verified) Expertise Models. Where they represent a new problem-solving task or a significant variation of an existing task, such Generic Task Models can be added to the portfolio of known Generic Task Models. This can facilitate a considerable degree of potential re-use. A current set of available Generic Task Models is presented in a library in Chapter 12.

A Generic Task Model may be thought of as a domain-independent version of the four-layer Expertise Model. It contains the Inference Layer, Task Layer and perhaps some Strategic knowledge, but no Domain Layer – Figure 4.29 shows this relationship. This figure also hints at one way in which Generic Task Models can be produced: by taking an existing Expertise Model and removing its Domain layer. This is a slight simplification, however, as to be as useful as possible in the future the Domain Roles (and perhaps Inference Types) documented in the Inference layer of the Expertise Model should also be generalized. (They will probably be couched in domain-specific terms for convenience in a real Expertise Model.) Alternatively, Generic Task Models can be built from scratch – but this is notoriously difficult where truly generic models are concerned. Some further general information on Generic Task

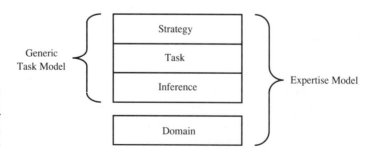

Figure 4.29
Simplified
relationship of
Generic Task Model to
Expertise Model

Models is presented in Chapter 12; see also Section 4.3.3.

Having introduced and described Expertise Models and Generic Task Models, the following sections of this chapter describe the activities which are used in the construction of Expertise Models.

4.3.2 *Analyze Static Knowledge*

The 'Analyze Static Knowledge' activity proceeds in parallel with, and is largely independent from, the 'Select/Construct Initial Generic Task Model' and 'Construct Expertise Model' activities in Expertise Analysis. The aim of the activity is to produce the set of Domain Structures which will make up the Domain Layer of the Expertise Model.

The analysis proceeds step by step. The basic list of domain terms is drawn up (if appropriate, by augmenting the Process Glossary); the terms are refined; the concepts are formalized; the Domain Structures are identified; concepts and relationships are defined and put into the structures.

A major input to this task will be background knowledge (in the form of reference books and background material), together with any definitions of domain terms and structures recorded by the Process Glossary, the System Overview and the Constraints Analysis activities and their documents – in particular, partial drafts of the 'Model of Present Situation', 'Functioning Objectives' and 'Functioning Problems' (see p. 107). However, a significant input will be obtained from interviews with the client and experts.

The techniques employed in the analysis of static knowledge can be split into four categories:

* *General reading* – (Self-explanatory).
* *Interviewing* – Collection of the raw data for analysis.
* *Interview analysis* – Identification of the relevant issues for the domain layer.
* *Knowledge representation* – Finding a suitable representation for the domain layer.

Note that the level of detail involved in the capture of static knowledge at this stage of the development is an issue that must be decided early on in performing this activity. The level largely depends on the type of system being built and how generic it should be. For example, should this activity capture *all* the knowledge items that will be stored in the first release of the system? Should it only capture the general classes of knowledge items? If the latter, does the project plan include an activity to capture and code up the actual knowledge that will go into the first release of the system? It does not really matter which approach is taken, but the project manager and knowledge engineer need to agree the approach to be taken for their particular project.

Interviewing for static knowledge analysis

This section provides a brief introduction to the interviewing techniques which may be used to support static knowledge analysis. Further details may be found in Chapter 10.

The primary methods for obtaining data for analyzing static knowledge are the focused interview, the structured interview and the tutorial interview:

> **The focused interview** – This is most suitable for eliciting factual domain knowledge. It will primarily be used to identify the important concepts and their definitions. See Section 10.5.1.
>
> **The structured interview** – The purpose of a structured interview is to gain detailed insights into parts of the static domain knowledge. It is primarily used for detailed, structured knowledge acquisition, not for becoming familiar with the domain. Therefore it is suited to the building of the Domain Structures. See Section 10.5.2.
>
> **The tutorial interview** – The purpose of a tutorial interview is to gain an initial understanding of the domain. It should only be used when there is a lack of textbooks or other reference material. Its primary use is in identifying domain concepts. See Section 10.5.4.

Apart from interviewing, a variety of non-verbal techniques exist to support static knowledge acquisition. These include the use of so-called repertory grids. See Section 10.7.1.

Analysis of interview results

The primary means of assessing the data obtained by interview will be by reviewing them. Reviewing consists of studying interview transcripts, correcting them (with the help of the expert if necessary) and identifying gaps in understanding. (Sometimes this is called 'protocol analysis'.) Reviewing will also enable inconsistencies in the information (whether real or only apparent) to be discovered at an early stage. The result of a review will often be a further interview with the expert, so the interview/ review process should not be seen as merely one-way. Acquisition will cycle through these activities until sufficient knowledge is gained to 'sign-off' the Domain Structures.

Knowledge representation

The final part of the 'Analyze Static Knowledge' activity is the representation of the knowledge. Generally, the way the domain concepts and relations are structured is selected on the basis of experience. In theory, the Domain Layer of the Expertise Model should be entirely inference-independent (for example, the same Domain Layer should be equally applicable to a diagnostic system or to an intelligent teaching system). In reality, the way the Domain Structure is represented will constrain the inferences which can be performed upon it.

A simple way of representing domain knowledge is in *consists-of*, *is-a* or similar hierarchies, or perhaps as frames. These will accommodate most domains' knowledge. A richer knowledge representation, chosen to suit the requirements of a particular domain, may also be used. (See also Section 13.2.) Entity Relationship Diagrams (ERDs) from conventional structured analysis methods may also be found useful, although they are best avoided for representing relatively complex knowledge as richer notations are available from the KBS world.

Many of the more advanced knowledge engineering toolkits, such as KEE, provide graphical facilities for structuring domain knowledge. Alternatively, conventional outlining or drawing tools may be used to draw up concept structures and hierarchies. CASE tools will generally have an ERD editor.

The Domain Modelling Language (DML)

The major support tool for the 'Analyze Static Knowledge' activity is the Domain Modelling Language (DML) – although its use within KADS is optional. The basic DML provides a set of eight general-purpose constructs with which to represent the static domain knowledge elicited:

Concept – An entity set or class. The term *concept* corresponds roughly to either *entity* or *class* in other data-modelling schemata.

Structure – An aggregate concept for which a set of parts is defined. Parts may be of types concept, set, structure; e.g. an 'address' has street number, street, postal district, town, country.

Set – A grouping of instances of other constructs. All members must be of the same construct type, i.e. relations, structures, concepts, logical expressions or sets. A cardinality range can be specified over a set; e.g. a 'family' is a set of people with two-plus members.

Relation – Relations specify roles for other constructs. An *n*-ary relation will have *n* roles. Each role may be assigned a cardinality; e.g. 'married(man[1,1],woman[1,1])'.

Sub-type relation – A binary relation used for building abstraction hierarchies of concepts, relations, sets and structures. All attribute-functions, parts or roles defined on the higher object are inherited on the lower one; e.g. 'sub-type-of(mammal,dog)'.

Atomic expression – A simple expression consisting of three parts: an operand, a logical operator and a value; e.g. 'temperature > 0'.

Attribute function – An attribute function operates on a single construct of type concept, relation, structure or is set to a value-set; e.g. 'age(man) → integer'.

Value-set – Value-sets are the ranges of attribute functions. Their members can be one of the value types: *string*, *natural number*, *integer*, *real* or *boolean*. Note that ranges cannot be other constructs; in these cases attributes are modelled as relations.

The Summary of Notations at the end of this book provides a complete BNF description of the Domain Modelling Language and also describes an alternative graphical notation.

It is important to note that the Domain Modelling Language allows models that are logically equivalent, but that use different combinations of constructs. For example, any structure could be defined by a set of *consists-of* relations emanating from a concept. This is a consequence of providing for ease of use and conciseness, rather than rigour and uniformity.

Prototyping the Domain Layer

Prototyping carried out during this part of Analysis may be concerned with choosing a suitable knowledge-representation formalism. It may be useful to animate a fragment of the data collected at an early stage to see how well dependencies can be captured. The selection of a good representation formalism will save time later on and prototyping can aid this choice.

Prototyping may also be more generally useful to aid many forms of knowledge elicitation, including eliciting static knowledge. It is particularly effective when used in an interview situation, either as a support for questions or as a focus for a discussion – but it should not be relied upon for one-off interviews. It is effective because the operationalizing of key system concepts can create many ideas in the expert and interviewer alike.

Example

Analyze Static Knowledge

The elicitation of static domain knowledge will proceed in parallel to the other Expertise Analysis activities ('Select Initial Generic Task Model' and 'Construct Expertise Model'). The resultant Domain Structures describe the domain concepts and relations in a graphical or textual form. A fragment of the routing knowledge for the Response Point Expert System is shown below. This is followed by part of the *is-a* hierarchy for Response Point problems (see Figure 4.30). Both of these are Domain Structures in KADS terms.

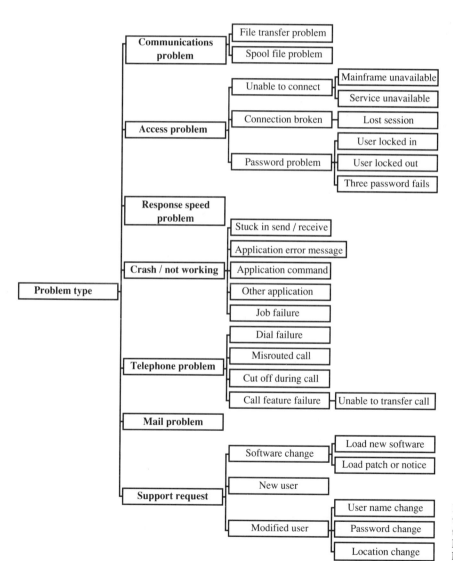

Figure 4.30 Part of the *is-a* hierarchy for types of problem handled by Response Point

Problem type	Hardware involved	Software involved	Front-line desk
Response speed slow	Mainframe	Any application	Desk 1
Response speed slow	Video conferencing	Any application	Desk 2
Stuck in send/receive	Any	Any application	Desk 3
Telephone problem	Internal phone N/W	Any application	Desk 4
Locked out	Mainframe	SALARY	Desk 5
Locked out	Mainframe	BULLETIN	Desk 2
Locked out	Mainframe	IP41	MISIP41
Locked out	Mainframe	IP21	Desk 1
Locked out	Mainframe	Others	File controller
Locked in	Mainframe	Known application	Desk 1
Locked in	Mainframe	Unknown application	File controller

4.3.3   Select/construct initial Generic Task Model

A Generic Task Model (GTM) provides a template for the structured analysis of expertise. GTM selection should be started in parallel with the 'Analyze Static Knowledge' activity, as soon as Process Analysis activities are reasonably complete. It should be completed before the 'Construct Expertise Model' activity commences. The latter activity uses the GTM(s) produced by this activity to focus further knowledge acquisition and representation in a structured and efficient manner. The GTM(s) consist of a sketch of the Inference, Task and Strategy Layers which will eventually become the major parts of the Expertise Model.

The major inputs for model selection are the Process Distribution (KBS tasks) and the Generic Task Model Library (GTML). The types of problem covered by the GTML fall into three main categories:

System analysis – Problem-solving proceeds from a description of a complex system to the identification or classification of some feature of the system. When problem solving is complete the original system is left unmodified.

System synthesis – In synthesis tasks the goal is to produce a description of a system (e.g. a design or plan) that meets some initial requirements.

System modification – Problem solving takes a system description as input and outputs a new system description in which at least one component has been changed. These tasks will usually contain both analysis and synthesis components.

The division of generic tasks into these three categories is shown in the GTML, where a detailed description of all the existing models is also given. The library, in its current version, is available in hard-copy format in Chapter 12 of this book. As more projects are conducted using KADS, the library should be expanded – readers should expand it locally for their own organizations and consider publishing any particularly successful models.

It must be borne in mind that, due to the inevitably incomplete nature of the library, an off-the-shelf GTM will not always be suitable for a project. In such cases, a new GTM can be built from fragments of existing ones. In any case, a familiarity with the existing GTML is required for this activity – and the more familiarity, the better.

The selection of the initial GTM is primarily an identification task for the knowledge engineer and is based mostly on familiarity with the GTML. It is made by the recognition of similarities with known tasks or by exploring possibilities based on the key characteristics of the task. An initial guideline is the input–output behaviour of the task. This will give an indication of which type of problem (system analysis, synthesis or modification) the system is closest to.

Once selected, the GTM(s) will need to be refined to 'fit' the characteristics of the expert task(s). This will involve removing or modifying parts of the model(s), and specializing the terminology to fit that of the chosen domain.

The final product of this activity is the chosen (or constructed) GTM. This is the primary input for the next stage of Analysis, 'Construct Expertise Model'. Because of the general nature of the library models, the knowledge engineer should continually test the model against a growing understanding of the task and domain. If necessary, the model should be further refined as analysis proceeds.

GTM construction

The models in the GTML are best seen as representing general-purpose, problem-solving tasks. For a specific case it may well be that no single library model fits the observed (or required) behaviour. In such cases the library models are used in a less 'top-down' manner. The knowledge engineer will need to identify problem-solving 'fragments' which are represented disparately in the library and synthesize these to form a new GTM.

For some tasks, notably for system modification and synthesis tasks where little support is provided, it will be necessary to build a GTM from the inference type primitives, or even to introduce new inference types. This approach will necessarily operate in a more data-driven or bottom-up manner than in cases where support from pre-existing models is available. Using the classification of inferences in the inference type categorization or 'typology' (see Chapter 11 for the categories of inference types (Section 11.2.1) and domain roles (Section 11.1.1)), the knowledge engineer imposes a typing of inferences in the observed problem-solving behaviour. For these cases, the acquisition phases of Analysis will probably first need to use introspection (Section 10.5.3) or self-report (Section 10.6.1) to obtain basic data, before using the other interview techniques once the GTM is drafted.

At the time of writing there are no tools available to support GTM refinement or construction specifically. If an electronic version of the GTML is available, this may be fed directly into a suitable word processor and/or drawing tool to facilitate modification.

Prototyping the GTM

In order to estimate the correctness of the selected GTM it may be useful to prototype the model. This will involve animating part of the results of the 'Analyze Static Knowledge' task and implementing some form of the inference and task layers. The advantage of a prototype is that this can be shown to the expert for verification – an expert is more likely to relate to a 'working system' than to an abstract four-layer model. As well as verifying the GTM, the cost of the prototyping exercise may also help to refine the estimation of the cost of building the complete system.

The Generic Task Model Document

This document should describe the GTM(s) which have been chosen or constructed for current use. It should follow the general style of the entries in the GTML in Chapter 12 (or be a simple reference to the model's source, e.g. this book) and the following should be covered:

1. *Domain roles* – A list of the names and descriptions of the domain roles to be used in the model, with cross-references to the Domain Structures onto which these can be mapped.
2. *Inference types* – A description of the inference types used in the model. They should be described using a frame structure consisting of the following slots:
    * The name and description (plain English) of the inference type.
    * The input domain role(s) (optional).
    * The output domain role(s) (optional).
    * The method of inference used by the inference type (if known).
    * The support knowledge needed by the inference type (if known).
    * A simple example of the inference step represented (optional).
3. *Inference structure* – A diagrammatic representation of the relation-

ships between inference types and domain roles, according to the rules outlined on p. 74.

4. *Task structure(s)* – A description of the problem-solving tasks that provide sequence over the Inference Structure. This is usually represented by 'pseudo-code', but other notations are reasonable (see p. 75).

5. *Strategies* – An indication of the potential contents of this layer, with guidance as to when particular strategies might be called upon.

Select Initial Generic Task Model(s)

Example

The selection or construction of the Generic Task Model(s) to drive analysis is based on the Process Decomposition of the Process Model, the knowledge thus far identified in the Domain Structures, and the experience of the analyst. We will show three examples of how to perform this activity for RPES. These serve to illustrate some typical ways to select or construct a Generic Task Model. The examples relate to three of the 'K' tasks in the Process Model for 'Resolve or Route Problem' (see Figure 4.9). They are:

- Compare Against Existing Problems (Task 2.5 in the Process Model).
- Compare Against Network Status (Task 2.4 in the Process Model).
- Decide Next Question (Task 2.2 in the Process Model).

The other knowledge-based task 'Attempt to Route Incident', is not covered in detail below (it demonstrates nothing new), but a summary description is provided at the end of the other examples for the sake of completion. To fully understand the examples in this section, the reader should refer to the Process Model examples presented earlier in this chapter (Section 4.1), including the data flow diagrams and the Process Glossary extracts.

Compare Against Existing Problems

This is a task where a large sub-set of a Generic Task Model can be used without any modification other than the refinement of domain role names. Our reasoning follows.

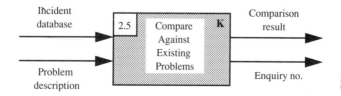

Figure 4.31 Inputs–outputs for 'Compare Against Existing Problems'

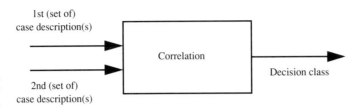

Figure 4.32 Inputs–outputs for Correlation

The task involves comparing the characteristics of the current problem with those of problems already reported in the incident database. The input–output relationships for this task are as shown in Figure 4.31. The Enquiry Number is a useful piece of information which is produced as a by-product of the result of a successful comparison. Otherwise, these input–output types suggest a correlation task, which has the input–output structure shown in Figure 4.32. 'Compare Against Existing Problems' can be seen to be a correlation task with:

Incident Database   → 2nd Set of Case Descriptions
[New] Problem Description → 1st Case Description
                                    (already decomposed into Case Parameters)
Comparison Result   → Decision Class

Figure 4.33 illustrates the chosen sub-set of the correlation inference structure (from the library) together with the necessary domain role name mappings shown alongside their corresponding domain roles from the original GTM.

Compare Against Network Status

This task involves the selection of a Generic Task Model and its adaptation by the modification of a single inference type. It compares the current Problem Description against the Network Status Information and attempts to find an explanation for the problem in terms of a reported network fault. The input–output relationships for the task are shown in Figure 4.34.

The task is similar to that for 'Compare Against Existing Problems', so the correlation GTM is a natural choice. However, an 'abstract' inference is needed (replacing the original correlation model's 'decompose 2', as highlighted in Figure 4.35) to turn the raw network status information into something more meaningful for the KBS. Figure 4.35 shows the resultant inference structure, as adapted from the correlation GTM.

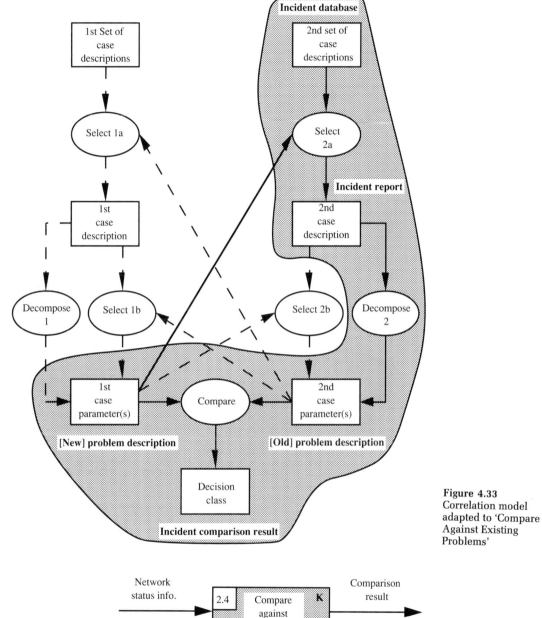

Figure 4.33
Correlation model
adapted to 'Compare
Against Existing
Problems'

Figure 4.34 Inputs–
outputs for 'Compare
Against Network
Status'

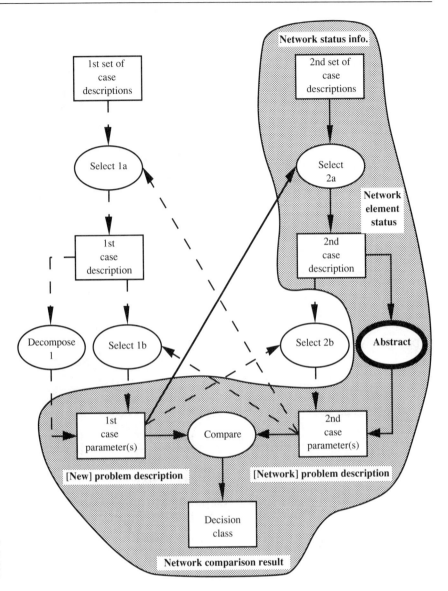

Figure 4.35 Inference Structure for 'Compare Against Network Status'

Decide Next Question

This task requires the construction of an inference structure from scratch. It takes the results of a set of unsuccessful comparisons and routing attempts and searches for the best question to ask the user in order to elicit helpful information. The input–output relationships for this task are shown in Figure 4.36.

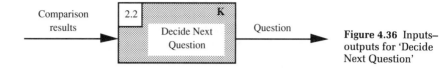

Figure 4.36 Inputs–outputs for 'Decide Next Question'

The task is analytic, but there is not a clear mapping onto a GTM. Fortunately, it is a simple matter to construct an inference structure from scratch. The task must choose a comparison result ('select 1') from the comparison attempts in other tasks, take from the selected comparison result a problem aspect (i.e. hardware type, software type or problem type) which needs to be refined ('select 2'), then map this onto a question to be asked ('match') as the system will only ask a question about a particular problem aspect. The inference structure is shown in Figure 4.37. Note in the figure that the 'Routing Result' Domain Role is the result of the 'K' task 'Attempt to Route Incident', Task 2.3 in the Process Model – see p. 92.

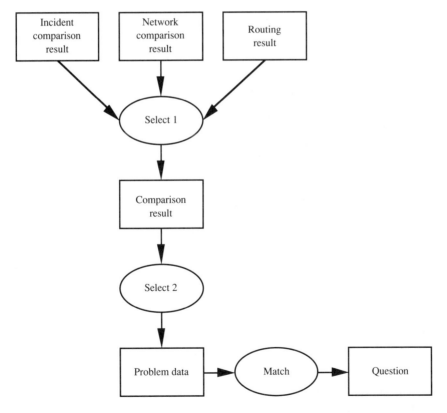

Figure 4.37 Inference Structure for 'Decide Next Question'

Attempt to Route Incident

Although we will not cover the selection of a Generic Task Model for the fourth and final KBS task in 'Resolve or Route Problem' in any detail, for the sake of completion it can be described as follows. The overall operation of the task is to take in increasingly refined Problem Descriptions, compare them with the problem description parts of Routing Knowledge items, output the differences, and, when no difference is found, output the matching front-line desk for the current Routing Knowledge item as the solution. (Remember that Routing Knowledge consists of hardware–software–problem triples, linked to front-line desks.)

Thus, the task can use the correlation GTM in a very similar way to 'Compare Against Existing Problems' (see Figure 4.33). 'New Problem Description' in that task is equivalent to the current Problem Description here; 'Incident Database' becomes the collection of Routing Knowledge; 'Incident Report' becomes a selected Routing Knowledge item; 'Old Problem Description' becomes the problem description part of the Routing Knowledge, i.e. the hardware–software–problem triple; the 'Incident Comparison Result' is just the 'Routing Result'.

To produce front-line desk solutions, however, an additional 'match' Inference Type is required, taking the problem description part of the Routing Knowledge and matching it onto a front-line desk solution, as defined by that Routing Knowledge element. (The match simply follows the link between the triple and its associated front-line desk in that element.) The task layer would fire this match when the result of the comparison showed no difference between the current Problem Description and the problem description in the current Routing Knowledge element.

4.3.4 *Construct Expertise Model*

The aim of the 'Construct Expertise Model' activity is to refine (and re-select as necessary) the chosen GTM; and, once it is sufficiently advanced, to link the Domain Layer produced by 'Analyze Static Knowledge' to the three layers of the GTM to form the Expertise Model. These objectives are achieved by a process of step-by-step refinement: the layers of the GTM are populated with more and more specific knowledge; finally, the Domain Layer is attached to the Inference Layer, thus making the model domain-specific. The following inputs are needed to start this task:

- The chosen or constructed GTM(s) – which will form a framework for filling out the four layers of the Expertise Model.

- The Process Model – which identifies the tasks and data stores which are owned by the KBS agent(s).
- The System Task Model – which provides a more detailed description of the interfaces between the KBS and other system agents.
- The results of initial static knowledge analysis – which feed into the Domain Layer of the Expertise Model. (The 'Construct Expertise Model' activity may proceed in parallel with 'Analyze Static Knowledge' at first, but later the domain knowledge will be required to add into the GTM framework.)

The output from 'Construct Expertise Model' will be the Expertise Model itself. This consists of the four layers: Domain, Inference, Task and Strategy. These are partly produced by the subsidiary activities: 'Construct Inference Layer', 'Construct Task Layer' and 'Construct Strategy Layer', which are described below. The Domain Layer comes from the 'Analyse Static Knowledge' activity. Where the completion of the Expertise Model cannot be achieved simply by collecting together the constituent layers, a small amount of additional work may be required. This is discussed in Section 4.3.5.

Prototyping the Expertise Model

In order to verify the Expertise Model it is recommended that at least part of the model is prototyped before the development proceeds to the Design phase. This prototyping, like any carried out in Expertise Analysis, is experimental. It tests the hypothesis that the Expertise Model is a model of the desired problem-solving behaviour. After this testing (ideally involving the human expert, and perhaps others in the client organization where appropriate), it may be necessary to redo parts of Expertise Analysis.

Construct Inference Layer

The activity of refining, extending and rationalizing the Inference Structure provided by the Generic Task Model(s) takes the form of more knowledge acquisition, analysis, and the construction of a final Inference Structure, with all its inference types and domain roles fully specified. The primary means of refining the Inference Structure will be the structured interview (see Section 10.5.2): the knowledge engineer will already have an idea of the basic inferences to be used from the GTM and will identify areas on which to question the expert more fully. A process of 'self-report' (see Section 10.6.1) may also be used to obtain detail about chains of inference for the purposes of specifying inference types. The Inference Structure should be completed by adding any inferences not shown in the GTM and populating the existing ones.

While the Inference Structure is being built, all the inference types and domain roles should be fully specified by filling the slots in their frame-based descriptions. (See p. 86 or the Summary of Notations at the end of this book.) Because domain roles are described in terms of their relationship to domain concepts, this requires some of the domain knowledge to be firmly in place at this stage.

Example

Construct Expertise Model: Construct Inference Layer

To build the Inference Layer, the knowledge engineer should elicit information about the inferences made in the domain by experts. Where inferences are of the same type as those made in the GTM, its terms and definitions may be modified appropriately, to fit the actual domain terminology.

Figure 4.38 shows how the separate Inference Structure fragments for the Response Point Expert System, discussed earlier, have been bolted together to form a single composite Inference Structure. (Only the links to the constituent Inference Structures are shown, not the *whole* resultant Inference Structure – the dashed arrows show connections to the rest of the constituent Inference Structures in each of the grey boxes.) Thus, this Inference Structure represents that required to support the KBS tasks in

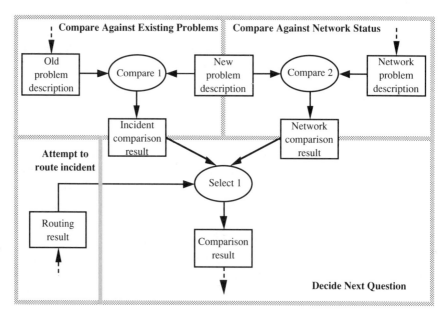

Figure 4.38
Conceptual view of Inference Structure for the KBS tasks in 'Resolve or Route Problem'

'Resolve or Route Problem' highlighted in the DFD in Figure 4.9, p. 47. Detailed definitions of the Inference Types and Domain Roles in Figure 4.38 are shown below, using the frame notation suggested in the text.

Inference Types

Compare1

The new problem description is compared against an existing problem description.

Inputs:	[New] Problem Description, [Old] Problem Description.
Outputs:	Incident Comparison Result.
Method:	Specialization and generalization. (Is the new problem a specialization or generalization of the existing one?)
Knowledge:	Problem Hierarchies.
Example:	New Problem Description = [h/w-A,application-B,access problem]
	Old Problem Description = [h/w-A,application-B,service unavailable]
	Comparison Result = INSUFFICIENT_DATA + access problem
	(i.e. more information is needed about the access problem).

Compare2

The new problem description is compared against the status of a network element.

Inputs:	[New] Problem Description, [Network] Problem Description.
Outputs:	Network Comparison Result.
Method:	Specialization, generalization and heuristic match.
Knowledge:	Problem Hierarchies; Heuristic relationships between network element status and problem descriptions.
Example:	New Problem Description = [h/w-?,application-B,access problem]
	Network Problem Description = [h/w-A = rebooting]
	Heuristic = (if h/w-A = rebooting & application-X on h/w-A then application-X has access problem)
	Comparison Result = INSUFFICIENT_DATA + h/w-?
	(i.e. find out which h/w application-B is running on).

Select1

A comparison result is chosen as the basis for question selection.

Inputs:	Incident Comparison, Network Comparison and Routing Results.

Outputs: [Selected] Comparison Result.

Method: Choose the comparison result which provides the least difference from the existing Problem Description to a solution or routing decision.

Knowledge: Problem Hierarchies.

Example: Incident Comparison Result = INSUFFICIENT_DATA + h/w-?

Network Comparison Result = INSUFFICIENT_DATA + h/w-?

Routing Result = INSUFFICIENT_DATA + password problem.

[Selected] Comparison Result = Routing Result (because it may be possible to route once the nature of the password problem has been refined].

Domain roles

[Old] Problem Description

A Problem Description (see Process Glossary) within a previously reported Incident Report,

e.g. [mainframe-A, application-B, access problem]

[New] Problem Description

The Problem Description which the customer is currently reporting,

e.g. [mainframe-A, application-?, unable to connect]

[Network] Problem Description

The abstract status of a network element such as a computer,

e.g. [mainframe-A = rebooting]

Incident Comparison Result

The result of comparing a new problem against a problem already recorded in the incident database (see Process Glossary), e.g.

SUCCESS,

FAILURE or

INSUFFICIENT_DATA + access problem

Network Comparison Result

The result of comparing a new problem against the abstract status of a network element, e.g.

SUCCESS,

FAILURE or

INSUFFICIENT_DATA + mainframe-?

Routing Result

The result of an attempt to route the current problem to a Front Line Desk, e.g.

SUCCESS,
FAILURE or
INSUFFICIENT_DATA + mainframe-? + problem-?
Comparison Result
One of: Incident Comparison Result, Network Comparison Result or
Routing Result.

Construct Task Layer

At this point the knowledge engineer is not concerned with what
knowledge is used, nor what the actual inferences are, but with *how* these
elements are used. A self-report (Section 10.6.1) or introspection
(Section 10.5.3) session with the expert will generally be the best method
of obtaining this knowledge.

The Generic Task Model may offer alternative strategies for problem
solving, such as data-driven versus solution-driven inferences. Once the
expert has been observed, a decision can be made as to which way(s) the
expert's own inference is driven. The expert may use different methods
on different occasions, so it will be necessary to question him or her
about this (a structured interview or introspection may be useful here) to
exhaust all possibilities. The Task Layer may then be refined to include
all problem-solving methods actually used in the domain. Note that the
purpose at this point is not to discover *why* the expert uses different
methods on different occasions, merely that he or she does so.

When the task to be performed has been decomposed to the level of
activating the inference types within the inference layer, the Task
Structure has reached the detail of general problem-solving strategies,
such as forward/backward chaining, etc. Further decomposition is in the
realms of Design.

Construct Expertise Model: Construct Task Layer   **Example**

There are several ways to navigate the correlation GTM, but the
Inference Structures for 'Compare Against Existing Problems' and
'Compare Against Network Status' restrict the set of possibilities for Task
Structures. The Task Structure for 'Decide Next Question' is much
simpler.

Compare Against Existing Problems
For 'Compare Against Existing Problems', the only real choice available
is whether to select all appropriate incident reports before the

'decompose' and 'compare' steps or whether to select each incident report individually. The two possible task structures are thus:

(T1) Compare Against Existing Problems by
  select2a (New Problem Description, Incident Database (set of)
   Incident Report)
  for each Incident Report until successful do
   decompose2 (Incident Report, Old Problem Description)
   compare (New Problem Description, Old Problem Description,
   Decision Class)
  loop

(T2) Compare Against Existing Problems by
  until successful or no more Incident Reports in Incident Database
  do
   select2a (New Problem Description, Incident Database, Incident Report)
   decompose2 (Incident Report, Old Problem Description)
   compare (New Problem Description, Old Problem Description,
   Decision Class)
  loop

The choice of which of these task structures to use depends in practice on issues such as the nature of the enquiry mechanisms supported within the incident database.

Compare Against Network Status

For 'Compare Against Network Status' there are again two choices of task structure, subtly different depending on whether the task is driven by (i) the customer problem or (ii) the network status:

(T3) Compare Against Network Status by
  select2a (New Problem Description, Network Status Info, Network Status Element),
  abstract (Network Status Element, Network Problem Description)
  compare (New Problem Description, Network Problem Description, Decision Class)

(T4) Compare Against Network Status by
  select2a (Network Status Info, Network Status Element),
  abstract (Network Status Element, Network Problem Description)
  compare (New Problem Description, Network Problem Description, Decision Class)

Decide Next Question

The task structure for 'Decide Next Question' is straightforward:

(T5) Decide Next Question by
   select1 (Incident Comparison Result, Network Comparison Result,
       Routing Result, Comparison Result),
   select2 (Comparison Result, Problem Data),
   match (Problem Data, Question)

Construct Strategy Layer

The Strategy Layer contains control knowledge for selecting, sequencing or configuring Task Structures. It allows for the avoidance and repair of problems, and high-level problem-solving plans. Depending on the project, this may contain a large amount of knowledge or very little.

The Strategy Layer is the 'why' of the goals in the Task Layer. It allows dynamic generation of goal trees (hierarchies of intermediate and final solutions) for the problem-solving process. It thus represents an attempt to capture the flexible approach that a real expert takes towards problem solving.

At a more simplistic level, however, it can be seen as managing the relationship between the information flows into or out of the KBS agent with the various structures in the Task Layer. Seen like this, it becomes clear that the Strategy Layer can also comprise quite trivial mappings between system-level events and task invocations in the Task Layer.

In most KADS projects to date there has been little knowledge to capture at the Strategy Layer. It may just amount to a depth-first search through the goals supported at the Task Layer. But as KBS tackle more complex and, traditionally, less well-suited domains, the need for advanced planning techniques to generate and fix goal trees from one consultation to the next will be needed.

Knowledge of the strategies an expert uses will be best gained from a self-report (Section 10.6.1) or introspection (Section 10.5.3) session. A useful technique is to ask the expert how he or she would solve a 'difficult' case. This will allow the knowledge engineer to see how the expert will plan and replan when faced with difficulties.

Construct Expertise Model: Construct Strategy Layer

Example

Because the System Task Model for the Response Point Expert System specifies a rigid control sequence between the four knowledge-based tasks, there is little scope for a rich strategy layer. However, there is potential for either static or dynamic choice of the alternative task structures described in the example on p. 97, thus:

(i) If the Incident Database supports structured queries
     Then
         Use 'Compare against Existing Problems' task structure (T1)
     Else
         Use 'Compare against Existing Problems' task structure (T2)

(ii) If the Network Status Info suggests a significant network problem
      Then
          Use 'Compare against Network Status' task structure (T4)
      Else
          Use 'Compare against Network Status' task structure (T3)

Other variations are possible. The knowledge engineer must examine the desired problem-solving capability of the system and make a judgement about the level of strategic knowledge needed for a particular application.

4.3.5   *Putting the Expertise Model together*

If the Expertise Model comprises a single task, then it is a simple matter to link the Domain, Inference, Task and Strategy layers together to form the final model. If, however, there are several tasks to be considered, then the knowledge engineer will need to choose whether to generate several discrete four-layer models or whether to 'glue' parts of these together in some way.

There are several ways to 'glue' four-layer models together. Figure 4.39 shows three possible options, which are discussed below.

Linking via the Strategy Layer

This is perhaps the most natural way to link several four-layer models together. As far as control linkage is concerned, this is already taken care of by the logic of the System Task Model. So in a sense this Model can been seen to encompass a high-level control strategy across the knowledge-based system tasks.

A common Strategy Layer also becomes important when the problem-solving tasks are sufficiently 'fine-grain' that their selection, repair and control are inextricably interwoven. In this situation it is unlikely that the System Task Model will provide the necessary degree of control, which itself is likely to require a knowledge-based approach.

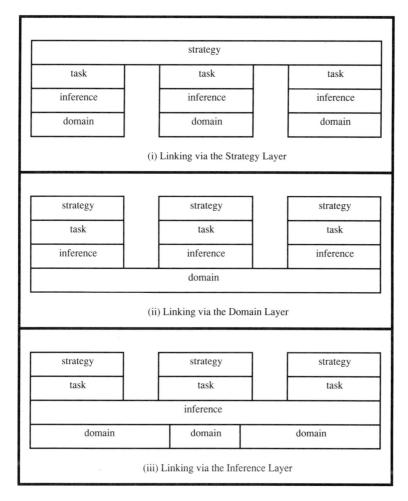

(i) Linking via the Strategy Layer

(ii) Linking via the Domain Layer

(iii) Linking via the Inference Layer

Figure 4.39 Linking several four-layer models together

Linking via the Domain Layer

The Domain Layer may be viewed as a shared resource, especially when domain roles from several tasks relate to the same domain knowledge. This form of linkage is especially pertinent when the knowledge base as a whole is expected to be stored in a single repository, such as a relational database.

Another form of linking via the Domain Layer occurs in the case of so-called blackboard architectures, where one task may post an item of information into a shared data resource for any other task to access and act upon. In this situation there is also likely to be linkage of other layers – especially the Strategy Layer – to provide scheduling across tasks.

Linking via the Inference Layer

Inference Structures and fragments of structures may be 'glued' together to provide a consolidated view of the inference capability. This is achieved by finding an inference in one structure whose output domain role is identical to an input domain role for an inference type within another structure. Note that linking together inference structures or fragments will also necessitate linking together parts of the Domain Layer since the shared domain roles will imply shared domain knowledge (see Figure 4.39).

4.4   Constraints Analysis

The Process, Cooperation and Expertise Analysis activities form the core of the KADS Analysis phase. However, there are important areas of Analysis which are not covered by these activities. These include the analysis of design constraints and context-dependent requirements upon the future system and its development – described collectively in KADS as the 'Constraints Analysis' stage.

Constraints Analysis is a background activity which is performed throughout the whole of the Analysis phase.[7] Figure 4.40 shows the temporal relationship of Constraints Analysis relative to the other Analysis stages. This highlights the 'in the background' nature of the stage.

The aim of Constraints Analysis is to record the constraints which arise during the other parts of Analysis and fill in any gaps as necessary. Constraints are the (mostly) non-functional requirements which will impact upon the system's design and the way the development phases in the project are performed. (The key functional requirements of the system are held in the System Overview – see Section 4.5.) Constraints are recorded in a structured result called the 'Constraints Document'. A checklist of potential contents of this document is the main topic of this section.

Constraints Analysis is more loosely structured and more pragmatic than Expertise, Process and Cooperation Analysis. It is also very 'conventional', in that it closely matches requirements engineering in conventional system development. The form and content of the documents produced are adapted to the special concerns of KBS development, but if the reader's organization already has an established requirements engineering process it may be more appropriate to extend or adapt that existing process rather than 're-invent the wheel'.

Constraints Analysis runs concurrently with all the other Analysis

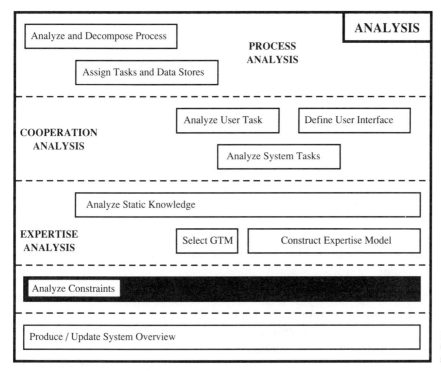

Figure 4.40 The Constraints Analysis stage

activities, and some parts may extend into the high-level design phases. This takes into account the fact that constraints often arise dynamically, sporadically, or change as the development progresses. In general, the component parts of the Constraints Document need not be produced in any particular order, although any specific project will probably require the imposition of some ordering, dependent upon its particular circumstances.

There is really only one activity within Constraints Analysis, 'Analyze Constraints', but this can be split into three (these are not described separately below, as they all progress and are performed in the same basic way):

- Analyze Environmental Constraints – concerned with organizational factors.
- Analyze Technical Constraints – concerned with system-specific factors.
- Analyze Policy Constraints – concerned with procedural factors.

The Constraints Document produced by performing these activities reflects this structure, consisting of three major parts: Environmental Constraints, Technical Constraints and Policy Constraints.

The primary input to Constraints Analysis will be work carried out in the pre-analysis phase(s), especially that done for a feasibility study. Inputs to Constraints Analysis will also include: interview transcripts, general domain literature, client documentation, developer documentation, and standards specifications.

Constraints Analysis as a form of conventional requirements engineering

Constraints Analysis in KADS is equivalent to requirements engineering for conventional software development, with an emphasis on non-functional requirements. In order to understand the contents and form of the Constraints Document, it is useful to recall the purpose and context of requirements analysis in general. (These points can also apply to the rest of Analysis.) First, general requirements analysis necessitates recording information which addresses:

- Models of the client's business activity, descriptions of the problem and chosen solution.
- Demands on the system, expressed as objectives and constraints.
- Solution details and consequences.
- Requirements on the way the phases of the development are carried out.

The record of requirements and constraints (sometimes called a 'requirements model') is produced and kept up to date by 'requirements engineering'. The record should satisfy the following conditions:

- It should only specify external system behaviour.
- It should specify constraints on the implementation.
- It should be easy to change.
- It should serve as a reference tool for system maintainers.
- It should record forethought about the lifecycle of the system.
- It should characterize acceptable responses to undesired events.

Two key factors influencing the record of requirements and constraints are:

- It will have a diverse audience.
- It should cope with the volatility of requirements.

These factors mean that the KADS Constraints Document needs to be especially well organized in order to facilitate ease of reading and regular changes.

These issues have influenced the way Constraints Analysis is described in KADS. The analyst is given a 'checklist' of smaller constraints/ requirements 'documents' that should be considered for any development (see Section 4.4.1.) and these are presented in detail below. The simple combination of all these small 'constraints documents' will form the final Constraints Document.

The checklist presented below is reasonably comprehensive, but it it should be extended and tailored to suit a particular project's needs. There will be potential constraints that we have not considered here.[8] Also, most programs do not require all the documents we havc listed to be filled in. Items from the complete checklist can be left off or, where appropriate, covered by a statement such as 'the following categories of constraint are not applicable to this project...'.

Techniques and tools for Constraints Analysis

Techniques used to produce the resultant requirements documents will include: interviewing domain experts and more general staff (most likely using a structured or focused interview), and reading the appropriate available literature. At the time of writing this book there are no dedicated tools with which to directly support the construction of the KADS Constraints Document, but there are more general-purpose ones which will be found useful. Obviously, there will be the usual tools used for interviewing. The analyst may also find storing transcripts (and text-based material from the literature) on a computer helpful, so that text searches and other indexing techniques can be applied.

Some conventional requirements engineering CASE tools are available (e.g. RqT or RTM – see Section 9.7.1), which may allow tighter management of constraints. For example, an important task recognized in requirements engineering is requirements traceability – the tracing of an elicited requirement throughout the system lifecycle. In theory, this allows one to check the origins of features in the final system code back to comments made by the client or future users, etc. Constraints Analysis in KADS could use an equivalent concept ('constraints traceability'). However, effective tool support is probably necessary for systems of any size.

4.4.1 The Constraints Document

The Constraints Document is a comprehensive store for all the external and internal non-functional constraints on the system and its development. It records all constraints: environmental, technical and political. It is highly structured, consisting of a hierarchy of component parts.

However, the contents of the document should be seen as fairly flexible, and new categories of constraint may be added if required.

The recommended contents of the Constraints Document are:

1. *Environmental Constraints*
   - Existing (Client) Environment
     - Model of present situation/system
     - Functioning objectives of user organization
     - Functioning problems of user organization
   - Development (Developer) Environment
     - Development environment requirements
     - Testing and validation procedures
   - Operational (Client) Environment
     - Operational environment requirements
     - Organizational consequences
     - Installation requirements
     - Acceptance procedures
     - Expected future enhancements
     - Maintenance procedures
2. *Technical Constraints*
   - General Technical Constraints
   - Knowledge Base and Other Storage Constraints
   - Database Constraints
   - User Interface Constraints
   - Communications Constraints
   - Hardware Constraints
3. *Policy Constraints*
   - Standards
   - Laws
   - Other Policies and Procedural Constraints.

These contents are described below. For ease of description, each item may be considered a 'document' in its own right. Their descriptions should serve as a minimum checklist of types of constraints that can be considered for documentation in a real project.

4.4.2 *Environmental Constraints*

The Environmental Constraints Document is a comprehensive store for all the 'environmentally oriented' constraints and other requirements on the system and its development, i.e. the various 'contexts' in which the system will be applied, developed or operated. The requirements are grouped according to the environment to which they are relevant:

- Existing Environment – which the system is being built to replace or enhance.
- Development Environment – where the system is being developed.
- Operational Environment – where the system will be situated once completed.

However, as with the rest of the Constraints Document, this structure should be seen as flexible.

Existing (Client) Environment

These documents are all optional. Their need is determined by the level of detail achieved in any pre-project analysis phase, compared with the level required to complete a satisfactory analysis. Process Analysis (see Section 4.1) may also overlap with certain areas included here. In addition, depending on the size and complexity of the project, the System Overview (see Section 4.5) may be sufficient to cover the issues addressed.

Model of present situation/system

This describes a model of the client's logical functional organization, as well as the formal organization. It should be possible to derive the latter from the client directly. The boundaries, interface and interaction with other systems/functions should be described in detail. It should be used by the project team to understand the environment and thus facilitate communication between the various parties involved with the project. An especially important and useful issue to address is the recording of all the relevant people in the present situation. This might be based on an organization chart which should say who is present and who does what. This information can help in the construction of the Process Model (see Section 4.1), and vice versa – the main difference is that the Process Model is more focused and formal than this Constraint Document. In the general case, every 'agent' in the present situation should be recorded – not just people. This would include major autonomous systems. The document may be an input to the 'Organizational Consequences' document, User Model (see p. 56) and System Overview (see Section 4.5).

Functioning objectives of user organization

This is produced from interviews with people who possess an overall view of the problem domain, and contributes to the construction of a description of the present situation. Functioning objectives are either measurable (e.g. deliver within two days) or immeasurable (e.g. solve the problem over the phone). This document is used to ensure that the system is built in line with the goals of the organization, and the system helps to fulfil unachieved objectives and avoid violating fulfilled ones. Hence, it has a number of parallels with Process Analysis (see Section 4.1). One basic format for this document is a table consisting of columns for objective name, description, yes/no to indicate if the objective is fulfilled or not, and a priority value field. It may be used as input to 'Functioning Problems of User Organization' and 'Model of Present Situation/System'.

Functioning problems of user organization

This contains a description of the client's problems in fulfilling the objectives of the document 'Functioning Objectives of User Organization', e.g. 'it takes three days for the order to arrive at the delivery department', 'there are constantly two calls waiting for the experts', etc. These problems can be collected without reference to the 'Functioning Objectives of User Organization' and then cross-referenced to identify objectives without a corresponding problem (missing problem?) or a problem without an objective (missing objective?). If it proves difficult to collect these problems then it might be advisable to base this section on 'Functioning Objectives of User Organization'. It is better to collect all the problems at an early stage and reserve judgement as to whether they are solvable by the system. For example, there may be a problem in that the environment is both too noisy and too warm, and although it does not seem relevant to the system, a less noisy fan-less terminal is a better solution than PCs with fans. As with the 'Functioning Objectives of User Organization', a table format can be used for this document, consisting of columns for problem name, description, priority (need to solve the problem). If cross-referencing is used, a column could be added to indicate the relevant items in the 'Functioning Problems of User Organization'. This document may feed into 'Model of Present Situation/System'.

Development (Developer) Environment

Development of environment requirements

This will describe the constraints and other requirements on the development environment, e.g. systems, tools, languages, shells, operating systems, etc. It will consist of two parts: the *constraints on* the choice of development environment and the *constraints imposed by* the particular development environment chosen. Issues to consider are compatibility, security, performance, etc. Compatibility issues will cover compatibility of the system's interface and peripherals with other systems (further constraints on the system arising from company strategies regarding its choice of languages, I–O-modules and operating system, etc., will be included in the 'Other Policies and Procedural Constraints' Document). Security issues will cover reliability, safety, user access control, fault-tolerance, etc. It must also take into account external constraints such as legal requirements, contracts, regulations, audit requirements, etc., some of which may already be detailed in the 'Policy Constraints' Documents. Performance issues will cover run-time speed constraints, disk/memory usage constraints, etc.

Testing and validation procedures

This is used to record all pre-installation testing procedures and validation tests, or references to those tests. It could include test plans and results of module tests, system and integration tests. These are important deliverables to accompany the system's design and code. Validation records for Analysis Models might be useful in some cases, such as recording when an Expertise Model has been agreed upon by a domain expert.

Operational (Client) Environment

Operational environment requirements

This will describe the constraints and other requirements on the operational environment, e.g. systems, tools, languages, shells, operating systems, etc. It will consist of two parts: the *constraints on* the choice of operational environment; and the *constraints imposed by* the particular operational environment chosen. Issues to consider are compatibility, security, performance, etc. (Cf. Development Environment Requirements above.) Special technical requirements on the operational environment might be usefully relocated to the Technical Constraints Document. Less technical requirements to be documented here will include reliability and usability measures.

Organizational consequences

This describes, on a global level, the consequences of the system on the organization, responsibility (re-)allocation, working conditions, tasks (new, changes or disappearing), software and hardware (choices, constraints, evolution), installation, operational use, maintenance, and training needs. It is in the same domain as the 'Model of Present Situation/System', but with three differences:

- It describes the structure of the organization after the information system has been implemented and identifies the changes.
- The information is more detailed, e.g. by decomposition in several layers describing interactions and relations within the system and its environment.
- It is focused on the domain in which the system will operate.

The level of detail of this document depends on the nature of the project as well as the methods used. In a simple form, it can be a schematic diagram of the system within the organization showing interactions between users, experts and other systems. Installation, acceptance testing and maintenance should not be covered in detail here, as there are specific documents for these (see below).

Installation requirements

This describes the procedures for installation and their associated requirements, some of which may relate to the operational and/or development environment requirements. It will cover such issues as when installation can take place, who should be involved, who should be informed, who will be responsible for the system in place, any special technical needs for installation, etc.

Acceptance procedures

This is used to record all post-installation testing procedures and validation tests, commonly termed 'acceptance tests'. It could include test plans and results of tests.

Expected future enhancements

This describes all known or expected enhancements of the system, and/or changes to the organization where it is installed.

Maintenance procedures

This describes the procedures for maintenance and their associated requirements, perhaps also considering the 'Expected Future Enhancements' (see above).

4.4.3   Technical Constraints

The Technical Constraints Document is a comprehensive store for all the 'technically oriented' constraints and other requirements on the system and its development. The documents below cover a wide scope and should be tailored as necessary.

General Technical Constraints

This is available to describe the general technical requirements on the system. For example, these would be performance-related issues, such as those arising from real-time considerations; it would contain compatibility constraints (what existing systems/processes the new development should work with); it would cover reliability constraints (e.g. maximum downtime, recovery periods, etc.); and it would cover capacity requirements (workload profiles for storage and processors, etc.).

Knowledge Base and Other Storage Constraints

This describes the requirements for the knowledge base, such as the size of the knowledge base, constraints on the knowledge base arising from the task and strategy layers (e.g. direction of reasoning), and the need for hypothetical reasoning and certain types of knowledge in order to accommodate the user. It could also include non-knowledge-based storage issues where necessary. The amount would depend on the degree of database content of the system, which could range from nil to dominant. Dominant database embedded KBS should consider using separate development methods outside of KADS for the database component(s), and use the 'Database Constraints' document below as its link to the knowledge-based component produced using KADS.

Database Constraints

This is available for recording the analysis of constraints for any substantial database component(s) of the complete system. It could be a description of the requirements for the interface between the knowledge-based and database component(s), or simply a reference to the appropriate document(s) produced for that component(s) as part of some method outside of KADS.

User Interface Constraints

This will cover topics such as: the level of system competence and the required user competence; the need for tutorial functions and help functions; the type of system messages, system input and output convenience (screen size, menus, mouse, function keys, logical graphics); robustness constraints; response-time constraints; and physical constraints (e.g. noise). It should form a strong complementary link with Cooperation Analysis (see Section 4.2; and in particular, Sections 4.2.1 and

4.2.3). General characteristics of users could be recorded here when a full-blown User Model (see p. 56) cannot be justified. Requirements to use certain user interface standards may be recorded here or in the special 'Standards' document.

Communications Constraints

This is available to describe requirements relating to data communications with the system. Typically, these would be performance-related issues, capacity and load-profile requirements. It should form a strong complementary link with Cooperation Analysis (see Section 4.2), where external agents must be interacted with over data communication links. Requirements to use certain communications standards may be recorded here or in the special 'Standards' Document.

Hardware Constraints

This is available for recording the analysis of constraints for any special hardware component(s) of the complete system. It could be a description of the requirements for the hardware, or just a reference to the appropriate document(s) produced as part of some method outside of KADS.

4.4.4 Policy Constraints

The Policy Constraints Document is a comprehensive store for all the 'policy-oriented' constraints and other requirements on the system and its development. The following documents are all optional.

Standards

This will detail the constraints imposed by any standards relevant or specified for the system and its development. This could include country-based or international standards, e.g. BSI (British standards) and ISO (international standards). It may also be used to record technically-related standards, such as user-interface standards (e.g. Motif on the X Window System graphical user-interface standard) or data communications standards (e.g. X.25 protocol). Alternatively, these references could be located in their appropriate Technical Constraints Documents.

Laws

This will detail the constraints imposed by any laws relevant to the system and its development. Sometimes this will relate to security requirements, as specified in 'Other Policies and Procedural Constraints'. An example of an important law in the UK to consider for many systems is the Data Protection Act.

Other Policies and Procedural Constraints

This will detail the constraints imposed by any other policies relevant to the system and its development. These may arise from the client, developer or sub-contractor(s). Typically, they are policies due to local management or business decisions. An example may be a local 'code of practice' or 'quality manual'.

Constraints Analysis

Example

It is difficult to give a good example of Constraints Analysis in a small space since it is inherently a broad area. However, the following should reinforce the idea that Constraints Analysis is quite straightforward. The following text shows three quoted extracts from the Constraints Analysis carried out for the Response Point Expert System. The first is part of the client-derived Environmental Constraints; the second is from the Technical Constraints; and the third is from the Policy Constraints.

'*Environmental Constraints – Existing environment*
Response Point forms a part of Command, Control and Communications (C3) within the Information Services (IS) Division of a large international corporation.
Response Point is the customers' access point into IS for information and problem resolution. Closely associated with Response Point are the Front Line Desks which provide the next line of support for problem solving.
IS supports a large number of applications and services running on a network of mainframes and other machines. Each Response Point operator acts as a first point of contact for customers requiring:

- Solutions to problems concerning IS services.
- Specific actions to be taken by service support staff.
- Information about the progress of calls already logged.
- Information about the status and availability of IS services.'

'*Technical Constraints – General – Software requirements*
Two options have been identified for the prototype system:

1. DecisionPower (Prolog plus user interface toolkit) with Sun OpenWindows version 2.0 & the X Window System X11r4.
2. Egeria (shell) plus KHS (user interface toolkit) with Sun OpenWindows version 2.0 & the X Window System X11r4.

Both of these will run on SunOS UNIX v4.0.3. or higher on Sun–3, Sun–4 or SparcStations. Option 1 provides most OpenLook 'level 2' client features.'

'*Policy Constraints – Standards*
User Interface software must be developed in line with the client company standards applicable to the chosen interface style.'

4.5   System Overview

The objective of the System Overview stage is to produce and maintain a comprehensive and concise summary of the whole system's objectives and functionality. It will be used primarily to aid communication between the project team members and the client, users and managers.

Like Constraints Analysis, the System Overview is a background activity which is performed throughout the whole of the Analysis phase. Figure 4.41 shows the temporal relationship of the System Overview relative to the other Analysis stages. This highlights the 'in the background' nature of the stage.

The starting point for the System Overview is any feasibility study or other work done prior to Analysis. This should contain a record of the system's objectives and functionality, as initially envisaged. Thus, the System Overview also acts as a repository of the key functional requirements of the system. (The non-functional requirements are captured and held in the Constraints Document – see Section 4.4.)

There is only one activity in the maintenance of the System Overview – 'Produce/Update System Overview'. This is described below.

4.5.1   *Produce/Update System Overview*

The Produce/Update System Overview activity (System Overview, for brevity) is best considered as a set of four constituent documents to produce and maintain, rather like the way the Constraints Document is constructed. Descriptions of the content of these System Overview documents are given in Section 4.5.2.

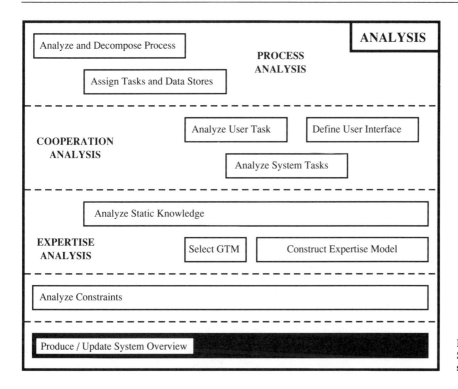

Figure 4.41 The System Overview stage

The System Overview activity should identify changes in objectives and functionality as they become known, draw up a sketch of the system's logical structure, and determine the input–output dependencies between system components (this last objective will draw upon other Analysis work, primarily Process Analysis – see Section 4.1).

The work of the other streams of Analysis (Process, Expertise and Cooperation) should be abstracted as they impact upon the System Overview. Constraints Analysis will also have a mutually dependent relationship with the System Overview. In particular, some of the information stored in the Constraints Document can alternatively be located in the System Overview. (See Section 4.4.)

The essential tool for this activity is the set of document descriptions given in Section 4.5.2. These should be used as checklists to ensure that the System Overview is up to date and complete in coverage.

Note that although Process Analysis is conventionally seen as the stage at which the 'meat' of a KADS Analysis starts, in practice we have found that starting (and also ending) Analysis with the System Overview activity results in a natural sequence of development activities (basically a top-down approach). This works either where the system objectives and functionality can be documented reasonably confidently at the start of

Analysis or, going to the other extreme, where it is found to be absolutely necessary to pin these down before detailed Analysis commences. For an alternative placement, see Section 9.2.1.

4.5.2 The System Overview Document

The System Overview Document should be a comprehensive but very concise summary of the proposed system's objectives and functionality. It is a top-level overview of the complete system to be built. In conventional Analysis these documents would assume a greater technical importance than here, since many of the core technical aspects of the Analysis in KADS are handled in the Process, Expertise and Cooperation stages.

The contents of the System Overview Document are:

- Objectives of Prospective System.
- System Functions.
- Provisional System Structure.
- Provisional Information Requirements.

These are described below. For ease of description, each item may be considered a 'document' in its own right. Their descriptions should serve as a minimum checklist of items for documentation in a real project.

Objectives of Prospective System

This describes what the aims and objectives of the prospective system are. Some of this information can be gleaned by abstracting the results of Process Analysis and it may also inherit the results of scoping or feasibility study activities prior to Analysis. It should also show the different agents' priorities of objectives: e.g. different classes of users, such as experts and end-users, might have different concerns, wishes and foci. Physically, it can be documented as a list of named objectives and summary descriptions. The document may be dependent upon 'Functioning Objectives of User Organization' and 'Functioning Problems of User Organization' in the Constraints Document (see pp. 107–8).

System Functions

This is a list and summary description of the complete set of functions that the system will support. Only the higher-level functions need be recorded. Physically, it may be documented as a straightforward annotated list, or free text. In pure KBS systems, it should be simply compiled by abstracting the results of Process Analysis (see Section 4.1) –

which should also act as a mutual consistency check. In embedded KBS, the document assumes greater importance, because while the problem-solving functionality can be obtained from the results of Process Analysis there will be other functions to record here. In such systems, this document acts as one of the key links between the KBS component and other components.

Provisional System Structure

This document describes the logical and/or functional decomposition of the system into sub-systems. The scope of 'system' here is left to the project manager's discretion, but it should generally represent a 'top-level' view, with the boundary of the proposed system clearly defined. Relevant external agents or other entities can be shown to show context. The main interactions between the sub-systems are specified (input–output), as well as communication with other existing or planned external systems and agents. The function of each sub-system is described, e.g. by reference to 'Development of Environment Requirements' and 'Objectives of Prospective System' in the Constraints Document (see p. 108 and p. 116). Physically, the usual form of the document is a simple schematic diagram, annotated in an informal style.

This document is optional and should primarily be used to aid communication with the client and/or management. It can, however, also form a useful input to Design, if treated carefully (see Section 8.2, for example). It is stressed that it should not represent a first level of design by default, at least until Analysis nears completion. If intended as an input to Design, the analyst should be careful to ensure that a form that is useful for communicating the system's structure to the client, say, is still appropriate for such a purpose. In general, this would not (and probably should not) be the case.

Provisional Information Requirements

This optional document supplements the 'Provisional System Structure' by summarizing the stored information and input–output information used in the functions and interactions shown in that document. Like the 'System Functions' Document, it will be more important in the case of embedded systems where Expertise Analysis does not consider the total functionality of the system. As in the case of the 'Provisional System Structure', this document should not be treated as a first level of design by default but primarily as an aid to communication. A useful input will be the Process Glossary (see p. 37). Physically, it may be documented as a straightforward annotated list. The following list indicates what should be considered for inclusion in this document (here, information = knowledge + data):

- Information to be communicated.
- Information to be stored.
- A top-level data dictionary or similar description of data.
- Information arising from different demands of user–system dialogues.

Example

System Overview

It is difficult to give a good example of a System Overview without presenting a complete one. However, despite the lack of space as with Constraints Analysis, the following should reinforce the idea that the System Overview is quite straightforward. The following text shows four quoted extracts from the System Overview for the Response Point Expert System.

'Objectives of prospective system
   The objective of the operational system will be to assist Response Point operators in performing their tasks. The expert system will support the determination of problem details and will assist in either clearing a problem immediately or routing a problem to the appropriate Front Line Desk. The expert system is also expected to act as a training aid, to familiarize new operators with the process involved when dealing with customer problems.'

'System functions
   The expert system will support the operator task by providing the following functions:

- Recording of customer details (name, location, telephone no., etc.).
- Determination of the customer's problem.
- Provision of immediate solutions by matching against previously reported Problems or against network status information.
- Automatic routing of problems to the appropriate Front Line Desk.
- Optional explanations of how the system arrived at its decision.
- Logging of all problems and subsequent retrieval of problem details.
- Facilities to abort problems or to retract problem details.'

'Provisional Information Requirements
   The following incident information currently held on the Incident Database may be useful for the expert system:

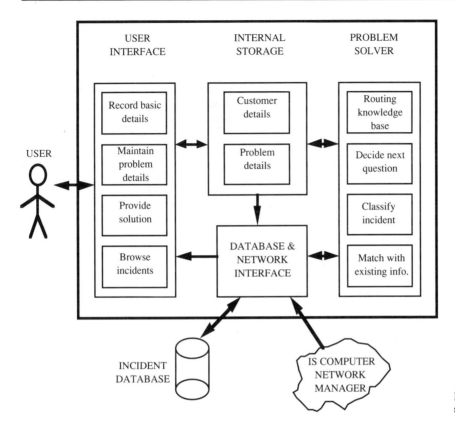

Figure 4.42
Provisional system
structure

- Customer information (name, site, extension): site is identified by the first three digits of the telephone number.
- Problem statement (with as much information as possible on the first line).
- Problem area (machine type, machine name, application name).
- Escalation type (service, application, hardware or blank).
- Priority: can be increased on customer request if a large (>20) number of users are affected, or if the problem is serious.
- Routing information – i.e. which Front Line Desk will investigate the incident.

Information about the proportions of mis-routed calls will need to be held on the Incident Database in order to evaluate the efficacy of the expert system approach.'

Notes

1. A popular conventional software development methodology in the UK – see Appendix 2.
2. Note that apart from these three there are other styles of interaction based on different roles played by the user and system, e.g. mixed initiative (user and system share taking control of the dialogue) and decision support (system provides one or more recommendations or solutions as an aid to a decision maker). However, KADS is less concerned with labelling these different scenarios and more with providing a framework for modelling the details of the diaglogue: who does what, to whom, and when.
3. These are a relatively new form of state machine notation, effectively like hierarchical state transition diagrams. They are becoming increasingly popular. See Harel (1988) in the Bibliography ('Documents about conventional software engineering').
4. An object-oriented dialogue language for use in such situations is described in Hayball (1991) – see Bibliography ('Other relevant KBS topics').
5. A simple glossary or word-list ('lexicon') is not really enough on its own, but it may be a good starting point for building more complete Domain Structures. This can be done using the Process Glossary from Process Analysis. (See p. 37.)
6. In fact, some people see the Strategy Layer as potentially containing an entire problem-solving task in itself, to model particularly sophisticated strategic capability. See also Section 4.3.5.
7. In fact, it is more accurate to say that the *majority* of the work is done on the activity in this phase. The Constraints Document produced by this stage should ideally be maintained throughout the development of the system. Some of the contents of the Constraints Document to be described below reflect this. They include such topics as test plans, most of which will not be produced until system design (including KADS Design) at the earliest.
8. An important set of constraints not covered by our list, but sometimes considered part of requirements engineering, are 'project management-type' requirements. These will cover items such as finances, project plans, staff assignments, quality assurance procedures, etc. These constraints are considered part of a 'project management framework' outside the scope of KADS – see Chapter 9. Other constraints found in conventional requirements engineering but not in the list here may be found in the KADS System Overview – see Section 4.5.

5 Analysis: the big picture

This chapter provides the reader with an overall view of KADS Analysis, showing how all its pieces fit together and why they are needed. It is the nearest thing to background theory that this book describes. (It should be all the theory that is required in order to put KADS into practice.) The preceding chapter described each Analysis activity to be performed, and result to be produced, on the basis of the overall framework presented in this one.

Recall that the Analysis phase in KADS is divided into five constituents, called 'stages', resulting in three models and two other results:

KADS Analysis stage		Result of stage
Process Analysis	→	Process Model
Cooperation Analysis	→	Cooperation Model
Expertise Analysis	→	Expertise Model
Constraints Analysis	→	Constraints Document
System Overview	→	System Overview Document

5.1 Levels of analysis – KADS Analysis models

In Chapter 2 we described how KADS is a methodology which takes a model-based approach to KBS development. The process of developing a KBS in KADS may be viewed largely as a progression through a set of models of the world, the system, the user(s) (and/or any other such 'agents'), and the expertise required in the system.

KADS Analysis takes as its foundation a 'conceptual modelling framework'. This simply means a set of interrelated models, with each model representing a particular aspect of the complete required behaviour of the system. Such aspects have been termed 'levels' of analysis, as they each focus on a different level of abstraction of the total analysis required for the future system – a different *scope* of analysis. There are three levels of analysis in KADS: process, system and KBS.

The **Process level** is concerned with analyzing the overall process within which the system will work. Analysis at this level considers what tasks are performed, what data/knowledge flows exist, what data/knowledge stores are required, who performs the tasks, and who owns the stores. We term the entities that perform tasks 'agents'. The entities in the outside world with which the system must deal are either (external) agents or stores; our system can be decomposed into a set of interacting internal agents and stores if it performs more than one trivial task. Sometimes the Process level needs to analyze and model the current situation in the domain, as well as the future situation when it will include the system to be built. It is concerned with *what* things are present in the domain.

The **System level** is concerned with analyzing how the system will interact with its immediate environment (i.e. with external agents) and how its first level of components will interact with each other on the basis of this (i.e. the internal agents). The Process level concerns itself only with identifying the tasks, agents and stores – the System level analyzes their cooperation in more detail, especially their dynamic behaviour. It is concerned with *when* things are done.

The **KBS level** is concerned with analyzing the precise expertise required to eventually be encoded within the system. Knowing that a knowledge-based agent in the system is needed to perform a certain task (from the Process level), and knowing how it interacts with its companion internal agents or the outside world, is obviously not enough to produce a good design. Thus, the KBS level uses special techniques, unique to KADS, to analyze and model the required problem-solving tasks in the system so that a quality design is possible. It uses the concept of a four-layer model of expertise. The KBS level is concerned with starting to define *how* things are done.

Within the above analysis framework KADS describes a particular set of models, together with the activities which are used to construct them. Table 5.1 shows the three levels of Analysis models in KADS together with their constituents.

An alternative view of the models is shown in Figure 5.1. This shows how the various models produced during Analysis correspond to cooperating (perhaps semi-) independent agents in the context of a conceptual view of a future working system.[1] The 'cooperating agents' include the user, the overall system to be built, the KBS component(s), other system components, etc. The scope of Analysis is also shown, as a boundary around part of the real world, representing part of an

Table 5.1 Analysis levels, models and constituents

Level	Model	Constituents
1: Process Level	Process Model	Process Task Data flow Data store Agent Agent assignment
2: System Level	Cooperation Model [User Task Model + System Task Model]	User state User event Control/information flow System action State transition
3: KBS Level	Expertise Model	Domain layer Inference layer Task layer Strategy layer

organization using the system, for example. Within the 'scope of Analysis' boundary, and within each of the agent's boxes, is shown the corresponding Analysis model.

Note from Figure 5.1 that the only external agent shown is the 'user'. This has a corresponding model, the User Task Model. This models the

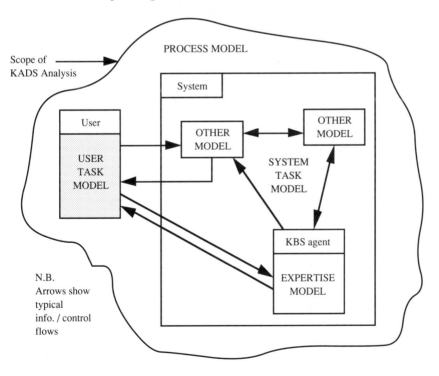

Figure 5.1 Analysis model relationships in terms of cooperating agents

cooperative behaviour of the system and user, from the user's point of view. However, this concept can be extended to *other external agents*. These agents, such as other systems or different classes of user (e.g. administrator versus ordinary user), should have their cooperative behaviour with the system modelled in the same way. In KADS Analysis described in this book we generally mention the User Task Model as the sole external agent task model. It should not be forgotten that this is just the minimal case, and that the systems built using KADS might often have other agents to deal with apart from a 'user'. Thus, one can envisage the generalization of the KADS activity 'Analyze User Tasks' and the optional concept of a 'User Model' – one could have 'Analyze <AGENT> Tasks' and '<AGENT> Models'.

5.2   Interdependencies in Analysis

Figure 5.2 shows how the models in KADS Analysis fit together in terms of their interdependencies.

5.3   Other parts of Analysis

Although KADS is a model-based methodology, a comprehensive approach to the Analysis phase of development needs other, supplementary activities. These are Constraints Analysis and the System Overview. Such activities are often taken for granted in conventional software development, as well as in KBS development.

KADS's **Constraints Analysis** is analogous to requirements engineering in conventional software development. It is concerned with the capture of new and changed requirements, and the maintenance of an up-to-date database of those requirements. As the requirements on the future system are defined, analysis of those requirements, as performed using KADS's model-based activities described in Section 5.1, can be performed. Thus, the model-based activities rely on Constraints Analysis to supply them with requirements ('constraints') to analyze and produce appropriate models. Other requirements constrain how the analysis should be performed, or how the whole project should be organized. Of particular note are those requirements which constrain the subsequent design of the system, such as user-interface and implementation platform requirements.

The **System Overview** is a place-holder in KADS for an overall view of the system to be developed. It helps to focus the development on a well-defined target, for communication to the development team, its management and its customer. It provides an essential focal point for a

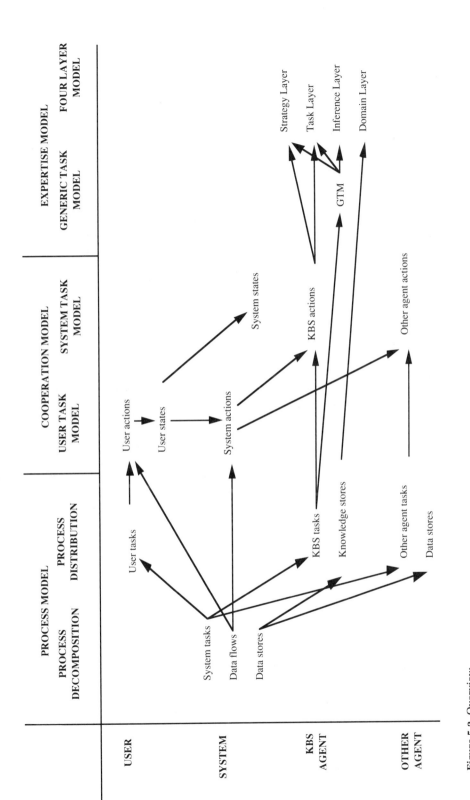

Figure 5.2 Overview of the principal interdependencies within Analysis

shared understanding of the system's concept and key functionality. (In general, although they are loosely defined terms, 'functional requirements' in KADS are documented in the System Overview and 'non-functional requirements' are documented under Constraints.)

Both the Constraints Analysis and System Overview activities can be described as 'maintenance-type' activities in KADS. What we mean by this is that, generally, they are background (but vitally important) activities that take an initial set of their inputs from the Pre-Analysis phase(s) of development and 'maintain' the documentation of their subject matter. Constraints Analysis takes an initial set of known requirements from Pre-Analysis, is performed throughout Analysis, in parallel with the modelling activities, and keeps the documentation of the Constraints on the system and its development up to date. Similarly, the System Overview takes some overall concept of the system from Pre-Analysis, and maintains an up-to-date overall view of the system throughout Analysis.

Note

1. This concept is central to KADS Analysis – the concept of a system consisting of a set of interacting (or cooperating) internal 'agents', working in a part of the real-world environment consisting of other, external agents, and interacting (or cooperating) with those external agents. Note that it is a concept useful during any Analysis, but it will not always carry over into the eventual design of a system – we do not say that *all* systems developed using KADS will have an architecture based on such cooperating agents (although they might). This would be unreasonably constraining. In KADS, it is purely an *Analysis concept*, but a very important one.

6 Overview of Design

This chapter presents a quick overview of the KADS Design phase. KADS Design can be used to support the 'System-level and Module-level Design' phase of a KBS product, equivalent to that required for conventional systems. For a more 'theoretical' description of how all the pieces of Design fit together, see Chapter 8.

6.1 Introduction

Design takes the analysis material produced using KADS Analysis and produces a design for a KBS at two levels. First, it provides an overall architecture for the complete system, consisting of KBS and non-KBS sub-systems. Second, it produces a detailed architecture for the KBS sub-system(s) and details of how the functions within them will be realized. (Non-KBS sub-systems identified at the first level are best designed using other, more established techniques.) Thus, the phase is split into two 'stages':

Global Design – Breaks down the overall system design problem into KBS and non-KBS sub-systems.

KBS Design – Designs the KBS sub-systems down to the level of modules of code, based on activities operating at the 'function', 'behaviour' and 'physical' levels of design; these are performed within the context of a particular design 'framework'.

The major KADS Design results are the *Global System Architecture* from Global Design; and three levels of result from the three levels of KBS design: *Functional Design Model*, *Behavioural Design Model* and *Physical Design Model*. In addition, a further result from KBS Design is the *KBS Design Framework* used to aid the rest of KBS Design – this framework can be thought of as a design 'paradigm'.

6.2   Design stages

The first stage of KADS design is **Global Design**. This produces a Global System Architecture, which is a model that describes the major sub-systems in terms of which functions they perform and how they interface to the other sub-systems. Design then continues independently for each sub-system on the basis that it can be treated as a 'black box'. KADS supports the design of the KBS sub-systems with the activities within KBS Design.

KBS Design takes the functional requirements for the KBS sub-system and transforms them into a Functional Design Model which is a hierarchical structure of the functional components of the system. These components, known as *function blocks*, are derived from a transformation of the analysis material. For components that store information, the equivalent to function blocks is the *domain model*, which details the data and knowledge to be stored. The KADS activity that performs Functional Design is **Decompose KBS Functions**.

Following on from the Functional Design Model, a Behavioural Design Model is built. Behavioural Design addresses the problem of how to realize the functions in terms of *design methods* and *knowledge representations*. There is a library of problem-solving methods (for knowledge-based functions) and knowledge representations in Chapter 13. Design methods can be decomposed into elements such as algorithms and data structures. These are collectively called *design elements*. The KADS activity that performs Behavioural Design is **Assign Design Methods**.

Finally, a Physical Design Model is built, which is concerned with defining the arrangement of the design elements and knowledge representations needed by the Behavioural Design. These components are arranged into modules of code and an architecture for the KBS sub-system. The KADS activity that performs Physical Design is **Assemble Design Elements**.

KBS Design operates within the Technical Constraints identified in Analysis (or an earlier phase). Of particular importance here are the constraints on the implementation platform available for the system. These constraints may restrict the choice of methods that are feasible. The design activity **Define KBS Design Framework** is partly concerned with carrying over these constraints to the Design phase, but is also useful in its own right. It defines a context or 'paradigm' to help the designer produce a design within an appropriate framework, taking into account the capabilities of any suggested or required implementation platform.

In parallel with the design of the KBS sub-system(s) an activity outside of the scope of KADS may need to be performed: *Design of Other Sub-*

Systems. This activity is a place-holder for conventional or special design activities needed by other non-KBS sub-systems.

In summary, KADS Design transforms the results of a KADS Analysis into a form that can be more readily transformed into program code: a physical architecture for the KBS sub-system(s) and specifications for its component modules. At the end of KADS Design, the various models and results are usually consolidated to form a single 'Design document'.

6.3 Design activities and results

Figures 6.1 and 6.2 show *consists-of* hierarchies summarizing the basic

- **DESIGN ACTIVITIES**
  - **Define Global System Architecture**
    - Specify Sub-Systems
    - Specify Sub-System Interfaces
  - **KBS Design**
    - Define KBS Design Framework
    - Decompose KBS Functions ('Functional Design')
    - Assign Design Methods ('Behavioural Design')
    - Assemble Design Elements ('Physical Design')
  - **[Design of Other Sub-Systems]** (not part of KADS)

Figure 6.1 Design activities summary

- **DESIGN RESULTS**
  - **Global System Architecture**
    - Sub-System Specifications
    - Sub-System Interface Specifications
  - **KBS Design Framework**
    - (KBS Design Guide-lines)
  - **KBS Functional Design Model**
    - Function Blocks
    - Domain/Data Model
  - **KBS Behavioural Design Model**
    - Design Methods
    - Design Elements
    - Knowledge Representations
  - **KBS Physical Design Model**
    - KBS Sub-system Architecture
    - Module Specifications
  - **[Other Sub-Systems Designs]** (not part of KADS)

Figure 6.2 Design results summary

Design activities and results respectively. They form a useful 'one page' summary of Design.

6.4   Design road map

Figure 6.3 shows the Design road map and all the basic Design activities in their hierarchical relationships, together with some indication of the potential parallelism between the activities, in a Gantt chart-like project plan format. (See Section 2.2 on how it has been derived.)

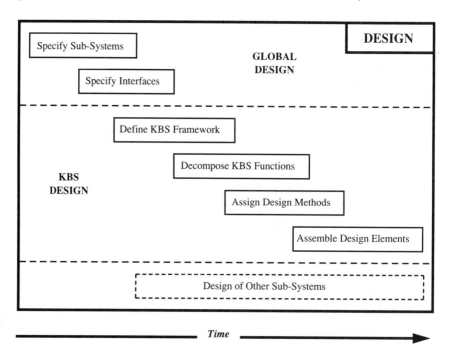

Figure 6.3 The basic KADS Design 'road map' diagram

The road map only gives a very rough guide as to the overlap of the various Design activities. It should *not* be taken as a literal statement of the optimum scheduling of the activities. (See Chapter 9.) It may be helpful to know that the order of describing the Design activities in this book is always the same, and is reflected in reading the road map diagram from top to bottom.

6.5   Design process

Figure 6.4 shows the Design process and illustrates the flow of development between Design activities and results, together with

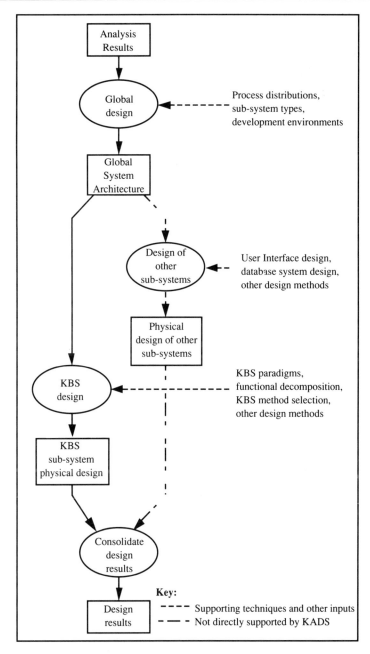

Figure 6.4 The Design Process (idealized)

information sources and techniques to support performance of the stages. It is, however, an idealistic view. It is just one way of illustrating the relationships between the activities and results, based on a dataflow diagram. (See the warning about the limitations of these types of diagrams in Section 3.5.) Refinements of this diagram, in the form of 'exploded' views of the bubbles, are given throughout Chapter 7. There is one resultant process diagram per modelling stage, e.g. Global Design (Figure 7.2) and KBS Design (Figure 7.10).

7 Design activities and results

7.1 Global Design

Global Design is the first stage of KADS Design. The activities within Global Design are concerned with dividing the total system functionality into a set of units, or sub-systems, each of which can then be designed and implemented relatively independently from each other. At its simplest, it is a re-mapping of the results of Analysis onto a practical system architecture, taking into account the non-functional constraints. Figure 7.1 shows the temporal relationship of Global Design relative to the other Design stages.

In Analysis, separation of concerns is expressed in terms of 'cooperating agents', allowing different problem aspects to be handled indepen-

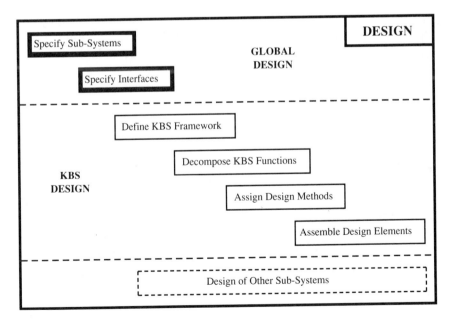

Figure 7.1 The Global Design stage

dently by development personnel with appropriate specialist skills. In Design, the same principle applies. However, here the separation of concerns is expressed in terms of *physical separation* of system functionality.

Global Design is of particular importance to the KBS designer, because it identifies which physical parts of the system will be knowledge-based or will embed knowledge-based components. Ideally, the design of a system will group similar or related functions together, so the norm is for the knowledge-based components to reside within a single sub-system. This makes sense because these components will usually require specialist design skills plus a particular implementation environment. However, there will often be a need to divide these components among several sub-systems (e.g. when the KBS components need to be physically distributed), so Global Design is not necessarily a trivial undertaking.

There are two activities within Global Design:

• Specify Sub-Systems.
• Specify Sub-System Interfaces.

The inputs to Global Design are the results produced in Analysis – particularly the Process Model (Section 4.1), the Cooperation Model (Section 4.2) and the System Overview (Section 4.5). The result of Global Design is the Global System Architecture, expressed as a set of sub-systems and sub-system interfaces. The Global System Architecture is the first of the four models produced by KADS Design. Figure 7.2 illustrates the relationships between the activities and results within Global Design, which are then described in further detail in the following sections.

7.1.1   Specify Sub-Systems

During this activity, the functions which the prospective system must support are divided and grouped into separate units, called sub-systems. This can be achieved as a general approach, either 'top-down' (define the sub-systems and then allocate each function to a sub-system) or 'bottom-up' (group similar or related functions together to define the sub-systems).

Most of the results from Analysis are useful in defining the Global System Architecture. However, the following are particularly significant:

• *The Process Model* – This defines the tasks and data stores which are assigned to each agent in Analysis. Each task and data store must be allocated to a sub-system in design. The agent assignments may be

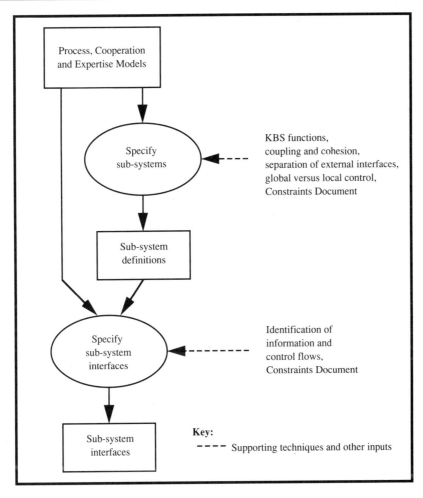

Figure 7.2 Global Design activities and results

useful in defining sub-systems, all other things being equal. (See Section 4.1.)

- *The System Task Model* – This provides a detailed description of the system functions which are invoked in response to each external trigger, e.g. a user event. Each system function must be considered during sub-system specification. (See Section 4.2.2.)
- *The Expertise Model* – This defines the required problem-solving capability of the knowledge-based system component(s). A decision must be taken as to whether the KBS components reside within a single sub-system or are distributed. (See Section 4.3.)
- *The System Overview* – This provides a further description of the system functions, including support functions which may not be detailed in the above models. The 'Provisional System Structure'

within the System Overview provides an early impression of the likely shape of the system and will almost certainly assist with sub-system specification. (See p. 117.)

- *Constraints Documents* – Constraints may restrict the possible assignments of functions to sub-systems. (See Section 4.4.)

The output of this activity is the Global System Architecture, defined as a set of sub-systems with an indication of how information or control flows between them. (See p. 138.)

Techniques for specification of sub-systems

There are no 'hard and fast' techniques to support this activity. However, the following guidelines should prove useful for most circumstances:

KBS functions – As has been indicated above, the 'norm' of system design is to group all the KBS functions together into a single subsystem. If this is achievable then the KBS components can be designed by a single KBS designer and implemented within a single specialist KBS environment (e.g. language, toolkit or shell). However, this is not always achievable. If the total system is *distributed* (e.g. physically separate management sub-systems within a computer network), then the KBS components may also have to be distributed across several sub-systems. In this case, care should be taken that the requisite skills are applied to the design of each of the KBS components and that the implementation of each KBS sub-system is supported by an appropriate environment. Figure 7.3 illustrates a distributed KBS architecture, where one KBS is monitoring an automatic process and passing significant events to a second KBS which diagnoses problems in cooperation with a human user.

Coupling and cohesion – In conventional software design, 'coupling' is defined as the degree of logical connection between modules; 'cohesion' is the degree of relationship between functions within a module. In general, it is good design practice to *minimize coupling* and to *maximize cohesion*. This ensures that the functions within a module (here, a sub-system) are closely related and that interconnections between modules (sub-systems) are reduced to the bare essentials. In other words, the Global System Architecture diagram should not look like spaghetti! (Of course, there is much more to it than this, but for extensive discussion, see note 1, p. 175.) Figure 7.4 contrasts good and bad design practice based on these principles. In the figure, functions prefixed with the same letter are taken to be related.

Separation of external interfaces – It is generally considered good

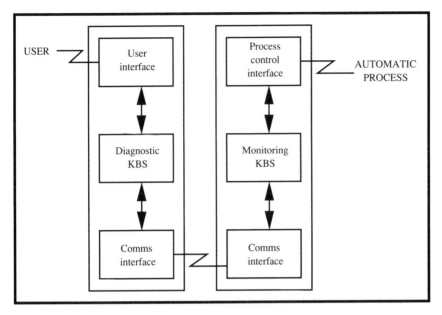

Figure 7.3 Example of a distributed KBS architecture

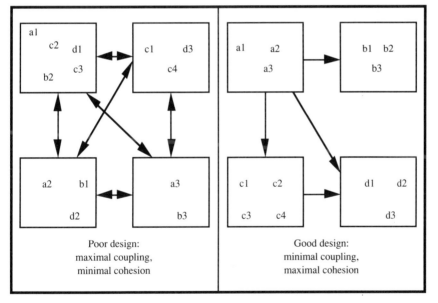

Figure 7.4 The impact of coupling and cohesion on Design

design practice to separate out the functions which are concerned with supporting the external system interfaces (especially the User Interface). Ideally, these should be placed into separate sub-systems. Many tools are becoming available to support the implementation of the User Interface, and their use will be facilitated if their functions are separated out in the design. Figure 7.3 illustrates a design which separates out interface functions.

Global or local control – The System Task Model from Analysis provides a specification of the highest level of control within the system. One way to achieve a good design is to provide a separate sub-system to handle this (global) control. In fact, several implementation environments now provide direct support for this kind of control under the guise of 'dialogue management'. Alternatively, the logic of the System Task Model may be spread across all sub-systems, leading to an implicit (local) realization of the contents of that model. Figure 7.5 illustrates the difference between global and local control.

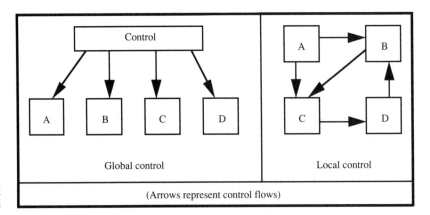

Figure 7.5 Global versus local control

Tools for specification of sub-systems

General-purpose drawing tools, such as MacDraw on the Apple Macintosh or similar PC-based packages, may be used to illustrate the Global System Architecture. Outliners and other hierarchical structure editors may be useful for documenting the *consists-of* nature of the Global System Architecture. CASE tools which provide notations such as Structure Charts may also be useful and bring their usual additional benefits beyond general-purpose tools.

The Global System Architecture

The result of the 'Specify Sub-Systems' activity is an outline Global System Architecture. This is expressed in terms of two relations. A *consists-of* relation is used to identify the sub-systems and their embedded functions; an *input–output* relation is used to show the flow of information or control between sub-systems. Alternatively, the flow of control may be

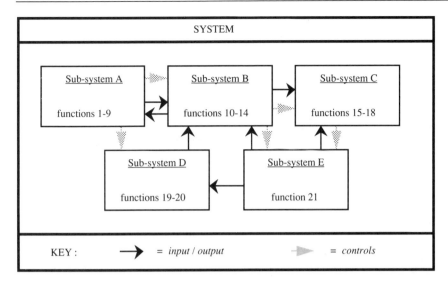

Figure 7.6 Example
Global System
Architecture

indicated separately from the input-output relation by means of a
separate *controls* relation. Figure 7.6 shows one way in which the three
relations may be provided in a single diagram.

Specify Sub-Systems

Example

In the Response Point Expert System development the 'Provisional
System Structure' from the System Overview was used as the basis for
Global Design. However, the following considerations prompted changes
to the original structure:

1. The decision was taken to have global, rather than local, control.
2. The database and network management interfaces were felt to be
    sufficiently independent to warrant separate sub-systems.
3. The decision to use a specialized user-interface toolkit meant that
    only display and control functions could be held in the user-interface
    sub-system. Some processing functions had to be placed in other sub-
    systems. The decision was taken to merge 'Obtain Problem Details'
    (Process Model Task 2.1) plus part of 'Provide Solution' (Task 3)
    with the internal storage block to form the Problem Manager; and to
    support 'Log/Browse Incidents' (Task 4) within the Database
    Interface.

Figure 7.7 illustrates the Response Point Expert System architecture.
Note that the Global Control sub-system is implicitly connected to every
other sub-system. Table 7.1 provides a breakdown of the top-level
functions within each sub-system.

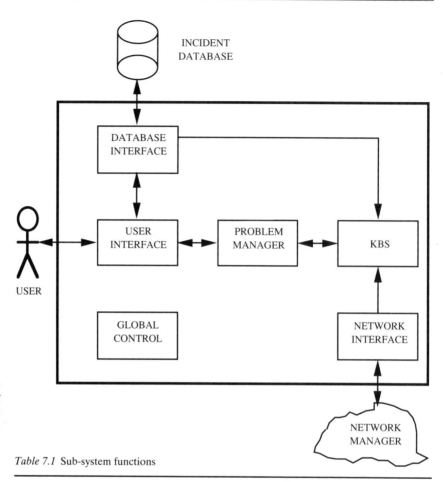

Figure 7.7
Architecture of
Response Point Expert
System

Table 7.1 Sub-system functions

User Interface
  Initialize basic screen support
  Support user interface control
    functions
  Input basic customer details
  Display questions and answers
  Display and input problem details
  Display problem solution
  Display explanation
  Input/display enquiry number
  Display incident log
  Display incident report

Problem Manager
  Store basic customer details
  Maintain problem description
  Maintain network status information
  Construct problem solution text(s)
  Construct question/answer text(s)

Global Control
  Manage system state
  Process user events

KBS
  Compare incident against existing problems
  Compare incident against network status
    information
  Attempt to route incident
  Decide next question

Network Interface
  Monitor network
  Input network status information

Database Interface
  Retrieve Incident Log
  Retrieve Incident(s)
  Log Incident

7.1.2   Specify Sub-System Interfaces

This activity basically follows on from 'Specify Sub-Systems' but can also be partly interleaved with it. Its aim is to specify what information flows between sub-systems and how the flows are controlled. Once the sub-systems and their respective functions have been identified and specified, the interfaces between sub-systems should be specified in detail. When this has been achieved, design of each sub-system can proceed relatively independently, allowing large systems to have their sub-systems designed in parallel.

The main input to this activity is the set of Sub-System Specifications from the outline Global System Architecture. This should be backed up with information from the Process Model (see Section 4.1) and the System Task Model (see Section 4.2.2), in order to determine the nature of the required interfaces.

Tools for specification of Sub-System interfaces

At the time of writing there are no specific tools to support this activity. Word processors and/or general-purpose drawing tools, such as MacDraw on the Apple Macintosh or similar PC-based packages, may be used. Frames, based on the details to be documented listed below, may be created and used as templates. A typical frame is shown in the case study example.

The Sub-System Interfaces

In documenting the Sub-System Interfaces the following details should be provided for each information or control flow:

- *Initiator*   The sub-system responsible for triggering the activity.
- *Request*   A description of the type of activity requested by the initiator (comparable to a function call).
- *Source*   Which sub-system (if any) provides information.
- *Destination*   Which sub-system (if any) receives information.
- *Information*   Specification of the information (if any) which flows.
- *Recipient*   Which sub-system (if any) receives control.
- *Result*   A description of any actions or state changes which result from the activity.

For simple systems, much of this information can be encapsulated into a compact pseudo-code description of the system. The close mapping between the System Task Model from Analysis and the system's control flow can then be used to generate pseudo-code quickly, which can be suitably annotated or rich enough to describe the key information from the list above. Alternatively, a frame or tabular structure can be built up and filled in.

The designer should expand and describe each control or information flow which is indicated in the outline Global System Architecture from 'Specify Sub-Systems'. The Process Model (see Section 4.1) and, more especially, the System Task Model (see Section 4.2.2) should be used to cross-check that all the important information and control flows have been considered. A special diagramming technique may be used to indicate which sub-system takes the initiative in information flow, as illustrated in Figure 7.8:

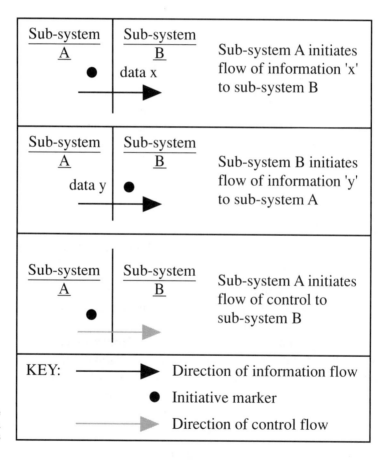

Figure 7.8 Example sub-system information flows

Specify Sub-System Interfaces

The example in this section details the interfaces to/from the Problem Manager sub-system of the Response Point Expert System (see Figure 7.7 in the previous example).

As can be seen from the Global System Architecture, the Problem Manager communicates only with the User Interface, KBS and (implicitly from the diagram) Global Control. The data flow in the latter is unidirectional from Global Control to the Problem Manager and bidirectional in the other cases.

The 'Requests' shown below will correspond to functions in the implemented system. The reader should be able to map each Request onto their overall parent functions shown per sub-system in Table 7.1. (For example, 'clear problem', 'store basic details', 'add data' and 'retract data' are all part of Global Control's 'Manage System State' functionality.) Ideally, such mappings should be clearly documented when doing this for real, to ensure that each functional area is fully covered. For simplification, only a sub-set of the possible information to be documented for the interfaces is shown below: entries for the 'source', 'destination' and 'recipient' are not included.

Requests to Problem Manager:

Initiator	Request	Information	Result
Global Control	Clear Problem	None	Problem Description is cleared
	Store Basic Details	Customer Details	Customer Details are stored
	Add Data	Problem Data	Problem Description is updated
	Retract Data	Problem Data	Problem Description is updated
User Interface	Get Data	None	Problem Data are provided
	Get Solution	None	Problem Solution is provided
	Get Explanation	None	Explanation is provided
KBS	Get Problem State	None	Problem Description is provided
	Add Solution	Solution	Solution is added
	Add Explanation	Explanation	Explanation is added

Requests from Problem Manager:

Initiator	Request	Information	Result
KBS	Get Question	None	Next Question is provided
User Interface	Display Data	Problem Data	Problem Data are highlighted
	Display Question	Q/A texts	Question on screen is updated

7.2 KBS Design

The KBS Design stage is concerned with the design of the problem-solving aspects of the prospective system. As indicated in Section 7.1.1, these aspects may reside within a single sub-system or may be physically distributed across more than one. Figure 7.9 shows the temporal relationship of KBS Design relative to the other Design stages.

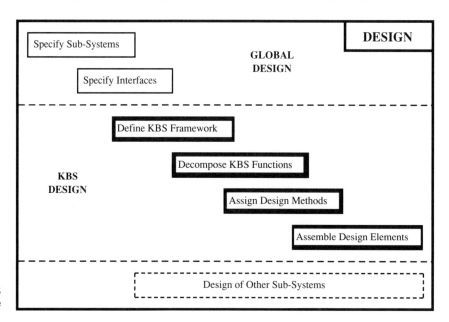

Figure 7.9 The KBS Design stage

The aim of KBS Design is to examine the problem-solving aspects of each knowledge-based sub-system individually and independently of other system functionality. Since the problem-solving capability of the prospective system has been captured during Analysis and has been represented in the form of the four-layer Expertise Model, a natural approach to KBS Design in KADS is to define a simple mapping from the Expertise Model onto a physical KBS design architecture. However, this is not always possible in practice, for a number of reasons.

First, the KBS sub-system is likely to embed functions which are strictly not part of the Expertise Model. Various functions may be needed to provide interfaces to other sub-systems or to support peripheral KBS tasks, such as the generation of explanations and house-keeping. Second, the layers of the Expertise Model may not provide an ideal mapping onto the chosen or imposed implementation environment. Most KBS implementation environments do not possess the richness of constructs to support all aspects of the Expertise Model directly. Third, the Expertise Model provides an idealized view of how expert problem solving is achieved. It will usually be necessary to choose between alternative implementation approaches, with subsequent impact upon the design elements which are necessary to realize the Expertise Model and the way in which these elements need to be grouped to provide the best solution. Fourth, the Constraints Document may place restrictions upon the way in which the Expertise Model may be realized, e.g. for reasons of system performance or security. Consequently, KADS provides a set of design activities and techniques to support transformation of the Expertise Model into a physical KBS design architecture.

There are four activities within KBS Design:

- Define KBS Design Framework.
- Decompose KBS Functions.
- Assign Design Methods.
- Assemble Design Elements.

The first activity to be performed is 'Define KBS Design Framework'. This identifies the technique, architecture or environment which will be used to support KBS Design. Following the definition of a Design Framework, KBS Design in KADS is achieved by:

1. Decomposing the functions which must be realized within the KBS sub-system (*'Functional Design'*).
2. Selecting 'Design Methods' and knowledge representations to realize those functions and identifying the Design Elements (basic computational components, such as algorithms and data structures) which support the Design Methods (*'Behavioural Design'*).
3. Assembling those Design Elements into modules to create the physical KBS sub-system architecture (*'Physical Design'*).

These three activities result in the KADS Functional, Behavioural and Physical Design Models. KADS provides a library of KBS Design Methods (see Chapter 13) plus some guidance on how implementation environments may be assessed for use as delivery vehicles (see Chapter 14). Figure 7.10 illustrates the relationship between the activities and results within KBS Design, which are then described in further detail in the following sections.

7.2.1 Define KBS Design Framework

The aim of this activity is to define a framework within which to carry out KBS Design. This could be a general problem-solving technique, such as

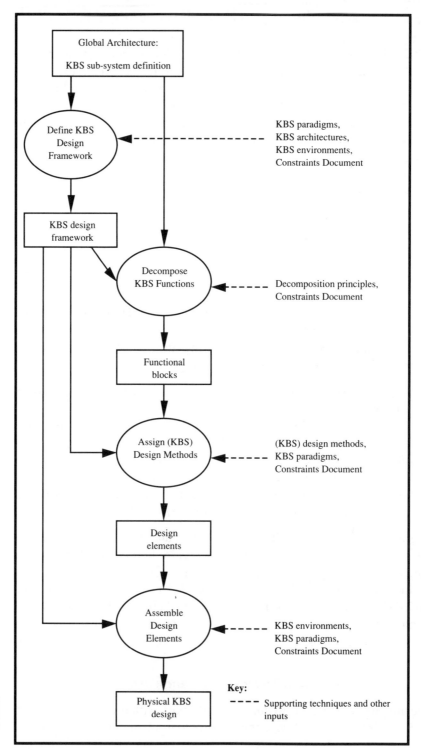

Figure 7.10 KBS
Design activities and
results

constraint-based logic or blackboard reasoning. Alternatively, it could be related to the chosen or dictated implementation environment, e.g. frame- or rule-based.

The main inputs to this activity are the Global System Architecture (see Section 7.1), the Expertise Model (see Section 4.3) and the Technical Constraints Document (see Section 4.4.3). The Global System Architecture defines the functions which must be realized within the KBS sub-system (as well as the other sub-systems). These may include support functions, as well as the problem-solving functions within the Expertise Model. The Expertise Model, together with the Global System Architecture, defines which problem-solving functions must be realized within the KBS sub-system. The Global System Architecture will define these at the level of trigger functions, while the Expertise Model will provide the Strategy, Task, Inference and Domain layers to support each such function. The Technical Constraints Document will define any restrictions on the way in which the KBS sub-system should be implemented, e.g. by dictating the preferred implementation environment.

Techniques for defining the KBS Design framework

If the Technical Constraints Document places restrictions on the implementation environment, then these should be used to define or to narrow the choice of environment. Each prospective environment should be characterized according to its knowledge representation and problem-solving capabilities. These characteristics should be matched against the characteristics of the Expertise Model. The KADS Generic Task Model Library (Chapter 12), Design Method Library (Chapter 13) and Implementation Environment assessment guide (Chapter 14) may be used to sustain this activity. Experimental prototyping may also provide valuable support.

If there is a good match between the characteristics of an implementation environment and those of the Expertise Model, this environment should be chosen and used to define the KBS design framework. If there is an implementation environment which provides some of the required capability, this should be chosen and extended to meet the problem-solving requirements. If there is no suitable implementation environment, this will need to be built from scratch, with consequent impact upon KBS implementation costs and timescales.

Note that implementation environments vary immensely with respect to the type of constructs they provide and how tailored they are to specific approaches. For example, most basic expert system 'shells' support various methods within the rule-based approach; some larger environments provide additional built-in features such as frame-based representation, probabilistic reasoning, truth-maintenance systems, constraint handling, the modularization of knowledge bases and object-oriented programming methods. Chapter 14 provides some guidance as to how to assess and choose environments on the basis of their capabilities in these respects.

With embedded KBS the choice is often constrained by requirements for interfaces to other system components. These requirements are often best met either by building the required problem-solving constructs from a lower-level language or by the use of a high-level language or shell which supports foreign function calls and/or database access routines.

Other constraints may arise from the user interface requirements (recorded in Technical Constraints). Often shells provide a set of communication primitives which may prove unsatisfactory for implementing the user interface design. This is particularly true of the cheaper PC-based environments.

The KBS Design Framework

The output from the 'Define KBS Design Framework' activity is the KBS Design Framework Document, which describes the technique, architecture and/or environment that has been chosen to support KBS Design. There is no fixed structure for this document, which will normally consist of free text. However, the following contents are recommended for inclusion:

- General characteristics of the desired problem-solving capability (from the Expertise Model).
- Description of the chosen framework (technique, architecture or environment).
- General characteristics of the chosen implementation environment (if any, to include the design elements which are supported).

Example

Define KBS Design Framework

The Technical Constraints document for the Response Point Expert System identified two possible implementation environments for the KBS – DecisionPower and Egeria. Of these, DecisionPower was chosen because of its general-purpose facilities and because the development team had considerable experience in its use.

Looking at the inference structure for the Response Point Expert System (see p. 93), an important element of problem solving is provided by the 'compare' inference type. This is used in three different circumstances and is based around the use of hierarchically structured concept sets.

Comparing the facilities offered by DecisionPower, which is Prolog-based, and the requirements of the 'compare' inferences, it was decided that a general approach using pattern matching, unification and traversal of hierarchies could be applied. This was confirmed by examining the other inference types and domain structures and finding no problems with this approach.

7.2.2 *Decompose KBS Functions (Functional Design)*

The aim of Functional Design is functional decomposition of the KBS sub-system. It should identify and describe the primitive functions which will be used as the basis for the KBS sub-system's design. This is achieved by decomposing the functions which must be supported by the KBS sub-system, as defined by the Global System Architecture, and analyzing their input–output relationships.

A fundamental input for this activity is the completed Expertise Model. The KBS Sub-System Specification from the Global System Architecture will also be needed, to provide details of the required overall functionality, together with the detailed problem-solving functionality.

The KBS functions are decomposed into sub-functions, which are then arranged in a *consists-of* hierarchy. The highest-level node in this hierarchy represents the complete KBS sub-system. The leaf nodes represent the primitive function blocks which will be used as the basis for further design (Behavioural design – see Section 7.2.3).

Figure 7.11 provides a clarification of KBS sub-system functions. (It also shows suggested symbols in parentheses for annotating the function types and an indication of the mapping between function types and their appropriate 'DDL frames' – see p. 152. These items are just documentation conventions and their use will be shown soon.)

The **Problem Solving** – function type is used to define functions which perform or support expert tasks, so these normally map onto one or more inference types within the inference layer of the Expertise Model. Two sub-types of this function type may be further identified:

The **Inference Function** – provides direct support for an individual inference type. The advantages of this direct mapping are a good degree of consistency between the structure of the Analysis and Design models coupled with good support for tracing and/or explanation.

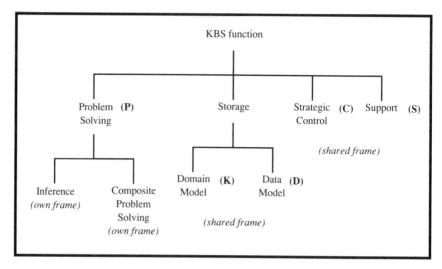

Figure 7.11 KBS function types

The **Composite Problem Solving (PS) Function** – allows for two or more inference steps (types) to be grouped together within a single function. This may be convenient where the inference steps in question are unique, are always used in the same sequence, and support a single task layer goal. The possible disadvantage of grouping inference steps in this manner is that the Composite PS Function is likely to hide details of individual inference steps which might be required to support explanation, etc.

The **Storage** function type is used to define static domain knowledge plus run-time data which are needed to support the KBS sub-system. Two sub-types of this function type may be further identified:

The **Domain Model** – describes static domain knowledge. This is derived from the domain layer of the Expertise Model. However, the Inference Layer provides a useful cross-check since both inference types and domain roles will provide associations with knowledge in the Domain Layer. Note that the purpose of the Domain Model description at this stage of design is to document the knowledge and data that are needed to support the KBS sub-system, but not how they are to be represented.

The **Data Model** – describes run-time storage information and other conventional (non-knowledge) data needed by the KBS sub-system.

The **Strategic Control** type describes higher-level overall KBS control functions. It is an optional component for facilitating the flexible use of the problem-solving behaviour of the system. Often only minimal control is required, and hence this type can be omitted as an explicit component, or specified quite simply. However, more advanced systems that require different sets of inference functions to be executed in different situations will probably require this component to be fully specified.

The functions described by a Strategic Control type normally require access to a run-time database in which data specific to the problem being solved are stored. The data are used to select agendas of goals for the problem-solver component of the sub-system. The following examples illustrate the types of function which may be represented within Strategic Control:

- *Identification of problem-solving goals* – This is best seen as generating an agenda of goals to be achieved by the problem solver given a problem description. This will be supported by an abstract model of the problem solver's competence. One way of representing this might be rules for the abstraction of problem features.
- *Identification of communication goals* – Communication goals are generated by the Strategic Control function when externally held data are required or when there is a requirement to inform the user of problem-solving results or to update an external system (e.g. database).
- *Invocation and monitoring of tasks for the problem solver* – Given a goal for the problem solver, the strategic function passes control messages to the relevant problem-solver function. During task execution, impasses or failures may occur. Where this cannot be solved at the lower level, new goal agendas may need to be generated by the strategic function.

The **Support Function** type is used to describe other (usually conventional) functions which are needed to support the KBS, including explanation and house-keeping.

The various types of function described above facilitate a breakdown of the required functionality of the KBS. Once the primitive functions have been identified and specified, the next step is to describe the input–output relations which hold between these functions – i.e. the information output from one function is needed as the input to another. The result of this step is (essentially) a detailed Data Flow Diagram (DFD) for the KBS. This will be needed later on in design, when decisions need to be taken about how to realize the functions and how to group the resultant components into modules.

Functional Design Techniques

The basic method of carrying out this activity is to perform a detailed review of the contents of the Expertise Model, in conjunction with the KBS Sub-System Specification from the Global System Architecture. The review should aim, wherever possible, to use corresponding function blocks, e.g. to map inference types onto Inference Functions. However, problem-solving tasks will be need to be re-evaluated and re-specified to ensure completeness at the required level of detail. The designer should remember that the ultimate aim is to represent the way in which the KBS is to be implemented within the chosen framework or environment. The KBS Design Framework should therefore be borne in mind, particularly when decomposing the problem-solving tasks into Inference and Composite PS Functions.

At its simplest, KBS Functional Design is a re-mapping of the contents of the Expertise Model. However, the activity gives the designer the opportunity to re-evaluate the detailed partitioning of the system's KBS functionality in terms of how the system code will be structured, using the additional inputs of the KBS Design Framework and the non-functional requirements of the Constraints. Being produced in Analysis, the Expertise Model will generally be described in terms of the original domain, and not in terms of an implementation. Here is where implementation concerns are imposed on the Expertise Model.

The Functional Design Model

The output from the 'Decompose KBS Functions' activity is a complete functional specification of the KBS, comprising function block specifications supported with input–output relations. This is also known as the Functional Design Model. The function block specifications can be described using KADS 'Design Description Language' (DDL) frames, supplemented by Data Flow Diagrams and a structure chart (for the function decomposition hierarchy).

The KADS Design Description Language (DDL)
– function block frames

There are four DDL frames to support the documentation of the Functional Design Model:

- Inference Function frame.
- Composite Problem-Solving Function frame.
- Domain/Data Model frame.
- Strategic Control/Support Function frame.

Figure 7.11 shows the mapping between function types and the DDL frames. (A fifth DDL frame is introduced in Behavioural Design for Inference Methods – see Section 7.2.3.)

The slots shown within any of the frames are to *support* rather than to constrain the designer. Thus, they should be treated as guidelines for the designer, who should feel free to add or remove slots if it is found *necessary* for the current development. However, note that compliance with the suggested slots is encouraged, as this will support the most consistent, and hence, widely comprehensible and maintainable documentation to be produced. Note in the frames below that the 'realized-by' and 'representation' slots are left empty until the next step of design, Behavioural Design; all the other slots are now filled in as part of Functional Design.

DDL description of inference functions
The following frame structure should be filled for each inference function

---

INFERENCE-FUNCTION *<name>*

Goal:
   Textual description of what the function achieves.
Input domain role(s):
   Pointer(s) to Domain/Data Model blocks used by this function.
Output domain role(s):
   Pointer(s) to Domain/Data Model blocks created by this function.
Activates:
   Pointer to any function block(s) invoked from within this function.
Activated by:
   Pointer to the function block(s) responsible for invoking this function.
Supports:
   Pointer to the inference type(s) the function is to realize.
Supported by:
   Pointer to the Domain Model blocks which support this function.
Realized-by:
   <Inference method name> – not used at this stage of design.
Side-effects:
   Textual description of possible side-effects such as sub-goals, bindings used in truth maintenance, interference with other inferences, etc.
Comments:
   An optional slot for general comments about the function that need to be noted.

---

identified. (The 'realized-by' slot is filled by the method selection activity described later in Design, in Section 7.2.3. The contents of the 'side effects' slot will also depend on the method selected.)

DDL description of composite problem-solving (PS) functions
Internal problem-solving control is required when composite problem-solving tasks are being performed, i.e. when lower-level composite tasks or two or more inference functions need to be invoked in order to achieve a goal. These sequences are referred to as composite problem-solving tasks or functions. In some cases it may be appropriate to define explicitly a fixed control regime for these tasks. In other cases, where a more

---

COMPOSITE PS FUNCTION *<name>*

Goal:
   Textual description of what the function achieves.
Input domain role(s):
   Pointer(s) to Domain/Data Model blocks used by this function.
Output domain role(s):
   Pointer(s) to Domain/Data Model blocks created by this function.
Activates:
   (list of) <inference function, composite ps function>
Activated by:
   (list of) <composite ps function>
Supports:
   Pointer(s) to the inference type(s) and/or task(s) the function is to realize.
Supported by:
   Pointer to the Domain Model blocks which support this function.
Control structure:
   A description of the sequencing of calls to component functions and lower-level functions.
Realized-by:
   <Design method name(s) > – not used at this stage of design.
Side-effects:
   Textual description of possible side-effects such as sub-goals, bindings used in truth maintenance, interference with other inferences, etc.
Comments:
   An optional slot for general comments about the function that need to be noted.

---

flexible approach is required, problem-solving plans may need to be generated at run-time by means of an 'inference planner'. This will then be described using a Strategic Control Function block. The following framework is used to describe inference control functions in fixed regimes:

DDL description of storage functions

Storage function blocks describe both static domain knowledge (from the domain layer of the Expertise Model – Domain Model) and run-time (Data Model) storage. Note that, in Functional Design, the intention is to describe *what* is required rather than *how* it is realized, so detailed knowledge and data representation is deferred until the next stage of design. The following framework is used to describe each Domain/Data Model block:

DOMAIN/DATA MODEL *<name>*

Use:
  Description of the purpose of the static knowledge or support data.
Composition:
  Specification of the contents (but not the representation) of the information.
Created by:
  Pointer to the function block (if any) which creates this information.
Used by:
  Pointer(s) to the function block(s) which use or modify the information.
Accessed by:
  Pointer(s) to the function block(s) which access the information.
Destroyed by:
  Pointer to the function block (if any) which destroys the information.
Representation:
  < Not filled in until the next stage of design >.

DDL description of strategic control functions and support functions

The DDL includes a framework to support the description of both Strategic Control Function and Support Function blocks. However, these should be used as guidelines only. Strategic Control Functions in particular will vary greatly in their range of capability and specification requirements, so the designer should be prepared to modify the existing notations or to invent new ones as the need arises. The Strategic Control Function and Support Function frameworks are as follows:

STRATEGIC CONTROL/SUPPORT FUNCTION *<name>*

Type:
Category of function supported, e.g. storage control, inference planner.

Description:
Textual description of what the function achieves.

Input:
Pointer(s) to Domain/Data Model blocks used by this function.

Output:
Pointer(s) to Domain/Data Model blocks created by this function.

Activates:
(list of) function blocks invoked by this one.

Activated by:
(list of) function blocks which invoke this one.

Control structure:
A description of the sequencing of calls to component functions and lower level functions.

Side-effects:
Textual description of possible side-effects.

Comments:
An optional slot for general comments about the function that need to be noted.

Example

Decompose KBS Functions (Functional Design)

The KBS sub-system functions for the Response Point Expert System are decomposed below. (Compare with the functional responsibilities of the KBS sub-system shown in Table 7.1.) The resultant functional blocks are indicated according to their type by a parenthesized letter to the right of the function block name – refer to Figure 7.11 for the mapping between function types and the letters P, S, K, C (D was not needed in this example).

Note that support knowledge for inference steps appears in the knowledge base, but is accessed by the relevant inference function, and that certain inference types have been designated support functions. This is because they represent trivial problem-solving steps for which the selection of a KBS method is considered unnecessary or trivial. (These two actions are typical.)

KBS sub-system function blocks

problem solving
  compare incident against existing problems
    select incident report (P)
    decompose into problem description (S)
    compare new and old problem descriptions (P)
  compare incident against network status information
    select network element status (P)
    abstract network problem description (P)
    compare new and network problem descriptions (P)
  attempt to route incident
    select front-line desk responsibility (P)
    decompose front line desk responsibility (S)
    compare new and FLD problem descriptions (P)
  decide next question (P)
    select comparison result
    select problem data
    match with question

Storage

knowledge base
  routing knowledge (K)
  question specifications (K)
  problem hierarchies (K)
  network knowledge (K)
run-time storage
  problem description (K)
  solution (routing decision, repeat or known problem) (K)
  question to ask (K)
  inference trail (K)
  explanation (K)
  comparison results (K)

Strategic control

choose network comparison task structure (C)
  check for updated network status information
interpret task structure (C)
  record inference trail

Support functions

initialize KBS sub-system	(S)
maintain current problem description	(S)
provide solution to problem manager	(S)
specify solution (repeat, known problem or routing information)	
provide next question to problem manager	(S)
provide explanation to problem manager	(S)
convert inference trail to explanation	
invoke network query	(S)
invoke incident database query	(S)

(Note that the KBS Design Framework example on p. 148 may help in interpreting why the above decomposition is the way it is.)

The primitive and composite Problem-Solving (PS) functions are suffixed with a '(P)'. These will be described in detail using Inference Function and Composite PS Function block DDL frame notation, respectively.

The 'Decide Next Question' task has been deemed a Composite PS function because there is no need to access the embedded inference types individually (e.g. no need to explain question generation) and it can be readily implemented as a single functional block. The other tasks have been split into function blocks for individual inference types in order to support explanation and to facilitate the grouping of similar functions.

Domain Model elements are suffixed with a '(K)'. They have been derived by looking at the Expertise Model's Domain Layer entities, as accessed by Domain Roles in the Inference Layer. They are described in detail in Domain Model DDL frame notation. Strategic control functions are suffixed with a '(C)' and are documented using Strategic Function block DDL frame notation. Support functions are suffixed with an '(S)' and are documented using Support Function block DDL frame notation.

Input/output relations of function blocks
Figure 7.12 gives an example of the description of an input–output relation – for explanation support functions. Remember that it is just a Data Flow Diagram and therefore only shows data dependencies, not control sequences.

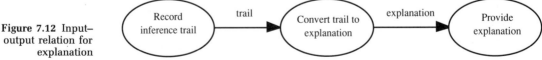

Figure 7.12 Input–output relation for explanation

If pseudo-code is used to specify the control structure of the system, or at least define the function calls, this may already show input–output relations in the parameters to the functions (cf. part of 'resolved' state in the System Task Model example on p. 60):

Explanation:

. . .

(during problem-solving)
  Record_inference_trail (out: trail);

. . .

(other things happen in the system)

. . .

IF explanation requested DO
  Convert_trail_to_explanation (in: trail; out: explanation);
  Provide_explanation (in: explanation).

Sample DDL frames for Function Blocks

Below are sample function block and Domain Model descriptions for a selection of the above functions.

COMPOSITE PS FUNCTION BLOCK DESCRIPTION: *Decide Next Question*
Goal:
  Use the comparison results from the other KBS tasks to determine the best question to ask to focus on a solution.
Input:
  One or more of 'Incident Comparison Result', 'Network Comparison Result' and 'Routing Result'.
Output:
  Question to ask.
Activates:
  None.
Activated by:
  Interpret Task Structure (Decide Next Question).
Supports:
  Problem Solving (task layer).
Supported by:
  Routing Knowledge, Problem Hierarchies, Question Specifications.
Control structure:
  < as per 'Decide Next Question' task structure >.
Side-effects:
  Creates and maintains a list of questions generated so far.

INFERENCE FUNCTION BLOCK DESCRIPTION: *Compare New and Old Problem Descriptions*

Goal:

Compare the aspects of the new problem against those within an existing incident report, recording the significant differences if the comparison is not exact.

Inputs:

New and Old Problem Descriptions (cf. Process Glossary).

Output:

Incident Comparison Result (cf. Process Glossary).

Activates:

None.

Activated by:

Interpret Task Structure (Compare Against Existing Incidents).

Supports:

'Compare 1' inference type (cf. p. 95).

Supported by:

Problem Hierarchies (cf. Static Domain Structures).

Side-effects:

If the comparison succeeds then the enquiry number of the existing incident is recorded. The comparison result may also be used to support explanation.

DOMAIN MODEL DESCRIPTION: *Problem Description*

Use:

To hold a composite description of the current type of problem which is being reported.

Composition:

Hardware Type + Software Type + Problem Type.

Created by:

'Maintain Current Problem Description' (support function).

Used by:

Compare New and Old Problem Descriptions.
Compare New and Network Problem Descriptions.
Compare New and FLD Problem Descriptions.

Accessed by:

Select Incident Report
Select Network Element Status
Select FLD Responsibility.

Destroyed by:

Initialize KBS sub-system.

STRATEGIC CONTROL BLOCK DESCRIPTION: *Choose Network Comparison Task Structure*

Type:

Task selection.

Description:

Choose an appropriate task structure for 'Compare Against Network Status' depending on whether new network status information is available.

Input:

Network Status Information.

Output:

Selected task structure.

Activates:

Check for updated network status information.

Activated by:

Interpret Task Structure (Strategic Control)

Control structure:

Check for updated network status information
Invoke network comparison selection rules
Interpret task (chosen task structure).

SUPPORT FUNCTION BLOCK DESCRIPTION: *Provide Solution to Problem Manager*

Type:

Interface support.

Description:

Provide the result from Problem Description comparison where successful to the Problem Manager sub-system.

Input:

Basic decision (Repeat Incident, Matched Network Characteristic, Routing Decision).

Output:

One of:

Repeat Incident Enquiry No. + Original Problem Description;
Network Characteristic + matched Problem Description;
FLD + responsible Problem Description which this desk handles.

Activates:

Specify Solution.

Activated by:

Interpret Task Structure (Strategic Control)

Control structures:

Specify Resolution from basic decision
Communicate Solution to Problem Manager.

7.2.3   Assign Design Methods (Behavioural Design)

The aim of Behavioural Design is to select the computational and representational methods which will be used to realize the problem-solving functions specified in Functional Design. Inevitably, in practice, the decisions required per function will depend upon the particular characteristics and facilities supported within the chosen implementation framework – hence the utility of the KBS Design Framework (see Section 7.2.1).

Behavioural Design takes as its input the Functional Model produced in Functional Design (see Section 7.2.2). Its result is a description of the computational and representational approaches which have been chosen to realize the required problem-solving functions, i.e. what actual methods/structures will be used to realize these functions. In practical terms, this means filling in the 'realized-by' and 'representation' slots in the DDL frames.

Once the methods and structures have been selected, the design elements (smaller components) needed by those methods and structures can be determined. These then form the main input to 'Assemble Design Elements' (Physical KBS Design) (see Section 7.2.4).

In Behavioural Design, the selection of methods and representation structures are inevitably intertwined. The selection of a method often impacts upon the choice of knowledge/data representation, and vice versa. Method selection and structure representation cannot be considered independently. There are therefore two complementary approaches within behavioural design: method-driven and representation-driven.

The *method-driven* approach involves selecting problem-solving methods and then using these, together with the KBS Design Framework and any relevant Technical Constraints, to choose appropriate representations. The *representation-driven* approach starts with the Domain Model frames from Functional Design and explores how best to represent the knowledge/data associated with the frames. The selection of problem-solving methods is then guided by the chosen representations. Figure 7.13 illustrates the various dependencies between the method- and representation-driven approaches. In practice, the designer will find it natural to interleave the two approaches, possibly iterating through several choices until the best practical solution is reached. It is a creative process.

Both the above approaches to Behavioural Design are supported by the library of problem-solving methods in Chapter 13. The library presents its methods categorized in these two ways. The first arises from the fact that known problem-solving methods can be classified by the types of inference they support. The second classification arises from the fact that

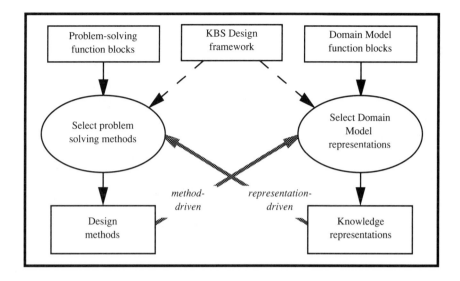

the domain constructs which support inference steps often 'suggest' certain knowledge-representation approaches.

Selecting problem-solving methods

The goal in selecting methods is to find, for each function, the most appropriate realization in terms of the algorithms and data structures required. Support for this activity in KADS is provided by a library of proven problem-solving computational methods (see Chapter 13). Selection of appropriate methods for the functions required can be achieved in two ways:

- On the basis of the type of inference(s) required.
- On the basis of the knowledge representation that is most appropriate.

The first approach is 'top-down': selection is driven purely by the functional requirements as recorded in the Functional Model. The second approach is 'bottom-up': selection is driven by the structure and characteristics of the knowledge which need to be processed (hence, the close relationship with the representation-driven method described below).

Obviously, the main input is the set of function frames from the Functional Model. Additionally, the Domain Model (see below) will aid method selection on the basis of knowledge/data representation. The Analysis results for Technical Constraints and the chosen KBS Design Framework will restrict the choice of methods.

The simplest output from this activity will be the values of the 'realized-by' slots in the Inference and Composite PS Function frames produced in the Functional Design activity (see p. 152). However, it will be prudent also to record more detailed specifications/descriptions of the methods required to realize the inference functions, including a list of the 'design elements' required by each method. An appropriate DDL frame is available to support this (see below).

The design elements are the basic components that are required, in turn, to realize the methods themselves, i.e. data structures and algorithms.

Problem-solving methods will be selected with the help of the Design Method library, as described above. Method selection can be achieved either by identifying the type of inference(s) required, by noting the Inference Type(s) to which the function applies; or by identifying an appropriate knowledge/data representation applicable to the function and its operands. The two classifications used within the Library will facilitate methods to be found using either approach.

Method selection may need to be revisited (and potentially revised) if the subsequent selection of knowledge-representation schemes conflicts with any of the selected methods.

The KADS Design Description Language (DDL) *– inference method frame*

The DDL description of inference methods
The following frame structure should be filled for each inference method required:

INFERENCE METHOD *<name>*

Realizes:
   (list of) <Inference Function, Composite PS Function or Strategic Control name>
Inference mechanism:
   <description or reference to an algorithm>
Domain-relation:
   <relation name> → <domain model construct>
[Design elements:] (optional)
   <algorithms and data structures>

Selecting Domain Model representations

The aim of this sub-activity is to find suitable knowledge representation schemes for each of the Domain Model blocks identified within Functional Design. This is also supported by the Design Methods library (see Chapter 13). Selection of appropriate representation schemes can be achieved in two ways:

● On the basis of the type of knowledge involved.
● Bearing in mind the requirements of the problem solving functions which the knowledge will have to support.

Finding an appropriate knowledge-representation scheme is an important issue in KBS design. For this reason the designer must be aware that the representation developed within this activity may be subject to revision on the basis of subsequent method selection (see above). Many representation techniques are available to support KBS design, and each technique should be chosen according to its suitability for the function(s) it must support within the chosen design framework.

The Domain Model is a specification of the ('static') knowledge base of the target KBS sub-system. It includes a more formal and 'refined' description of the Domain Layer of the four-layer Expertise Model. The Domain Model is developed by filling out the 'representation' slots of the Domain Model description frames which were produced during Functional Design.

In terms of systems designed using KADS, the expert knowledge in the Inference, Task and Strategy layers of the Expertise Model is not strictly stored in the system's knowledge base. This is in contrast to most conventional KBS, where knowledge at all four levels of abstraction is often stored in a single knowledge base – the classic situation of mixing control and domain knowledge. KADS avoids this by reflecting the different levels of knowledge in different system aspects. This separation of concerns within the Expertise Model will normally persist into Physical Design – unless the chosen design framework dictates otherwise.

The main input to this activity is the set of Domain Model description frames produced within Functional Design. Other DDL frames for functions which reference Domain Model constructs will be needed as these will place constraints on the possible representation techniques which can be used. The KBS Design Framework is another important input to this activity.

The output of the activity is a specification of the structure of the static domain knowledge to be stored in the knowledge base of the KBS sub-system, together with details of other data structures required for support purposes. This is described in more formal terms than in the Functional Model, using an appropriate representation notation.

Domain Model representation may need to be revisited (and possibly revised) on the basis of any subsequent method selection for problem-solving functions which access the knowledge concerned.

Identifying the design elements

When all the required problem-solving methods and knowledge-representation schemes have been chosen, the final step in Behavioural Design is to identify and record the design elements (algorithms and data structures) which are needed. These will primarily support the Inference Function and Composite PS Function blocks. The Design Methods Library provides support for this (see Chapter 13). For example, a 'parse' method requires two design elements – a grammar (data structure) and a parsing algorithm (note that this method also constrains knowledge representation as the output should normally be a parse tree). In many situations the designer will need to be creative, as the set of methods and design elements in the library is by no means exhaustive.

For Strategic Control and Support Function blocks, the design elements may be synonymous with the function block itself, since this will provide all the necessary control structure information to support detailed design and implementation. For the Domain Model and Data Model blocks the knowledge representations and data schemas are considered to be the design elements.

The Behavioural Design Model

The document produced from Behavioural Design represents a 'Behavioural Model' of the KBS under development. The final outputs of Behavioural Design are:

- A description of the methods which will realize the problem-solving functions, i.e. augmented Function Block descriptions.
- A description of the representations to be used to support static knowledge and data, i.e. augmented Domain Model descriptions.
- Details of the design elements (algorithms and data structures) required.
- A diagrammatic representation of the relationships between functions, methods and design elements. [optional]

Figure 7.14 illustrates how the functions, methods and design elements may be related diagrammatically, as suggested in the last output. (A further example is provided in the case study example which follows.)

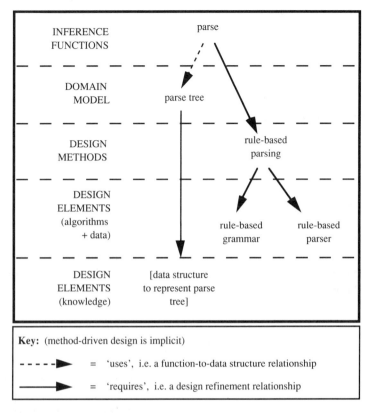

Key: (method-driven design is implicit)

- - - - ▶   = 'uses', i.e. a function-to-data structure relationship

———▶   = 'requires', i.e. a design refinement relationship

Figure 7.14 Relating functions, methods and design elements

Assign Design Methods (Behavioural Design)

This example of Behavioural Design is based on the 'compare' inference function blocks identified in the previous section. To select the most appropriate realization for these functions we need to address three key issues:

- What kind of inference step is being performed and what inference mechanism does this suggest?
- What kind of domain knowledge is used to support the inference and how is this best represented?
- What kinds of representation formalisms and inference mechanisms are available or can be built into the chosen KBS Design Framework?

Identification of Design Methods

The KADS Design Method Library suggests unification as the most frequently used method to support the 'compare' inference type. Given the chosen KBS Design Framework based on pattern matching and unification within Prolog, the unification method for this inference type is therefore an obvious choice.

Compare New and Old Problem Descriptions

For the 'Compare New and Old Problem Descriptions' inference function the comparison should only succeed if the new and old problem descriptions are identical. However, the inference function must also return a result of INSUFFICIENT_DATA if the new problem is a generalization of the old one, e.g. if the old problem refers to a specific mainframe but the new problem description does not as yet specify the particular mainframe involved. Thus, a generalization method is also needed to support the comparison and it is this method which uses the problem hierarchies as support knowledge. Thus the 'Compare New and Old Problem Descriptions' inference function requires two methods – unification and generalization – plus the problem hierarchies as support knowledge.

Compare New and Network Problem Descriptions

The 'Compare New and Network Problem Descriptions' inference function embeds a set of heuristics which map abstract network problem descriptions onto new problem descriptions, e.g. [mainframe-X, cpu = overloaded] maps onto [mainframe-X, application-Y, response_speed_ slow] for any Y. Within the chosen KBS design framework, this is best achieved by a mixture of unification (to match problem descriptions with the left- and right-hand sides of rules) and modus ponens (to generate potential problem descriptions from abstract network status information by firing the rules). Generalization is again needed to support the generation of INSUFFICIENT_DATA results.

Thus the 'Compare New and Network Problem Descriptions' inference function requires three methods – unification, modus ponens and generalization – plus the problem hierarchies and mapping rules as support knowledge.

Compare New and FLD Problem Descriptions

The 'Compare New and FLD Problem Descriptions' succeeds if the FLD problem description is a generalization of the new problem description. Similarly, a result of INSUFFICIENT_DATA is returned if the new problem description is a generalization of the FLD problem description.

Thus the 'Compare New and FLD Problem Descriptions' inference function requires two methods – unification and generalization – plus the problem hierarchies as support knowledge.

Identification of design elements

The next step in Behavioural Design is to identify the design elements needed to realize the methods and support knowledge identified above. Unification is built into the Prolog language and so will not entail additional design. Generalization will need to be realized with an algorithm based on the recursive traversal of the problem hierarchies. Modus ponens will be realized in Prolog by pattern matching across the mapping rules.

The problem hierarchies will be represented by three separate predicates in Prolog for hardware, software and problem type respectively. The mapping rules will also be represented in Prolog by a set of facts grouped together by a common predicate name. Figure 7.15 shows the relationships between these Response Point Expert System inference functions, design methods and design elements.

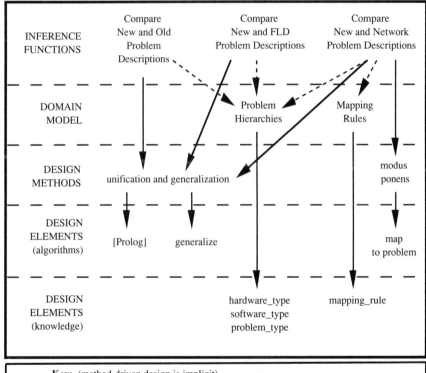

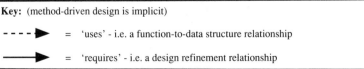

Figure 7.15 Example mappings between inference functions and design elements

Augmented slots for the Function Block frames and a Design Method frame are shown below. To save duplication, the full frames are not presented, only the newly filled-in slots. Also, the frames seen in the previous case study example are not all represented below only 'Compare New and Old Problem Descriptions' and 'Problem Description' are common to this and the Functional Design case study. A single Inference Method frame is shown at the end.

INFERENCE FUNCTION BLOCK DESCRIPTION
Compare New and Old Problem Descriptions

Realized by:
   generalization and unification over problem hierarchies.

INFERENCE FUNCTION BLOCK DESCRIPTION
Compare New and FLD Problem Descriptions

Realized by:
   generalization and unification over problem hierarchies.

INFERENCE FUNCTION BLOCK DESCRIPTION
Compare New and Network Problem Descriptions

Realized by:
   generalization and unification over problem hierarchies, modus ponens to map network element status to problem description.

DOMAIN MODEL DESCRIPTION
Problem Description

Representation:
   problem_description (Role, Hardware_Type, Software_Type, Incident_Type),
   where Role = new, old, network or fld_resp.

DOMAIN MODEL DESCRIPTION
problem hierarchies

Representation:
hardware_type (Class, Subclass),
software_type(Class, Subclass),
problem_type(Class, Subclass).

DOMAIN MODEL DESCRIPTION
mapping rules

Representation:
mapping_rule (status(Element, Status = Value),
problem(Hardware, Software, Problem)).

INFERENCE METHOD DESCRIPTION
generalisation and unification

Realises:
Compare New and Old Problem Descriptions
Compare New and FLD Problem Descriptions
Compare New and Network Problem Descriptions (partially).
Mechanism:
unify with a problem type which is a generalization of the given one.
Domain relation:
Problem Hierarchies.

7.2.4 *Assemble Design Elements (Physical Design)*

The final activity of KBS Design is concerned with bringing together the design elements (from the Behavioural Design Model) to form physical code modules that contain related functionality. Additionally, an architecture for the KBS should be specified, showing the structure and interrelationships of these modules. This architecture (known as the Physical Design Model) is expressed as a structure of modules, interconnected by interfaces.

The input to this activity will be the design elements from Behavioural Design (see Section 7.2.3), together with a description of the implementation environment support for those elements from the KBS Design Framework (see Section 7.2.1). The Functional Model should be included as an input to ensure that its structure is reflected in the physical architecture of the system, wherever possible.

The design elements include those components required to implement the problem-solver inference methods and knowledge structures, together with the required strategic control and support functions. These design elements fall into four categories:

- *Algorithms* – to implement all function methods.
- *Data Structures* – to support the algorithms.
- *Knowledge-Base* – to support inference, task and strategic function methods.
- *Data-Base* – to support other functions within the KBS.

Some design elements may be provided within the chosen implementation environment. These need not be repeated within other code modules.

Physical KBS Design techniques

The activity involves two types of consideration:

- How functionality is to be partitioned into code modules.
- Within these modules, how the design elements are to be realized using the constructs of the implementation environment.

The modularization within physical KBS design should reflect such good design practice as maximizing cohesion within modules and minimizing coupling between modules (cf. Section 7.1).

Wherever possible, the structure of the Functional Model should be preserved in the physical KBS architecture. With the Functional Model already reflecting the Analysis Models, a flowing consistency is then preserved in the system's representations used throughout the development. The benefits of this approach are greater the more complex the KBS. The four-layer Expertise Model provides a natural modularization of knowledge: both 'vertically' in terms of levels of abstraction and 'horizontally' in terms of discrete inference types and domain concepts. If this is exploited in the physical architecture, maintenance of and enhancements to the system will be more straightforward, as the documentation of the system's development will reflect the physical arrangement of the system.

The amount of further work required before an implementation (coding) can proceed will depend upon the size and nature of the system under development. KADS Design is considered to go to a relatively detailed level, so little further work should be required to obtain a working system.

Note that the first pass at this activity is not necessarily the last activity in KBS Design, due to the iterative nature of the design stages. But it will be the general 'exit point' of a KADS Design.

The Physical Design Model

The document produced during Physical Design represents a 'Physical Model' of the KBS under development. It should contain:

- The KBS sub-system architecture (a set of physical code modules).
- Detailed module specifications.

The architecture will be a *consists-of* structure of some form, possibly including input–output relations between modules shown diagrammatically. Each module description should include:

- A list of the Function Blocks covered by the module.
- A list of the design elements (algorithms, data structures and knowledge representations) used within the module.
- Interface definitions covering who calls the module and what modules it calls.

Typical (types of) code modules to consider are as follows (they can only be suggestions, as the precise choice of modules will be highly specific to each system):

- Domain Roles used in the Inference Layer may become explicit modules in the design. They will contain groups of data used to represent domain knowledge (e.g. rules), stored in a 'static' knowledge base.
- An *Inference Type 'interpreter'* module will contain the algorithmic design elements which realize the inference steps. This module might itself be decomposed to atomic inferences.
- A *'task control'* module may be used to control the execution of inference steps by referencing a task structure representation based on that recorded in the Task Layer of the Expertise Model.

- A *strategic level 'system executive'* can potentially control both the problem-solver and the interfaces to other sub-systems.

Physical Design tools

At the time of writing there are no tools which specifically support this activity. The implementation environment assessment guide presented in Chapter 14 may, however, be found useful. This stage of design is one of the most creative, so little external support is possible. The description of this last phase of design may use yet more frames (of an appropriate structure to the system under development), or even pseudo-code, as appropriate. (One example of such a frame is shown in the case study example below.)

Example

Assemble Design Elements (Physical Design)

An important requirement for the Response Point Expert System was that the domain knowledge (especially the routing knowledge) should be capable of rapid and frequent change. This led to the decision to separate out the domain knowledge elements into a separate module from the rest of the KBS. The other design elements were grouped according to type and interrelationship. The major physical design decisions were as follows:

- Place all static domain knowledge into a single module – the 'Knowledge Base'.
- Group the common elements which support comparison into a single module – the 'Comparator'.
- Otherwise group all the elements which support a particular task into a module for that task – giving modules for 'Compare Against Existing Problems', 'Compare Against Network Status', 'Attempt Routing Result' and 'Decide Next Question'.
- Place the elements which support explanation into module 'Explanation'.
- Place strategic control elements (including initialization) into module 'Strategy'.
- Place run-time storage elements into the modules which control them, e.g. 'Question to Ask' into 'Decide Next Question', 'Solution' into 'Comparator', etc.

Figure 7.16 illustrates the Response Point Expert System physical KBS architecture. Compare it with the Global System Architecture diagram in Figure 7.7 and see how the contents of the KBS module have now been

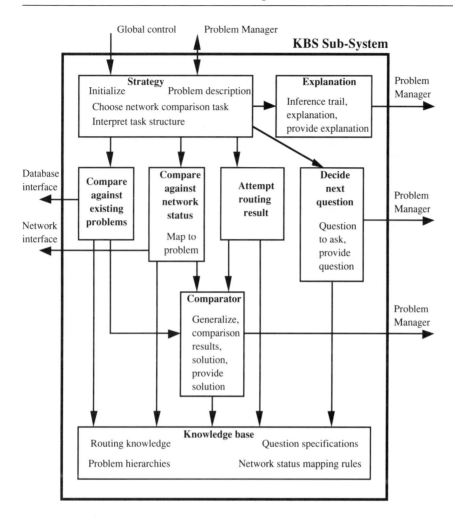

Figure 7.16 Physical architecture of the RPES KBS

defined; the reader should be able to see that the inputs–outputs of the KBS module correspond across both diagrams. The physical KBS architecture diagram is followed by a sample module specification frame.

MODULE SPECIFICATION
Comparator

Description:
General-purpose module supporting generalization and comparison of problem descriptions.
Elements:
Generalize, Comparison Result, Solution, Provide Solution.
Called by:
Compare Against Existing Problems:
compare new and old problem descriptions
Compare Against Network Status
compare new and network problem descriptions
Attempt Routing Result
compare new and FLD problem descriptions
Calls:
Problem Manager: Add Solution
Problem Manager: Add Comparison Result
Knowledge Base: Problem Hierarchies
Algorithms:
Compare(Problem Description 1, Problem Description 2, Comparison Type, Comparison Data):

(example):
CASE
  Problem Description 1 is a generalization of Problem Description 2:
    add comparison result (INSUFFICIENT_DATA + Differences)
  Problem Description 1 same as Problem Description 2:
    add solution (Comparison Type, Comparison Data)
  Problem Description 2 is a generalization of Problem Description 1:
    if Comparison Type = new-old
      then
        return FAILURE
      else
        add solution (Comparison Type, Comparison Data)

Data:
    Comparison Type ::= new-old | new-network | new-FLD
    Comparison   Data   ::=   enquiry_number | status_info |
    front_line_desk
    Differences ::= problem_data*.

(Note that the frame is not proposed as a standard KADS frame, as module specification requirements for each project may be quite different. However, the general structure could be used as a template to be tailored to the specific needs of readers' projects.)

Note

1. For detailed discussion of these and related conventional software design concepts, see, for example, Page-Jones (1988) in the Bibliography ('Documents about conventional software engineering').

8 Design: the big picture

This chapter provides the reader with an overall view of KADS Design, showing how all its pieces fit together and why they are needed. It is the nearest thing to background theory that this book describes. (It should be all the theory that is required into order to put KADS into practice.) The preceding chapter described each Design activity to perform, and result to produce, on the basis of the overall framework presented in this chapter.

Recall that the Design phase in KADS is split into two constituents, called 'stages', and with the KBS Design stage further decomposed it results in four models and one other result:[1]

KADS Design stage		Result of stage
Global Design	→	Global System Architecture (Model)
KBS Design	→	(KBS Sub-System Design)
Define KBS Design Framework	→	KBS Design Framework
Functional Design	→	Functional Design Model
Behavioural Design	→	Behavioural Design Model
Physical Design	→	Physical Design Model

Note: In KADS we prefer to use more specific names for the three main activities within KBS Design. 'Functional', 'Behavioural' and 'Physical' are rather generic terms, and can also be applied to the design of non-KBS sub-systems. The KADS mapping is as follows:

General type of KBS Design		Actual KADS Design Activity
Functional Design	→	Decompose KBS Functions
Behavioural Design	→	Assign Design Methods
Physical Design	→	Assemble Design Elements

8.1   Levels of Design – KADS Design models

In Chapter 2 we described how KADS is a methodology which takes a model-based approach to KBS development. The process of developing a KBS in KADS may be viewed largely as a progression through a set of models of the world, the system, the user(s) (and/or any other such 'agents'), and the expertise required in the system.

While this 'model-driven' approach is perhaps most usefully considered in Analysis, KADS Design can also be viewed as a progression through a series of models. The design of systems is a less well-understood process, however, because a more creative approach is needed: system design involves the idea of *synthesis*, as opposed to *analysis*.[2] Perhaps even more than in Analysis, KADS Design is intended to *support* this process, not constrain it to a particular path. With this rider, we can still describe the series of Design models in the same way as we did for Analysis in Section 5.1.

For Analysis we showed the KADS 'conceptual modelling framework'. Analogously, we can describe KADS Design based on different 'levels' of design, containing a set of interrelated models, with each model representing a particular aspect of the complete required behaviour of the system. In the same way as for Analysis, different levels of design focus on different levels of abstraction of the future system's total design – a different *scope* of design. There are four levels of design in KADS: global, KBS sub-system functional, KBS sub-system behavioural, and KBS sub-system physical. (Note that we generally drop the 'KBS sub-system' from the latter three, to avoid verbosity.)

The **Global Level** is concerned with the design of the overall system, including KBS and non-KBS sub-systems, and how the sub-systems are interfaced. This is needed in order to partition the complete system for various reasons. One reason is that it distinguishes parts of the system which need special design techniques, separating, for example, the KBS parts from the conventional parts, such as database components. KADS KBS Design can then be applied to the KBS components, and appropriate specialist database design techniques on the database components. This avoids imposing inappropriate design techniques on some components of the system, where the system is non-trivial. The Global level may also take into account technical constraints (as documented in Constraints Analysis) which impose a particular sub-system architecture. For example, certain components (functions) of the system may have to reside in a group, perhaps corresponding to a particular processor in the final delivery hardware.

Once the KBS component(s) have been distinguished, KADS Design uses a three-level split also found in the design of conventional software, but specially adapted here for KBS: functional, behavioural and physical.

The **Functional Level** is concerned with the design of the KBS sub-system(s) in terms of the functions required of it, primarily on the basis of the Expertise Model produced during Analysis. KADS distinguishes four types of functional blocks (categories of function): problem solving (for reasoning functions), storage (for manipulating knowledge and data stores), strategic control (for controlling other functions), and support (for non-knowledge-based functions in the KBS sub-system).

The **Behavioural Level** is concerned with the design of the KBS sub-system(s) in terms of how the functions at the Functional level are to be realized by appropriate design methods, and what knowledge representations to use for the knowledge-based stores. Design methods are called 'problem-solving methods' in the case of knowledge-based functions. Methods can be decomposed into 'design elements', which are basically algorithms and data structures. In the case of the functions, the designer must choose, or devise, computational techniques that will enable the functions of the KBS sub-system to work in practice. Such computational techniques are called 'methods'. The task of the designer is aided by the four-way categorization of functions performed at the Functional level – the behavioural design of the different function types are decided in different ways. For example, the behavioural design of problem-solving functions may be aided by the library of problem-solving methods presented in Chapter 13; the behavioural design of support and strategic control functions may be supported by a conventional approach.

In the case of knowledge-base storage functions, the critical design decision is in choosing an appropriate knowledge representation for the underlying store. This may be aided by the library of knowledge representations in Chapter 13. In the case of conventional stores, their schemas would also have to be defined (but this is not strictly part of KADS).

The **Physical Level** is concerned with the design of the KBS sub-system(s) in terms of how the algorithms and data structures ('design elements') needed to support the Behavioural level's methods are to be arranged in a structure of modules of code. The modules will also contain the data and knowledge stores whose schemas or representations were decided at the Behavioural level. Thus, the Physical level of Design will result in a set of specifications for modules of code that will serve as input to a detailed design phase, or even straight into the coding phase ('implementation', in the 'V' model lifecycle shown in Chapter 2).

Within the above design framework KADS describes a particular set of models, together with the activities which are used to construct them. Table 8.1 shows the four levels of Design models in KADS together with their constituents.

Table 8.1 Design levels, models and constituents

Level	Model	Constituents
1: Global Level	Global System Architecture	Sub-systems (KBS, non-KBS, etc.) Inter-sub-system interfaces
2: KBS Functional Level	Functional Design Model	KBS Functional Blocks: Problem solving Storage Strategic Control Support
3: KBS Behavioural Level	Behavioural Design Model	KBS Methods and Knowledge Representations: Design elements: algorithms + structures Storage schemas
4: KBS Physical Level	Physical Design Model	KBS Modules and Sub-system Architecture: Module specifications Interface definitions

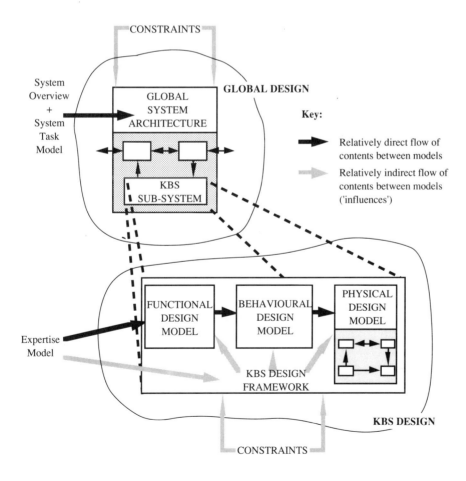

Figure 8.1 Design model relationships

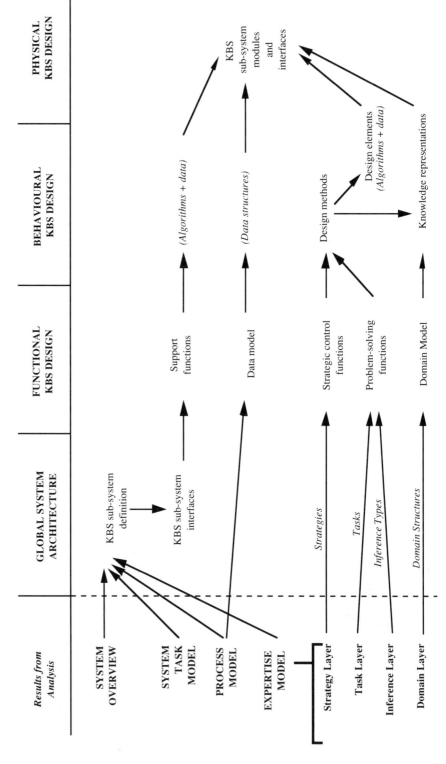

Figure 8.2 Overview of the principal interdependencies within Design

An alternative view of the Design models is shown in Figure 8.1. This illustrates how the various models are interrelated. It gives a schematic view of a Global System Architecture and an exploded view of a KBS sub-system distinguished within that architecture. The exploded view shows the process of KBS Design used to specify the contents of the KBS sub-system. KBS Design takes the Expertise Model and Constraints as important inputs from Analysis. Constraints influence how the Functional, Behavioural and Physical levels of design are performed in KBS Design, as well as how the overall Global Design is performed. The KBS Design Framework (see Section 8.3) is defined as part of KBS Design, and only influences the three KBS Design levels, as a set of 'local' constraints.

8.2   Interdependencies in Design

Figure 8.2 shows how the main parts of KADS Design fit together in terms of their interdependencies. (The KBS Design Framework is not shown, nor is non-KBS sub-system design.)

8.3   Other parts of Design

Although the Models described above cover the bulk of Design, there is one significant other part of KBS Design to explain: the KBS Design Framework. In addition, we need to consider the design of sub-systems other than the KBS sub-system, and how this fits in with the rest of KADS Design.

The **KBS Design Framework** is complementary to the three other KBS Design activities: the KBS Design levels Functional, Behavioural and Physical. Its presence recognizes that these three levels of design are rarely performed in isolation – either the designer is constrained by some requirement(s) on the system or its development, or they constrain *themselves*, which can actually aid the design process. The KBS Design Framework is thus the 'paradigm' or context in which the designer performs these three levels of design. It often corresponds to the capabilities of the chosen, or enforced, implementation platform for the system; or it may be a particular architectural-based framework, such as specifying the use of a blackboard system architecture. The KBS Design Framework is therefore an important part of KBS Design, but it is orthogonal to the levels described in Section 8.1.

The other important issue in Design is that KADS only fully supports the design of the KBS components of the system. Where a system is not wholly knowledge-based (and this is the general case, of course), and there are *non-knowledge-based sub-systems* distinguished in Global Design, KADS does not support further design of those sub-systems. In addition, where the design of a KBS sub-system involves *non-knowledge-based algorithms and data stores* KADS does not provide special techniques to help specify them.

To design non-knowledge-based components or smaller elements, conventional design techniques should be used. A functional/behavioural/physical approach analogous to that used by KADS would be a natural choice for designing some conventional sub-systems. More specialized techniques would be preferable in other cases, such as for substantial database sub-systems or sub-systems based on other specialized architectures.

Notes

1. The 'KBS Sub-System Design' is usually excluded as an explicit result of the KBS Design stage, as it is simply a collective name for all the constituent results produced within that stage.
2. Note we are not saying that design is *purely* synthesis, or even, by analogy, that requirements analysis involves *no* synthesis. System design in general, and KADS Design in particular, simply places more *emphasis* on synthesis, compared with analysis; and requirements analysis, as embodied in KADS Analysis, *concentrates* on analyzing. Thus, even Analysis inevitably involves some synthesizing of ideas – for example, whenever the analyst takes a decision or makes a choice in how the analysis is to proceed. System development is not black and white with respect to analysis and synthesis, but there are clear differences in emphasis, nonetheless. (See also Section 2.1.4.)

Part III
KADS for day-to-day use

This part of the book is specially designed for the KADS practitioner. It introduces 'project management'-type issues for KADS and provides a set of libraries and a 'checklist' description of KADS Analysis and Design, all of which are intended to support the day-to-day use of KADS.

Chapter 9's objectives

- To describe the separation of technical development from project management.
- To summarize project management issues special to projects using KADS.
- To provide a starting point for running projects using KADS.

Chapter 10's objectives

- To provide advice and guidance in performing knowledge acquisition.
- To relate knowledge acquisition techniques to KADS activities.
- To present a library of techniques to support knowledge acquisition.

Chapter 11's objectives

- To present a classified library of roles that static domain knowledge can play in problem-solving, for use in KADS Expertise Analysis.
- To present a classified library of types of basic reasoning steps that can be used in problem-solving, for use in KADS Expertise Analysis.

Chapter 12's objectives

- To present a classified library of models of generic problem-solving tasks for use in KADS Expertise Analysis.

Chapter 13's objectives

- To present a classified library of models of generic problem-solving approaches and algorithms, and knowledge representations, for use in KADS KBS Design.

Chapter 14's objectives

- To introduce the issue of KBS implementation environments in a KADS context.
- To present ideas for helping in the assessment and selection of such environments.

Chapter 15's objectives

- To present an easy-to-use description of KADS Analysis in a memory-jogging structured format – a KADS Analysis checklist.

Chapter 16's objectives

- To present an easy-to-use description of KADS Design in a memory-jogging structured format – a KADS Design checklist.

Chapters 10–13 are the libraries which can be used to support the use of KADS. They are not intended to be prescriptive nor completely comprehensive. Some of the topics covered would take *at least* a whole book in themselves! Only summary descriptions of the non-KADS-specific topics can be presented, such as knowledge acquisition and general KBS design techniques. These chapters also assume some familiarity with KBS technology and terminology. Pointers to more complete descriptions may be found in the Bibliography at the end of the book. For the KADS-specific topics, *as with the whole methodology*, the KADS user should be *pragmatic* – taking appropriate care if method standardization is important, of course. The **golden rules** are:

- *Only use what is found to be useful in practice.*
- *Adapt the suggested objects, frameworks and approaches where necessary.*
- *Use familiar tools and techniques if they are better than those suggested here.*
- *Ignore anything found to be a cost with no benefit.*

9 Putting KADS into practice: project management-type issues

Putting KADS into practice for a project will involve performing some of the activities, and producing some of the results, that were described in detail in Part II. In some ways, this whole book can be seen as a 'library' of techniques, and not just some of the chapters in this Part III – KADS is not a 'take it or leave it', single indivisible whole. It will depend upon the particular context, domain and many other circumstances, which activities and results might be left out, or even replaced by established analysis and design methods in the reader's own organization; also, KADS will have its own constraints on what dependencies exist between the methods described (see Chapters 5 and 8). However, these 'technical' issues of what technical development activities are performed and results produced are not the full story when it comes to embarking on a project using KADS – there are all the 'non-technical' issues of a software development project.

This chapter presents advice in this area, which may be broadly classified under the heading of 'project management', i.e. issues primarily that the project manager of a project using KADS needs to consider. Seven separate topics are covered:

- The concept of 'project management frameworks'
- Planning
- Scheduling
- Staff assignments
- Quality assessment and control
- Prototyping
- Tool support

The first part of this chapter introduces the topic of project management in a KADS context. It presents the concept of a *project management* framework, as distinguished from a *technical development* framework. Next, the issues of planning KADS projects, scheduling the activities to perform and assigning staff to those activities are considered. Following this, the issue of quality in producing KADS deliverables is covered. Then the issue of prototyping in relation to KADS is summarized. Finally, some advice on the use of software and non-software tools in KADS projects is presented.

9.1 Management of KADS projects

A major thrust in the software development industry is to make its products reach a higher quality and be more cost effective, just as the established engineering fields aim to do. Similarly, software development has tended towards using procedures and processes analogous to those found in established engineering disciplines. The use of a structured method like KADS is just *part* of the means to achieve this goal. KADS, like most other structured methods, is a collection of inter-working *technical* development methods. To put such technical structured methods into practice requires a disciplined approach to the non-technical aspects of software development – that is, good practice must be followed in the *management* of projects.

The problem of managing software development projects has been widely recognized as being particularly difficult, and is frequently discussed in the literature. The main potential problems found in projects are: badly defined objectives, bad planning, bad estimation, bad communication, low-quality deliverables, and lack of shared commitment. To address these, a good project management process will consider: a clear development lifecycle, defined roles of people on the project or related to it, planning, control and monitoring, and documentation. However, what help can we offer the manager of a project using KADS at this time?

Help with specific problems, such as how to plan KADS-based projects, and schedule the activities to perform, is presented later in this chapter. First, though, an important concept must be made clear if the message presented in this book is to be understood. The concept was hinted at above: KADS is a set of technical development methods, with some defined interdependencies; to make KADS 'work', one needs a complementary overall framework or process to follow for a particular project.[1] This is sometimes called a '*project management framework*'.

Other specialized 'frameworks' or processes may be distinguished along these lines, such as a quality management process (e.g. ISO 9000 – see Bibliography, 'Miscellaneous'), or one for controlling risk (e.g. CRAMM, the UK government-approved CCTA Risk Analysis and Management Methodology – see Section 9.1.1). However, for the purposes of this book we cover all of these in the idea that there is KADS, and then there are all the other things one must do in order to make KADS, or any other technical development methodology, work in practice. Thus, we say:

- A successful software development project needs at least two process frameworks:
  - *Technical development framework(s)* – e.g. KADS
    - Activities
    - Results
    - Interrelationships
  - *Project management framework* – e.g. PRINCE (see below)
    - Generic development lifecycle
    - People's roles
    - Planning
    - Control and monitoring
    - Documentation

This book concentrates on describing the technical development framework, KADS. We will not describe the other frameworks in any detail because they are well covered elsewhere by others. However, few words are relevant to summarizing some of the key characteristics of project management frameworks which are presented next.

9.1.1　*Project management frameworks*

There are two primary sources of project management frameworks: public domain publications and proprietary frameworks, e.g. from within the reader's own organization perhaps, or from consultancies. We suggest that KADS can be used quite straightforwardly with such existing frameworks, with few changes on either side. This is because (1) we have striven to present KADS in a form which is compatible with such frameworks – i.e. like a conventional technical development methodology and (2) KBS software is not so very different from conventional software, when considered at the *overall project* level.

Few complete project management frameworks are to be found in the public domain at the time of writing, although a particularly important one in the UK (and perhaps to come in Europe via EUROMETHOD, and even in the rest of the world on the coat-tails of SSADM's increasing popularity) is *PRINCE*.[2]

If readers go on to use KADS for a major project requiring a full-blown project management framework they should apply their own in-house framework, if one is available, go to a consultancy, or investigate one like PRINCE. (Sources for PRINCE are listed in the Bibliography, 'Documents about other related methods'.)

PRINCE is published by the CCTA (Central Computing and Telecommunications Agency – a UK government body), and has been specially developed to be the standard project management framework for SSADM (the CCTA's popular conventional software development methodology). (The CCTA also supply the risk analysis and management methodology, CRAMM, which is also compatible with SSADM – see Section 9.1.) For illustrative purposes only, and to compare with other project management frameworks, PRINCE supplies the following guidelines:

- Overall: project and quality management throughout the lifecycle
- Concept of a lifecycle split into stages (phases[3]) – but none pre-defined
- Project organization – roles of people
- Plans at the overall project and stage (phase) level
- Control points, to offer more than monitoring
- Documentation requirements

KADS's Analysis and Design phases are readily mappable onto the generic lifecycle PRINCE offers.[4] (Although KADS only covers these parts of the lifecycle – other (structured) methods should be employed to address the other phases.) Figure 9.1 shows KADS in a typical PRINCE lifecycle with familiar phases. KADS will fit into other project management frameworks in an analogous way.

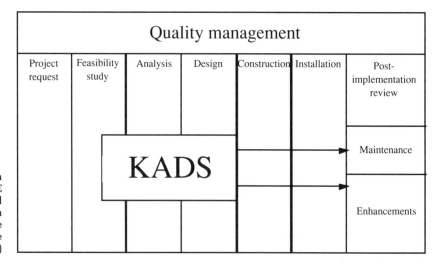

Figure 9.1 KADS in a typical PRINCE lifecycle. (Reproduced and adapted with permission from The Informatics Resource Centre, London.)

The project organization (roles of people) suggested by PRINCE is based on the following structure, which can be easily mapped over a KADS-based project:

- Project board
  [*approvals; organisation; reviews; sign-offs*]
  – Senior user + Senior technical adviser + Executive (business) adviser
- Project, or if project complex enough, stage (phase) managers
  [*plans; day-to-day control; ensure quality deliverables produced*]
- Team leaders and teams
  [*produce deliverables; review between teams*]
- Project assurance team
  [*advise and consult only; to support project/stage manager, teams and project board*]
  – Business assurance coordinator + Technical assurance coordinator + User assurance coordinator + Configuration librarian

Figure 9.2 shows this structure schematically.

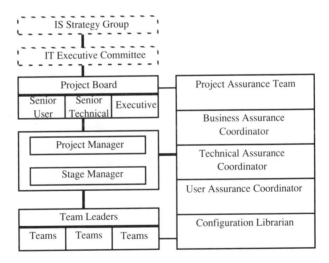

Figure 9.2 Project structure when using PRINCE, showing roles of people. (Reproduced and adapted with permission from The Informatics Resource Centre, London.)

PRINCE's planning framework distinguishes planning at the project level and at the stage (phase) level. There are many types of plan distinguished: a general description (including assumptions, prerequisites and risks); 'product'-based plans; activity network; technical plan; tabular resource plan; graphical summary; and quality plan. Additionally at the project level a 'business case' is considered part of the plan documentation set, justifying the project and its continuation. This consists of: cost-benefit analysis and investment appraisal; risk analysis; and sensitivity analysis. Planning KADS projects is specifically described in Section 9.2, and can be readily structured within the PRINCE framework. Section 9.3 on scheduling activities and Section 9.4 on staff assignments may also be useful to refer to in planning.

PRINCE defines eight control points or mechanisms: project initiation; end-of-stage assessment; mid-stage assessment; checkpoint meetings; highlight reports; tolerance; quality reviews; and project closure. Quality reviews are especially well defined in PRINCE. With respect to KADS, quality checklists have been included in this book for each result to produce from a KADS activity. These can be used as the basis for larger quality checks. We also summarize some general quality procedures suitable for use with KADS in Section 9.5.

PRINCE defines a rich set of documentation to produce, based on the idea of four 'guides': management guide (per stage – job descriptions, plans, reports, approvals, etc.); technical guide (per end-product – strategies, specifications, test results, etc.); quality guide (quality method definitions, results of reviews, etc.); and configuration guide (issues, requests for change, version documentation, etc.) The documents produced by KADS, such as the Analysis and Design models, are easily slotted into this framework.

The reader is strongly recommended to seek full documentation of PRINCE, *or any other project management framework*, if a KADS-based project of any significant size (say, greater than one person-year) is expected to be undertaken. In particular, we suspect that many organizations will have their own in-house standards for such frameworks, at least in the form of established project procedures and quality management. To duplicate further description here would therefore be unnecessary.

9.2   Project planning

This section provides very basic guidance on planning a KBS project using KADS. Part II of the book has described the KADS activities, and included Gantt chart-type views of the activities in the form of our 'road maps'. The potential for overlapping in performing KADS activities, highlighted by the Gantt chart representation, is described in more detail in Section 9.3. Here, however, we assume a simple case, where we can overlap all the activities that can be overlapped and consider two new issues:

- PERT chart view of KADS – a 'generic KADS plan'
- Simple guide for estimating the duration of KADS activities

(This section assumes that a new development is being considered. However, maintenance and enhancements to existing KBSs can be planned in similar ways, because they can be viewed as special types of project based on subsets of the same form of lifecycle – see Appendix 2, Section A2.1.4.)

9.2.1   A generic project plan for KADS

A generic project plan for KADS would show the dependencies between activities as generic ordering of activities – a sequence of things to do. The Gantt chart-like road map diagrams can be viewed as a simple form of generic KADS project plan, as they can be read as an ordering over the activities.

An alternative representation is the complementary PERT chart view. This uses boxes to represent activities, and has a dependency network of lines between them to show ordering. Figure 9.3 shows such a PERT (or 'schedule') chart, with the critical activities and dependencies highlighted. It is not a true generic plan but an example of a typical real-life KADS project plan. It is generalizable. A generic plan for KADS can be derived by abstracting and adapting this PERT chart, with consideration also given to the Gantt chart road maps.

To produce a particular project plan (scheduling of activities) for a project, the project manager can use this example PERT chart as a starting point. The road map diagrams should also be considered, and the process diagrams shown for each stage in Chapters 4 and 7, and each phase in Chapters 3 and 6, will also help in producing a reasonable sequence of activities. Taking these representations of KADS activities in conjunction with the particular characteristics of a development project will enable the project manager to build an accurate plan.

Obviously the plan in Figure 9.3 should not be viewed as a template for *all* kinds of KBS development but rather as guidance for the 'average' project. Note that some activities are not standard KADS – this would be typical of a real project plan using KADS. Most are standard KADS activities, but these are supplemented with special or adapted activities to reflect the particular characteristics of the development.

The criticality of the KBS-specific activities is clearly shown on this plan. The stages of Process, Cooperation and Expertise Analysis are on the critical path (marked in bold in Figure 9.3), as is KBS Design.

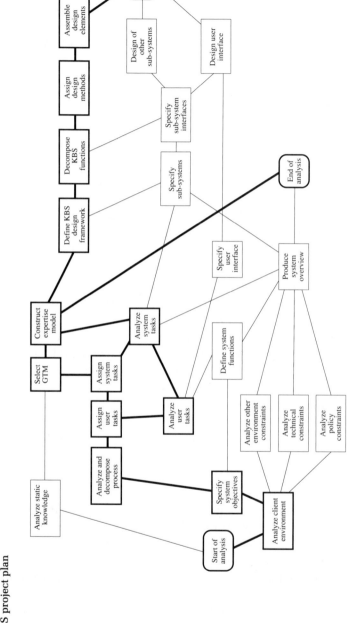

Figure 9.3 A basic
KADS project plan

9.2.2 Estimating the duration of KADS activities

In order to put some 'flesh' onto the plan shown in Figure 9.3, Table 9.2 provides example elapsed times for each of the development activities. (Note: 'Analyze Client Environment' in Table 9.2 is not a standard KADS activity but should be self-explanatory. Its purpose is to make explicit the initial task in performing Constraints Analysis and the System Overview. Likewise, in this example plan, the Provisional Information Requirements activity has not been included, for other project reasons. It could easily be added as a, say, 1-week task.)

Essentially, then, the basic use of KADS can be gleaned by following the descriptions presented in Chapters 4 and 7 (or even 15 and 16), in conjunction with the project plan shown in Figure 9.3, instantiated with figures based on those presented in Table 9.2. If an uncomplicated project follows this approach, it should result in a successful development.

We have employed this approach on our own projects (for example, the case study system used in Part II) with success. However, readers are

Table 9.2 Example of 1-person-year breakdown of durations across activities

KADS stage	Activity name	Duration in weeks
Constraints Analysis	Analyze Client Environment	2 (15%)
	Analyze Environment Constraints	2
	Analyze Technical Constraints	2
	Analyze Policy Constraints	2
System Overview	Specify System Objectives	1 (7.5%)
	Define System Functions	1
	Produce System Overview	2
Process Analysis	Analyze and Decompose Process	2 (7.5%)
	Assign User Tasks	1
	Assign System Tasks	1
Cooperation Analysis	Analyze User Tasks	1 (11%)
	Analyze System Tasks	1
	Specify User Interface	4
Expertise Analysis	Analyze Static Knowledge	4 (25%)
	Select Generic Task Model	1
	Construct Expertise Model	8
Global Design	Specify Sub-Systems	1 (4%)
	Specify Sub-System Interfaces	1
KBS Design	Define KBS Design Framework	1 (11%)
	Decompose KBS Functions	2
	Assign Design Methods	2
	Assemble Design Elements	1
Other Design	Design User Interface	2 (19%)
	Design Other Sub-Systems	8
Total		53 weeks

warned that caution is obviously required when scaling the estimates for their own projects – any such scaling must be done intelligently and with care, taking into account any special circumstances of the particular development under consideration (including simple factors like particular ways of doing things in a particular organization, which may be quite different from ours). For the future, we advise each organization using KADS to build its own local 'library' of experiences using the method, which should include a summary of the success of planning estimates. In time, it should be possible to build a localized set of metrics[5] which can be used with a great deal more confidence than with those presented here.

Before we leave the issue of planning, the reader should recall Section 2.1.4, where we highlighted the somewhat artificial split between Analysis and Design. In practice, as conventionally, project managers can plan assuming that there is a clean break. However, they should recognize that, also as conventionally, there will inevitably be some overlapping between the completion of Analysis and the commencement of Design in terms of the technical effort. The project manager should be careful to minimize this, but accept some overlap as normal and healthy. This will take experience to gauge well.

9.3   How to schedule activities

Although it is impossible to give specific advice about the precise ordering and overlapping of KADS activities in a particular project, this section will tell the reader where to find the appropriate general information in this book. There are three sources:

- Road map diagrams – for showing starting points in relation to other activities.
- Gantt chart view – for showing overall dependencies between activities.
- The 'When should I do it?' slot in the guided tour frames in Chapters 15 and 16.

Chapter 2 introduced the idea the 'road map' diagrams used extensively in the book – Gantt chart form of presenting the KADS activities derived from the 'V' model lifecycle. One of the obvious characteristics of these diagrams is the potential for overlapping activities. We will not repeat the diagrams here (see Figures 3.3 and 6.1) but, for example, Constraints Analysis and Update System Overview in Analysis are 'background' activities to be performed in parallel (potentially) with all the other

Analysis activities; Process, Cooperation and Expertise Analysis all can overlap to some degree. In Design, the primary parallelism is the potential to overlap the KBS sub-system design with the design of any other sub-systems; there is also potential to overlap all the activities within KBS Design, for example. The key point about these diagrams, however, is that although they illustrate parallelism and the relative starting points of activities, the *degree* of overlap is only very roughly shown. This is because the timescale on the horizontal axis of these diagrams is not linear – they are only schematic diagrams.

The Gantt chart view presented in Figure 9.3 shows the interdependencies between the activities, as derived from knowing which activities need the results of other activities to proceed or complete.

Finally, in the 'guided tour' descriptions of KADS presented in Chapters 15 and 16 a slot in the frames there is entitled 'When should I do it?', i.e. information saying when the activity should or could be performed. These slots give precise and succinct statements of when an activity can be started.

9.4   How to make appropriate staff assignments

Traditionally, KBS development has been viewed as a specialist activity, requiring specialist skills. While there are certainly areas within KBS development that do benefit from having specialist knowledge (and it is nearly always the case that the more experience a developer has, the better), we believe KADS helps to reduce the dependency upon specialist skills across the *whole* project. This is a simple point, but may prove important for some readers.

One way to think about the different skills requirements across KADS is according to the precise type of KADS activity to be performed. Different activities have different objectives. They require different tasks to be performed and different techniques to be used.

Another way to look at this issue is to consider that KADS splits software development into two main streams: KBS (sub-system) development and non-KBS (sub-system) development. (The sub-systems may be plural, of course.) For simple systems, with very little conventional components, the development may be considered pure KBS. However, in the great majority of practical and useful KBSs a mixture of KBS and non-KBS components will need to be analyzed and designed. This split enables the project manager to consider whether to assign staff with different skills to different parts of the development.

The following checklist summarizes a set of skills profiles for KADS (note, in general, that having KBS knowledge will not hinder any stage or activity, but is sometimes not an important prerequisite to perform the stage or activity):

Analysis

- *Process Analysis*
  - Analyze and Decompose Process – does not require specialist KBS knowledge. Conventional software experience using process modelling with DFDs is a benefit.
  - Assign Tasks and Data Stores – requires some KBS experience to know which tasks and stores are likely to be knowledge-based and which are not.
- *Cooperation Analysis*
  - Analyze User Task(s) – does not require specialist KBS knowledge. Conventional software experience using something like state machines is a benefit, and event-driven analysis experience would be useful. Some appreciation of the concepts in human–computer interaction (HCI) is also helpful, such as task analysis.
  - Analyze System Task(s) – requires some KBS experience to know which system tasks are likely to be knowledge-based and which are not.
  - Define User Interface – specialist HCI skills would be very beneficial, but not essential. Some experience of specifying and building user interfaces of the same type to be used by the prospective system is necessary.
  - (Define Other Agent Interfaces) – depends on the nature of the external agent.
  - User Modelling – specialist HCI skills would be beneficial, but not essential.
  - (Other Agent Modelling) – depends on the nature of the external agent.
- *Expertise Analysis* – all the activities within this stage ideally require previous KBS experience.
- *Constraints Analysis* – little specialist KBS knowledge is required. A KBS specialist should be assigned to check for KBS-specific requirements in the project, but most of this activity can be performed by people with conventional software and analytical experience. An attention to detail is a helpful personal attribute, although this should really apply across the whole project, of course.
- *Produce/Update System Overview* – some KBS experience may be helpful in thinking about the schematic architecture of the future system (but this could also be seen as a handicap to communication!). Good communication skills are the main prerequisite.

Design

- *Global Design* – KBS experience will be necessary to determine an appropriate sub-system architecture where the KBS functionality of the system cannot be clearly isolated from the rest of the system. For systems with a substantial non-KBS element there is potential for much of the partitioning to be done by non-KBS specialists. Knowledge of 'good design principles' and specific design experience will be helpful.
- *KBS Design*
  - Define KBS Framework – this generally requires solid, and preferably wide, KBS experience.
  - Decompose KBS Functions – some of this activity could be performed by those with less KBS experience, but it will require a specialist to complete it.
  - Assign Design Methods – requires solid, and preferably wide, KBS experience.
  - Assemble Design Elements – KBS experience is helpful but also necessary is knowledge of 'good design principles' and specific design experience.

9.5 Quality assessment and control (QAC)

Finding and fixing errors as early as possible in the development of KBS, as of other systems, can reduce considerably the overall development effort and subsequent expense. Quality assessment and control (QAC) describes the activity of identifying and fixing errors occurring in the outputs from development activities. We provide here a summary of QAC techniques that are recommended in projects that use KADS. We are concerned with *internal* QAC procedures, that is, assessment and control prior to delivery for formal external review at project milestones.

Also in this book we describe QAC specifically with respect to the production of each activity's result. These are presented as 'QA checklists' within the guided tour frames in Chapters 15 and 16 and consist of specific points to check to assure quality per activity. These checklists are important in using KADS, but are not the main topic of this section.

A large commercial project's full QAC will involve the use of the QA checklists, the general internal QAC techniques presented below, and *external* QAC procedures. The last should be provided by a project management framework – see Section 9.1.1.

9.5.1 QAC in KADS

From the QAC perspective, the KADS models and other types of result constitute a set of standards to which the outputs from activities must conform. Assessment of conformance is viewed from three perspectives:

1. Part of the assessment entails ensuring that structures are *correctly filled* – that syntactic rules are obeyed in models and that documents contain the correct type of information.
2. The reviewers must ensure that the contents are *consistent* – that there are no contradictory statements in the documents and that no terms are used with varying meanings.
3. It must be ensured that the output is *complete* with respect to the requirements. This is achieved by comparing the outputs with the inputs to ensure that the transformation has not omitted anything.

The extent to which minor errors and their fixes need to be recorded depends on a number of factors. The most important of these is the amount of shared work in the project. The project manager needs to establish a change-control policy as part of the project scoping. It is important not to restrict the creativity of development personnel by imposing over-extensive recording policies, while at the same time it is very important that major errors and fixes are logged, particularly in major reviews. In larger projects this will entail a proper configuration-management process and someone responsible for its management.

9.5.2 QAC techniques

The recommended techniques for QAC on project deliverables are:

- Fagan inspections[6]
- Examinations
- Walkthroughs
- Random fault finding
- Testing

Fagan inspections and examinations are the main procedures for formal reviews. For less formal reviews conducted by development personnel, walkthroughs are used, and random fault finding will eliminate some errors.

The most complex and rigidly defined technique is the Fagan inspection. This will be covered in the most detail here, but there is much more to it than we can describe in this book. It is recommended that the project controllers choose those techniques from the selection presented which are most appropriate for the project in hand. Because KADS developments are concerned with domains in which there is much specialized knowledge, there is a great emphasis on examinations, particularly during the analysis phase.

Fagan inspections

Fagan inspections are a general and powerful QAC technique, typical of that provided by many project management frameworks. They are presented here primarily for projects that do not have a similar technique already provided by such a framework.

Fagan inspections occur at fixed points in the development. They are the final activity of the phase in which they occur, and are carried out by a team of between three and six people, each with a specific role to play. The procedure has six stages, at the end of which the activity output under inspection is signed off. Errors found should be recorded in a database which will provide input for guiding future inspections.

The three roles of personnel in Fagan inspections are (quantities in parentheses):

- *Moderator* (1): The moderator is responsible for organizing and chairing meetings. He or she will not be a member of the development team.
- *Author* (1): The author is the person responsible for the development activity whose result is under inspection.
- *Inspector* (1–3): Inspectors are tasked with identifying the errors. Where there are more than one they will be assigned different areas for inspection.

There are six stages in a Fagan inspection:

1. *Planning*: Appointment of the inspection team and scheduling of meetings.
2. *Overview*: A brief meeting to introduce participants to the item under inspection.
3. *Preparation*: All team members examine the documents.
4. *Inspection meeting*: A step-by-step examination of the item against an appropriate checklist, yielding a set of errors to be fixed. If the estimated rework required exceeds 5 per cent of the original work then a re-inspection will be needed.
5. *Re-work*: The correction of all errors by the author.
6. *Follow-up*: Where it has been deemed necessary a re-inspection will take place. Otherwise, the author informs the moderator that the rework is complete.

Checklists for the KADS models and other results are detailed in the 'QA checklist' slots in the guided tour Chapters 15 and 16.

Examinations

Examinations are a kind of inspection where specialist expertise is required in order to carry out the process successfully. An examination is a formal review of a deliverable, performed by a party or panel in isolation from the author(s) of the document. The results of an examination are passed back to the author(s) on completion of the examination. In KADS, a good example of where examination rather than Fagan inspection is needed is in the validation of the Expertise Model by domain expert(s). This task could not be carried out by peers of the author of the model, as is suggested for Fagan inspections.

Walkthroughs

Walkthroughs are less formal reviews carried out by development staff. The author of an item presents the results (either complete or partial) to other members of the team, after which any misunderstandings or problems are dealt with. Walkthroughs serve the purpose of both identifying faults and educating team members who are or will be working on activities dependent on the results that are explained.

Random fault finding

Errors are often discovered in an *ad hoc* manner during development activities. If the extent of the error merits it then the errors and consequent changes made should be recorded. A history of such errors and fixes will be a valuable asset to this and/or future projects.

Testing

The term 'testing' is used for the testing of code against its specification, in either full implementations or prototype systems. The prime example in KADS of such a prototype is a user interface prototype. The main test of this will be done by performing trials with the future users. Other prototypes produced could be tested in analogous ways.

9.6 Prototyping in KADS

This section discusses prototyping as a development technique in general, and gives an overview of the roles of prototyping using KADS. However, specific opportunities for prototyping using the methods are noted in the Analysis and Design parts of this book, primarily in Chapters 4 and 7.

Prototyping can be broadly defined as the rapid implementation of a part of the target system functionality or a simulation of the full system. For some, 'rapid prototyping' is vital to expert system development, while for others it is viewed as something of a necessary evil, arising from the limitations of formal techniques in software engineering. In order to clarify some of these issues we use a set of commonly used classes of prototyping and show how and when they can be usefully employed in projects using the KADS methods. These are defined in Section 9.6.1.

The view taken in Section 9.6.2 is that prototypes are operational descriptions of (parts of) KADS models. Thus, the role of any prototyping activity relates to the development phase whose output is the model that is operationalized. The exception is the operationalization of the physical design model, which can be considered the actual system implementation.

9.6.1   Types of prototyping

Unfortunately, there is much ambiguous terminology used in the field about prototyping, resulting in many misunderstandings. This section defines the terms as used in this book:[7]

- Evolutionary prototyping
- Throwaway prototyping
  - Exploratory prototyping
  - Experimental prototyping

Although widely used, the term 'rapid' prototyping does not appear to provide a useful distinction from any other type (slow prototyping?) in a KBS context – although perhaps it is most often used to mean 'evolutionary' or 'incremental' prototyping. Here we see all prototyping as rapid compared to the full system development.

'Evolutionary prototyping' is problematic because most systems are evolutionary to some degree. 'Incremental prototyping' has been distinguished from evolutionary, by saying that in the latter the stages of development are not predefined. (Thus it is evolutionary prototyping that is so different from the process of software development supported by structured methods such as KADS.)

Another widely used general term is 'throwaway' prototyping. We define that a throwaway prototype is used for a clearly defined purpose. Once this is achieved, the prototype has no further role in the development. There are two kinds of throwaway prototypes: exploratory and experimental. These are distinguished by the way the prototypes are used. Both approaches are viewed as support activities for model-building in KADS, and are discussed below.

A summary of the major types of prototyping and their usefulness in KADS is as follows:

- *Evolutionary prototyping* (not very useful with KADS)[8]: This describes an approach where the system evolves from a series of analysis and implementation cycles. Many KBS development environments are tailored around an evolutionary model of development, providing easily modifiable and extendable primitive constructs. This approach does not complement the KADS modelling approach well, as the models are at a higher level of abstraction.

- *Exploratory prototyping* (useful with KADS): The purpose of exploratory prototyping is to gather and refine data from the requirements perspective. The prototypes produced are best thought of as 'mock-ups'. Feedback from the evaluation of these systems is used to refine KADS analysis models (either the model of expertise or the model of cooperation). The need to perform these kinds of exercises is dependent on the complexity of the models in question. For example, a relatively straightforward problem solver with a large set of modalities ('modes of user interaction') is best supported by the development of a user-interface mock-up. This technique has been found to be particularly useful for the analysis of user interface requirements, for example.

- *Experimental prototyping* (useful with KADS): Experimental prototyping aims to evaluate options for the implementation of the system. A precondition of this activity is that the functional requirements are known. This activity is used to assess the feasibility of design options. A good example of the use of this technique in a KADS context is the operationalization of (a part of) the behavioural design model in order to establish how well a specific implementation environment supports a selected problem-solving method. Where there is a detailed knowledge of implementation environments this exercise may not be necessary. Often this approach is used in a 'benchmarking' context in order to assess the relative performance of two or more possible implementations.

Note that, in general, exploratory prototyping is integral to analysis activities – it serves as a support activity *within* the modelling of expertise and interaction. Experimental prototyping is best viewed as a technical feasibility exercise occurring *between* design phases.

In conclusion, the most useful forms of prototyping in KADS are of the 'throwaway' type, i.e. those produced for a clearly defined purpose – exploratory and experimental. However, the breadth of this purpose, and the time to actually 'throw away' the prototype or use (part of) it in further prototypes, is left to the discretion of the project manager.

9.6.2   *KADS models and prototypes*

One way of understanding the opportunities for prototypes in KADS is to view them as *operational* descriptions of (parts of) KADS models. Some KADS models and examples of their corresponding operational descriptions are as follows:

KADS models		*Operational descriptions*
Process Model	→	Process simulation
Cooperation Model	→	User-interface mock-up
	→	Storyboard
Expertise Model	→	Problem-solver prototype
	→	Implemented domain model (e.g. frames)
Global System Architecture	→	Control simulation
Functional Design Model	→	Functional simulation
Behavioural Design Model	→	Implemented method
	→	User-interface object implementation
	→	Control simulation
Physical Design Model	→	Target system

9.7   Support tools

This section discusses the general issue of tools to support the use of the KADS methods. Essentially, it summarizes what types of tool are available. The pros and cons of particular tools or types of tool cannot be discussed in any detail due to space constraints. Specific opportunities for using various tools are noted in the appropriate sections in the Analysis and Design parts of this book.

There are many opportunities for using computer-based and other tools to support KADS activities. There are also many forms of such tools, from various sources. The software-based tools include commercial general-purpose packages such as drawing packages, structured text processing packages and hypertext systems, running on machines such as the Apple Macintosh and PCs, as well as simple generic and purpose-built UNIX utilities.

9.7.1   Types of support tools for KADS

The following is a taxonomy of support tools with respect to KADS:

- Software-based support tools
  - KADS-specific tools
  - Conventional CASE tools
  - General-purpose tools
  - Project management tools
  - KBS-specific tools
    - Knowledge-acquisition tools
    - KBS implementation environments
- Non-software-based support tools
  - KADS-specific tools
  - General purpose tools

Covering these from top to bottom, first let us take software support tools, and *KADS-specific tools* in particular. At the time of writing there are no commercially available KADS-specific software tools, although a number are known to be under development. An experimental prototype of such a tool, called 'Shelley', was produced as part of the ESPRIT project that originally produced KADS. We understand that the ESPRIT II project under way at the time of writing is producing a KADS-specific software tool, which will be a commercially available product. First versions of this tool may be based on the Shelley prototype, and could be available by the time this book is being read. (See Appendix 4.)

The lack of a KADS-specific tool is not as important as it may at first appear, as other software tools can be readily applied in using KADS. Suggestions for the use of such tools are mainly presented in the major Analysis and Design sections of this book (Chapters 4 and 7) and also in the guided tours (Chapters 15 and 16).

One type of non-KADS-specific tool is the *conventional CASE tool*. These have the advantage that they are becoming increasingly widespread and may be already available in the reader's organization. They include: standalone tools with a specific purpose (e.g. the requirements engineering tools, RTM (Requirements Traceability Manager) from Marconi Systems Technology and RqT from Cadre Technologies); loosely connected modular toolsets, allowing the combination of more than one function in different configurations (available from various manufacturers); and fully integrated toolsets.

Two major international products typical of the latter genre, primarily used in the field of technical software development, are: IDE's 'Software through Pictures' and Cadre's 'TeamWork'. These have different strengths and weaknesses and different styles and characteristics. However, they are both similar by being integrated collections of diagram editors centred around a common data store. The editors are tailored to support drawing specific types of conventional software diagrams, such as DFDs, state transition diagrams and structure charts. In addition to basic drawing support, they also provide rudimentary syntax and validity checking for diagrams drawn. Finally, the tools form much more of an 'environment' for conventional software development by providing a means to navigate around the diagram editors in such a way that is compatible with the semantics of a particular structured method, such as SA/SD. All these features make such tools very powerful and are especially effective on larger projects, although at a price.

While it is true that the full potential of these tools cannot be realized immediately when supporting KADS, compared with their original structured method, they can be used in a rudimentary fashion as basic diagramming tools. However, with relatively simple changes to the tools, which is technically feasible given their built-in flexibility, it should be possible to create a reasonable version of these tools tailored to KADS. (At the time of writing the authors are working on such a project for their own use.) Indeed, the trend in these tools is to build in more and more flexibility, the tool vendors being market-driven (reluctantly) towards the concept of a 'meta-tool' – a CASE tool fully programmable to support 'any' method. Thus support for KADS will become even easier with new releases of these tools.

There is a wider benefit to this approach. The existing capabilities of the tool to support conventional methods, such as SA/SD, should still be available for use alongside any additional KADS capability. This will facilitate the use of conventional techniques for the parts of a hybrid system that are not knowledge-based, and KADS techniques in those that are knowledge-based. Thus, a single tool should be able to capture the whole of a complex mixed KBS *and* non-KBS system in its database, providing a powerful integrated repository for such developments. The separation of KBS and non-KBS concerns in KADS, particularly in the Process Analysis stage, was designed to cope with exactly these sorts of situations.

General-purpose tools are also mentioned in this book as being potentially useful to support KADS. A particular advantage of such tools is that they are becoming ubiquitous. For smaller projects, where the benefits of true CASE tools are not so important, general-purpose drawing packages and word-processors are very effective. In addition, some of the more specialized tools, such as outliners (hierarchy manipulation) and hypertext systems have also found a place in our use of

KADS. The simple but powerful UNIX (and similar) text-processing utilities can also prove useful for information filtering and manipulation operations. For example, they can prove helpful when attempting to extract specific knowledge from on-line files such as interview protocols.

Project management has been distinguished from KADS in Section 9.1. Thus, *tools to support project management* are outside the scope of this book.

KBS-specific tools for knowledge acquisition may become increasing important during the lifetime of this book. At the moment, there are few available, but an ESPRIT project[9] (completely separate from KADS) is working towards producing 'ACKnowledge', a powerful and flexible toolset for knowledge acquisition. Other tools are available to support some of the knowledge-acquisition techniques summarized in Chapter 10.

KBS implementation environments have an obvious purpose as a delivery vehicle for KADS-based projects and as prototyping vehicles. However, in the case of the powerful ones they may have knowledge structure editors, for example, which would be very useful in document-ing some of the KADS models – particularly the Expertise Model or some of its layers.

Finally, the *non-software tools* should not be forgotten. This book is a tool in itself for KADS, but also contains many more specific tools, in the form of its frames, checklists and libraries. Non-software general-purpose tools are just as important in KADS developments as in conventional software – the reader should not need reminding of whiteboards and flipcharts, but have you considered the usefulness of the 'paper CASE tool' in the form of a set of yellow sticky notes and a large piece of paper? It sounds trivial, but it can be surprisingly effective!

Notes

1. Appendix 2 shows that this approach is comparable to that taken in con-ventional structured methods such as SSADM and SA/SD.
2. Another, soon to be published in the UK at the time of writing, is GEMINI – see Appendix 4. An experimental and rather complex framework was specially developed for KADS in the original ESPRIT project, known as 'CONCH'. Unfortunately, it requires further refinement. This is actually being done, as part of an ESPRIT II project – see Appendix 4. In its favour is that it is based on a modern 'risk-driven' approach to software development. However, one might question the *need* for a KADS-specific framework. When the technical development method KADS is distinguishable from a project management framework as we describe, the latter can be relatively generic. KBS technology requires special techniques at the technical development level, as provided by KADS, but the special needs at the project management level seem much less.
3. PRINCE uses the term 'stage' to refer to the major divisions of the lifecycle,

such as analysis and design. We have used 'phase' in this book for these. However, because PRINCE has no concept of any particular predefined divisions of the lifecycle, its 'stages' could equally map onto KADS's stages, if one so chooses.

4. See Section 2.1 and Appendices 1, 2 and 4 for further comments on KADS and lifecycles.

5. Metrics specific to KADS are still at the research stage at the time of writing.

6. The original source is Fagan (1976) – see Bibliography ('Miscellaneous'). There are alternative techniques, of course, and both the IEE in the UK and the IEEE in the USA publish useful documents describing good ones, Fagan-based or otherwise.

7. Our terminology is similar to that used in Floyd (1984). However, many other classifications have been produced – for one résumé, see Bates (1989). (See the Bibliography ('Miscellaneous') for both of these references.)

8. Usually in software development a prototype is taken to mean some trial executable code. KADS *is* naturally evolutionary at the model level (the models are built and successively refined), but *not* at the implementation level (the models are not written in program code).

9. ESPRIT project number 2576.

10 Library of knowledge-acquisition techniques

This chapter presents a basic set of techniques for knowledge acquisition. These are primarily used during Expertise Analysis in KADS (see Section 4.3), although they may be found useful for the other Analysis activities, including Process Analysis (Section 4.1), Cooperation Analysis (Section 4.2) and even Constraints Analysis[1] (Section 4.4). (However, for simplicity the techniques are still considered 'knowledge-acquisition' techniques.)

This chapter is divided into five basic parts:

- What is knowledge acquisition?
- Preparing for knowledge-acquisition sessions
- Common pitfalls in knowledge acquisition
- Matrix of knowledge-acquisition techniques for KADS Analysis
- Summary guide to knowledge-acquisition techniques (split into three main groups – interviewing, observational, multidimensional – plus a final general technique)

The first part introduces the topic of knowledge acquisition and distinguishes the three different types of knowledge-acquisition techniques. Next, some ˙practical general advice is presented, including preparing for knowledge-acquisition sessions and advice on some common pitfalls. Following this, a summary table is presented, showing where the techniques can best be applied in KADS. Finally, each of the three groups of techniques is presented in turn, with, for each individual technique, a short description, when to use the technique, pros and cons, and variations of the basic technique.

Like the other libraries in this book, this one is not meant to be taken as prescriptive. It is mainly intended to be useful when the analyst is unsure what technique to use. The library should also not be taken as a comprehensive guide to knowledge-acquisition techniques. Only summary descriptions of some of the most common are presented. Pointers to more complete descriptions of knowledge acquisition can be found in the Bibliography ('Knowledge acquisition').

10.1   What is knowledge acquisition?

'Knowledge acquisition' and 'knowledge elicitation' are loosely regarded as being synonymous in the literature (sometimes, however, the latter is seen as referring to a subset of the activities involved in acquisition). The phrase 'knowledge acquisition' as used in this book means the extraction of material to be modelled. 'Knowledge' is used in a broad sense, including not only problem-solving knowledge but also knowledge of the process context of the future system and its cooperative behaviour. Even when the desired problem-solving behaviour (say) of the system is not always present in the real world, the modelling paradigm still applies.

Some understanding of the nature of expertise is essential in order to be able to choose from and use the acquisition techniques available. It is also important in appreciating the differences between knowledge acquisition and conventional systems analysis.

Expertise underlies much of the routine intelligent behaviour that we observe in people ('human agents') in many diverse situations. It can be characterized as the possession of appropriate specialized knowledge coupled with the techniques and rules for using this knowledge in a particular domain. Experts utilize their knowledge to solve problems effectively with an acceptable rate of success, efficiently producing useful solutions and determining the most relevant information quickly. Generally, they also recognize their own limitations and refer problems that lie outside their field of expertise to other experts who possess the required knowledge. These abilities are recognized by others who then use the expert to provide information, solutions to problems and explanations.

In many ways the objectives of systems analysis and knowledge acquisition are similar and the same problems can be encountered in each (e.g. the failure to ask the right questions, the making of wrong assumptions, the misunderstanding of terms and jargon). Many of the techniques used in systems analysis (e.g. observation, sampling from existing records, interviews, group discussions, questionnaires) are available for use in knowledge acquisition. The differences between systems analysis and knowledge acquisition, however, mean that these techniques are not sufficient on their own.

The knowledge engineer's task is less clear than that of the systems analyst, often being less routine and less well defined. The expert in the particular domain under consideration will have built up expertise, usually through years of experience. Many of his or her particular experiences will have been due to specific and personal combinations of events and will not be found in textbooks. In addition, judgements are often made on intuition; and knowledge is often over-learned, procedural and not available for direct verbal report. To overcome some of these problems there are a number of techniques available that have been drawn from psychology and other disciplines, which enable the knowledge held by an expert to be accessed and expressed.

The knowledge engineer should have available a battery of techniques and ways of assessing the benefits and drawbacks of each in order to judge when best to use them. The techniques differ in the kinds of data they produce (verbal or non-verbal), and also in the kind of expertise that they are best suited to capturing (e.g. some make available hierarchies of domain objects, and others, more strategic information about how and when to use rules). The techniques are all the same in that they aim to produce valid and reliable data, and add rigour and structure to a vague and ill-defined area. This is important in the context of a structured method like KADS, if the contributions from knowledge acquisition are to be married with the results from other phases of the analysis and design process; it is also necessary in order to develop quality systems reliably.

Three main types of techniques have been distinguished, and form the bulk of this chapter:

> **Interviewing techniques** – These are verbal techniques where the expert, removed from the actual problem-solving situation, is required to reflect upon, recall and explain his or her own behaviour.
> **Observational techniques** – Here the expert is in a real-life or simulated problem-solving situation. These techniques may or may not involve the generation of a verbal protocol (i.e. a transcript).
> **Multidimensional techniques** – These are contrived techniques which provide non-verbal data. They often force the expert to think about the domain in a new way and so may seem unrelated to the actual tasks he or she performs.

These three groups are used later in the chapter. The general technique of 'reviewing' in knowledge acquisition is presented after these, and is the last section in the chapter.

We omit discussion here of public data, such as books, manuals and reports. These generally contain static, support knowledge, and do not represent expertise in action. However, these sources are *very important* in domain orientation, and such public data should be collected as early as possible in the project. The 'background' knowledge that can be obtained in this way is invaluable in facilitating communication with the expert, and saving time and effort for all concerned. The kinds of sources available will vary considerably between projects, but the knowledge engineer is strongly advised to spend some time determining their existence, content, position, extent and nature of use.

Finally, there are two general points to note for the rest of this chapter. First, following convention, the interviewee or subject will be referred to as the 'expert', although in many cases in KADS Analysis 'user' or 'client', etc. would be equally valid; second, acquisition techniques are referred to assuming a single expert source of information.

10.2   Preparing for knowledge-acquisition sessions

A major point in the preparation for knowledge acquisition, and that most often ignored, is the question of securing a session and ensuring that there is sufficient time available for it. As the experts needed for acquisition are often senior personnel with many demands on their time, it can be difficult to secure sessions of longer than an hour or so. This stresses the need for careful preparation before going into the session. With KADS in particular, there will often be follow-up sessions (for example, to verify the Generic Task Model with the expert) and so it is important to make sure that the resource of the expert's time is used as efficiently as possible. Also, one should be careful not to fall into the trap of polluting a knowledge-acquisition session with discussion of other (e.g. project management) issues – a *specific* knowledge-acquisition session should be arranged.

The next important preparation for a knowledge-acquisition session is to know beforehand precisely what kind of knowledge needs to be obtained. In Process, Cooperation and Expertise Analysis there are several occasions when knowledge acquisition is required. Sometimes the session is a preliminary one, the aim may be to get a grasp of the basic domain concepts (as when producing a lexicon or glossary in preparing static domain knowledge); or it may be to validate or populate the chosen Generic Task Model for the system. The KADS methods ensure that acquisition will take place at carefully specified times within development. The knowledge engineer will be aided by this in deciding exactly what he or she needs to know from a given meeting and which acquisition technique is most suitable for the task in hand. The descriptions of techniques in this chapter provide guidance as to which techniques are most suitable where in KADS; also, Section 10.4 presents a summary table.

Finally, the knowledge engineer should be as familiar as possible with the basic terminology of the domain (if a significant part of the static domain knowledge has been elicited by the time of the session, this would be ideal, otherwise as much background documentation as possible should be read before the session). There is nothing worse than an interview where the expert thinks the knowledge engineer is a fool simply because the knowledge engineer does not understand the basic domain terms.

In summary, there are four main points for the knowledge engineer to remember:

- Arrange a specific knowledge-acquisition session with the expert.
- Ensure that enough time is made available – agreed by expert and knowledge engineer.
- Plan for the type of knowledge under consideration and choose an appropriate technique or subset of techniques.
- Be as familiar as possible with the domain terminology.

10.3   Common pitfalls in knowledge acquisition

If a knowledge-acquisition session is to be successful there are certain problems which must be anticipated, and avoided, by the knowledge engineer. There are five issues to consider, which are discussed in detail below:

- Recording
- Reliability and validity
- Technique appropriateness
- Data completeness
- Expert's motivation

10.3.1   Recording the session

Conducting a successful knowledge-acquisition session involves more than asking the right questions at the right time – it includes the use of reliable recording techniques and obtaining subsequent documentation. Often audio recording will be sufficient, but sometimes video recording will also be required. Note-taking alone is rarely desirable, because the knowledge engineer is selectively filtering the material before it is recorded, and human memory can never be relied on to recapture what was omitted. Some general points to remember about recording sessions are:

- The knowledge engineer should be familiar with the equipment that is to be used in the session.
- Equipment should be kept as unobtrusive as possible.
- The knowledge engineer should ensure that there are enough power sockets for the equipment and that there is enough length of lead to

reach comfortably, or batteries (and spares) used are in good condition; similarly some spare blank tapes should be available.

- The equipment and recording levels should be checked immediately prior to the expert's arrival.
- The expert must always be informed that the session is to be recorded and must give his or her consent; this must all be made as natural as possible, to ensure that the expert is at ease.

Recordings should be at least partially (if not fully) transcribed, and enough time (up to eight times the recording time) should be allowed for this. Transcriptions can sometimes be difficult to interpret when removed from the context of the knowledge-acquisition session (owing to the characteristics of natural speech, and the absence of body language and inaudible stimuli). Supplementary notes taken by the experimenter during the session can be of use in disambiguating and clarifying points in the transcript.

Recording, rather than note-taking, frees the knowledge engineer to concentrate during the session. This means that he or she is more likely to pick up contradictions, clarify points and probe for more detail, and will save having to return to the expert for this purpose at a later date. It may be beneficial to have two knowledge engineers in a session; one acting as the main elicitor while the other takes notes, occasionally adding additional probes and comments.

10.3.2 *Reliability and validity of the data*

Any data elicited must be both 'reliable' and 'valid': reliable in the sense that a similar acquisition would yield similar results; and valid in that the data obtained are accurate. In straightforward question-and-answer interviews the reliability will generally be very high; an expert is likely to respond consistently to simple questions. Validity is more difficult to ensure, particularly where procedural (as opposed to declarative) knowledge is concerned. In cases such as these the knowledge engineer should consider the use of non-interview techniques more suitable for capturing this kind of data (e.g. observational or multidimensional techniques).

There are certain corrective and preventive procedures that can be employed by the knowledge engineer in attempt to ensure the validity of the data collected.

Mechanical techniques

- *Visual props* – allowing the expert to select from, create and compare visual representations (rather than verbal expressions) can help to capture knowledge that is difficult to verbalize.
- *Response mode changes* – varying the format of the requested information can help to identify inconsistencies and allow the expert to find the most natural means of expressing his or her knowledge.
- *Scoring rules* – a function of the discrepancy between actual and observed values can be used to recalibrate assessments after collection, or to motivate the expert to attempt to provide more valid data.
- *Consensus weighting* – data from many experts can be combined, and weighted means of numeric values can be obtained.

Behavioural techniques

- *Focusing* – structuring the task and the method of acquisition can help the expert to identify areas prone to invalidity and take corrective action.
- *Decomposition* – relationships and domain concepts can be easier to assess when broken down into their sub-components than when presented as a whole.
- *Logic challenges* – requesting the expert to provide justifications of the data he or she provides can highlight areas of invalidity and force the expert to reconsider his or her reasoning.
- *Consensus interaction* – knowledge can be acquired in a group setting, and feedback from all the group members can encourage negotiation until a consensus is reached.

10.3.3   *Appropriateness of the technique*

The issue of the validity of data raises the question of the appropriateness of techniques. There is no generally applicable knowledge-acquisition technique that will be suitable for every occasion. Rather, the knowledge engineer must be aware of a range of techniques and be able to choose the one best suited to the needs of the moment (e.g. the kinds of data to be captured, the stage of KADS reached, and limits on resources). The techniques available are described in detail later in this chapter, and a useful summary is shown in Table 10.1.

10.3.4 *Completeness of the data*

Data may be reliable, valid, have been acquired using the appropriate technique, but still be incomplete. This is a common problem faced by knowledge engineers; many verbal explanations given by experts will miss things out – things that the expert may consider too obvious to need mentioning but which are actually important steps in the reasoning process. Incompleteness may also occur where the expert knows the answer but is unable to express it in a way useful to the knowledge engineer.

There are a number of ways in which the knowledge engineer can try to increase the completeness of coverage of the domain:

- *Feedback* – Feeding back the data the expert has supplied, and asking if there are other points that should be mentioned can prompt the expert to supply details that had previously been considered unimportant.
- *Multidimensional techniques* – Making use of multidimensional techniques, which are non-verbal, can help the knowledge engineer to access knowledge that the expert cannot verbalize.
- *Multi-expert acquisition* – Carrying out additional acquisition sessions with other experts can increase the coverage of the domain. A problem with this approach can be combining the data from the different sessions, to form a single view of the domain. This can be achieved by asking experts to validate accounts other than their own, or by the knowledge engineer adopting critical threshold values and including only data obtained from two or more independent sources. Independent judges can also be used in this process.

10.3.5 *Motivation of the expert*

Another cause of incomplete data may be the lack of motivation of the expert. There can be many reasons why an expert does not give his full cooperation in an acquisition session, for example, fear that the aim of the KBS is to replace the expert with a computer, and so he or she may be out of a job if it is successful. Alternatively, the expert may have gaps in his own knowledge which, for reasons of professional pride, he does not wish to be exposed. Other reasons for reticence include suspicion of the motivations of management and a lack of belief in the relevance of the KBS.

There are certain behaviours that an expert might demonstrate which should indicate to the knowledge engineer that motivation is a problem.

Table 10.1 Summary table of techniques supporting KADS Analysis

	Context	Facts	Relationships	Procedure	Structure	Sequence	Concepts	Strategy	Reasoning
Focused interview	Con	E (sk)	P/E (sk)	P	P/E (sk)	E (task)			E (inf)
Structured interview	Con	E (sk)	P/E (sk)	P	P/E (sk)	E (task)	E (sk)	E (strat)	E (inf)
Introspection	Con			P		E (task)		E (strat)	
Tutorial interview	Con						E (sk)		E (inf)
Self-report				P/E (task)	P			E (strat)	
Participant observation				P/E (task)				E (strat)	
User–expert dialogue			Coop	P				E (strat)	
Repertory grid		E (sk)	E (sk)		E (sk)				E (inf)
Card sort		E (sk)	E (sk)		E (sk)				E (inf)
Matrix generation		E (sk)[a]	E (sk)[a]		E (sk)[a]		E (sk)[a]		

KEY:

P	Process Analysis
Con	Constraints Analysis
Coop	Cooperation Analysis
E (sk)	Expertise Analysis – Analyze Static Knowledge
E (task)	Expertise Analysis – Construct Task Layer
E (inf)	Expertise Analysis – Construct Inference Layer
E (strat)	Expertise Analysis – Contruct Strategy Layer

[a] This technique is not suitable for use on its own

These include under-reporting, the expert taking control of the session and steering the topics, and an eagerness to look for diversions. These are problems long known to knowledge engineering and cannot always be solved by the correct selection of an acquisition method. However, a few simple precautions can avoid many of these issues of motivation: be open with the expert, state the objectives of the project and make him feel the worth of his contributions. Do not be afraid if the expert becomes interested in the technical aspects of the system, and do not attempt to shield him or her from some knowledge of the intricacies. It is important that the expert continues to feel involved in the project, and to this end the results of sessions should be fed back to him regularly. The expert should also be kept notified of the stage of development of the system.

10.4   Knowledge-acquisition techniques in KADS

Table 10.1 is a matrix showing knowledge-acquisition techniques (at the side) against different forms of knowledge (along the top), with KADS activities and stages plotted at their intersections. It can be used to select appropriate-acquisition techniques.

10.5   Interviewing techniques

KAT

10.5.1   *The focused interview*

The focused is the most widely used form of knowledge-acquisition interview. It is the technique most akin to normal conversation; the interviewer asks the expert a series of questions on topics prepared in advance (the 'focused' part) and the expert responds. The overall structure of the interview consists of three parts:

- *An introduction* – Where the purpose of the interview is explained to the interviewee, what the proposed system is about and where the expert's contribution fits in. It will lay out an agenda for the rest of the interview – this allows the expert to assess what depth of knowledge will be required from him or her in the session.
- *The main part of the interview* – Consisting of the questions and their answers.
- *A summary* – By summarizing what has been covered in the interview (as opposed to what was intended to be covered) the success of the interview can, in the first instance, be evaluated. An appointment may be made for another interview, if necessary.

When to use

The focused interview is most suitable for eliciting the following types of data: factual domain knowledge, especially for domains where the static knowledge is not well documented; the type of problems to be solved; and the role of expertise in the intended environment (this may well cover a lot of the expert's existing job description). Thus, the activities it will most likely be used in are:

- Analyse Static Knowledge (Expertise Analysis)
- Constraints Analysis

The focused interview can also be of use (but perhaps to a lesser extent) in:

- Analyze and Decompose Process (Process Analysis)
- Construct Task Layer (Expertise Analysis)
- Construct Inference Layer (Expertise Analysis)

Pros and cons

This technique should seem natural to the expert and should not cause him or her too much discomfort. As the interview is not too rigorously controlled there is room for interesting and unanticipated topics to come to light and be discussed.

The main problem of this technique (and often of interviewing techniques in general) is the large amount of data that is obtained and must be transcribed and analyzed. Natural speech is characterized by incomplete sentences, contradictions and repetitions. This can make the transcripts difficult to understand after the event and out of context. Body language and other inaudible stimuli or events will also be lost. Another problem arises if the interview is used for investigating procedural information as the data obtained are often inaccurate or even totally spurious.

Variations

There are variations on the focused interview which provide different ways of focusing on the domain and obtaining specific kinds of data. All the techniques can be used to prompt an expert to give explanations at a finer level of granularity.

- *Distinction of goals* – the expert is presented with a goal (e.g. a diagnosis) and asked what evidence is necessary and sufficient to distinguish this goal from alternatives. This technique can be repeated for final and intermediate goals. The distinctions that emerge will help the knowledge engineer to structure the domain, classes of goals will be revealed and this will help to identify the types of problems that are encountered.

- *Re-classification* – each of the set of possible goals is re-classified in terms of the pieces of evidence supporting it. The evidence is then re-classified into a set of sub-goals and the process is repeated until all evidence has been broken down into facts directly observable by the expert. This can be used to establish the links between evidence and facts. In this way the structure of the domain can be addressed and problem definitions can be built.

- *Dividing the domain* – this is the reverse of the above technique. The expert starts with the set of facts and groups them until a final goal is obtained. Whether this technique or the previous one is used will depend on the way of addressing the domain with which the expert is most comfortable. Both can be used, and the results compared if some kind of generic structure (especially across experts) is required.

- *Systematic symptom to fault links* – given a set of all the possible faults in a system the expert would provide links indicating which faults would lead to which symptoms. The explanations provided by the expert while performing this can give insight into the kinds of reasoning he or she is employing. This can also provide pointers to areas for further questioning.

- *Intermediate reasoning steps* – the expert takes each step in the symptom to fault link and indicates what evidence points to the next step in the link. This will again give insight into the nature of the expert's reasoning and indicate dependencies between pieces of evidence.

10.5.2 The structured interview

KAT

The purpose of a structured interview is to obtain detailed insights into parts of the static domain knowledge. It is primarily used for detailed, structured knowledge acquisition, not for becoming familiar with the domain.

In a structured interview the knowledge engineer tries to elicit *all* the knowledge relating to some aspect of the domain by continuously asking for clarification, justifications, instances, explanations and even counter-examples. The difference between this and the focused interview is that the knowledge engineer probes a few topics in depth, rather than a number of topics at a high level. As in the focused interview, the interviewer will start with a list of questions, but the style is more like interrogation.

When to use

The activities a structured interview is most likely to be used in are:

- Analyze Static Knowledge (Expertise Analysis)
- Construct Inference Layer (Expertise Analysis)
- Constraints Analysis

The technique can also be used in

- Analyze and Decompose Process (Process Analysis)
- Construct Task Layer (Expertise Analysis)
- Construct Strategy Layer (Expertise Analysis)

Pros and cons

One drawback to the structured interview is that it is difficult for the knowledge engineer to be sure that the answers obtained are accurate, rather than just *ad hoc* guesses produced under the pressure of questioning. A warning to the prospective interviewer is that too much probing can lead to increasingly unreliable results.

The structured interview, like the focused, also suffers from the fact that the knowledge engineer must be fairly well acquainted with the domain in order to conduct the session. An advantage of the structured interview over the focused interview, however, is that there will have been some order and discipline injected into the session. This will reflect itself in the transcript, which should be easier to analyse.

Variations

There are two variations of this technique which provide different ways of structuring the interview in order to obtain different kinds of data:

- *Twenty questions* – the knowledge engineer picks one of a set of items known to the expert (e.g. a diagnosis). The expert then has to guess which one the engineer has in mind by asking a series of questions which can be answered 'yes' or 'no' by the engineer. This technique provides heuristic rules and information requirements used by the expert and indicates which questions dominate as the expert searches through a problem space. The results of this technique can be used in the construction of the Inference Layer and Strategy Layer of the Expertise Model. Problems with this technique are that the inferences and heuristics obtained will not have been provided directly and should, therefore, be fed back to the expert for confirmation. The knowledge engineer has also to be familiar with all aspects of the domain in order to ensure that he or she will be able to answer any question the expert asks. Experts are often reluctant to participate in this technique, complaining that thcy are not used to thinking about the domain in this way and that they cannot see the point. It should be noted, though, that the degree of expert resistance bears no relation to the efficacy of the technique.

- *Laddered grid* – This technique uses a set of predefined questions to move systematically throughout the domain. It is particularly useful when there is a hierarchical structure to the domain. From a 'seed' point provided by the knowledge engineer, the space is examined using questions such as: 'What is X an example of?' 'What is an example of X?' 'Can you give me any other examples of X?' 'What features distinguish X from Y?' In this way a map of the domain can quickly be drawn. Again there may be some resistance from the expert.

10.5.3 Introspection

KAT

Introspection is closest in everyday terms to telling stories, thinking aloud or giving testimony. The expert is asked to imagine and describe *how* he or she would solve a given problem (or class of problems). This form of acquisition may well happen spontaneously in a focused interview, but 'introspection' is the name that will be used to refer to this phenomenon when the expert is explicitly asked for it. The expert should be asked to focus on a problem that is concrete and familiar (in order that the memory of it be more reliable), and the interventions of the knowledge engineer should be confined to asking 'how' (probing for more information). Asking 'why' may introduce inaccuracy into the report because the expert might infer an answer without reference to a specific memory.

During introspection the expert is asked to describe how he or she would go about solving a certain problem. When this is done, the expert is asked to name all the thought processes he would consciously apply. Note that the expert does not undertake any actual problem solving but only describes what it would involve.

When to use

Introspection can be best used to elicit global descriptions of the strategies the expert uses (or believes that he or she uses) in solving problems; justifications for decisions in the process; some global information about the *types* of knowledge the expert uses. Care should be taken, however, to seek validation of data yielded from introspection.

Introspection, and its variants, will be usually employed in the following activities:

- Construct Task Layer (Expertise Analysis)
- Construct Strategy Layer (Expertise Analysis)
- Analyze and Decompose Process (Process Analysis)

Pros and cons

The main problem with introspection is the lack of reliability of the data obtained; it is an often acknowledged fact that what experts *think* they do and what they *actually* do are sometimes very far apart. It is also very important to note the kind of problem that is being solved, as the problem-solving methods the expert describes may vary between routine, interesting and rare cases.

Variations

- *Retrospective case description* – the expert is asked to describe how he or she solved one or more typical cases in the recent past. This technique attempts to anchor the generation of the report to an actual case to increase accuracy. The problems with this technique are that the knowledge engineer must assess how typical the case is; judge whether the memory of the case is accurate; be aware that essential details may be omitted from reports of mundane cases; and assess the extent to which hindsight has affected the expert's justifications of his or her actions.
- *Critical incident* – the expert is asked to choose a difficult or unusual case for description. This technique usually provides more detailed and accurate data than retrospective case descriptions, but problems may be encountered because the features of the expert's performance cannot be immediately generalized to other, more everyday cases.
- *Forward scenario generation* – here the expert describes in detail a hypothetical case chosen either by himself or the knowledge engineer. This technique has many problems associated with it: the validity of the account may be poor with respect to real-world instances and the

account may contain *post hoc* justification leading to spurious decision rules. In some domains, however, there will not be any real examples to work with (e.g. emergency shut-down procedures of large operating plants), and this technique could then be employed.

10.5.4   *The tutorial interview*

This is the simplest kind of acquisition. The expert is asked to prepare an introductory talk outlining the main themes and ideas of the domain, lasting about an hour. This is recorded and the concepts are subsequently extracted from the transcripts.

When to use

The technique should be restricted to use when a lack of textbooks, or other reference material, has prevented the knowledge engineer from gaining a preparatory understanding of the domain. The technique should, therefore, be used for domain orientation. The results of the tutorial interview may provide data that can be fed into:

- Constraints Analysis
- Analyze Static Knowledge (Expertise Analysis)

Pros and cons

This can be useful for gaining 'working' definitions of words including the connotative meaning that experts bring to domain concepts. Subtle distinctions and personal experiences will be missing from dictionary and textbook definitions. A drawback of this technique is that the knowledge engineer has no control over what is covered, and little idea of how complete the coverage has been. The expert may also regard his or her part of the job as being completed after this technique and may be unwilling to be interviewed again, feeling that he or she is only being asked to repeat what has been said before. If a tutorial interview is used for domain orientation, then it may be necessary to use a different expert for subsequent acquisition sessions.

Variations

- *Compiled list* – here the expert is asked to write out specific areas of knowledge as lists of information. This is best employed for well-defined areas where the knowledge engineer can be reasonably sure that complete coverage of the domain has been obtained. The advantage of this approach is that the expert can prepare such a document in his or her own time. The knowledge engineer is then free to perform other activities while awaiting the results.

KAT

10.6   Observational techniques

10.6.1   Self-report

Of all the techniques mentioned in this book, self-report (also referred to as protocol analysis) is the one closest to investigating expertise in action, being a report of ongoing, or directly preceding, events. In a self-report session the expert thinks aloud while actually solving a problem. This is the main difference between self-report and introspection: an actual problem is being solved during the session. The report here is secondary to the problem-solving process. In a self-report situation the interviewer should take an unobtrusive stance, interjections should only be used to keep the expert talking.

When to use

The self-report technique is best employed to elicit information about when and how certain knowledge is used; the task structure and strategies used in problem solving; evaluation criteria and procedures; and detailed chains of inference. Some of these data will be implicit and the knowledge engineer should seek validation of his or her assumptions, both by observing the actions that the expert performs and feeding back data in a subsequent session.

A self-report consultation may also be useful in validating an existing prototype. Thus, in KADS it is recommended that self-report is used at an early stage: as soon as a strong contender is found for the Generic Task Model.

Self-reports, and selective reports, may be used in the following activities:

- Analyze and Decompose Process (Process Analysis)
- Construct Inference Layer (Expertise Analysis)
- Construct Task Layer (Expertise Analysis)
- Construct Strategy Layer (Expertise Analysis)

Pros and cons

The main advantage of self-report over introspection is the validity of the *observed* data. The expert must be doing the right thing or the problem would not get solved. The unconstrained verbalizations of the expert may reveal knowledge that he or she could not articulate in an interview situation. However, the information gathered may be less generally applicable than that from introspection; the expert will only be talking about the specific problem in hand in self-report, whereas he may give much more general comments in an introspection session.

Another problem with this technique is that the generation of a verbal report, while simultaneously performing a task, might interfere with one or both of the processes. Although the validity of the expert's actions can be checked, that of the report is hard to evaluate. This technique is also limited in the kind of tasks to which it can be applied (e.g. an expert cannot generate a verbal report while performing a verbal task at the same time).

Variations

- *Selective report* – this is used in a situation where the problem solving happens very quickly, and there is no time for the expert to report everything he or she does; in this case the knowledge engineer will ask the expert to report on events of a certain type – the ones he is most interested in.
- *Retrospective self-report* – here the expert watches a video recording of himself performing a task and talks the knowledge engineer through it, explaining the goals he held at various stages and the plan that he was following. The advantage of this is that the task performance is not disturbed by verbal report and the report can be made while referring to actual happenings. This should increase accuracy but cannot overcome the problem of *post hoc* rationalization.

10.6.2   *Participant Observation*

KAT

In this technique the expert is observed performing the domain tasks. No verbal report is required from the expert, the knowledge engineer must instead infer what is going on. The technique can be of use in acquiring tacit knowledge which the expert cannot verbalize.

When to use

The technique is of most use when the nature of the expert's task is verbal (an expert-generated verbal report would, therefore, be impossible to obtain). It is also of use when the expert's time is very valuable and access is difficult to negotiate. In this way the knowledge engineer can collect as much information as possible and reduce the number of sessions needed with the expert to just those for validating his or her assumptions. The knowledge engineer will be able to observe the task order and decomposition and will be able to infer the reasoning processes and strategies of the expert.

Participant Observation may be used to support the following activities:

- Analyze and Decompose Processes (Process Analysis)
- Construct Task Layer (Expertise Analysis)
- Construct Strategy Layer (Expertise Analysis)

Pros and cons

It can be difficult for the knowledge engineer to infer the meaning of the expert's actions or the typicality of the observed interaction. The transcription and analysis of any dialogues produced by the expert in the course of performing his or her task is time consuming, and it is essential for the knowledge engineer to secure a session with the expert in order to validate extracted data. This method can be useful when there are strict time and access constraints.

Variation

- *Intermediary reporting* – this is a variation of this technique which can reduce the amount of inference about actions that the knowledge engineer has to make. One expert performs the task while another looks on and explains what is happening. Although this is preferable to guesswork on the part of the knowledge engineer, there are still problems due to the possibility of actor–observer discrepancy. Again the original expert should be consulted for a validation session.

10.6.3   *User–Expert Dialogues*

This technique is one where the potential user and the existing expert simulate the proposed system. They may do this via Teletypes or terminals, or simply be separated by a screen. This is useful in analyzing cooperation in the KBS. Here the knowledge engineer plays an even more passive role than in self-report; he or she may not say anything at all but may be required only to analyze the transcripts afterwards.

When to use

User–expert dialogues, mock-ups and the Wizard-of-Oz technique can be used as part of the following activities:

- Analyze and Decompose Process (Process Analysis)
- Analyze User Task(s) (Cooperation Analysis)
- Construct Strategy Layer (Expertise Analysis)

Pros and cons

The advantages of this technique are that it is less costly and time consuming than building a prototype; the use of a mechanical intermediary forces both actors to 'think aloud'; and there will generally be a log-file or transcript available for analysis afterwards. Finally, when a prototype has been built, it can be used in tests with the user to validate decisions about cooperation.

Variation

- *Wizard-of-Oz* – this is a simple mock-up technique which might involve the expert simulating the system separated from the prospective users by a screen. In such a case the actions of all parties can be recorded for later analysis. In the mock-up technique the expert is in one room, the user or developer in another, and they communicate via a terminal or Teletype.

10.7 Multidimensional techniques

KAT

10.7.1 Repertory Grid

This technique can capture the expert's view of a problem and its domain, with respect to experience and the personal understanding that he or she has developed of it. The Repertory Grid is composed of constructs and elements, where a construct is a bipolar characteristic possessed to some extent by each element in the domain.

The first stage is for the knowledge engineer to define clearly the problem under investigation. This is important in order to set the context for the expert so that his or her constructs and ratings can accurately represent his view of the problem.

Groups of three domain elements (triads) are chosen at random (or systematically) from the set of elements. The expert is asked to choose the two that are most similar and then name the attribute that makes them similar. He is then asked what the opposite of this attribute is which describes the third (dissimilar) element. This process provides the bipolar construct along which all other items in the set are rated (a numeric scale is required for the analysis, but ratings may be described by names rather than numbers during the acquisition if this is easier for the expert). It is important to keep the same scale (i.e. 1 to 5, or 1 to 3) throughout the session, although the terms used to describe the particular ratings might vary from construct to construct.

New triads are selected until all permutations (or those identified by the knowledge engineer as of special interest) have been presented. In this way a grid describing all the elements considered relevant to the problem under discussion is obtained. The expert can add or remove constructs and elements at any time during the session. The grid is complete when the expert is satisfied that it represents his or her view of the problem.

When to use

This technique is of particular use when experts are having difficulty articulating the decision criteria they use for discriminating closely related elements within a domain. The grid can be analyzed statistically to reveal the underlying patterns relating elements, and also to derive the decision rules an expert uses in the problem. The Repertory Grid obtains finer-grain criteria than interviewing techniques and is particularly suitable for accessing implicit knowledge.

Repertory Grid can be used to identify the structure in a domain and so can support:

- Analyze Static Knowledge (Expertise Analysis)
- Analyze and Decompose Process (Process Analysis)
- Construct Inference Layer (Expertise Analysis)

Pros and cons

Repertory Grids take a long time to administer and are often difficult to analyze and interpret; they also become quickly unmanageable with many more than ten elements. It is open to debate whether it is valid to expect experts to view a problem in terms of bipolar constructs, and often resistance will be encountered. This method has been used with success, however, and its ability as a non-verbal technique to access implicit knowledge is valuable.

Variation

- *Multidimensional scaling* – this is a technique for use with a set of objects assumed to vary along only a few dimensions. Each element is compared with each of the others in the set and an estimation of their similarity is given. The resulting similarity matrix is then subjected to statistical analysis to reveal the structure among the elements.

10.7.1 *Card Sort*

KAT

This is a similar technique to the Repertory Grid but is simpler both for the knowledge engineer and for the expert. The price of simplicity is that the data are not as rich or complex as that from other (more complex) multi-dimensional techniques.

The knowledge engineer prepares a set of cards, each bearing the name of one concept from the domain. These are placed in a random configuration on the table. The expert is asked to pick a dimension and then classify each element according to this dimension by placing the cards in relevant piles. When all cards have been allocated to a pile the expert names the dimension and each of the piles. The knowledge engineer records these, also noting which elements occur in which pile.

For example, consider a Card Sort to determine how people classify fruit. The expert might be provided with cards bearing the names 'tomato', 'plum', 'banana', 'orange', 'lemon', 'pear', 'lime'.

The expert might do the first sort along the dimension of colour and the results might be:

```
sort one, dimension = colour
   pile one = red (tomato, plum)
   pile two = green (pear, lime)
   pile three = yellow (banana, lemon)
   pile four = orange (orange)
```

It should be emphasized to the expert that they can have a category 'does not fit' since it is often difficult to find dimensions that encompass every concept.

After sorting along a dimension, the cards are collected up, shuffled and laid out for sorting along another dimension. This is repeated until the expert can think of no more dimensions to sort along.

When to use

The Card Sort can be used to build up definitions of concepts in the domain (by compiling a list of all the values a particular concept has across the dimensions) and also for deriving rules of classification. This technique could be of particular use in:

- Analyze Static Knowledge (Expertise Analysis)
- Construct Inference Layer (Expertise Analysis)

Pros and cons

The knowledge engineer needs to be familiar with the domain in order to identify the concepts to be used on the cards. The technique is useful in cases where the expert is having problems verbalizing his or her knowledge, since it is non-verbal in its nature and can capture some implicit procedural knowledge.

The data are captured in a structured form and lengthy transcription is avoided, but the rules that can be extracted from this technique are often cumbersome and clauses may be redundant. They can provide a good starting point for an interview, however, since in the process of refinement and validation with the expert other kinds of knowledge, including strategic knowledge about how the rules are used, may come to light.

The technique can also be used to investigate the structure of a domain by studying which concepts are associated with each other. This requires the use of statistical analysis using techniques such as cluster analysis. Expert resistance is often encountered with this technique and the knowledge engineer may find that he or she has to justify its use in the acquisition session.

Variation

- *Card Sort for hierarchical knowledge* – in cases where the number of concepts covering the domain is large and in need of structuring to become manageable a variation of the Card Sort can be employed. This involves presenting the expert with all of the concepts and asking him or her to divide them into as many small piles as possible until no further subdivision is possible. The expert provides a label for each group and then merges them into slightly larger groups. The groups are again labelled. This is repeated until no further amalgamation is possible. Encouraging the expert to think aloud while performing this task helps the knowledge engineer to understand the processes governing the grouping of domain items. This technique requires that the domain has an inherent hierarchical structure, otherwise a meaningless and tangled net will result. Class duplication within a hierarchy can also be a problem, and can cause confusion when trying to interpret the results.

10.7.3   *Matrix Generation*

KAT

This technique is particularly useful with experts who are used to providing information in a tabulated form. A grid is drawn, for example, with symptoms as column headings and faults as row names. Pairs are then considered along such dimensions as whether or not a relationship exists, the strength of the association, and the type of fit. The matrix is then filled with the elicited responses.

This method can produce a large number of propositional relationships between concepts in a short space of time. It is particularly good for forcing consideration of combinations that would not otherwise have come to mind, and identifying elements which never co-occur or have no relationship. Explanations about the non-occurrence of certain combinations can provide valuable insight into the nature of the domain.

When to use

This technique is unlikely ever to be used alone, but is useful in combination with interviewing techniques (where it can be used to measure the completeness of coverage of the domain) and multidimensional scaling (where it can be employed to preserve information on local structuring of domain elements).

Pros and cons

Matrix Generation is of little use as a technique on its own, but is valuable in complementing other techniques and improving the quality of the data obtained from them.

Variation

None.

KAT

10.8 Reviews

Reviews are a very general technique, supplementary, but necessary, to the effectiveness of the other techniques described previously. A review is where the knowledge engineer and expert revisit the data elicited to date, or from a specific session or series of sessions. The purpose is for the knowledge engineer to get the expert to assess the data, to check that it is correct and complete.

Reviews may be used for the correcting of transcripts (by taking them to the expert), repairing gaps in self-report results and validating assumptions that the knowledge engineer has made. They are a necessary stage of knowledge acquisition, as the gaps may well contain information needed to complete the system.

Reviewing is also required if the information collected from the expert is inconsistent in any way. These inconsistencies may be only apparent – the result of the different interviewing techniques used – or they may reflect genuinely muddled explanations. Whatever the cause, it is imperative to clear up confusions before analysis proceeds too far.

Reviewing may occur at all stages of the knowledge-acquisition process, as at any stage gaps and inconsistencies may appear in the information so far assessed. For instance, once a Generic Task Model for the project has been chosen or built, it should – if at all possible – be reviewed extensively with the expert. Reviews are also useful politically, and help to keep the expert's motivation high.

Note

1. Increasingly, techniques that were once seen as special for use in eliciting 'knowledge' have been recognized as also usable as better general requirements capture techniques – perhaps an example of where KBS technology has improved the range of general software development techniques.

11 Library of Domain Roles and Inference Types

This chapter presents a library of Domain Roles and Inference Types. These are the primary components of the Inference Layer in a KADS four-layer Expertise Model, as described in Section 4.3.1. The reader should consider using selections from this library as elements in the Inference Layers of the Expertise Models that they build. Reading this chapter will also help them to understand the Generic Task Models presented in Chapter 12 and how their own Generic Task and Expertise Models can be constructed.

This chapter is divided into two parts:

- Domain Roles
- Inference Types

Both sections are structured in similar ways, consisting of an introduction, a classification and complete list, and descriptions of the Domain Roles or Inference Types themselves. After the Inference Types descriptions, a comprehensive set of examples of Inference Types in use in Inference Structure fragments is presented.

This library covers all the Inference Types and Domain Roles used in the Generic Task Model library, and more. In our experience, it is rare to need to use a new Inference Type that is not presented below (although, less rarely, a new Domain Role). However, the set described is not intended to be prescriptive. So if there is some gain in clarity or fidelity by representing the inference behaviour required by the system using a new type of Inference Type or Domain Role, then go ahead! One could even consider creating one's own (organization's) addendum to this library – ours should be treated as just a good starting point.

11.1 Domain Roles

Domain Roles define packets of static knowledge taken from the Domain Layer. They represent the roles that these pieces of knowledge play within the Inference Layer of the Expertise Model. Thus, they are more than just simple named groupings of the static knowledge, such as those obtainable from domain structures already defined in the Domain Layer. Here, for the Inference Layer, they define *how that static knowledge is used*, by identifying what actual groupings (or single items) are required for problem solving. See p. 72 for a full discussion.

Note that Domain Roles are abstractions at the Inference Layer level. When the Expertise Model is made executable via KBS Design, or when describing the 'execution' of Domain Roles during the problem-solving process, they will be realized by knowledge structures and other elements of actual static domain knowledge that they represent.

Naturally, (the names of) Domain Roles will tend to be dependent upon the particular problem domain that the future system is addressing. However, there are some common themes, and a list of these is presented below.

11.1.1   *Classification of Domain Roles*

A hierarchical classification of Domain Roles is shown in Figure 11.1. (Domain Roles are in bold type; 'bases' for roles in parentheses – see below.) This categorization can hardly be described as complete. The knowledge engineer should feel free to expand this as necessary by using appropriate named groupings of the static knowledge in his or her Expertise Model's Domain Layer.

The classification is based on the different roles knowledge and data can play in the problem-solving process. However, the groupings shown are not rigorous and some names shown could be situated in more than one place in the hierarchy in some cases. The first-levels of groupings mean:

- *Typical Input roles* – Roles usually used as the inputs to Inference Structures, to initiate problem solving.
- *Typical Intermediary roles* – Roles normally used within the body of Inference Structures, to be used during problem solving.
- *Typical Output roles* – Roles usually produced as outputs from Inference Structures, as the results of problem solving.

Apart from Domain Roles, also included in the classification in Figure 11.1 are some '*bases for roles*' (parenthesized). These are names which, *in general*, are poor choices for Domain Roles, but do describe valid types of domain knowledge frequently used in problem solving. However these pieces of knowledge are used, whatever *roles* they play, *those* are the terms that should be used for the corresponding Domain Roles. (A detailed description of the contents of Figure 11.1 appears in Section 11.1.2.)

Domain Roles (or Bases for Roles)

   Typical Input Roles

      Problem [-Statement]

        Question

     Intention

     Data

        Structured Data

           Case [-Description]

           System [-Description]

           Structural [-Description]

           Specification [Formal-]

           (State [-Description])

        Individual Datum

           Constraint

           Requirement

           Symptom

             Complaint

           Observable

           [Universum of] Possible Observables

           (Variable)

           (Value)

   Typical Intermediary Roles

      Intermediary Role of Data/Problem

        Element

        Differential

        Component

        Finding

          Evidence

        (Parameter)

        (Factor)

        (Relation)

        (Attribute)

        (Object)

        (Mathematical Model/Equation)

        (Function)

Intermediary Role of Domain Knowledge

    System Model

    Hypothesis

     Focus

    Norm

    Criterion/Criteria

    Assertion

    Action

    Method

    Model

    Conceptual Model

    Skeletal Model

    (Framework)

    (Term)

    (Database [Historical-])

  Typical Output Roles

    Solution

    Result

    Conclusion

    Decision [-Class]

    Discrepancy [-Class]

    Difference

    Results of Tasks

      Diagnosis

      Classification

      Prediction

      Design

      Plan

      Configuration

      Resource Allocation

      Schedule

      (Single Inference Type Result)

Figure 11.1
A hierarchy of
Domain Roles

Finally, a special form of Domain Role is called (because, in fact, it contains) '*support knowledge*'. This is sometimes distinguished from other Domain Roles in Inference Structures (e.g. using dashed connections to Inference Types), but is also often treated just like any other Domain Role. Support knowledge is generally associated with a single Inference Type, but could apply to more than one. It is used to control or otherwise facilitate an inference step in its processing of input knowledge to produce the output – it is the knowledge used to process other knowledge. For example, in a selection inference, the support knowledge would be the selection criterion which controls what precisely is selected from the input.

Support knowledge does not fit into the classification of Domain Roles used in this chapter and it is often debatable as to what is and what is not support knowledge. Further, it is not treated any differently in KADS in general, and hence we will not dwell on it further. But it may be useful for the reader to be aware of this special type of Domain Role in case it is found to have an influence on their developments.

For future reference the main types of support knowledge that will be encountered in this book, and their associated Inference Types, are as follows (see also Section 11.2). Note, however, that it is possible to imagine support knowledge for *most* Inference Types:

Support knowledge	Associated Inference Type
Comparison criteria →	Compare
Selection criteria →	Select
Match criteria →	Match
Grammar →	Parse
Sorting criteria →	Sort

11.1.2 Descriptions of Domain Roles

This section consists of a brief description of each of the Domain Roles as presented in the hierarchical classification shown in Figure 11.1. Remember, Domain Roles, and hence the names a knowledge engineer chooses for them, should be very dependent upon the system under consideration. However, we have tried to be generic in our descriptions below so that they can be applied and adapted easily for real systems.

Although keeping to the generic descriptions below will facilitate some standardization across the system documentation the reader will produce, sometimes one will need to use the name of one of the 'generic' Domain Roles for something more specific in the real domain. For example, if the real domain is some aspect of chemistry, and one requires a Domain Role called 'element' in their Inference Structure, then the reader should feel free to use the name 'element', even though we provide a different description below. However, to avoid confusion for those who know KADS but not the system's domain when they come to read the system documentation, this situation should be clearly noted in the documentation, e.g. 'Domain Role: "element" (not standard KADS meaning)'. In general, use our generic names for new Generic Task Models, and use as precise names as possible within Expertise Models.

The list below describes each of the Domain Roles, and bases for roles, shown in Figure 11.1. As in the figure, bases for roles are shown parenthesized – and should be avoided as names for actual Domain Roles (although they *may* describe legitimate roles, of course, if they truly exist in the domain). Examples are shown where possible. (For other examples, if rather generic ones, see the Generic Task Models in their library in Chapter 12.) The reader should be careful not to be constrained by our choice of descriptions, which are really just examples in themselves. There may be many possible uses for the Domain Role term described than we have suggested below. Use discretion and do not use the descriptions slavishly.

Typical Input Roles

Problem [-Statement]   A situation or concept requiring problem solving by reasoning; a statement describing this. (See also Complaint and Case.) For example, the description or statement of a system's failure mode. (But note that this Domain Role may not necessarily be used in failure mode situations.)

Question   A specific form of Problem Statement, consisting of a sentence expressed in order to seek information. For example, a request for a diagnosis in a system in some failure mode. (But note that this Domain Role may not necessarily be used in failure mode situations.)

Intention   A concept that has an aim or purpose to be fulfilled in the future. For example, an action to be performed by a system, as selected from a known plan.

Typical Input Roles: Data: Structured Data

Case [-Description]   A list of features and/or their relationships describing a situation; the context description of some mode of a system. (See also Problem and System.) For example, the set of values describing an object to be measured or assessed; a value or set of values of some parameter of a system that has failed.

System [-Description]   A list of functions, components and/or their relationships, describing a system of interconnected elements. Could include (descriptions of) systems ranging from biological (such as people) to computer systems. For example, a schematic of the lymphatic system in humans; a blueprint of a telecommunications network.

Structural Description   A description of the structure of a system. (See also Skeletal Model.) For example, the architecture of a computer system; the topology of a telecommunications network.

Specification [Formal-]   A detailed static or behavioural description of a system; a formal (mathematically provable) description. (Cf. System Model, which is not necessarily formal; see also System Description.)

(State [-Description])   A concept representing a well-defined condition of a system; all activity may occur on transitions between states (as in Mealy machines), or on first entering states (as in Moore machines); a description of such a condition(s). For example, the description of a failure mode of a system.

Typical Input Roles: Data: Individual Datum

Constraint   A limitation or set of limitations on some concept. (See also Requirements.) For example, the restricted range of values that a variable parameter can take during problem solving; or a heuristic rule limiting the way parts can be arranged in a framework during a configuration problem.

Requirement   A statement (partially) describing what a system or concept needs to achieve before some status is reached or capability is attained. (Cf. Constraint and Criteria.) For example, the functions a system to be configured must be able to perform.

Symptom   A concept having a known or suspected relationship with a faulty or other well-defined condition of a system. (Cf. Complaint, which does not have this latter association.) For example, a value of a parameter, or values for a set of parameters, representing the physical condition of an ill person, and associated with a disease; the set of values of alarms for a telecommunications network, associated with a state such as 'overloaded'.

Complaint   A statement representing something that has gone wrong with a system; something awry from the normal condition (as measured against a System Model, say). (See also Problem.) For example, a value or set of values for parameters of a system that is in a failure mode; a statement or set of statements about the condition of such a system.

Observable   A particular measurable concept of a system. For example, a value or set of values representing the dimensions of an entity; the value or set of values of some dynamic parameter of a system.

[Universum of] Possible Observables The complete set of concepts (i.e. parameters, variables, attributes, etc.) of a system that it is possible to measure or otherwise observe the value of. (See Observable.)

(Variable) A concept that can be associated with another concept called its value – may be distinguished from a Parameter by making Variables able to be instantiated with a new value at any time.

(Value) (See Variable.)

Typical Intermediary Roles: Intermediary Role of Data/ Problem

Element Usually defined to be the smallest component of a system or structure. For example, the concept represented by a leaf node in a *consists-of* or *part-of* hierarchy. (See Component.)

Differential The subset of things remaining in a collection after it has been filtered or selected from, or added to (i.e. like a Difference, but for collections). For example, during a diagnosis, the set of hypotheses remaining after some have been rejected.

Component A part of some system or structure. For example, a concept representing a node in a *consists-of* or *part-of* hierarchy.

Finding An (intermediary) conclusion reached by an inquiry. For example, could be used for generating an explanation whereby intermediary results of the problem solving are recorded for later recall.

Evidence A concept supporting or denying a hypothesis. (See also Symptom.) For example, a value or set of values that are consistent with a known type of failure.

(Parameter) (See Variable.)

(Factor) A concept which contributes to a result by some set of relationships; or just another word for Parameter or Variable.

(Relation) A concept representing the association between other concepts. For example, the association between neighbouring nodes used to construct a knowledge structure such as an *is-a* hierarchy.

(**Attribute**) Generally, an element of a concept or object that represents a particular aspect of that thing; attributes also can be identifiers (perhaps typed), associated with values. (See also Value and Object.)

(**Object**) A concept defining a single entity, collection of entities, or a relationship between entities; often considered in the form of a frame structure, with an identity and a set of attribute-value pairs. (See also Attribute.)

(**Mathematical Model/Equation**) A model described in terms of mathematics. (See also Formal Specification.)

(**Function**) Generally, a particular capability of a system.

Typical Intermediary Roles: Intermediary Role of Domain Knowledge

System Model   Like a System Description, but in the form of a working model of the behaviour (or whatever) of the system. System Models are used for reference purposes, such as testing against a real-world example of the system. For example, a model of the human lymphatic system in the form of a set of mathematical equations; a computer-based dynamic representation of a telecommunications network; simpler examples often used in Generic Task Models include *part-of* or *is-a* hierarchies.

Hypothesis   A proposition made as a basis for reasoning, without knowing whether it is true or not. An assumption of the solution or partial solution, made or derived during problem solving in order to continue the process through to completion (such as a 'confirmed' hypothesis). For example, possible reasons for the observed problems in a network, obtained from the knowledge of the 'most frequent causes', such as 'physical break in cable A'.

Focus   A concept which is distinguished from a collection of other concepts by being selected for some kind of special treatment. For example, a hypothesis, from a set of possible hypotheses considered during a diagnosis, which is currently the most likely and will be attempted to be verified next.

Norm A standard, reference, normal, or expected value of some concept. (Perhaps determined from some reference system, or a reference model of the system – see System Model.) For example, a value or set of values found or measured under the non-failure condition(s) of a system.

Criterion/Criteria A concept describing the aspect(s) upon which an entity can be assessed. Often used in conjunction with a term to associate it more closely with some inference or other entity, such as 'success criteria', 'comparison criteria' or 'match criteria', etc. For example, a value (or set of values) of some parameter of a system which, if it matches a value measured in the real world, implies that some state has been reached.

Assertion A statement or description of some condition or system, made for the purposes of its assessment in some way. For example, a previous diagnosis to be confirmed (verified).

Action An element of a plan that represents some behaviour that will change some part of the world. (See also Intention.) For example, any step in some plan a system knows about or which is being constructed.

Method An algorithm or approach to solving a problem.

Model A representation of a concept (usually complex), that is designed to exhibit some subset of the behaviour or other properties of the actual concept. (See also System Model.)

Conceptual Model A model of a system which only describes (i.e. 'models') what the system does and not how the system does it. A model describing a system in a fashion which is independent of representation. For example, the results of the requirements analysis for a software system.

Skeletal Model A model of a system in which the framework or structure of the system is considered, but not its contents. (See also Framework.)

(Framework) The structural relationship between components in a system, as opposed to the components themselves – how the components are connected together. For example, the form of a knowledge structure, such as a hierarchy.

(Term)   Part of or the whole subject of a predicate of a proposition.

(Database [Historical-])   A collection of facts, perhaps about the past. For example, the record of previous failures (including causes and actions, perhaps) of a system.

Typical Output Roles

Solution   The result of problem solving or reasoning. (Cf. Problem.)

Result   (See Solution.)

Conclusion   (See Solution.)

Decision [-Class]   A concept which can take the possible values resulting from a comparison between other concepts. For example, either the difference between some reference concept and a real-world concept, which represents what must be done to the real-world concept in order to make it equivalent to the reference concept; or simply what is different about the two concepts, or what is similar; the suitability of a candidate for a job, which may take the values 'accept', 'reject' or 'further interview'.

Discrepancy [-Class]   A concept representing the degree of dissimilarity between other concepts representing the expected or predicted case, and the actual case. (See also Difference, which is more general.)

Difference   A concept representing the degree of dissimilarity between other concepts. For example, a value representing the difference between the current value and the required value in some task involving searching a knowledge structure, such as in localization (see p. 000).

Typical Output Roles: Results of Tasks

Diagnosis   The result of an identification task in the search for the cause of a failure condition in some system. For example, a value or set of values representing a known type of failure which has been verified.

Classification   The result of an identification task in the search for the class or a class of some system.

Prediction   The result of a prediction task in the search for the future value(s) of some system or its future behaviour.

Design   The general or detailed arrangement or layout of the components of a system. (See also Component.) For example, the result of a design task, such as for a piece of software.

Plan   A sequence of actions to be carried out. (See Action.) For example, the sequence of actions to be carried out to perform remedial action in the event of a failure condition.

Configuration   The result of a configuration task in the search for an arrangement of components of some system which satisfies functional requirements and constraints. For example, the arrangement of printed circuit boards of different types in the shelves of a rack-style electronics cabinet.

Resource Allocation   A concept representing the assignment of an agent(s) or object(s) to an action. For example, the assignment of an action in a plan (as produced by a planning task) to a resource.

Schedule   (See Plan and Resource Allocation.)

(Single Inference Type Result)   The result of any Inference Type can easily be expressed in terms of the name of the Inference Type. For example, the output of an 'abstract' will be an 'abstraction'; the output of 'decompose' will be a 'decomposition', etc.

11.2   Inference Types

Inference Types define small packets of reasoning within the Inference Layer of the KADS four-layer Expertise Model. By 'small', we mean 'a step of inference beyond which we decide we have no need to describe in more detail'. In the Inference Layer, one creates one or more Inference Structures. These are directional graphs connecting Domain Roles together via Inference Types. (See p. 72 for a full discussion.)

Note that Inference Types are abstractions at the Inference Layer level – when the Expertise Model is made executable via KBS Design they will be realized by problem-solving functions (usually). However, when describing the general 'execution' of Inference Types during the problem-solving process they are described as performing an '*Inference Step*', i.e. an Inference Type described at the level of the domain knowledge it processes.

As with Domain Roles, (the names of) Inference Types will tend to be dependent upon the particular problem domain that the future system is addressing. However, in the case of Inference Types it has been found that there is less need to devise new ones beyond the list presented below.

11.2.1   Classification of Inference Types

A hierarchical classification of Inference Types is shown in Figure 11.2. (Inference Types are in bold.) As for the Domain Roles, the knowledge engineer should feel free to expand this as necessary by defining names appropriate to the types of reasoning required in their Inference Structures.

The classification in Figure 11.2 is based on the different ways in which domain concepts or structures of concepts (as defined by a Domain Role) are manipulated. However, there is no formality or rigour implied in this categorization – it is purely for convenience of use. In overview, the first levels mean:

- *Generate concept* – An existing concept(s) can generate a new, related concept.

```
Inference Types
        Concept Manipulation
                Generate Concept
                        Instantiate
                        Generalize
                        Classify (Identify)
                Change Concept
                        Abstract
                        Specialize (Refine, Specify)
                        Assign_Value (Change_Value)
                        Compute (Evaluate)
                Distinguish Between Concepts
                        Compare
                                Confirm
                Filter, or Home-in on Concepts
                        Select
                Associate Concepts
                        Match (Associate, Relate, Map)
        Structure Manipulation
                Build or Destroy Structure
                        Assemble (Aggregate, Compose, Augment)
                        Decompose
                Re-arrange Structure
                        Transform
                        Sort
                        Parse
```

Figure 11.2 A hierarchy of Inference Types

- *Change concept* – The values of an existing concept, or the concept itself, can change.
- *Distinguish concepts* – Concepts can be distinguished from each other.
- *Filter concepts* – Concepts may be separated out from a group.
- *Associate concepts* – Concepts may be associated with each other.
- *Build/Destroy structures* – Structured arrangements of concepts may be built or broken down.
- *Re-arrange structures* – Structured arrangements of concepts may be re-arranged.

A detailed description of the contents of Figure 11.2 appears in the next section.

11.2.2 Descriptions of Inference Types

This section consists of a brief description of each of the Inference Types as presented in the hierarchical classification shown in Figure 11.2. We describe them in terms of the things they process – their inputs and outputs. In the descriptions bear in mind that the inference process actually occurs in terms of Domain Layer elements. Thus, examples will centre on entities such as concepts, relations and structures, rather than Domain Roles. Table 11.1 at the end of the section provides a summary of all the Inference Types described in 'expressions' showing their input/outputs.

As with the classification in Figure 11.2, there is no implied formal basis for the descriptions of the Inference Types given below – we have simply tried to describe them in as precise a way as possible, without over-constraining their application. This especially applies to the example inference 'expressions' we show, using such terms as 'object', 'concept' and 'structure'. Necessarily, these are very general terms, but we have tried to make the descriptions usable. Be aware also that we have only given initial guidance on the so-called 'control knowledge' ('criteria') possible for certain Inference Types – it is possible to envisage control knowledge for Inference Types other than those we have suggested. Yet again, the reader should be careful to use his or her discretion in using the Inference Types as we describe them, according to the domain's requirements.

In the descriptions below, the following notation and semi-formal terms are used:[1]

- *(1,*)* means 'one or more'; *(*)* means 'more than one'; $\rightarrow$ means 'via the operation of the Inference Type, produces...'.

- *'Concept'* means 'a general item of knowledge or piece of information' or 'the description or name of that knowledge/information'; a concept will represent a single entity, but that entity may be singular, plural or a structured arrangement of smaller elements. (In Smalltalk-based object-oriented terminology, a concept would be an 'object' or a 'description/name of an object' – everything is an object in Smalltalk.)
- *'Object'* means 'a concept with attributes', or the name of such a concept. It is a type of variable containing other variables. It is *not* the same as a Smalltalk 'object'.
- *'Structure'* means 'a well-defined arrangement of concepts', or when without contents, the pattern/framework for such.
- *'Variable'* means 'a place-holder for a value'; *'Value'* means 'a specific concept', representing any arbitrary concept.
- *'Instance'* means 'a specific concept' which is a member of a 'class'; *'Class'* means 'a concept representing the general description or format for other concepts sharing certain common characteristics'.

Concept Manipulation: Generate Concept

Instantiate
General concept or place-holder (class/variable) → *A particular thing (instance/value)*
Instantiation consists of the assignment of value(s) to the attribute(s) of, or to the concept/structure itself, when initially, no or only some value(s) have been previously assigned. In many cases this inference is trivial, and only involves copying values into attribute slots; in others, it may be truly knowledge-based. To achieve complete instantiation, all attributes should have values assigned, and default values may be used to ensure this. Instantiation includes such things as the object-oriented notion of producing an instance from a class, and the assignment of a value to a variable in logic programming. It can be understood as a more general case of Assign_value (which is like 'instantiate (variable → value)'). It is like the opposite of Classify.

Generalize
Collection of instances (1, *) → *New concept (common to all instances)*
Generalization focuses on the common feature(s) in a collection of instances and attempts to generate a *new* concept from them, associated with the common feature(s). It may be realized using induction methods. (Cf. Classify, where common features are mapped onto an *existing* classification concept.)

Classify (Identify)
A particular thing (object + attributes) → General concept or place-holder (class)
Classification is the identification of a class description which suffices to describe the attributes of the given object. It is like the opposite of Instantiate. (Cf. Generalize, where common features are mapped onto a *new* classification concept.)

Concept Manipulation: Change Concept

Abstract
Existing instance → New instance of a more general (existing or not) class
Existing class → New more abstract class (existing or not)
Abstraction is the collecting together of a subset of the attributes from an existing concept to form a new concept; the other attributes are ignored. It is the equivalent to taking an instance of some class and generating the instance of a more general class. It is the opposite of Specialize.

Specialize (Refine, Specify)
Existing instance → New instance of a more specific class (existing or not)
Existing class → New more specific class (existing or not)
Specialization ('to make something more specific') is the addition of one or more attributes and/or values to the attributes of an existing concept to form a new concept. It is the equivalent to taking an instance of some class and generating the instance of a more specific class. It is the opposite of Abstract. It is also known as refinement ('refine') or even specification ('specify'), but the latter can be misleading.[2]

Assign_Value (Change_Value)
Concept with attribute(s) → Concept with attribute(s) with new/changed values
This consists of giving a value(s) to the attribute(s) of a concept. It can be applied either when initially no value(s) has been assigned or when existing values are simply overwritten. 'Change_Value' can be used to make the latter explicit. Like instantiation, in many cases this inference is trivial, and only involves copying values into attribute slots; in others, it may be truly knowledge-based. To achieve complete instantiation, all attributes should have values assigned, and default values may be used to ensure this. It can thus be understood as a more specific case of Instantiate.

Compute (Evaluate)

Structure (expression) → *concept of structure (result of expression's evaluation)*

Computation is the production of a value on the basis of a structure of concepts (instantiated expression) – evaluation of the structure produces the value. It does not necessarily imply an arithmetic operation. This inference often includes implicit instantiation (of the result, particularly). 'Evaluate' may be considered a less arithmetic-biased form of the inference, but this is not a formal definition. A typical use of evaluate is in the evaluation of a condition, e.g. 'A = B', or 'X is_larger_than Y', etc. In this case, two possible inputs might be first the condition structure, containing place-holders for values, and then the values themselves as the second input.

Concept Manipulation: Distinguish Between Concepts

Compare

Concepts (usually two) → *Difference value*

Comparison takes two (usually, but could be more) concepts and results in a measure of the difference(s) between them. Control knowledge ('comparison criteria') may be used as an additional input to the inference, which defines the basis for comparison, and the valid outputs from the comparison (possible 'difference values'). Typical difference values might be: 'no difference', 'insignificant difference', 'significant difference'; or 'accept', 're-evaluate', 'reject'; or 'different', 'same'. Difference values may be chosen from binary, tertiary, or n-ary sets of possible values.

Confirm

Hypothesis (possible conclusion) → *Confirmed hypothesis (conclusion)*
Concept → *Confirmed concept*

Confirm is used where a hypothesis has been found to be true thus far in problem solving, but which needs additional final checking to confirm that it is actually the conclusion. For example, one may need to check that the hypothesis corresponds to a leaf node in a hierarchy before stopping the inference process; alternatively, one may simply wish to check that there are no other true hypotheses and that this is the only one which could possibly be the conclusion. A stylistic note: although one usually wants the binary ('confirmed', 'not confirmed') output of this inference, perhaps to use to control the problem-solving sequence, in practice we usually show the output Domain Role on an Inference Structure as the confirmed hypothesis, i.e. the conclusion. Confirm can also be used for purposes other than conclusion checking, in the middle of problem solving.

Concept Manipulation: Filter, or Home-in on Concepts

Select

Collection (structured/unstructured) of objects (*) → Filtered collection of objects

This Inference Type chooses one or more objects from a collection of several objects (removing or copying the chosen object(s) from the collection). Control knowledge ('selection criteria') may be used as an additional input to the inference, to define the basis for selection. For example, it may define what attributes of the objects in the collection are examined. In the case of a selection directly upon a structured arrangement of objects there may be an implicit decomposition required first. (See Decompose.)

Concept Manipulation: Associate Concepts

Match (Associate, Relate, Map)

Collection (structured/unstructured) of objects (1,*) → Collection (structured/unstructured) of objects (1,*)

Matching means taking one or more objects and producing one or more objects which are associated with the first object(s). This is a mapping procedure. The simple case where the match is based on heuristic rules associating pairs of concepts is the most frequently used. It works by looking at the left-hand side of some expression, and where there is a match with the input to the inference, the right-hand side of the expression is output (or added to the output collection). It is also often used for bridging between different pairs of knowledge structures, such as two hierarchies. Control knowledge ('match criteria') may be used as an additional input to the inference, to define the basis for making the match. For example, it may define what attributes of the objects in the collection are to be examined or which particular heuristics are used. Match has also been called 'associate' or 'relate'.

Structure Manipulation: Build or Destroy Structure

Assemble (Aggregate, Compose, Augment)

Collection of objects (*) → Structured arrangement of objects

Assembly takes an unstructured or partially structured collection of objects and results in a more or completely structured arrangement of the objects. This inference is typically used for building knowledge structures such as hierarchies. Construction sequence, like the construction mechanism, is defined within the inference itself and hidden from the rest of the Inference Layer. Assemble can have many alternative names, depending on its context. Assemble is the opposite of Decompose.

Decompose

Structured arrangement of objects → Collection of objects (*)
(Structured arrangement of objects → Filtered collection of objects (1,))*
Decompose takes a structured or partially structured collection of objects and results in a less or completely unstructured arrangement of the objects. In its simplest form, decomposition results in no loss of objects and only the structure is removed (or ignored). However, Decompose can also result in either a single sub-assembly or even a single object, where the other sub-assemblies or objects in the input structure are ignored – this is like a combination of a Decompose followed by a Select. Decompose is typically used for breaking down existing knowledge structures such as hierarchies. Decompose, at least in its simpler form, is like the opposite of Assemble.

Structure Manipulation: Re-arrange Structure

Transform

Structured arrangement of objects → Re-arrangement of objects
A transform Inference Type converts one structure into another. There are two types of transformation. One leaves the structure the same, only re-ordering or re-positioning the elements within it; examples of this are some sorting procedures. The other assigns a new structure to the elements; an example of this is a parse operation, where a linear structure is converted to a hierarchical structure. There are many possible applications of such transformations. Note that complex forms of transformation may need to be decomposed into finer-grain inferences.

Parse

Linear arrangement of objects → Hierarchical structure of objects
Parsing involves building a hierarchy (commonly called a 'parse tree') for a linear arrangement of objects. Control knowledge ('grammar') may be defined to control the basis upon which the parsing procedure is to be carried out.

Sort

Collection of objects (*) → Sorted collection of objects
Sorting involves (re-)ordering the elements of a structured or unstructured collection of objects to form a sorted collection of those objects. At least two types may be distinguished: the sorting of an unstructured collection of objects, where the analyst may include an implicit Assemble, to build a sorted structure; or the sorting of a previously structured and perhaps partially ordered collection of objects, to form a re-arrangement

of the same structure (this latter form of sort may be considered a type of Transform). Typically, Sort will be used on lists or hierarchies. Control knowledge ('sorting criteria') may be used to define the basis for the sorting procedure.

Table 11.1 summarizes the Inference Types described above together with their associated example inference expressions.

Table 11.1 Summary of Inference Types

Inference Type	Example Inference Expression
Instantiate	General concept or place-holder (class/variable) → A particular thing (instance/value).
Generalize	Collection of instances (1, *) → New concept (common to all instances).
Classify (Identify)	A particular thing (instance) → General concept or place-holder (class).
Abstract	Existing instance → New instance of a more general (existing or not) class. Existing class → New more abstract class (existing or not).
Specialize (Refine, Specify)	Existing instance → New instance of a more specific class (existing or not). Existing class → New more specific class (existing or not).
Assign_Value (Change_Value)	Concept with attribute(s) → Concept with attribute(s) with new/changed values.
Compute (Evaluate)	Structure (expression) → concept of structure (result of expression's evaluation).
Compare	Concepts (usually two) → Difference value.
Confirm	Hypothesis (possible conclusion) → Confirmed hypothesis (conclusion). Concept → Confirmed concept.
Select	Collection (structured/unstructured) of objects (*) → Filtered collection of objects.
Match (Associate, Relate, Map)	Collection (structured/unstructured) of objects (1,*) → Collection (structured/unstructured) of objects (1,*).
Assemble (Aggregate, Compose, Augment)	Collection of objects (*) → Structured arrangement of objects.
Decompose	Structured arrangement of objects → Collection of objects (*). (Structured arrangement of objects → Filtered collection of objects (1,*)).
Transform	Structured arrangement of objects → Rearrangement of objects.
Parse	Linear arrangement of objects → Hierarchical structure of objects.
Sort	Collection of objects (*) → Sorted collection of objects.

11.2.3 Examples of Inference Types in use –
Inference Structure fragments

The diagrams in Figure 11.4 later in this section show 'Domain Roles' (see below) connected by Inference Types in *Inference Structure fragments*.[3] These illustrate the action of Inference Types in a simple format.

The Inference Structure fragments are shown alongside hypothetical examples from an imaginary problem domain (relating to cars and their owners). The examples can be viewed as representing a typical instantiation of the corresponding Inference Structure fragment, describing the fragment in typical Domain Layer (i.e. domain knowledge) terms. Figure 11.3 shows the format of the fragments (on the left-hand side) and their examples (on the right-hand side).

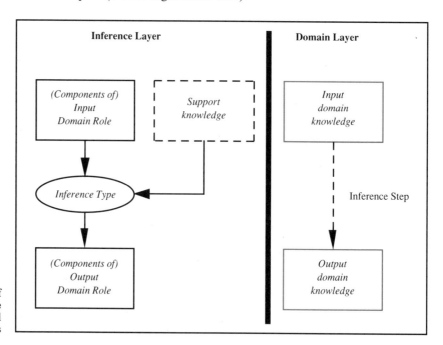

Figure 11.3 Format of Inference Structure fragments and examples

There are three important points to note about the Inference Structure fragments, concerning: Domain Roles; Support knowledge; and the 'Domain Layer' notation:

- *Domain Roles* – The words used in the boxes for Domain Roles in this section are actually not good examples of names for real Domain Roles, as they are not true *roles*. In fact, they describe the components

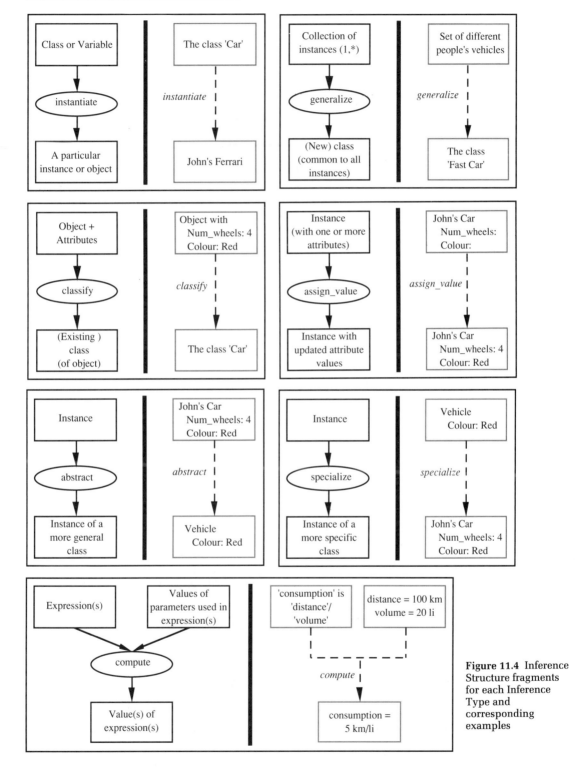

Figure 11.4 Inference Structure fragments for each Inference Type and corresponding examples

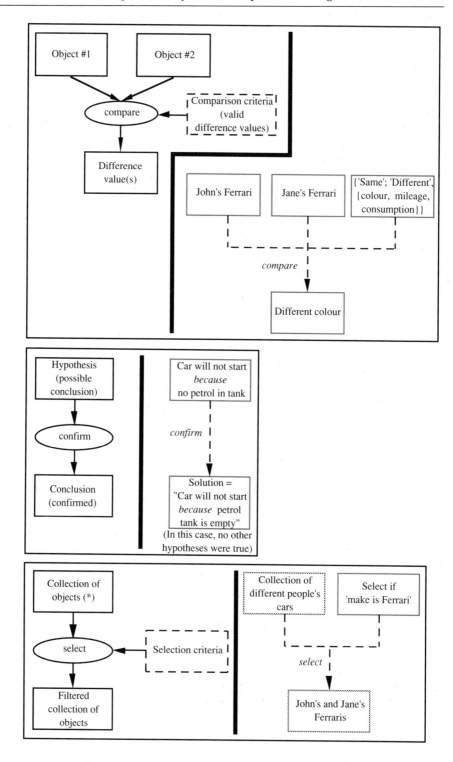

Figure 11.4
Continued

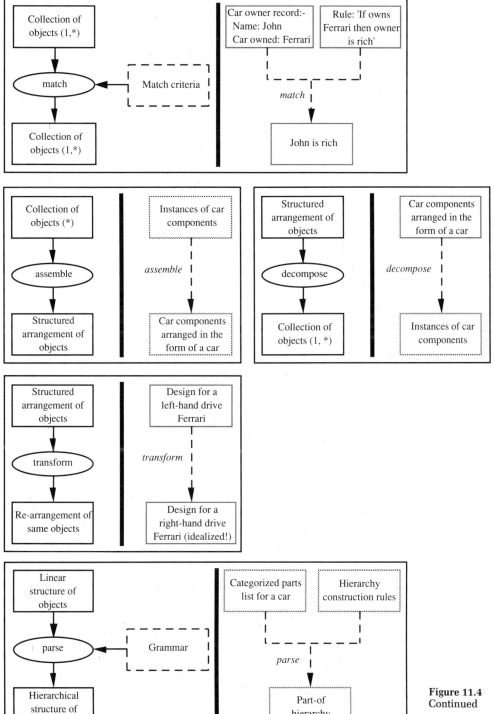

Figure 11.4
Continued

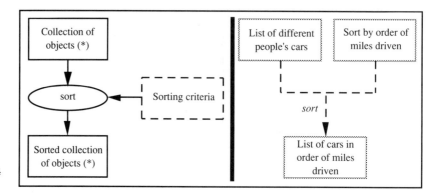

Figure 11.4
Continued

that make up an appropriate role, but *not* the role itself. This has been done to make the operation of the Inference Type clearer. (For examples of true if rather generic names for Domain Roles, see the Generic Task Models library in Chapter 12.)

- *Support Knowledge* – 'Support knowledge' Domain Role boxes are shown in some of the fragments. Support knowledge can be viewed as 'control knowledge' required by certain Inference Types in order to determine their precise inferencing operation – as opposed to the input Domain Role(s), which are the main subject of the inference. Support knowledge is not consistently shown in Inference Structures. In Figure 11.4 we have shown it explicitly, but have used a box with a dashed border to distinguish support knowledge Domain Roles from the others. In the Generic Task Model library in Chapter 12 it is generally not shown, unless the support knowledge Domain Role is produced by an Inference Type within the same Inference Structure. A similar convention could be used in the reader's own Expertise and Generic Task Models, as explicitly showing such roles tends to clutter the diagrams.[4] (See also notes on support knowledge in Section 11.1.1.)

- *'Domain Layer' notation* – The notation used in Figure 11.4 for the examples representing equivalent Domain Layer action of the Inference Type (where it then becomes an inference step processing domain knowledge) is *not* part of KADS. We have simply used it for these examples to distinguish it from the Inference Structure fragments themselves. Note that Support Knowledge is not distinguished in the 'Domain Layer' notation – it is just like other domain knowledge and shown in the same grey boxes.

Figure 11.4 shows the Inference Structure fragments and associated examples. A similar order is used for the diagrams as for the descriptions in Section 11.2.2.

Notes

1. It is sometimes useful to think of examples from the object-oriented technology world for these items, but one must bear in mind the narrower scope of its similar terms. (See Appendix 3.)
2. 'Specify' has been used in KADS models in very different ways over the years and needs careful interpretation. Frequently it has been used for inferences other than specialization. Because of this, its use in new models is best avoided if possible.
3. i.e. subsets of complete Inference Structures which contain a single Inference Type. They are really only useful to illustrate the action of the Inference Type, and not to perform any useful step of inference. Also, see p. 72 for a description of the notation for Inference Structures.
4. But the support knowledge Domain Roles should be defined in the frame descriptions for the Inference Types, at least.

12 Library of Generic Task Models

12.1 Introduction

This chapter presents a library of Generic Task Models (GTMs). These are models of problem-solving tasks that are not tied to a single domain. Instead, they have the potential to be applied to many different ones. To enable this, they are KADS Expertise Models with no Domain Layer – they consist only of Inference, Task and Strategy Layers.

Generic Task Models are used to initiate and drive the knowledge-acquisition process in Expertise Analysis, for producing Expertise Model layers other than the Domain Layer. The main aim of this library is to support the selection of appropriate Generic Task Models. (See Section 4.3.1 for more details.)

In overview, the contents of this chapter are as follows:

- This introduction, including a note on terminology in the library.
- Hierarchical summary of the models in the library, and where they sit.
- Input/output descriptions of generic tasks.
- The models themselves, split into:
  - System Analysis Models
  - System Modification Models
  - System Synthesis Models.

The origins of the models in this library vary. Some are quite old (in KADS terms); some are newly published in this book. Sometimes they have been derived from real system developments, by generalizing the Expertise Model built for such systems and removing the Domain Layer. Others have been built by carefully thinking through how the problem-solving tasks are performed, either when done by humans or, if this was particularly poorly understood, how they could be performed by some mechanism.

Readers may find this chapter quite hard going (although they should remember it is a *library*, and is not designed to be read straight through), despite the measures we have taken to aid them. It takes time and experience to think in the generic frame of reference of these models – practice makes perfect!

12.1.1 Note on terminology

The models are described using the notations for the components of the Inference, Task and Strategy Layers that were introduced in Section 4.3.1. This format should be used as a pattern for documenting these layers of the reader's own Expertise Models. However, a slightly more formal notation is used to describe Task Structures, using the following conventions:

Symbol	Meaning
'+'	Instantiated Domain Role, i.e. input or input/output.
'−'	Uninstantiated Domain Role, i.e. output only.
':'	Separates inferences (or groups) that can be carried out in parallel.
'←'	Replace left-hand side with right-hand side.
KEYWORDS	Conventional procedural statements are written in capitals.

Few of the models have detailed Strategy Layer knowledge described. This is not really a deficiency of the library but a reflection of the fact that strategic knowledge, although 'high level', is nonetheless often strongly domain-dependent. This makes it extremely hard to describe for generic tasks in a sensible, usable fashion (see Figure 12.1).

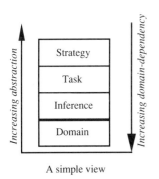

A simple view

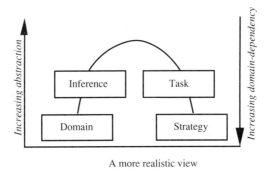

A more realistic view

Figure 12.1 Two views of levels of abstraction in KADS four-layer models

The terminology used in the Generic Task Models may seem quite difficult. This is due to the abstract and semi-formal nature of the models. Chapter 11's descriptions of Inference Types and Domain Roles should help. The names of the models themselves may provoke some difficulty, however. This will usually be because a widely used word like 'classify', say, has been used in a semi-formal way within the library, but the reader may have a different understanding of what 'classify' means. Likewise, our hierarchical breakdown of Generic Task Models is not definitive and neither are our input/output definitions of the models.

This sort of problem is inevitable while English is used to describe the models. One day, a formal notation may be developed for specifying Generic Task Models (probably bringing its own problems of readability!). Until then, we believe the different levels of description of the models presented below will be sufficient.

Table 12.1 A hierarchy of Generic Task Models in the library

Generic Task Models	Section
● SYSTEM ANALYSIS	12.4
● Identification	12.4.1
– Diagnosis	12.4.1
– Single Model Diagnosis	12.4.1
– **Systematic Diagnosis**	12.4.1
– **Localization**	12.4.1
– **Causal Tracing**	12.4.1
– Multiple Model Diagnosis	12.4.1
– **Mixed Mode Diagnosis**	12.4.1
– **Verification**	12.4.2
– **Correlation**	12.4.3
– **Assessment**	12.4.3
– **Monitoring**	12.4.4
– Classification	12.4.5
– **Simple Classification**	12.4.5
– **Heuristic Classification**	12.4.5
– **Systematic Refinement**	12.4.5
● **Prediction**	12.4.6
– **Prediction of Behaviour**	12.4.6
– **Prediction of Values**	12.4.6
● SYSTEM MODIFICATION	12.5
● Repair	12.5.1
● Remedy	12.5.2
● Control	12.5.3
● Maintenance	12.5.4
● SYSTEM SYNTHESIS	12.6
● **Design**	12.6.1
– **Hierarchical Design**	12.6.1
– **Incremental Design**	12.6.1
● Configuration	12.6.2
– **Simple Configuration**	12.6.2
– **Incremental Configuration**	12.6.2
● **Planning**	12.6.3
● **Scheduling**	12.6.4
● Modelling	12.6.5

12.2   Contents of the library – a hierarchy

Table 12.1 shows a list of the Generic Task Models in the library, in roughly the same order as presented. The models that have complete, or effectively complete models, are highlighted in bold.[1] The corresponding section/page number that contains the model, or at minimum its input/output description (see Section 12.3), is also shown.

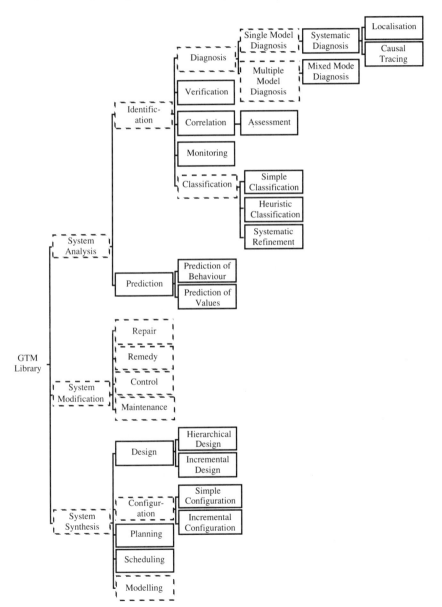

Figure 12.2 A graphical hierarchy of the Generic Task Models in the library

A graphical version of this same hierarchical classification of Generic Task Models is presented in Figure 12.2. This may be a better overview 'map' of the semantics of the arrangement of the tasks, whereas Table 12.1 will probably be more useful to help navigate this chapter.

The hierarchy, in either form, is a *type-of* hierarchy – each child task is a type of the parent task. The three main branches are:

> **System Analysis** – covers those GTMs which deal with analytic tasks – the detailed examination of the elements or structure of some entity.
> **System Modification** – covers those tasks which change a system (sometimes these are combinations of analysis and synthesis tasks, but which go on to modify the system after finding a solution) – the process of updating the attributes, structure or behaviour of some entity.
> **System Synthesis** – covers those which deal with synthesis tasks – the process of building up separate elements into a coherent single connected structure.

At the time of writing, some of the GTMs are better defined than others – notably, more work has been done with the System Analysis tasks than with the others. In Figure 12.2, the models enclosed in solid boxes are those for which a reasonably complete model exists, as listed in bold in Table 12.1; the others are given a more speculative description as they occur in sequence within the library, or are just a label for a group.

12.2.1   Aside: note on the hierarchy

There is nothing 'definitive' or 'objective' about the hierarchical format and its precise arrangement. If it is presented on its own, it usually satisfies few people – most dispute the positioning of one task or another. Its current arrangement, though, should be less controversial than most. This is because the number of 'dimensions' embedded within the hierarchy has been purposely reduced.

One possible dimension of a hierarchy is the relationship between the nodes across levels. One can have more than one such dimension in a single hierarchy, and there are many possible. The formality of dimensions also varies. In Table 12.1 and Figure 12.2 the basic dimension used is 'type of task', a relatively informal dimension ('informal' here means 'open to debate'). Other possible dimensions include: level of detail, or scope of task; quantity of data processed or under consideration; type of agent performing the task; the input/output of the task; the role of the task.

Hierarchies of generic tasks often mix different dimensions at different

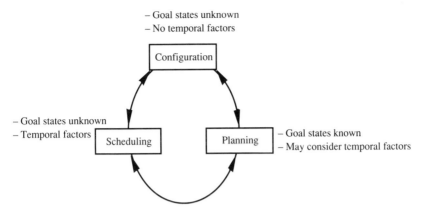

– Goal states unknown
– No temporal factors

Configuration

– Goal states unknown
– Temporal factors

Scheduling

Planning

– Goal states known
– May consider temporal factors

Figure 12.3 The typical tripartite relationship between three generic tasks: Configuration, Scheduling and Planning

levels. It is very difficult not to, as there are no 'independent variables' for generic tasks. Figure 12.3 illustrates one typical situation, where three generic tasks have a three-way relationship in the dimension of 'goal states known or unknown' and 'temporal factors considered or not'. Each box represents a task; distinguishing characteristics are shown alongside each box.

The current hierarchy of GTMs is an attempt to reduce the mixing of dimensions and reduce the confusion that results, while accepting that there is no universally accepted formal breakdown at the time of writing. They should therefore give the new reader a way into understanding the contents of the GTM library.

But we stress: *do not take the hierarchies too literally*. Because a model is placed in the 'Diagnosis' sub-tree does not mean that it can *only* be used for diagnosis – do not select GTMs solely on this basis. We have tried to minimize problematic cases, but if we were to eliminate them all, a less useful, very flat hierarchy would result. The current one is a compromise to provide a first level of guidance.

12.3   Input/output descriptions of generic tasks

There are two forms of input/output descriptions of generic tasks used in the library: an informal diagrammatic form and a summary table. Instances of the former are scattered throughout the library and the latter is presented at the end of this section.

The diagrams are shown for each major branch of the hierarchies shown in Table 12.1 and Figure 12.2, in the introduction to the corresponding section in the text. They are not a standard part of KADS, but they may be found useful nonetheless. They may help in selecting a Generic Task Model for a system by encouraging the knowledge engineer

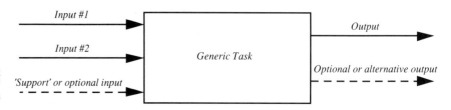

Figure 12.4 Format for generic task input/ output diagrams

to think about the knowledge-based tasks in the Process Model in terms of the pattern of their inputs and outputs. The inputs/outputs described in the Process Model might map onto some of the inputs/outputs for the generic tasks described below. They are also intended as an aid to navigating among the models.

Each input/output diagram shows a generic task represented as a box. To the left of the box are shown annotated arrows representing the inputs to the task. To the right are the outputs of the task (see Figure 12.4).

The terms used for the inputs and outputs are abstract. However, the knowledge engineer should find a good mapping between them and the corresponding Domain Roles used in the descriptions of the Inference and Task Structures of the GTMs themselves (where a model exists). For example, for a particular generic task, the inputs shown will correspond with the Domain Roles which are only ever used as inputs to Inference Types in the appropriate GTM; the outputs will correspond with Domain Roles that are only outputs from Inference Types.[2]

The reader is warned, however, that it is easy to underestimate the power of the generic models when they are presented in this form. Unfortunately, this is a factor of the abstraction performed to produce the diagrams and the limitations of the English language. For a reasonable understanding, one needs to become familiar with at least a few models in the library. This takes time, but will evolve naturally as one uses KADS.

Remember: the knowledge engineer is not trying to make a *one-to-one* mapping between GTMs and the future system's problem-solving requirements – a *close enough* match is sufficient to drive knowledge acquisition (see Section 4.3.3). Be reassured that if the knowledge engineer selects any of a subset of 'appropriate' GTMs initially, they will usually get a good final Expertise Model by refinement during subsequent analysis. GTMs exist just to get you started in the 'right direction'.

Table 12.2 shows a summary of the input/output descriptions of all of the GTMs in the library in a shorthand format using their true Domain Roles. (As in the Task Structures, '+' means the Domain Role is an input, *or* input/output[3]; '−' means it is an output only.)

Table 12.2 Summary of Generic Task Model input/ouput descriptions

Generic task	Input/output domain roles
Systematic Diagnosis	+complaint, +possible observables, −hypothesis
Localization	+faulty system description, +observable output values, −fault location
Causal Tracing	+faulty state description, +observable states, −fault cause
Mixed Mode Diagnosis	+symptoms, −possible faults
Verification	+assertion, +possible observables, −decision class
Correlation	+actual system, +reference system, −decision class
Assessment	+case description, +system model, −decision class
Monitoring	+system model, +possible observables, +selection criteria, +historical database, −decision class
Simple Classification	+observables, −variables
Heuristic Classification	+observables, −solutions
Systematic Refinement	+object description, +object attributes, −hypothesis
Prediction	+system description, +system model, −predicted system description
Prediction of Behaviour	+system description, +system model, −predicted state description
Prediction of Values	+system description, +system model, +math. model(s), +methods, −predicted values
Design	+informal problem statement, −detailed design
Hierarchical Design	+formal specification, +models, −detailed model and final spec.
Incremental Design	+conceptual model, −detailed design
Simple Configuration	+requirements, +detailed design, −difference
Incremental Configuration	+current detailed design, +requirements, −new detailed design
Planning	+plan, −resource allocation
Scheduling	+plan, +requirement

12.4   System Analysis models

These Generic Task Models are concerned with decomposing existing models of 'systems' (i.e. models of non-trivial things in the real world) into their constituent elements and observing their function, behaviour or attributes (of the whole system or its parts). They include the familiar expert tasks of fault diagnosis and classification, but also more sophisticated tasks such as qualitative reasoning (prediction).

The following is a relevant extract from the hierarchy of tasks/models shown in Table 12.1:

- SYSTEM ANALYSIS
  - *Identification*
    - Diagnosis
    - Verification
    - Correlation
    - Monitoring
    - Classification
  - *Prediction*
    - Prediction of Behaviour
    - Prediction of Values

We distinguish two major types of task in system analysis: identification and prediction. **Identification** is concerned with establishing the identity (perhaps a name or class) of a system, some aspect of a system (such as its behaviour), or of the state of a system, where the identity is selected from options already known to the task. **Prediction** is concerned with suggesting what will happen next to a system, or some aspect of it. Both tasks operate on the basis of analysing the current situation of the system. (Prediction is discussed in more detail in Section 12.4.6.) Figure 12.5 shows the appropriate input/output descriptions for the first level of these tasks/models.

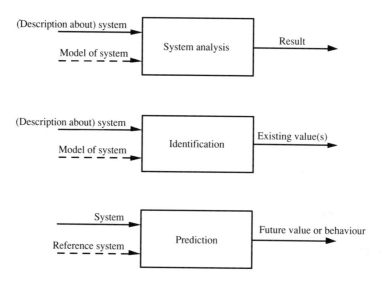

Figure 12.5

12.4.1 *System Analysis – Identification – Diagnosis*

Diagnosis is concerned with locating the cause of a difference in the observed state or behaviour of a system, compared with the expected state or behaviour. It is a specialization of 'identification'.

There is often a close relationship between diagnosis tasks and classification tasks. Basically, this means that diagnosis tasks can be used in the role of classification (and similarly, classification tasks can be used in the role of diagnosis). Two obvious examples of this are that Heuristic Classification can be used as 'heuristic diagnosis' (in fact, it was originally derived from a task playing this role); and Systematic Diagnosis is Systematic Refinement playing a diagnosis role.

The following is a relevant extract from the hierarchy of tasks/models shown in Table 12.1:

- SYSTEM ANALYSIS
  - Identification
    - *Diagnosis*
      - *Single Model Diagnosis*
        - *Systematic Diagnosis*
          - *Localization*
          - *Causal Tracing*
      - *Multiple Model Diagnosis*
        - *Mixed Mode Diagnosis*
    - Verification
    - Correlation
    - Monitoring
    - Classification
  - Prediction

There are two forms of diagnosis described in this book: single- and multiple-model-based. **Single-model diagnosis** tasks use a single type of Inference Structure. There is one basic type, Systematic Diagnosis, which has two variations, Localization and Causal Tracing. **Multiple-model diagnosis** tasks use a mixture of types of Inference Structure. Put another way, multiple-model diagnosis tasks involve an embedded combination of the single-model diagnosis tasks – for example, they may include localization, causal tracing, and even a 'classification' task, like heuristic classification. At the time of writing, there is only one multiple-model diagnosis task: Mixed Mode Diagnosis. Figure 12.6 shows the appropriate input/output descriptions for these tasks/models.

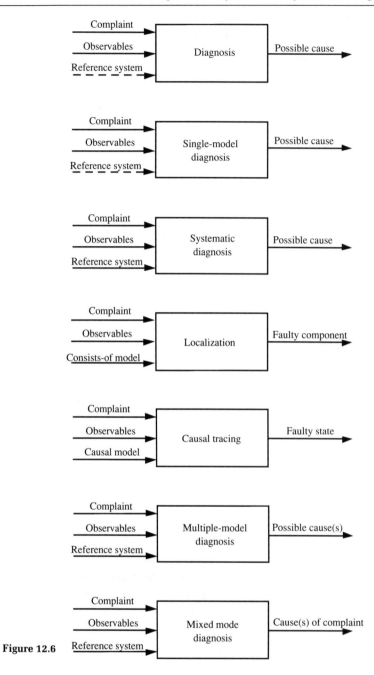

Figure 12.6

System Analysis – Identification – Systematic Diagnosis

GTM

The **Systematic Diagnosis** Generic Task Model can be sub-divided into **Localization** and **Causal Tracing**. Both have the same basic Inference Structure, shown in Figure 12.7. (In fact, yet another model uses this: Systematic Refinement[3] – p. 308.

Systematic Diagnosis is not necessarily used in isolation. For example, a classification task such as Heuristic Classification may be used initially – heuristics may be employed to focus on likely problems, then Localization or Causal Tracing may follow in order to pin down the diagnosis. Localization and Causal Tracing may also work together, alternating to systematically eliminate hypotheses. This combining of generic tasks should be considered where a single form of model is inadequate to cover

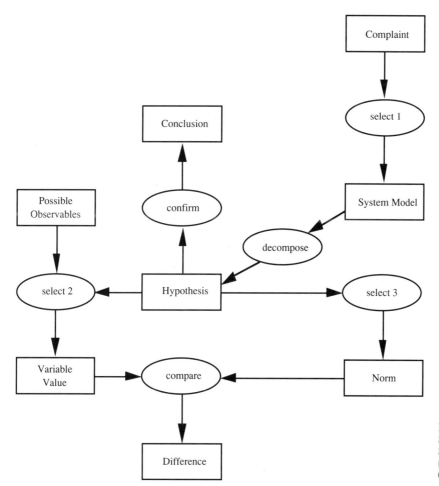

Figure 12.7 Inference Structure for Systematic Diagnosis (Localization and Causal Tracing)

the complete required problem-solving behaviour. (See Multiple Model Diagnosis in Section 12.4.1 and Mixed Mode Diagnosis on p. 280.)

Inference Structure

See Figure 12.7.

Domain Roles

The different Domain Roles for the two guises of Systematic Diagnosis are summarized in Table 12.3.

Table 12.3

Domain Role	Localization	Causal Tracing
Complaint	Faulty system description	Faulty state description
System model	*Consists-of* model	*Causes* model
Possible observables	Observable output variables	Observable states
Hypothesis	(Sub-)system containing faulty component	Sub-network of causal model
Variable value	Observed output value	Observed state
Norm[a]	Expected output	Expected state
Difference	Decision class	Decision class
Conclusion[b]	Yes/no (+fault location)	Yes/no (+fault cause)

Notes:
[a] This can be the expected value obtained under failure conditions or, equally, the expected value when in operational mode – it will depend on the structure of the knowledge used in the system model.
[b] The conclusion is really just the boolean result of checking that the hypothesis can be refined no further. The actual result of the tasks is the current hypothesis when the conclusion confirms that no further refinement is possible.

Inference Types

Although based on the same Inference Structure, the Inference Types for Systematic Diagnosis are best described separately for the two generic tasks, Localization (see p. 273) and Causal Tracing (see p. 277).

Task structure

Diagnosis starts with the selection of a system model. This will be either a *causes* network (Causal Tracing) or a *consists-of* tree (Localization). A hypothesis is generated by decomposing the model to the next increased level of detail and implicitly selecting one of the nodes (the combination of decomposed system model and selected hypothesis is sometimes referred to as the 'differential'). If the hypothesis consists of a primitive part of the original model which cannot be broken down any further, this is confirmed and the result is the faulty component; otherwise, the hypotheses in the differential are tested by comparing the variable values with the norm. If a difference is found, all other hypotheses are rejected and the sub-model is decomposed again. The process is repeated until the lowest level of decomposition is reached.

In Localization, a conclusion means that for the current hypothesis the primitives of the *consists-of* model have been reached and the location of the offending part(s) identified. In Causal Tracing a conclusion means that for the current hypothesis the state(s) responsible for the complaint has been identified.

The Task Structure, like the Inference Structure, is the same for both the Localization and Causal Tracing forms of Systematic Diagnosis. The general Task Structure is as follows:

> *Systematic Diagnosis (+complaint, +possible observables, −hypothesis) by*
>   *select 1 (+complaint, −system model)*
>   *REPEAT*
>   *decompose (+system model, −hypothesis)*
>   *WHILE number of hypotheses > 1*
>   *select 2 (+possible observables, −variable value)*
>   *select 3 (+hypothesis, −norm)*
>   *compare (+variable value, +norm, −difference)*
>   *system model ← current decomposition level of system model*
>   *UNTIL confirm (+hypothesis), i.e. system model can be decomposed*
>   *no further*

Strategies
None defined.

Example
Examples for Systematic Diagnosis are best described separately for the separate generic tasks, Localization (see p. 273) and Causal Tracing (see p. 277).

System Analysis – Identification – Localization

GTM

Localization is a type of Systematic Diagnosis (see p. 271). A typical case for the use of diagnosis by Localization is a troubleshooting task where the device in question has a specified design: for example, electro/mechanical systems. The design structure of the faulty device may be used as a basis for a Domain Layer *consists-of* model; separate components may be tested locally, independently of each other. In general, the following points may be used to identify suitable domains for its use:

- The domain knowledge is easily expressed in terms of a *consists-of* model.
- Tests may be performed on elements of the system independently of the rest.
- There is a detailed specification of system behaviour in input/output terms.

Inference Structure

Because Localization is a type of Systematic Diagnosis it uses the Inference Structure shown in Figure 12.7. Remember that the Domain Roles in that Inference Structure should be replaced with those described on p. 271.

Inference Types and Domain Roles

Select 1

The diagnosis starts with the selection of a *consists-of* model.

Input:	*Complaint.* Problem statement about a system with at least one faulty component.
Output:	*System Model.* A *consists-of* hierarchy of components, or a sub-model thereof.
Method:	Direct association.
Knowledge:	Knowledge of system's behaviour and structure, and available System Models.

Decompose

The model is decomposed into sub-models at the next level of the hierarchy, and one node is selected as the hypothesis.

Input:	*System Model.* As above.
Output:	*Hypothesis.* A part (sub-model) of the system containing the faulty component.
Method:	Descending *consists-of* tree.
Knowledge:	*Consists-of* structure of system.

Select 2

A variable value is selected from the observable values output from (part of) the system at the current level of analysis.

Input:	*Hypothesis.* As above.
	Possible Observables. All possible observable output variables (at the current level).

Output: *Variable Value.* The selected, observed output variable.
Method: Generate and test.
Knowledge: Knowledge of test methods.

Select 3
The output norm (i.e. the expected, correct output for a given input to
the faulty component) is identified.
Input: *Hypothesis.* As above.
Output: *Norm.* The expected output.
Method: Direct association.
Knowledge: Knowledge of system behaviour. May use the System
             Model for this.

Compare
Compares the variable value with the norm.
Input: *Variable Value.* As above.
             Norm. As above.
Output: *Difference.* The difference between the expected and the
             observed output. Used to iterate the procedure by
             detecting whether the current hypothesis is nearer the
             solution or not.
Method: Compares values or functions.
Knowledge: Significance of differences.

Confirm
Confirms that a hypothesis is the conclusion, i.e. the bottom of the
decomposition process has been reached and the fault found.
Input: *Hypothesis.* As above.
Output: *Conclusion.* Yes or no; the part of the system at fault
             may be output as a side effect of 'yes' – it is the current
             hypothesis.
Method: Primitive part of model reached. Could use a verification
             task, if required.
Knowledge: Knowledge of system structure.

Task Structure
The Task Structure, like the Inference Structure, is the same for both
Localization and Causal Tracing within Systematic Diagnosis (see p. 271).

Strategies
None defined.

Example
Typical applications of Localization might be in the diagnosis of a faulty

car, video recorder or computer. Taking the faulty car case, the task proceeds as follows:

1. The car will not start. First, select an appropriate *consists-of* system model for a faulty car, e.g. a repair manual describing a breakdown of all the parts of the car.
2. Decompose the description of the car by one level, i.e. major sub-systems such as bodywork, engine, transmission, electrics, etc. Select one to focus on as a hypothesis, e.g. electrics. (We could choose more than one to check at a time if we like.)
3. Select from the possible observations we could make about the actual state of the car, one appropriate to the current hypothesis, e.g. since we are looking at electrics, we could choose any of: operation of the lights, operation of the starter motor, operation of the horn, etc.
4. Select from the current hypothesis, electrics, normal values for the attributes of that sub-system, i.e. the expected operation of the lights (they should come on), starter motor (it should turn), horn (it should honk), etc.
5. Compare these expected values with their actual values; where there is a difference, this indicates that the fault probably does lie in the electrics sub-system, the current hypothesis; where there is not, either try another pair of attributes in this sub-system or backtrack to look at another sub-system, re-selecting another hypothesis at the current level of decomposition of the system model, e.g. the engine.
6. Assuming we found that the lights did not operate, suggesting that the electrics sub-system is faulty, now confirm whether the hypothesis '(fault in) electrics' is the conclusion by seeing whether it is at its lowest level of decomposition. Of course, it is not, since we could break down the sub-system further using the system model into lights, switches, wiring, etc.
7. Hence, taking 'electrics' as the new system model, go back to step 2 and decompose the electrics sub-system one level and select a new hypothesis, e.g. lights. And so on...
8. As soon as a confirmed hypothesis is found, by the fact of it corresponding to a lowest level of decomposition (e.g. the repair manual describes no further detail in this area of its parts breakdown), stop, and the current hypothesis is the fault's location. (There could be other reasons to stop, such as reaching the most economic repair level – no point in changing components in an engine management unit, just replace the whole unit.)
9. If no confirmed hypothesis is ever found, the task has failed.

System Analysis – Identification – Causal Tracing

Causal Tracing is a type of Systematic Diagnosis (see p. 271) and is typically used in the troubleshooting of electromechanical devices, like Localization. However, unlike Localization, a *consists-of* model (such as a design description) of the faulty system is not needed; instead, a *causes* model is used. Prediction (see Section 12.4.6) could be used to generate this. Pointers to the suitable use of Causal Tracing are:

- The possibility of explaining the system in terms of causal relations, i.e. when you need to explain what causes what – in order to better prescribe a solution: for example, the mechanical interactions in an engine or the causal relations in a medical domain.
- The possibility of obtaining data on a significant number of the states the model may progress through, i.e. when you need to search for as many reasons as possible: for example, any safety-critical system or possible reasons for an aircraft to have crashed.

Inference Structure

Because Causal Tracing is a type of Systematic Diagnosis it uses the Inference Structure shown in Figure 12.7. Remember that the Domain Roles in that Inference Structure should be replaced with those described on p. 271.

Inference Types and Domain Roles

Select 1

The diagnosis starts with the selection of a causal network.

Input: *Complaint.* Problem statement describing a system's faulty state.

Output: *System Model.* (Part of) the causal net – a network linking the possible states of a system by 'causes' relationships.

Method: Match faulty state to full model; may use heuristics.

Knowledge: Causal links between states of the model.

Decompose

Divides the causal net into sub-nets by taking a state and decomposing it into sub-states, and one state is selected as the hypothesis.

Input: *System Model.* As above.

Output: *Hypothesis.* A sub-net containing the faulty state.

Method: Direct association.

Knowledge: Knowledge of the causal net.

Select 2

Selects a state from the set of possible observable states at the current level of analysis.

Input: *Hypothesis*. Generally, the top state of the current subnet (i.e. its root).

Possible Observables. All possible observable states of the system (at the current level).

Output: *Variable Value*. The selected, observed output variable.

Method: Generate and test.

Knowledge: Causal net, and test methods.

Select 3

The norm (i.e. correct, expected value of the state) is identified.

Input: *System Model*. As above.

Output: *Norm*. The expected state.

Method: Direct association.

Knowledge: Knowledge of system behaviour. May use the System Model for this.

Compare

Compares the variable value with the norm.

Input: *Variable Value*. As above.

Norm.   As above.

Output: *Difference*. The difference between the expected and the observed. Used to iterate the procedure by detecting whether the current hypothesis is nearer the solution or not.

Method: Compares values of states.

Knowledge: Significance of differences.

Confirm

Confirms that a hypothesis is the conclusion, i.e. the bottom of the decomposition process has been reached and the fault found.

Input: *Hypothesis*. As above.

Output: *Conclusion*. Yes or no; the faulty state may be output as a side effect of 'yes' – it is the current hypothesis.

Method: Test for bottom of sub-net.

Knowledge: Knowledge of system structure.

Task Structure

The Task Structure, like the Inference Structure, is the same for both Localization and Causal Tracing within Systematic Diagnosis (see p. 271).

Strategies

None defined.

Example

Typical applications of Causal Tracing might be just as those for Localization. Taking the faulty car case again, the task proceeds as follows:

1. The car won't start (engine won't fire). First, select an appropriate *causes* system model for a faulty car, e.g. a set of fault consequences along the lines of:

    {starter motor stuck} OR {no power to starter motor} → {starter motor won't turn} → {engine won't turn} → {engine won't fire}

    {no petrol in tank} OR {leak in petrol feed} OR {petrol pump not working} → {no petrol in engine) → {engine won't fire} OR {engine stops}.

2. Decompose the causal model by backing up one level from the complaint (observed symptom(s)), giving a set of possible hypotheses about why the engine won't fire, e.g. {engine won't turn} OR {no petrol in engine} OR {no spark to plugs}

3. Select from the possible observations or tests we could make about the actual state of the car, any which can be used to confirm or deny any of these current hypotheses, e.g. to test {no petrol in engine}, disconnect the feed from the petrol pump and observe what happens when the ignition is turned on.

4. Select from the same hypothesis, i.e. {no petrol in engine}, normal values for the selected test or observation, in this case 'no flow of petrol when ignition is turned on'.

5. Compare these expected values with the actual values found; where there is a match (no difference), this indicates that the hypothesis {no petrol in engine} is confirmed; where there is a difference, either try another test on the same hypothesis or select another hypothesis at the current level of decomposition of the causal model, e.g. {no spark to plugs}.

6. Assuming we found a lack of petrol flow, suggesting {no petrol in engine} is true, now confirm whether this hypothesis is the conclusion by seeing whether it is at its lowest level of decomposition (i.e. whether it represents a 'root cause' within the model). Of course, it is not, since we could trace the fault state back further using the system model into {no petrol in tank} OR {leak in petrol feed} OR {petrol pump not working}, etc.

7. Hence, taking {no petrol in engine} as the new system model, go back to step 2 and decompose this state one level and select a new

hypothesis, e.g. {no petrol in tank}. And so on... .

8. As soon as a confirmed hypothesis is found, by the fact of it corresponding to a lowest level of decomposition (i.e. the system model describes no possible underlying cause of {no petrol in tank}), stop, and the current hypothesis is the fault's cause.

9. If no confirmed hypothesis is ever found, the task has failed.

GTM

System Analysis – Identification – Mixed Mode Diagnosis

Mixed Mode Diagnosis is the single form of Multiple Model Diagnosis – see Section 12.4.1. Multiple Model Diagnosis means diagnosis through the (implicit) use of a combination of more than one single-model-based diagnosis task.

This task is concerned with identifying faults with a system, given a set of complaints, using a combination of the essence of the Localization and Causal Tracing tasks, together with Heuristic Classification (although the derivation of this is not immediately apparent nor important). It supports the transformation of more than one simultaneous complaint into hypotheses.

Inference Structure

See Figure 12.8.

Inference Types and Domain Roles

Transform

An observable symptom is transformed into a structure which can act as a hypothesis. (This can be analogous to the English-language convention of making a question out of a statement by the addition of a question mark.)

Input: *Symptoms*. A statement of any problem requiring attention by the system. Where several symptoms have been observed, this is expected to be the most obvious or important one. Other symptoms may be viewed as separate complaints (if thought to be independent) or a part of the possible observables (if not).

Output: *New Hypotheses*. Statements of belief about the fault, e.g. that it lies within a particular sub-system or is of a particular type.

Method: Abstraction or specification (to fill in the default slots).

Knowledge: Knowledge about the characteristics of particular symptoms.

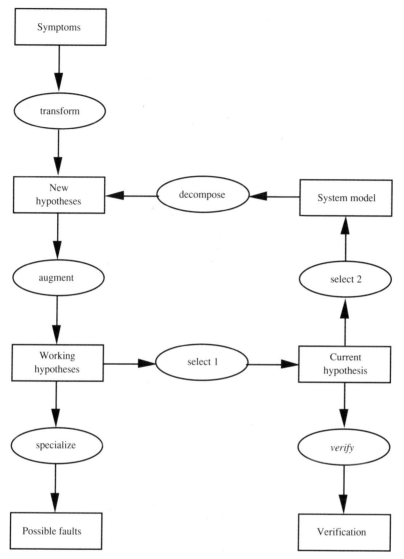

Figure 12.8 Inference Structure for Mixed Mode Diagnosis (call to Verification task shown in italics)

Augment

The number of hypotheses in the working set of hypotheses is increased by the addition of a new hypothesis. This is a special case of the transform.

Input: *New Hypotheses.* As above.

Output: *Working Hypotheses.* A set of hypotheses which have been identified but not yet ruled out. These may be given degrees of likelihood. This domain role may also contain some dependency information, e.g. H1 and H2 are mutually exclusive (so affirming one would rule out the other automatically). Sometimes called the 'differential'.

Method: Insert, in order.

Knowledge: Knowledge about the structure of the differential, knowledge about the relationships between hypotheses.

Select 1

A particular hypothesis is chosen from the set of working hypotheses on the basis of priority, suitability, details, etc.

Input: *Working Hypotheses.* As above.

Output: *Current Hypothesis.* A hypothesis which forms the current focus of attention (and is therefore sometimes called the 'focus'), e.g.

1. potentially faulty sub-system
2. potential fault type
3. potential fault specification

Method: Possibly heuristic match plus some kind of ordering.

Knowledge: Knowledge about priorities of hypotheses and knowledge about preferability of hypotheses.

Select 2

A new system model is chosen on the basis of the type of the current hypothesis under consideration, from a library of models or from the previously decomposed system model.

Input: *Current Hypothesis.* As above.

Output: *System Model*: e.g. a graph of possible causes of faults (causal network) or part-of model, etc., used at the current level of decomposition (see Decompose).

Method: Possibly heuristic match.

Knowledge: Knowledge about types of system model available.

Decompose

A new hypothesis is generated by decomposing the system model down by one level of abstraction. (The decomposed system model is used next time around instead of the system model, thus taking a more precise viewpoint each time.)

Input: *System Model.* As above.

Output: *New Hypotheses.* As above.

Method: For models expressed as relations, the match is by association, using the root node as a selector. For models expressed as a rule base, it is a process of matching all rules which relate to the given focus (equivalent to specifying a conflict set).

Knowledge: System model (causal, part-of, etc.).

Specialize

The (hopefully reduced) set of working hypotheses is used to generate a solution in terms of the most likely fault definitions (possibly ordered in some way). These definitions may be associated with remedies.

Input: *Working Hypotheses*. As above. Although only verified hypotheses are bothered to be specialized by this inference.

Output: *Possible Faults*. An ordered set of verified hypotheses which form the result of the diagnostic task.

Method: Hierarchical or rule-based specialization.

Knowledge: Knowledge on how to order and present fault definitions; knowledge about remedies.

Verify

Checks to see if the current hypothesis conflicts with the observed behaviour or state of the faulty system. If it does not, the current (verified) working hypotheses can be specialized into a diagnosis and the task concluded; otherwise the task must continue.

Input: *Current Hypothesis*. As above.

Output: *Verification*. Two alternatives: the current hypothesis is or is not consistent with the system's observables.

Method: Use 'Verification' task – see Section 12.4.2.

Knowledge: Heuristics defining how to confirm a hypothesis.

Task Structure

Mixed Mode Diagnosis starts by a transformation of a set of symptoms into hypotheses which are then used to augment a set of working hypotheses. A particular hypothesis can then be selected from this set to help generate a new hypothesis. This is done by decomposing an appropriate system model or sub-model (if previously decomposed). A solution is generated ('specialized') when the system model can no longer be decomposed and hence the lowest level of decomposition has been reached; alternatively, completion may be defined to occur when the current hypothesis is verified.

The Inference Structure allows for more than one fault to be handled by the system. Thus, a solution that is generated ('specialized') from the working hypotheses may leave other hypotheses still active that correspond to pending complaints. Different system models can also be used (chosen first time around the task), depending upon the forms of hypotheses generated by the symptoms.

Mixed Mode Diagnosis (+symptoms, −possible faults) by
  Create working hypotheses set by
    FOR each symptom DO
      transform (+symptom, −new hypothesis)
      augment (+new hypothesis, +working hypotheses)
  Refine working hypotheses set by
    UNTIL working hypotheses specializable and verified DO
      select 1 (+working hypotheses, −current hypothesis)
      (verify (+current hypothesis, −verification) OR
        (select 2 (+current hypothesis, −system model)
        decompose (+system model, −new hypothesis)
        augment (+new hypothesis, +differential)))
  Produce diagnosis by
    specialize (+working hypotheses, −possible faults)

For a description of the Task and Inference Layers for 'verify', refer to the Verification Generic Task Model described in Section 12.4.2.

Strategies

This is a complex task as it can work with a rich set of hypotheses and corresponding system models, resulting in a sophisticated run-time behaviour. The strategic knowledge should attempt to capture and separate out the different ways of operating the task according to the types of hypotheses being dealt with in its particular application. However, no particular strategic guidance has been defined in the current state of the art.

Example

Typical applications of Mixed Mode Diagnosis might be in the diagnosis of multiple faults reported on a production line or other complex control system, such as a nuclear power station. Taking the production line case, the task proceeds as follows:

1. A series of fault conditions are reported. First, build an initial working hypotheses set by transforming these symptoms into a form which can be processed (as hypotheses), e.g. 'overload alarm on conveyor 1' is rewritten as 'conveyor 1: state: overload'.
2. Add the new hypotheses to the current set of working hypotheses; the first time around this means that the working hypotheses just consist of ['conveyor 1: state: overload']. Do this for each symptom, augmenting the working hypotheses set.
3. Now try to refine the working hypotheses to reach a diagnosis by selecting one of them according to some criterion such as 'most

urgent'. This becomes the current hypothesis, e.g. 'conveyor 1: state: overload'.

4. Take the current hypothesis and either (i) verify that it does not conflict with the observed state of the production line (clearly in this case it does not – although conflicting alarms are feasible) or (ii) derive new hypotheses.

5. Derive new hypotheses by first selecting a reference description of the production line appropriate to the current hypothesis, e.g. select a causal model of the production line because the current hypothesis has an instantiated state variable (equally, one could select a *consists of* model to localize the problem with conveyor 1, rather than causal trace). Decompose the causal model by one level of increased detail and pick the first state at this level as a new hypothesis, e.g. 'conveyor motor turns gearbox, gearbox turns drive pulley, drive pulley turns belt...', new hypothesis is 'conveyor motor turns gearbox?' Augment the working hypotheses set with this new hypothesis, so that it now contains ['conveyor motor turns gearbox?', 'conveyor 1: state: overload'].

6. Continue refining the working hypotheses, further decomposing the current system model and/or selecting new system models.

7. As soon as one or more hypotheses are verified and specializable into diagnoses, the task can output results.

12.4.2   *System Analysis – Identification – Verification*

Verification determines whether an assertion made about a system is consistent with (at least some of) the actual values of the observables of the system. It is frequently used as an adjunct to other tasks, typically in the guise of a 'verify' Inference Type – for example, see Mixed Mode Diagnosis on p. 280. It can also be thought of as a more general case of the 'confirm' Inference Type – see Section 11.2.

The following is a relevant extract from the hierarchy of tasks/models shown in Table 12.1:

*   SYSTEM ANALYSIS
    *   Identification
        *   Diagnosis
        *   *Verification*
        *   Correlation
        *   Monitoring
        *   Classification
    *   Prediction

Figure 12.9 shows the appropriate input/output descriptions for this task/model.

Figure 12.9

Inference Structure
See Figure 12.10.

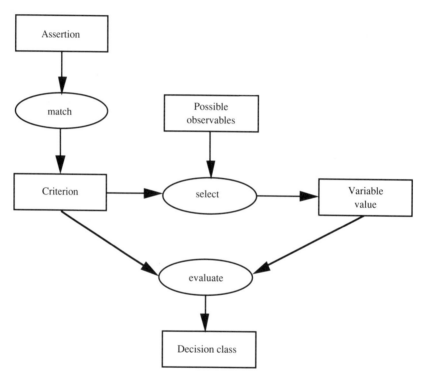

Figure 12.10
Inference
Structure for
Verification

Inference Types and Domain Roles
Match
The assertion is associated with a condition for affirmation or denial.

Input:	*Assertion*. A fact that require verification.
Output:	*Criterion*. A condition, possibly involving many variables and tests, which affirms or denies the assertion.
Method:	Heuristic match.
Knowledge:	Matching rules for association of criteria with hypotheses.

Select

The criterion is used to select one or more variables which can be used to verify or negate the assertion.

Input: *Criterion*. As above.

Possible Observables. Any observable parameter or state, the value of which can be used to deny or substantiate the assertion.

Output: *Variable Value*. The value of a particular observable parameter.

Method: Generate and test.

Knowledge: Knowledge about test methods, knowledge about how to obtain variable values.

Evaluate

The variable value is checked against the criterion by evaluating the condition with the variable value.

Input: *Criterion*. As above.

Output: *Decision Class*. The result of evaluating a criterion – usually produces an 'accept', 'reject' or 'unable to evaluate' type result, but there are many other possibilities.

Method: Expression evaluation (perhaps lazy evaluation) using the instantiated variable values to evaluate the criterion.

Knowledge: Significance of difference (e.g. tolerances).

Task Structure

There are three main possible Task Structures for the verification of assertions against observables:

- *Goal-driven* – Criteria cause the appropriate observables to be obtained.
- *Data-driven* – Criteria are evaluated according to whatever observables are available – the 'select' is ignored.
- *Mixture of both* – Criteria cause the appropriate observables to be obtained, but (other) criteria can be evaluated if different observables are available – also called 'mixed initiative'.

```
/* Goal-driven */
Verification (+assertion, +possible observables, −decision class) by
    match (+assertion, −criterion)
    UNTIL conclusion reached DO
        select (+criterion, +possible observables, −variable value)
        Obtain selected variable value
        evaluate (+criterion, +variable value, −decision class)
```

```
/* Data-driven */
Verification (+assertion, +possible observables, −decision class) by
    match (+assertion, −criterion)
    UNTIL conclusion reached DO
      Obtain variable value
      evaluate (+criterion, +variable value, −decision class)
```

(Note: the data-driven task could also cause the selection of a particular criterion, documentable by reversing the left-to-right arrows on the 'select' in the inference structure. Alternatively, it could have the available observables influencing the match from the original assertion, i.e. the data driving which assertion to verify. In this case, one would rewrite the above Task Structure to obtain the variable value(s) at the start of the task and possibly amend the inference structure to link the possible observables to the assertion via a 'select' inference type.)

```
/* Mixed initiative */
Verification (+assertion, +possible observables, −decision class) by
    match (+assertion, −criterion)
    UNTIL conclusion reached DO
      select (+criterion, +possible observables, −variable value)
      Obtain selected or other variable value
      evaluate (+criterion, +variable value, −decision class)
```

(Note: as in the data-driven task, the result of obtaining a different value from that selected could be defined to cause the selection of a different criterion (implicitly reversing and then re-firing the 'select' inference), or even cause a different assertion to be considered.)

Strategies

Given the three basic Task Structures for verification, strategic knowledge should describe if and when choices should be made between them. Otherwise, a fixed strategy should be documented, i.e. the use of just one of the Task Structures.

Example

Verification has very wide applicability. Taking the production line example used for Mixed Mode Diagnosis (see p. 280), in goal-driven form the task proceeds as follows:

1. The assertion is 'conveyor motor turns gearbox?'
2. Match this onto the criterion 'gearbox speed > 0?'
3. Select 'gearbox speed' from the possible observables; obtain the data; return its value '100 rpm'.

4. Instantiate the criterion 'gearbox speed > 0?' with the value obtained, giving '100 > 0?'; evaluate it, giving 'VERIFIED', say.
5. Since this was the only condition found in the criterion, the task stops, returning this result.
6. Obviously, if the gearbox speed was found to be '0 rpm', the task would instead return the result 'CONFLICT', say; alternatively, if the gearbox speed could not be determined, the task would return the result 'CANNOT_DETERMINE', say.

12.4.3 System Analysis – Identification – Correlation

GTM

Correlation is concerned with comparing two (or more, but primarily two) entities (systems), and producing some result on the basis of that comparison. It is particularly familiar in the guise of one of its specializations, **Assessment** – see p. 294.

The following is a relevant extract from the hierarchy of tasks/models shown in Table 12.1:

- SYSTEM ANALYSIS
  - Identification
    - Diagnosis
    - Verification
    - *Correlation*
      - *Assessment*
    - Monitoring
    - Classification
  - Prediction

Figure 12.11 shows the appropriate input/output descriptions for these tasks/models.

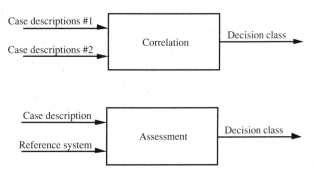

Figure 12.11

For Correlation itself, note that the Generic Task is of a particularly general nature. It is very useful whenever a problem-solving process involves a non-trivial comparison between two (or more) concepts, states, systems, etc. Essentially, it centres around a compare inference, but with potentially very flexible pre-processing of the entities to be compared. (Cf. Heuristic classification, which wraps general pre- and post-processing inferences around a core heuristic match inference – see p. 305.) It could be used where one of the inputs is derived from a measurement in the real world and the other is derived from some internal reference model ('system model'); alternatively, it could be used to compare the similarities/dissimilarities between two real-life concepts. Correlation model is described below.

Inference Structure
See Figure 12.12.

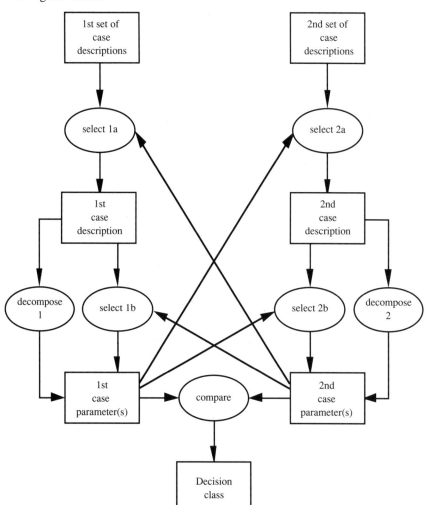

Figure 12.12 Inference Structure for Correlation

Domain Roles

1st/2nd Set of Case Descriptions

A set of statements describing particular instances or circumstances.

1st/2nd Case Description

A statement describing a particular instance or circumstance.

1st/2nd Case Parameters

A set of parameters describing some part of a particular instance or circumstance.

Decision Class

The result of the correlation – a measure of the similarity or difference between the two cases.

Inference Types

Select1a and 2a

Selects a particular case description from the full input set, perhaps on the basis of the other case's parameters.

Input:	*1st/2nd set of case descriptions.*
Output:	*1st/2nd case description.*
Method:	Heuristic association, unification, etc.
Knowledge:	Selection criteria.

Select1b & 2b

Selects a parameter or set of parameters from a particular case description, perhaps on the basis of the other case's parameters.

Input:	*1st/2nd case description.*
Output:	*1st/2nd case parameters.*
Method:	Heuristic association, unification, etc.
Knowledge:	Selection criteria.

Decompose 1 and 2

Decomposes a particular case description in order to produce a parameter or set of parameters contained within it.

Input:	*1st/2nd dase description.*
Output:	*1st/2nd case parameters.*
Method:	Heuristic association, navigation of a *part-of* hierarchy, etc.
Knowledge:	Structural knowledge of how the case descriptions are constructed.

Compare

Compares the parameters from the two cases in order to produce a description of the similarities or differences between the cases.

Input:	*1st/2nd case parameters.*

Output: *Decision class.*
Method: Attribute matching, structure matching, heuristic match-
               ing, etc.
Knowledge: Comparison criteria.

Task Structure

Correlation is a particularly general task, and any individual Task
Structure used will be only one of many possible. Two main modes of
operation are as follows.

The first is when one of the case descriptions is based in the real world
and the other is based in a model of part of the real world. Correlation is
then attempting to compare reality with expectations. The second mode
of operation is when correlation receives two (or more – but the
Inference Structure shown above is for two) sets of case descriptions,
both derived from the real world. Correlation is then attempting to
compare two different realities.

Another important variation in the way Correlation will work is
whether the two branches leading to the comparison will operate in a
pair-wise fashion (both doing similar operations in parallel), or whether
all or some of the preparation for one or other cases can be done up-
front. There are also built-in redundancies in the task. For example, the
decompose Inference Types are only needed if the case descriptions being
processed are structured in some way. Another example of redundancy is
if single case descriptions can be input to Correlation, or if only one of
them is in a set. Then select1a and/or select2a may not be required.

There are too many possibilities for Task Structures to give detailed
examples, but the following gives an idea of one possible variation of the
general approach. First, note that in the Task Structure below we have
rewritten the Domain Roles to be more readable (if slightly less generic),
in the form of correlating the state of some real-world system with that of
a reference system by examining the state variables:

1st set of case descriptions → Reference system (description)
1st case description   → Reference state (description)
1st case parameter   → Reference state variable
2nd set of case descriptions → Actual system (description)
2nd case description   → Actual state (description)
2nd case parameter   → Actual state variable

Correlation (+actual system, +reference system, −decision class) by
    select1a (+reference system, −reference state)
    select2a (+actual system, −actual state)
    REPEAT

select1b (+reference state, −reference state variable)
select2b (+actual state, −actual state variable)
compare (+reference state variable, +actual state variable, −decision class)
UNTIL no more parameters in reference state

Strategies

Because the correlation Inference Structure is particularly flexible and there are many possible Task Structures, there is great potential for having strategic knowledge determine the particular Task Structure used. This knowledge could be based on such factors as the availability of data, the format or structure of the data, the level of abstraction of the data, changes in these factors over time, etc.

Example

We used the Correlation Generic Task Model in the case study example in Chapter 4 – see Section 4.3.3. Taking the particular example of correlating a problem description against the list of previous incidents stored in the incident database ('Compare Against Existing Problems', Task 2.5 in the Process Model for the case study), the task proceeds as follows:

1. In this case the current problem description is in a form which requires no pre-processing before comparison (described in terms of a hardware–software–problem-type tuple – see case study examples in Chapter 4). Thus, the current problem description can map straight onto the '1st case parameters' in the correlation Inference Structure. None of the preceding inferences on the left-hand side are required.
2. On the right-hand side, though, a previous incident is obtained from the incident database in a more general form. The entire incident database corresponds to the '2nd set of case descriptions' in the Inference Structure. A particular incident is selected by 'select 2a' to be checked against the current problem description. However, the selected incident first needs to be decomposed into its hardware–software–problem-type tuple, which is done by 'decompose 2'.
3. The two sets of case parameters in their tuple forms are then in a comparable state. They are compared and the 'decision class' is an incident comparison result, i.e. the label 'INCIDENT_COMPARISON' plus one of 'SUCCESS, 'FAILURE' or 'INSUFFICIENT_DATA' + Problem Data. (See the Process Glossary examples in Section 4.1 to check these results.)

GTM

System Analysis – Identification – Assessment

Assessment is a type of Correlation task. A case is assessed against and in terms of a system model so that it may be classified as belonging to one of a set of decision classes. These are specified in advance and depend upon the type of assessment required. Examples of situations where this Generic Task Model might be appropriate include the assessment of: the suitability of an applicant for a job; the legal status of a company or individual with respect to liability in a bankruptcy case; or the suitability of a tool to be used in support of some activity.

Assessment can be understood as two classification tasks: the finding of applicable categories in the case description for assessment (abstraction), and classifying this new description according to the norms of the system model (classification). This differs from a 'simple classification' Generic Task Model in that the correct classification of the case is not 'given' but must be *interpreted* in terms of the system model.

There are three main elements to assessment: (1) abstract the case description (optionally in terms of a selected norm); (2) select the norms for the system model (optionally according to an abstracted case description); (3) compare these two.

The assessment process may be either *model driven* or *case driven*. If there is sufficient need the assessment task may be done recursively or embedded in other assessment tasks. The Inference Structure for assessment is shown in Figure 12.13.

Inference Structure
See Figure 12.13.

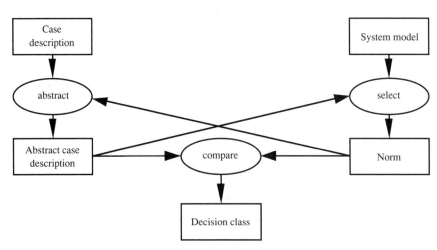

Figure 12.13
Inference Structure for
Assessment

Inference Types and Domain Roles

Abstract

The abstraction selects and presents the attributes of the case description which are also attributes of the system model.

Input: *Case description.* A structure containing specific attribute-object pairs.

    Norm. The appropriate attributes and typical or crucial values for the assessment to be performed.

Output: *Abstract case description.* Concepts in the *Case description* are replaced by more general concepts, allowing for comparison with the system norms.

Method: Inheritance, association, parsing, etc.

Knowledge: Concept hierarchies, classification rules, 'grammars', etc.

Select

Concepts in the system model are selected to accommodate individual cases.

Input: *System model.* The classification principles. It may be simple or complex; ranging from a simple list of typical attributes to a layered, justified model.

    Abstract Case Description. As above.

Output: *Norm.* As above.

Method: Heuristic match.

Knowledge: Hierarchies of concepts.

Compare

The abstracted case description and the norms are compared in such a way as to allow a decision-statement to be made.

Input: *Abstract case description.* As above.

    Norm.   As above.

Output: *Decision class.* A decision class may be a simple yes–no result of the assessment or it may involve a rating system.

Method: The method of comparison will vary greatly depending on the type of structures used as input and the type of decision needed. It may just be a simple, top-down comparison of elements in the norms and abstract case description, and the output a specification of where they differ.

Knowledge: Comparison criteria, rules, constraints, value restrictions, etc.

Note that in cases where a simple decision is not sufficient for the result of the assessment process at the Task Layer, the Inference Structure may be extended to produce a *Discrepancy Class* as well as a decision class. This Domain Role will be a description of the ways in which the norm and abstract case description do not match. Usually such data will be used in the control of further abstractions and assessments.

Task Structure

The Task Structure for Assessment may be top-down (model-driven) or bottom-up (case-driven) in approach, or even a mixture of both (mixed initiative). A top-down approach specifies the norms from the system model before abstracting the case description; in a bottom-up approach, the case description is abstracted (in some default way) first, and then matched against the system's norms; in a mixed initiative approach, information may be offered to the problem-solving process as well as it specifically requesting information.

```
/* Top-down */
Assessment (+case description, +system model, −decision class) by
    WHILE concepts still to be processed in case description DO
        select (+system model, −norm)
        abstract (+case description, +norm, −abstract case description)
        compare (+abstract case description, +norm(s), −decision class)

/* Bottom-up */
Assessment (+case description, +system model, −decision class) by
    WHILE concepts still to be processed in case description DO
        abstract (+case description, −abstract case description)
        select (+system model, +abstract case description, −norm)
        compare (+abstract case description, +norm(s), −decision class)
```

Strategies

Many issues arise for this task at the Strategy Layer. First, one should take account of cases which go beyond the range of the values expected by the system. If cases are simple it may not be necessary to use an assessment task as a simple classification procedure is more appropriate; on the other hand, atypical cases may require a pre-assessment abstraction in order to be tractable by assessment (cf. Correlation). Second, there is the strategic aspect of top-down versus bottom-up approaches. If the system model is a layered model then a bottom-up approach may be most effective: the assessment may work on the lower levels first; on the other hand, a bottom-up approach may also lead to greater discrepancies than a top-down one.

Example

An example of an Assessment task is the matching of a job applicant's skills to the job's requirements, in top-down form:

1. The job's requirements are a specification which maps onto the System Model, e.g. the job description as specified in a newspaper.
2. All the applicant's skills and other relevant attributes are the Case Description, e.g. this is the combination of the applicant's curriculum vitae, covering letter, qualification certificates, references, etc.
3. Norms are selected from the job specification in the form of single or groups of skills and other attributes required of a suitable candidate, e.g. 'at least 2 years experience of X'.
4. The job applicant's actual skills are abstracted into the terms of the job specification skills (because in the general case there will not be a simple one-to-one match) as specified by the Norm – these form the Abstract Case Description, e.g. '3 years experience of X'.
5. Then the Norm (required skills in part of the job) and the Abstract Case Description (actual skills in this area) are compared to reach a decision such as 'reject', 'request second interview', 'subject to aptitude tests', etc. In this case, 'exceeds requirement' might be a suitable response (3 years actual versus 2 years required).
6. The task would iterate over the possible Norms until a rejection or other terminating condition is reached.

12.4.4 *System Analysis – Identification – Monitoring*

GTM

Monitoring (also known as chronicling) is concerned with taking measurements of some aspect of an operational system and comparing those measurements with a reference model of the system. Whether the measurements are made continuously or at specified intervals is outside the scope of the generic task. Optionally, it may take into account historical data in order to arrive at some discrepancy between current performance compared with past performance.

The following is a relevant extract from the hierarchy of tasks/models shown in Table 12.1:

*   SYSTEM ANALYSIS
    *   Identification
        *   Diagnosis
        *   Verification
        *   Correlation
        *   *Monitoring*
        *   Classification
    *   Prediction

Figure 12.14 shows the appropriate input/output descriptions for this task/model:

Figure 12.14

Inference Structure
See Figure 12.15.

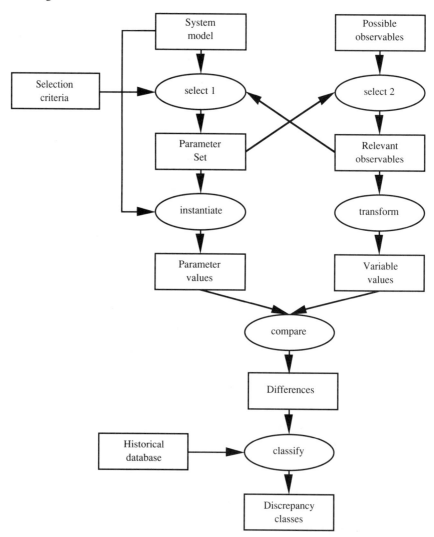

Figure 12.15
Inference Structure for
Monitoring

Inference Types and Domain Roles

Select 1

A set of parameters is selected at the start of monitoring; indeed the result of monitoring might be to select a further set of parameters.

Input: *System model.* A model of the system to be monitored.

                      Selection criteria. These are input from the Strategy Layer of the Generic Task Model (see below).

                      Relevant Observables. The relevant observations of the faulty system may help select the correct parameters for monitoring.

Output: *Parameter set.* The parameters are the parts of the system the monitoring task is concerned with.

Method: This will depend on the task, examples of methods are: generate and test, decision trees, etc.

Knowledge: System Knowledge.

Select 2

This will perform a similar task to *Select 1* except that it is concerned with the observed state of the system, rather than system model.

Input: *Possible observables.* All observed data about the system.

                      Parameter set. The chosen areas for monitoring may help select the relevant data.

Output: *Relevant observables.* The relevant data from the *Possible Observables.*

Method: This will depend on the task in hand.

Knowledge: Real-world knowledge.

Transform

Relevant observable system data are transformed into variable values by data abstraction.

Input: *Relevant observables.* As above.

Output: *Variable values.* The actual values of the parameters in the running system.

Method: Definitional abstraction, qualitative abstraction, generalization.

Knowledge: Definitional knowledge.

Instantiate

The expected values of the parameter set are inferred.

Input: *Parameter set.* As above.

                      System model. As above.

Output: *Parameter values.* The expected values for the system.

Method: Specialization.
Knowledge: System knowledge.

Compare
The desired values (parameters) are compared with the actual values (variables).

Input: Parameter values. As above.
             Variable values. As above.
Output: *Differences*, e.g. abnormalities, distance from norm, etc.
Method: Attribute matching.
Knowledge: Support knowledge will vary depending on the domain.

Classify
The differences between desired and expected system behaviour are classified according to information already known.

Input: *Differences*. As above.
             Historical database. Information about previous system
             behaviour.
Output: *Discrepancy classes*. The classified differences.
Method: Heuristic association.
Knowledge: Historical data.

Task Structure

The inference process for monitoring may be either model-driven (backward) or data-driven (forward). Both are shown below; which is chosen is a strategic issue – see Strategies.

```
/* Model-driven */
Monitoring
    (+system model, +possible observables, +selection criteria, +historical
    database, −decision class) by
      REPEAT
        select 1 (+system model, +selection criteria, −parameter set)
          (instantiate (+system model, +parameter set, −parameter values) :
            (select 2 (+possible observables, +parameter set, −relevant
            observables)
            Obtain data (for relevant observables)
            transform (+relevant observables, −variable values)))
          compare (+parameter values, +variable values, −differences)
          classify (+differences, +historical data, −discrepancy classes)

/* Data-driven */
Monitoring
    (+system model, +possible observables, +selection criteria, +historical
```

```
         database, −decision class) by
           REPEAT
             select 2 (+possible observables, −relevant observables)
               (Obtain data (for relevant observables) :
               select 1 (+system model, +relevant observables, −parameter set))
               (transform (+relevant observables, −variable values) :
               instantiate (+system model, +parameter set, −parameter values))
             compare (+parameter values, +variable values, −differences)
             classify (+differences, +historical data, −discrepancy classes)
```

Strategies

The inputs to the Strategy Layer are the system model and the discrepancy classes. The strategy of the monitoring task is concerned with the following issues:

- *Whether to use a data- or model-driven approach* – if the obtaining of data is straightforward and low cost, then a data-driven approach should be considered.
- *The selection criteria* – these are rules which determine which parameters should be selected from the system model for monitoring. Should these be fixed at the beginning of monitoring or changed by the Strategy Layer according to the results of a monitoring cycle?
- *The timing aspects* – the system will need to be monitored at regular intervals and the length of these depends on the type of system under consideration. The Strategy Layer may be able to alter the regularity of monitoring; for instance, if discrepancies are found it may be a good idea to shorten the time intervals.
- *Actions to be taken* – rules at the Strategy Layer should relate discrepancy classes to any decision as to whether to start a diagnosis and/or remedy task.

Example

A typical application of Monitoring is in the medical domain of patient care. In its model-driven form, the task proceeds as follows:

1. An ill patient is examined. First, select a set of reference parameters over which to perform the monitoring function from the range possible in the system model. The latter will be a physiological model of the patient's condition. The parameters may include an electrocardiogram or changes in the body's fluid patterns, for example.
2. Instantiate the selected reference parameters to determine what their expected values are, e.g. using the physiological model, find the

expected body fluid changes or the expected characteristics of the electrocardiogram.

3. Meanwhile, select from all the possible things we can measure about the patient the actual parameters corresponding to the reference parameters selected from the physiological model, e.g. obtain the output from an electrocardiogram or listings of body fluid intake and secretion.

4. Transform these raw data into parameters at the same level of abstraction as the expected values of the reference parameters, e.g. determine the essential characteristics of the electrocardiogram or the difference between fluid intake and secretion.

5. Compare the expected values of the reference parameters with those actually found in order to produce a difference value, e.g. there are abnormal characteristics in the measured electrocardiogram or there is excessive fluid consumption.

6. Classify the difference value based on historical data such as the patient's medical record or graphs of recent behaviour. This will produce a result such as 'no change', 'getting better', 'getting worse', etc.

7. The result of the classification may terminate the task until manually called again; or it may drive the re-selection of different system model parameters (leading to the selection of other things to measure about the patient); or the task may simply go round again after some suitable time interval.

12.4.5   System Analysis – Identification – Classification

Classification is concerned with categorizing a system, some aspect of a system (such as its behaviour), or the state of a system, where the name or class is selected from one already known to the task. It is thus a simple specialization of Identification.

There is often a close relationship between classification tasks and diagnosis tasks. Basically, this means that classification tasks can be used in the role of diagnosis and vice versa. Two examples of this are that Heuristic Classification can be used as 'heuristic diagnosis' and Systematic Refinement is Systematic Diagnosis playing a classification role.

The following is a relevant extract from the hierarchy of tasks/models shown in Table 12.1:

- SYSTEM ANALYSIS
  - Identification
    - Diagnosis
    - Verification
    - Correlation
    - Monitoring
    - *Classification*
      - *Simple Classification*
      - *Heuristic Classification*
      - *Systematic Refinement*
  - Prediction

Figure 12.16 shows the appropriate input/output descriptions for these tasks/models.

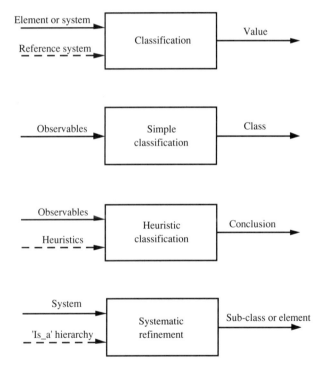

Figure 12.16

System Analysis – Identification – Simple Classification

Simple Classification is an example of the simplest form of Inference Structure that a task would employ. It sits at the boundary of a full-blown problem-solving task and an Inference Type, as it consists of a single

Inference Type. It is possible to envisage other such simple generic tasks based on other single Inference Types.[4] Simple Classification is the only one covered in the library, however.

Simple Classification is employed if the straightforward transformation of observables into variables is sufficient for a solution. Otherwise, a more sophisticated classification task will be needed. The Inference Structure is shown in Figure 12.17.

Inference Structure

See Figure 12.17.

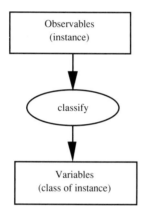

Figure 12.17
Inference Structure for
Simple Classification

Domain Roles

Observables

A set of real-world data to be classified.

Variables

The data described in terms that the system recognizes, based on a value from some internal model of the world, e.g. a classification hierarchy.

Inference Types

Classify

Simple classification transforms observables into variables recognized by the system. It is the opposite of Instantiation.

Input:	*Observables*.
Output:	*Variables*.
Method:	Abstraction, generalization, pattern matching, aggregation, etc.
Knowledge:	Knowledge of how observables are defined and their accuracy, etc.

Task Structure

The Inference Structure for simple classification has only one obvious way of being used, and so the Task Structure is trivial, consisting of a single call. This is a data-driven approach. However, note that it is also possible to run the task in reverse in a goal-driven fashion.

```
/* Data-driven */
Simple Classification (+observables, −variables) by
    classify (+observables, −variables)
```

Strategies

None defined.

Example

The following are three simple examples of the application of simple classification:

1. Classification of vehicles:
    Input: The instance "John's Ferrari" →
    Output: The class 'Car'.
2. Classification of people:
    Input: The observable "Car's max. speed is 150 mph" →
    Output: The class 'Fast car'.
3. Classification of car states:
    Input: The set of cars in the car park →
    Output: The class 'Parked cars'.

System Analysis – Identification – Heuristic Classification

Heuristic Classification is a particularly well-established model in KADS, being based on Clancey's original (see Clancey, 1985, in the Bibliography 'Problem Solving Methods and Knowledge Representation'). This task has wide applicability in classification as well as in diagnosis and other types of generic task. This is because the heuristic match inference at the heart of the task is frequently found to be useful in many applications of problem solving. Like the correlation generic task (see Section 12.4.3), which wraps optional data pre-processing around a core 'compare' inference, heuristic classification wraps pre- and post-processing inferences around its core 'match' inference. The Inference Structure (with Domain Roles suitable for Classification) is shown in Figure 12.18.

Inference Structure

See Figure 12.18.

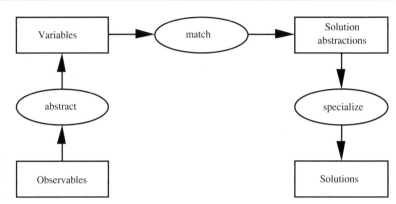

Figure 12.18
Inference Structure for
Heuristic
Classification

Domain Roles

Observables

An observable phenomenon.

Variables

The value placed on the observed data, from the system's perspective.

Solution Abstractions

An abstract classification of a problem (or other concept).

Solutions

A specific, identified solution.

Inference Types

Abstract

Observable data are abstracted into variables.

Input:	*Observables*.
Output:	*Variables*.
Method:	Definitional abstraction, qualitative abstraction, generalization.
Knowledge:	Definitional knowledge.

Match

Abstracted data (variables) are matched heuristically by direct, non-hierarchical association with a concept in another classification hierarchy. The heuristics here typically show only 'shallow' knowledge.

Input:	*Variables*.
Output:	*Solution abstractions*.
Method:	Heuristic matching.
Knowledge:	Heuristic rules.

Specialize

Abstract solutions are refined into more specific solutions.

Input:	*Solution abstractions.*
Output:	*Solutions.*
Method:	Heuristic specialization.
Knowledge:	Heuristic knowledge.

Task Structure

In simple terms, Heuristic Classification may be either data-driven (forward reasoning) or solution-driven (backward reasoning). However, in practice it is possible to imagine many intermediate forms, as with many of the generic tasks. Thus, these two merely represent the ends of a spectrum of possible task structures, with varying times and aggregations of data ('observables') input to the task. The Task Structures, in pseudo-code, for the two extremes for heuristic classification, are as follows:

```
/* Forward Reasoning */
Heuristic Classification (+observables, −solutions) by
    Obtain data (for observables)
    abstract (+observables, −variables)
    match (+variables, −solution abstractions)
    specialize (+solution abstractions, −solutions)

/* Backward Reasoning */
Heuristic Classification (+observables, −solutions) by
    specialize (−solutions, −solution abstractions)
        match (−solution abstractions, −variables)
            abstract (−variables, +observables)
                Obtain data (for observables)
```

(Note that the latter pseudo-code means that each call, which is indented, is made with uninstantiated variables until the call is made to obtain the observables, hence the uninstantiated variables become instantiated one by one on the way back.)

Strategies

In determining knowledge for the Strategy Layer when using this generic task, at least two aspects one should consider are:

- *The choice of the Task Structure* – The cost of obtaining data is the most important factor in choosing a Task Structure; if the cost is high, a more backward-reasoning approach is more suitable, as this only obtains data as required.
- *The level of refinement* – How accurate the solution must be, or to what level of classification. In a diagnostic application, for example, in some cases only superficial diagnosis is needed; then different types of

call to the 'specialize' Inference Type may be required, depending on the accuracy required.

Example

1. From measurements of a patient's blood pressure and temperature, say, abstract the observables 'temperature = 40°C', 'diastolic blood pressure = 100 mm Hg' into a variable, e.g. '(patient has) a fever'.
2. Match this variable onto an abstract solution, e.g. 'a fever' is matched onto the abstract solution, 'bacterial infection'.
3. Specialize the abstract solution into a particular suggested solution (i.e. a hypothesis), e.g. 'bacterial infection' is specialized onto '(pneumonia caused by) infection with pneumococcea'.

GTM

System Analysis – Identification – Systematic Refinement

Systematic Refinement is a classification task which works with an *is-a* knowledge structure. It enables traversal of the *is-a* structure in order to determine a refinement (a more detailed view) of an existing system. Its Inference Structure is essentially the same as that used by the two variations of Systematic Diagnosis (see pp. 271–7). The difference is that those work with a *consists-of* or *causes* structure.

Inference Structure
See Figure 12.19.

Inference Types and Domain Roles

Select 1
The refinement starts with the selection of a system model.

Input:	*Object description*. Statement about an entity that requires a more detailed (refined) description.
Output:	*System model*. An *is-a* hierarchy of concepts, or a sub-model thereof.
Method:	Direct association.
Knowledge:	Knowledge of object's structure.

Decompose
The model is decomposed into sub-models at the next level of the hierarchy, and one node is selected as the hypothesis.

Input:	*System model*. As above.
Output:	*Hypothesis*. A part (sub-model) of the system containing a refinement of the object.
Method:	Descending *is-a* tree.
Knowledge:	*Is-a* structure of system.

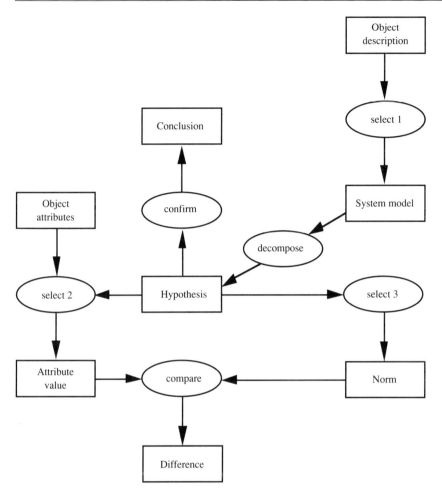

Figure 12.19
Inference Structure for
Systematic
Refinement

Select 2

An attribute value is selected from the possible object attributes at the
current level of analysis.

Input:	*Hypothesis*. As above.
	Object attributes. The attribute value pairs of an object (at the current level).
Output:	*Attribute value*. The selected attribute value.
Method:	Heuristic selection, unification, etc.
Knowledge:	Selection criteria.

Select 3

The attribute norm (i.e. the attribute value that is normally associated
with the hypothesized object) is identified.

Input:	*Hypothesis*. As above.

Output: *Norm.* The expected value.
Method: Heuristic selection, unification, etc.
Knowledge: Selection criteria.

Compare
Compares the attribute value with the norm.

Input: *Attribute value.* As above.
             Norm.   As above.
Output: *Difference.* The difference between the expected and the
             observed value. Used to iterate the procedure by
             detecting whether the current hypothesis is nearer the
             solution or not.
Method: Compares values or functions.
Knowledge: Significance of differences.

Confirm
Confirms that a hypothesis is the conclusion, i.e. the bottom of the
decomposition process has been reached and the object description has
been refined.

Input: *Hypothesis.* As above.
Output: *Conclusion.* Yes or no; the refined object description
             may be output as a side effect of 'yes' – it is the current
             hypothesis.
Method: Check for leaf (or other defined) node of *is-a* hierarchy
             reached.
Knowledge: Knowledge of system structure.

Task Structure

The Task Structure for Systematic Refinement is analogous to that within
Systematic Diagnosis (see p. 271).

```
Systematic  Refinement  (+object  description,  +object  attributes,
−hypothesis) by
   select 1 (+object description, −system model)
   REPEAT
      decompose (+system model, −hypothesis)
      WHILE number of hypotheses > 1
         select 2 (+object attributes, −attribute value)
         select 3 (+hypothesis, −norm)
         compare (+attribute value, +norm, −difference)
      system model ← current decomposition level of system model
   UNTIL confirm (+hypothesis), i.e. system model can be decomposed
   no further
```

Strategies
None defined.

Example
Typical applications of Systematic Refinement might be in the identification of part of a machine given a set of its characteristics or properties or of animals given descriptions of their appearance and behaviour. An illustrative, if not entirely practical, example is its use in the domain of bird watching to identify an unknown bird. The task proceeds as follows:

1. A strange bird has been spotted. First, select an appropriate *is-a* system model for the identification of a bird, e.g. a hierarchical classification of birds as found in a bird-watcher's field guide.
2. Decompose the bird classification by one level, i.e. major groupings of birds such as birds of prey, songbirds, seabirds, etc. Select one to focus on as a hypothesis, e.g. birds of prey. (We could choose more than one to check at a time if we like.)
3. Select from the possible observations we could make about the bird one appropriate to the current hypothesis, e.g. since we are looking at birds of prey, we could choose any of: beak shape, type of feet, etc.
4. Select from the current hypothesis, birds of prey, normal values for the attributes of that class, i.e. hooked beak, clawed feet, etc.
5. Compare these expected values with their actual values; where there is no difference, this indicates that the bird is probably a bird of prey, the current hypothesis; where there is one, either try another pair of attributes or backtrack to look at another type of bird, re-selecting another hypothesis at the current level of decomposition of the system model, e.g. songbird.
6. Assuming that we found the bird had a hooked beak and clawed feet, suggesting a bird of prey, now confirm whether the hypothesis '(the bird is a) bird of prey' is the conclusion by seeing whether it is at its lowest level of decomposition. Of course, it is not, since we could break it down further using the system model into eagle, hawk, owl, etc.
7. Hence, taking 'bird of prey' as the new system model, go back to step 2 and decompose the bird of prey type one level and select a new hypothesis, e.g. eagle. And so on...
8. As soon as a confirmed hypothesis is found, by the fact of it corresponding to a lowest level of decomposition (e.g. the field guide describes no further detail in this area of bird types), stop, and the current hypothesis is the type of bird.
9. If no confirmed hypothesis is ever found, the task has failed.

GTM

12.4.6 System Analysis – Prediction (including qualitative reasoning)

Prediction covers those tasks whose aim it is to determine what will happen next, to, or within, a system in a certain situation. Therefore, prerequisite to any prediction task is a description of the current state of the system: the system description. How the system is analysed depends on the constraints on the system, but essentially the solution will consist of description(s) of processes and objects which can take place or come to exist. There are two specializations of generic Prediction: *prediction of future behaviour* of a system and *prediction of future values* of a system.

In many applications precise prediction is either not required or is not feasible due to the size of the problem. In these situations *qualitative reasoning* is often appropriate. Qualitative reasoning eschews conventional, quantitative mathematics in favour of a simpler qualitative mathematical theory. This allows for much simpler and quicker problem solving. Another thrust of qualitative reasoning is modelling. Most approaches encourage the use of a library of modelling elements from which system models can be built. Qualitative reasoning is discussed later in this section as a special note.

The output of prediction will depend on what there is of interest about the system. Is only the final state of the system required or is a description of how the system will get to this state what is wanted? If a ball is thrown against a window there are a number or things that can occur: the ball may bounce safely off; it may crack the window; or even smash it and sail right through. Should the prediction task merely state where the ball ends up or should it describe the way it got there? What is needed is a way of constraining the inference process so that only the required outcome is deduced. This constraining must be done at the Strategy Layer (see below).

The following is a relevant extract from the hierarchy of tasks/models shown in Table 12.1:

- SYSTEM ANALYSIS
  - Identification
    - Diagnosis
    - Verification
    - Correlation
    - Monitoring
    - Classification
  - *Prediction*
    - *Prediction of Behaviour*
    - *Prediction of Values*

Figure 12.20 shows the appropriate input/output descriptions for these tasks/models.

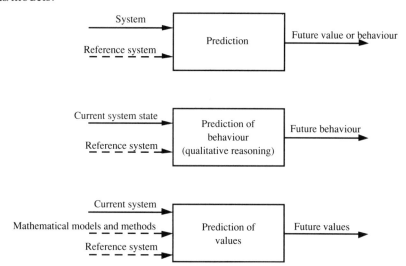

Figure 12.20

The prediction model is described below.

Inference Structure
See Figure 12.21.

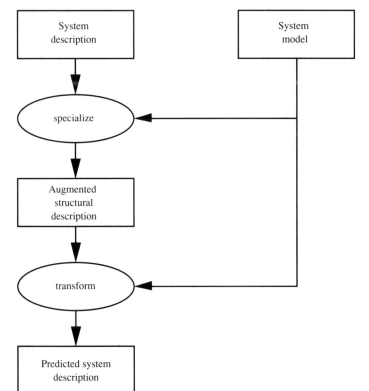

Figure 12.21
Inference Structure for
Prediction (Generic)

Domain Roles

Apart from the *System Model*, the Domain Roles in the Inference Structure are all forms of system description; they have been given different names to indicate the state of that description, but they all contain the same type of information: descriptions of processes, objects and the way they interact.

Inference Types

The Inference Types in the Inference Structure are not the usual primitive steps of inference but are *compound* inference types – they each consist of more than one primitive inference type. This is an allowable technique in the KADS methods, but care must be employed when using it, as the grouping together of Inference Types like this tends to make the reasoning inside them opaque.

Specialize

The system description is augmented with knowledge about processes and objects which are part of the description. It includes adding new attributes, values to concepts and relations between concepts.

Input: *System description.* A description of the processes and objects which are to be used to make the prediction. The formalism used will vary, as will the representation of time. Time may be presented as either a fixed (t^1) where the state of the system does not change, or a sequence of states ($t^1. . .t^n$).

                 System model. The knowledge about the way the system can behave; how the processes and objects interact.

Output: *Augmented system description.* The same as the *System description,* except that it is augmented with more knowledge of the objects and processes.

Method: All specialization methods are possible: refinement, inheritance, heuristic association, etc.

Knowledge: The knowledge used will depend on what domain is being dealt with: hierarchies, causal relations, classification, etc.

Transform

Transforms the current system description into the predicted system description: i.e. the system state which necessarily follows.

Input: *Augmented system description.* As above.

                 System model. As above.

Output: *Predicted system description.* If the *Augmented system description* is the system at t^n, then this will be the system at t^{n+1}, etc. It may be a single state of the system, or a sequence of states.

Method: All methods are possible: heuristic association, means–end analysis, constraint propagation, etc.

Knowledge: The knowledge used will depend on the domain involved.

Task Structure

As the Inference Structure is fairly simple, the possible Task Structures for prediction do not differ greatly – in fact the only difference will be between the depth of recursion of the task, whether the prediction is exhaustive or not. The overall form is trivial:

Prediction (+system description, +system model, −predicted system description) by

    specialize (+system description, +system model, −augmented structural description)

    transform (+augmented structural description, −predicted system description)

Strategies

The Strategy Layer controls the execution of the Task Structure by first planning the structure (the depth of recursion), then monitoring its execution, and finally making any changes to it (increasing or decreasing the depth) arising from the results of the prediction.

Special note: approaches to qualitative reasoning

There are generally considered to be three distinct kinds of qualitative reasoning, differentiated by their modelling paradigm, sometimes called their 'ontologies' (see the Bibliography):

1. Constraint-centred approach
2. Component-centred approach
3. Process-centred approach

The main thrust of qualitative reasoning is to provide a modelling paradigm and inference engine in which systems can be easily modelled, and state behaviours and values of variables can be predicted. The difference between this and conventional techniques is that a precise prediction of behaviour and values is not required. A qualitative description is all that is needed. Qualitative reasoning has been called many things, including 'commonsense reasoning' and 'naive physics'. These names stem from the ability of humans to predict behaviours of systems without knowing the mathematics of the problem.

The modelling approach usually allows for a highly restricted value set for variables, normally the set $\{+,0,-\}$. Their derivatives, representing the direction of change of the variable, take the set {increasing,steady, decreasing} (both sets are often labelled as $\{+,0,-\}$). Some forms of qualitative reasoning allow the specification of other values in the quantity spaces. These qualitative reasoning approaches allow for a much simpler mathematical description of the system under investigation.

The *Constraint-centred* approach provides a structural description of a system derived from an abstraction of the conventional differential equation representation of the system. The ontology makes it possible to represent algebraic and functional relationships between variables. What distinguishes this approach is its ability to generate landmarks, which are new values added to the value set. This ability to generate new values gives a greater granularity of description to the prediction, as more values can be referred to. There are several problems with this approach. The construction of the model is mathematical, and it is often difficult to generate a correct model. The inference engine often generates spurious behaviours, which through recent work can now be decreased. The approach is complete, and as such it is guaranteed to generate the set of possible behaviours of the system.

The *Component-centred* approach provides for a library of generic components which can be connected together and instantiated to form a (more complex) system. Each component has one or more states, and each state has preconditions for entry to the state, and a set of equations ('confluences') which define the behaviour in the state. The total number of states that the system can possibly enter is the cross-product of the states for each component. Thus this approach is seen to be complete, as all possible states are generated. The inference engine uses the initial conditions to the system and the state descriptions to generate a set of possible state transitions. These are filtered to remove any redundant transitions, and the final result is the set of states and the possible transitions between them.

The *Process-centred* approach represents processes acting on objects to modify them. Processes can be concepts such as 'boiling' or 'freezing'. A process is said to 'influence' variables. This approach draws on the idea of a library of possible objects and processes in order to generate a model of the system under investigation. This approach uses a more complex quantity space including landmarks, but these are not generated during inference. The main problem with this approach is the complexity of the inference algorithm. The algorithm has yet to be satisfactorily implemented, although it is widely believed that this approach is the best step forward in producing a methodology for representing and reasoning with commonsense knowledge.

System Analysis – Prediction of Behaviour (qualitative reasoning)

The prediction of the future behaviour of a system is achieved by analysing its current state and determining what its behaviour will be next. It follows the following steps:

- Abstraction of the system model. The system is abstracted so that it can be used by the prediction task.
- The resulting description is then analyzed by a process of qualitative reasoning.
- A behavioural description of the system is then produced. This describes the system's behaviour in its succeeding states.

It is the qualitative reasoning aspect of prediction that will be considered here. Note, however, that all three approaches to qualitative reasoning are shown on the Inference Structure. This is because the inference structures are similar for all three approaches. The main differences between the approaches will be at the Task Layer, as the task can be either depth- or breadth-first, and the approach may or may not allow for the generation of landmarks dynamically.

Inference Structure

The Inference Structure for the Prediction of Behaviour task is shown in Figure 12.22. Note that in this Inference Structure the usual domain role *System Model* (or, more correctly, *Abstracted System Model*) has not been explicitly represented. This is because it is relevant to most of the Inference Types in the structure, and fills a role more as background knowledge to the Inference Types.

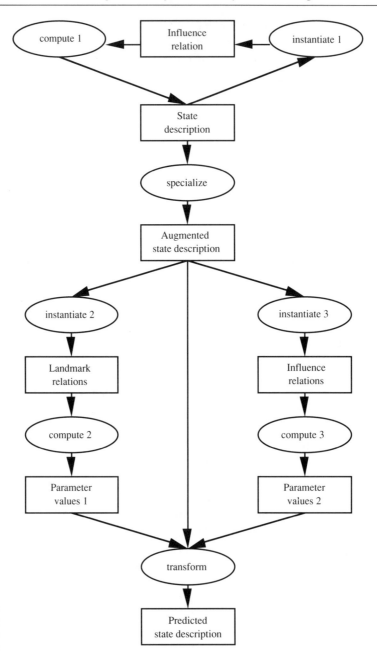

Figure 12.22
Inference Structure for
Prediction of
Behaviour (Qualitative
Reasoning)

Inference Types and Domain Roles

Specialize

Augments the current state description with knowledge of its processes and objects. It can be the adding of new attributes or the defining of new relationships between concepts.

Input: *State description.* Not a single Domain Role but a collection of the Domain Roles which describe the processes and objects that must be used to make the qualitative prediction. The collection covers the following types of knowledge: parameter values (the values which describe parts of the system's behaviour); causal parameter relations (the effect one parameter may have on another); and system elements (the objects and their relations).

Output: *Augmented state description.* Takes the same form as the *State description* but it differs in that the description is augmented with more knowledge about the processes and objects in the system. It also contains influences: a representation of the effect a process has on a quantity, e.g. freezing reduces the volume of water.

Method: Refinement, inheritance, heuristic association, etc.

Knowledge: Hierarchies of concepts, causal relations and classification rules, and from the *System model*: knowledge about processes, objects and the way they interact: parameter values and parameter relations (see above); causal parameter relations and quantity parameter relations; tendencies, representations of changes in parameter relations; influence relations, how the value of a parameter may be influenced; and knowledge of system elements.

Instantiate 1, 2, 3

The instantiate domain roles are broadly similar. They take some form of state description and supply values for influence relations or landmark relations.

Input: *State description* (1). As above.
              Augmented state description (2 and 3). As above.

Output: *Influence relation* (1). An instantiated influence relation that can be used to compute the effect of an influence on a quantity.

              Landmark relations (2). A landmark is a choice point in the process of qualitative reasoning, a point at which the overall state may change; a landmark relation is the combination of parameters which define this landmark.

              Influence relations (3). The set of influence relations from the augmented state description, see above.

Method: Filling in attribute slots according to their value restric-
            tions.

Knowledge: From the *System model* (see above).

Compute 1, 2, 3

The compute domain roles are broadly similar. They take some relation
and compute unknown values of that relation.

Input: *Influence relation* (1). As above.

            Landmark relations (2). As above.

            Influence relations (3). As above.

Output: *State description* (1). The computation provides a new
            parameter value for the state description.

            Parameter values 1 and 2 (Compute 2 and 3). The result
            of an influence on a quantity (2) is a new parameter
            value, e.g. increasing or decreasing. A value which
            represents the quantity of a value when it reaches a
            landmark, i.e. a maximum or minimum.

Method: Computation.

Knowledge: Knowledge of how to compute relations of various kinds.

Transform

After the operations on the influence relation and landmark relations, the
augmented state description will no longer be the correct state
description; the system will have changed. Therefore, the state description must be changed into the predicted state description.

Input: *Augmented state description*. As above.

            Parameter values 1. The result of the defined landmarks;
            used as a guide to aid transformation, and also become
            part of the predicted state.

            Parameter values 2. The results of influences; used as a
            guide to aid transformation, and also become part of the
            predicted state.

Output: *Predicted state description*. This is the same type as the
            initial state description (above); it consists of the same
            components and may be used for further qualitative
            prediction tasks.

Method: Many different methods are possible, e.g. heuristic
            association, default reasoning, etc.

Knowledge: Hierarchies of concepts, causal relations, classification
            rules and others.

Task Structure

The Inference Structure described above may be used by several different Task Structures. Here are two examples:

1. The task starts by trying to compute more values in the state description; system model parts are selected from the system model and computed. Then, the computed values are integrated into the *Augmented State Description*. The next stage is to find landmarks. Again, there is a selection of system model parts: influence and landmark relations. The defined tendencies within the model are used to compute the landmark values. Once these parameters have been defined, the augmented state description may be transformed into a predicted state description. Finally, this predicted state is used recursively for further qualitative predictions; the full prediction task is complete when there is no prediction that can be, or needs to be, made. The process can be summarized as:
    *   Compute more parameter values.
    *   Find landmarks.
    *   Match landmarks to state description.
    *   Do another prediction.

2. The task starts by specializing the state description and arriving at the augmented state description. Parameter values are then computed: landmarks and influence relations. The augmented state description is no longer an adequate description and must be transformed into a new state description; this transformation is guided by the calculated parameter values. Finally, the predicted state description may be used as an input to a further prediction task. The process can be summarized as:
    *   Specialize current description.
    *   Compute more parameter values.
    *   Find landmarks.
    *   Find influences.
    *   Transform current state.
    *   Do another prediction.

Strategies

The Strategy Layer controls the prediction task by planning or choosing a Task Structure, then by monitoring the execution, and finally by updating or changing the Task Structure. The choice of Task Structure will depend on the domain. Other generic tasks (e.g. Monitoring and Diagnosis) are needed to develop a complete strategy.

System Analysis – prediction of values

Prediction of values is the identification of the values of variables in a system at a certain point in time. The process starts with an informal model of the system which is transformed into a formal one. The values wanted (generally quantitative) are derived from this formal, mathematical model of the system.

Inference Structure

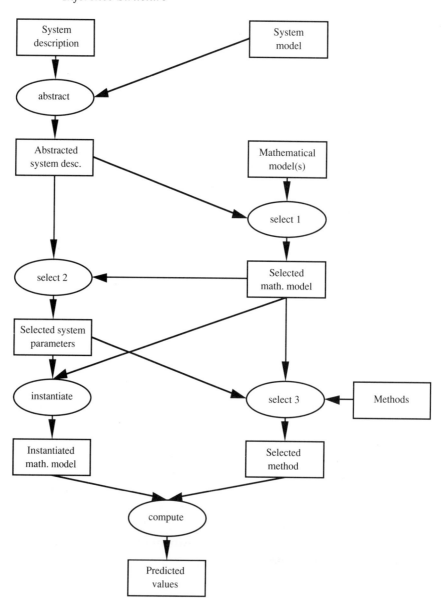

Figure 12.23
Inference Structure for
Prediction of Values

Inference Types and Domain Roles

Abstract

Scans the system description for elements which can be abstracted and fit into a canonical form.

Input:	*System description.* See the description in the general prediction task.
	System model. Standard descriptions of systems or parts of systems which allow the application of mathematical formalisms.
Output:	*Abstracted system description.* This is a formalized version of the system description. The informal description has been mapped onto the formal theory.
Method:	Refinement, inheritance, heuristic classification, etc.
Knowledge:	Hierarchies of concepts, classification rules, etc.

Select 1

Selects mathematical models from those available; guided by the canonical descriptions in the abstracted system description.

Input:	*Mathematical models.* Standard mathematical formalisms which can be used to describe relations in the system.
	Abstracted system description. As above.
Output:	*Selected mathematical model.* A model chosen from the set of models.
Method:	Heuristic classification.
Knowledge:	Selection criteria.

Select 2

Selects the relevant parameters from the available ones. The selection process may be guided by a mathematical model if selected.

Input:	*Abstracted system description.* As above.
	Selected mathematical model. There is an interaction between the selection of system parameters and the mathematical model; sometimes a number of parameters will be chosen before the mathematical model, although the converse will usually be the case.
Output:	*Selected system parameters.* The actual parameters chosen.
Method:	Heuristic classification, etc.
Knowledge:	Selection criteria.

Instantiate

Gives the parameters their values.

Input:	*Selected mathematical model.* As above.
	Selected system parameters. As above.

Output: *Instantiated mathematical model.* A complete formalized description of the system.

Method: Filling the attribute slots of formalisms according to value restrictions.

Knowledge: None.

Select 3

Selects from various methods one that is best suited to the selected mathematical model. A particular mathematical model may have various calculating procedures associated with it; this Inference Type selects the most appropriate one.

Input: *Selected mathematical model.* As above.

Selected system parameters. As above.

Methods. A set of formal calculating procedures which can be used to solve the mathematical model.

Output: *Selected method.* The method chosen.

Method: Various approaches may be employed to select the right method.

Knowledge: Selection criteria.

Compute

Computes the actual values the prediction task requires.

Input: *Instantiated mathematical model.* As above.

Selected Method. As above.

Output: *Predicted values.* The previously unknown values, which have now been predicted.

Method: The method is provided by the *Selected Method* domain role.

Knowledge: Mathematical knowledge.

Task Structure

The following is one way to use the Inference Structure illustrated above:

Prediction of Values

(+system description, +system model, +math. model(s), +methods, −predicted values) by

abstract (+system description, +system model, −abstracted system desc.)

select 1 (+mathematical model, +abstracted system desc., −selected math. model)

select 2 (+abstracted system desc., +selected math. model, −selected sys. parameters)

instantiate (+selected sys. parameters, +selected math. model, −inst. math. model)

> *select 3 (+selected math. model, +selected sys. param, +methods,*
> *−selected method)*
> *compute (+inst. math. model, +selected method, −predicted values)*

Strategies

The Strategy Layer should generate or choose an appropriate Task Structure for the required prediction task. This is then monitored and updated as necessary.

12.5   System Modification models

These Generic Task Models are concerned with taking an existing 'system' (i.e. a non-trivial thing in the real or conceptual world) and changing its characteristics, such as its behaviour, or potential behaviour. (It could also be used for 'changing the system model' – where the 'system model' in KADS is an idealized description of some system in the real world, used as a reference. See Section 11.1.)

The following is a relevant extract from the hierarchy of tasks/models shown in Table 12.1:

- SYSTEM MODIFICATION
  - *Repair*
  - *Remedy*
  - *Control*
  - *Maintenance*

System modification tasks are usually dependent on system analysis tasks. An analysis task will detect a fault, say, and a modification task will 'repair' it; alternatively, an analysis task will detect some threshold condition in a system, such as a certain temperature level, and a modification task like 'control' will act accordingly, perhaps initiating the shut-down of valves or a heater. Possible relationships between analysis tasks and modification tasks are as follows:

System Analysis		System Modification
Heuristic Classification	→	Remedy, Repair
Causal Tracing	→	Remedy, Repair
Localization	→	Repair
Monitoring	→	Control, Maintain
Prediction	→	Control

In real-world applications, modification tasks are usually trivial or very complex. This makes them hard to describe as generic tasks. For example, in a medical diagnosis the associated treatment (by modification) required is usually simply associated with a disease (by analysis); if it is not, the treatment will be a complex task itself: it may include experimental treatments, new medicines, etc. These could involve many steps of complex problem solving. Thus, there are no complete Generic Task Models for system modification tasks at the time of writing. Figure 12.24 shows the appropriate input/output descriptions for these tasks.

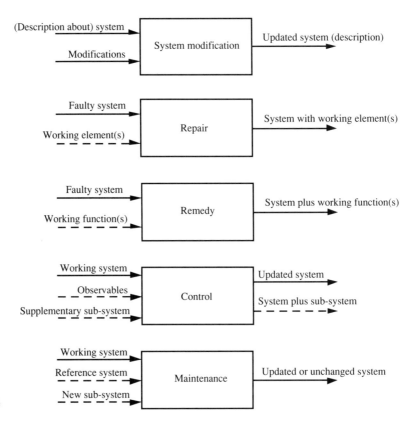

Figure 12.24

12.5.1 *System Modification – Repair*

A repair task is the replacement of a defective element of the system. If it is non-trivial it will require the disassembling of the old component and the reassembling of it, or even finding a functional equivalent. These may involve planning tasks, etc. An example is performing an operation on a patient with a disease.

12.5.2 System Modification – Remedy

Remedy is the counteracting of a malfunction in one process by initiating another. It is usually only a temporary measure; a repair should be used for longer-term solutions. An example is the administration of a drug to a patient with a disease.

12.5.3 System Modification – Control

Control is a simple form of system modification, usually relying on feedback. Modification is driven by the occurrence of external events. For instance, if the temperature gets too high in some hypothetical system a cooler might be applied to it. It is easy to see how this could work with a monitoring task – control would be fired as an action from that task.

12.5.4 System Modification – Maintenance

Maintenance is concerned with ensuring that a system behaves (continues to behave) according to some reference model. It can also be interpreted as a type of control task, initiated by regular events, perhaps internally generated. Generic control tasks are driven by external, 'random' events, as well as regular events.

12.6 System Synthesis models

These Generic Task Models are concerned with forming (synthesizing) a new 'system' (i.e. a non-trivial thing in the real or conceptual world), given a set of elements and constraints. The elements are the components used to build the system (often best considered as a 'structure'); the constraints, also called requirements, constrain how the elements must be put together to form the system.

The following is a relevant extract from the hierarchy of tasks/models shown in Table 12.1:

- SYSTEM SYNTHESIS
  - *Design*
    - Hierarchical Design
    - Incremental Design
  - *Configuration*
  - *Planning*
  - *Scheduling*
  - *Modelling*

All the Generic Task Models for synthesis tasks presented in this section rely on a general two-stage model: first, the problem statement is *analysed*, giving a formal specification of the structure (system); second, the structure (system) is actually generated *(synthesized)*. Figure 12.25 shows the appropriate input/output descriptions for these tasks/models.

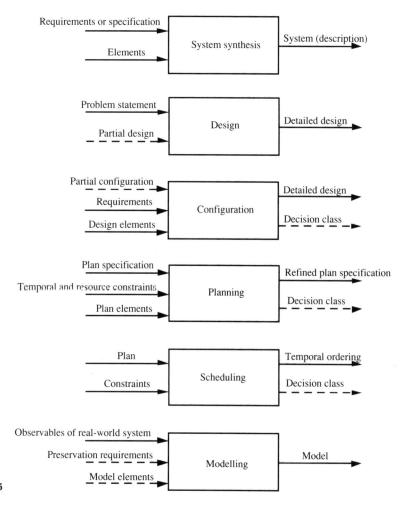

Figure 12.25

12.6.1   *System Synthesis – Design*

Design is the specifying of the components and architecture of some artifact, given a statement of the role that that artifact must fulfil. The basic framework for any design task consists of taking an informal problem statement, analyzing it to produce a formal specification of the artifact, and then synthesizing this to produce a detailed design. A distinction can be made between single- and multiple-stream design problems: in a single-stream design one structure is generated; in a multiple-stream problem several structures are generated concurrently.

Most design tasks have a model, known as the 'conceptual model', of the artifact to be designed. This will be true whenever the global structure of the artifact is not specified beforehand. There are two specializations of the (Gencric) Design task: Hierarchical Design and Incremental Design.

The following is a relevant extract from the hierarchy of tasks/models shown in Table 12.1:

- SYSTEM SYNTHESIS
  - *Design*
    - *Hierarchical Design*
    - *Incremental Design*
  - Configuration
  - Planning
  - Scheduling
  - Modelling

Figure 12.26 shows the appropriate input/output descriptions for these tasks/models.

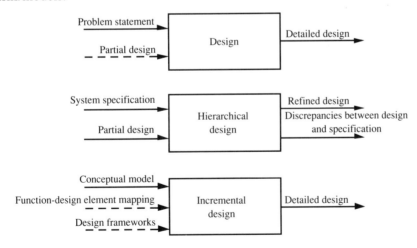

Figure 12.26

The Design model is described below.

Inference Structure
See Figure 12.27.

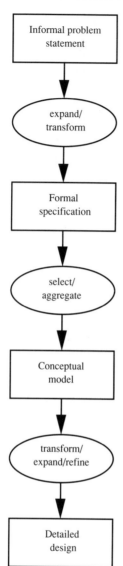

Figure 12.27
Inference Structure for
(Generic) Design

Domain Roles

Informal Problem Statement

An informal specification of the structure to be designed. It may be an I/O specification, a functional specification, the major parameters, functions and constraints, etc.

Formal Specification

A description of the artifact in the language of the domain. It is an elaboration and/or transformation of the *Informal problem statement* in terms of engineering concepts: design criteria, design variables, etc. An initial description in the appropriate domain language.

Conceptual Model

A first high-level structure of the artifact. It may be a sketch, an algorithm, etc.

Detailed Design

A fully detailed model of the artifact. No further elaboration should be required. It may be a technical drawing, an electric circuit layout, etc.

Inference Types

Expand/Transform

Build a formal specification of the desired artifact.

Input:	*Informal problem statement.*
Output:	*Formal specification.*
Method:	This will be domain dependent.
Knowledge:	The functions of the required artifact, knowledge of what is achievable.

Select/Aggregate

The requirements in the *Formal specification* indicate design decisions which must be taken. Some of these must be made at a high level. This inference type selects and structures such decisions.

Input:	*Formal specification.*
Output:	*Conceptual model.*
Method:	Domain-specific.
Knowledge:	Domain-specific.

Transform/Expand/Refine

Produces the *Detailed design model* from the *Conceptual model.* This may be a straight transformation or may involve an expansion of elements of the *Conceptual model.*

Input:	*Conceptual model.*
Output:	*Detailed design model.*
Method:	Domain-specific.
Knowledge:	Partial models may be used to guide the design process.

Task Structure

The generic design Inference Structure follows a linear progression, therefore the basic Task Structure simply follows the arrows top to bottom. However, there may be many subtleties in practice as there are plenty of opportunities for the inferences to overlap to various degrees.

(Generic) Design (+informal problem statement,-detailed design) by
expand/transform (+informal problem statement,-formal specification)
select/aggregate (+formal specification,-conceptual model)
transform/expand/refine (+conceptual model,-detailed design)

Strategies

Strategic knowledge could control the degree of overlap between the inferences, as mentioned in the Task Structure above. This control knowledge could be based on externally arising constraints on the design process and/or the constraints of designing according to a particular set of guidelines or 'paradigm'.

Example

Although rather indulgent with respect to the subject of this book, software design can be used as an example of the generic design task. In particular, we can roughly map KADS onto this task as follows:

1. An informal statement of requirements for a software system is presented. First, expand/transform this to produce a (relatively) formal specification, i.e. in KADS terms, perform the Analysis activities to produce a set of Analysis models.
2. Select/aggregate this formal specification into a conceptual model, i.e. in KADS terms, map the results of Analysis onto a global design.
3. Transform/expand/refine this conceptual model into a detailed design, i.e. in KADS terms, perform the Design activities to produce a detailed physical design.

GTM

System Synthesis – Hierarchical Design

The distinguishing characteristic of **Hierarchical Design** from other design tasks is that a model of the artifact is first built and then modified: the design works at different levels of abstraction by recursion. If the domain is well understood then the design may be undertaken in a structured manner. More difficult problems may be solved by filling skeletal models.

The Hierarchical Design model is a special case of the Generic Design model. It is not fully refined and should be used more cautiously than most of the other models in this library.

Inference Structure

See Figure 12.28. This should be used in conjunction with the Generic Design Inference Structure shown in Figure 12.27.

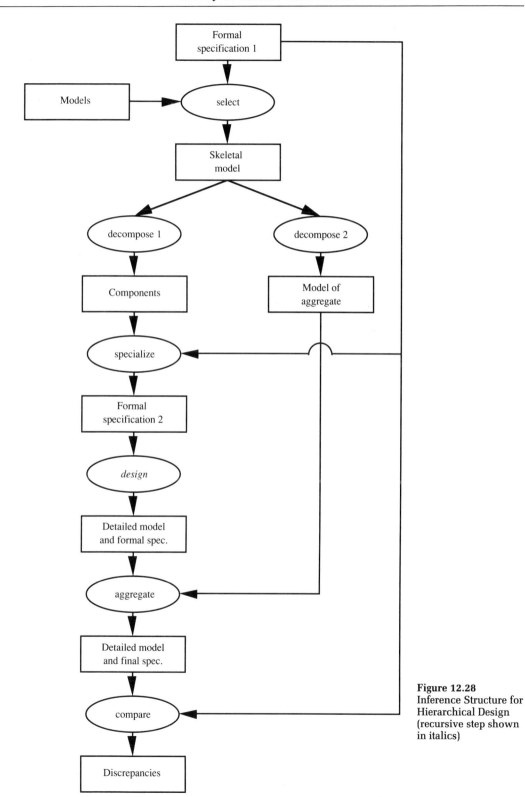

Figure 12.28
Inference Structure for
Hierarchical Design
(recursive step shown
in italics)

Inference Types and Domain Roles

Select

Matches the artifact's formal specification with the skeletal models in the database, and picks the most appropriate one.

Input: *Formal specification 1*. This is the domain role output from the generic design task Inference Structure.

Models. Not really a domain role, but a database of skeletal models for design. A skeletal model is an aggregate of components, and the relation between the components and the aggregate. This should be sufficient to (1) build a formal specification for each of the components, given a formal specification for the aggregate; and (2) infer the full specification of the aggregate, given the full specifications of its components.

Output: *Skeletal model*. One of the models in the database.

Method: Heuristic association, constraint satisfaction.

Knowledge: Knowledge of the models in the database.

Decompose 1

Outputs the components only of the skeletal model.

Input: *Skeletal model*. As above.

Output: *Components*. A functional specification for each component in the skeletal model, but not all the parameters are specified.

Method: Heuristic association, etc.

Knowledge: Knowledge of the structure of the models in the database.

Decompose 2

As *Decompose 1* except that relations between the component and the aggregate are abstracted.

Input: *Skeletal model*. As above.

Output: *Model of aggregate*. A description of the way the components interact.

Method: Heuristic association, etc.

Knowledge: Knowledge of the structure of the models in the database.

Specialize

Takes the original formal specification for the artifact as a whole and the functional specifications of the components and produces a formal specification for each of the components.

Input: *Formal specification 1*. As above.

Components. As above.

Output: *Formal specification 2.* A formal specification of the components.

Method: Inheritance, top-down refinement, etc.

Knowledge: Relations between components.

Design

The design task indicates the start of the recursive design process on each of the components. The recursion will continue until the components are described at the lowest level possible.

Input: *Formal specification 2.* As above.

Output: *Detailed model and formal specification.* The components described in terms of software language statements, industry-standard primitive components, etc.

Method: (Not applicable.)

Knowledge: (Not applicable.)

Aggregate

Takes the designed components and links them together into a complete system, such as a floor plan design or a circuit diagram.

Input: *Detailed model and formal specification.* As above.
                Model of aggregate. As above.

Output: *Detailed model and final specification.* The completed design of the artifact and its final specification.

Method: Constraint satisfaction, by applying the relations in the aggregate to the components.

Knowledge: (None defined.)

Compare

Validates the model by comparing the finished design against the original formal specification.

Input: *Detailed model and final specification.* As above.
                Formal Specification 1. As above.

Output: *Discrepancies.* Inconsistencies between the two input domain roles – does the design match its original specification?

Method: Heuristic association, unification, etc. with discrepancy measurement.

Knowledge: Comparison criteria, tolerances.

Task Structure

The Task Structure for Hierarchical Design is fairly straightforward, being only a special case of the Generic Design task. However, the main difference is that the Inference Structure is recursive: the design process will use the 'design' Inference Type to start the whole process again at a lower level for each component. Recursion will cease when the skeletal model can be decomposed no further, or it is not necessary to do so, e.g. when primitive elements have been reached in the composition of the design. On the way back up the recursion, all the models of aggregates, and detailed models and formal specifications, are gathered up and presented to the 'aggregate' Inference Type to be composed into the proposed final design. The proposed final design is validated against the original specification by 'compare' to confirm it is the final design when it is within tolerance.

> *Hierarchical Design (+formal specification 1, +models, −detailed model & final spec.) by*
>   *REPEAT*
>   *select (+formal specification, +models, −skeletal model)*
>   *IF skeletal model is decomposable to more primitive elements THEN*
>   *(decompose 2 (+skeletal model, −model of aggregate) :*
>   *decompose 1 (+skeletal model, −components)*
>   *specialize (+components, +formal specification 1, −formal specification 2)*
>   *design (+formal specification 2, −detailed model & formal spec.)))*
>   *ELSE return*
>   *aggregate (+detailed model & formal spec., +model(s) of aggregate(s), -detailed model & final spec.)*
>   *compare (+detailed model & final spec., +formal specification 1, −discrepancies)*
>   *UNTIL discrepancies within tolerance*

Strategies

None defined. (But see Strategies for Generic Design, in Section 12.6.1.)

Example

Continuing the theme of using software design as an example of this task (see the generic design task in Section 12.6.1) and, in particular, KADS, we can roughly map one approach to the KADS Design phase onto this task as follows (functional decomposition):

1. A formal specification for a software system is presented (perhaps as the result of performing the first step in the Generic Design task). First, select an appropriate skeletal model, i.e. in KADS Design terms, a global system architecture.
2. If the current skeletal model is decomposable, which initially it

should be, decompose it into a model of the way the sub-systems will cooperate.

3.   At the same time, decompose the skeletal model into its components, i.e. the sub-systems. Then, specialize the component specifications, taking into account the original overall formal specification, in order to produce a formal specification of the components, i.e. specifications for functional blocks. Next, recursively call the task again, taking the last level of specifications as the main input. This process is basically functional decomposition. The process will stop when primitive components have been reached and the current skeletal model is no longer (reasonably) decomposable, i.e. function specifications no longer need to be refined.

4.   When the recursion has ceased, aggregate the completely detailed functional specifications with the completely detailed model of how they will cooperate, in order to form the final description of the system design.

5.   Finally, check the last design with the original specification to ensure that it matches.

System Synthesis – Incremental Design

GTM

The **Incremental Design** task is an expansion of the compound inference type *Transform/Expand/Refine* found in the Generic Design model – see Section 12.6.1. Incremental Design is where there is no straightforward transformation of the conceptual model to the detailed design model; rather, elements of the conceptual model are transformed individually while the structure of the design is constructed from skeletal models.

The Incremental Design model, like Hierarchical Design, is a special case of the Generic Design model. Also likewise, it is not fully refined and should be used more cautiously than most of the other models in this library.

Inference Structure
See Figure 12.29. This should be used in conjunction with the Generic Design Inference Structure shown in Figure 12.27.

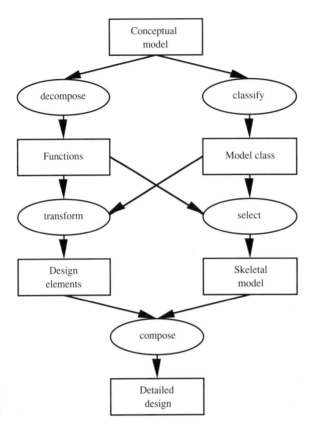

Figure 12.29
Inference Structure for
Incremental Design

Inference Types and Domain Roles

Decompose

Breaks down the conceptual model into functions (functional areas).

Input: *Conceptual model.* As for Generic Design.

Output: *Functions.* The required capability of the system or artifact described by the conceptual model in terms of specific functions or groups of functions.

Method: Heuristic association, etc.

Knowledge: Knowledge of the structure of the system or artifact described by the conceptual model.

Transform

Transforms the required functions into specific implementation components (design elements), optionally controlled by the type of conceptual model under consideration.

Input: *Functions.* As above.

             Model class. The type of conceptual model, i.e. its form, structure, paradigm, etc.

Output: *Design elements.* Components of the final system written in terms of the implementation (i.e. or more generally, at whatever level of description is required by the detailed design).

Method: Heuristic association, unification, etc.

Knowledge: Relationships between functions and design elements.

Classify

Determines the type of conceptual model under consideration.

Input: *Conceptual model.* As for Generic Design.

Output: *Model class.* As above.

Method: Heuristic association or classification tasks.

Knowledge: Knowledge describing possible types of models.

Select

Selects a skeletal model framework for specifying the structure of the detailed design according to the type of conceptual model, and optionally, also its functional decomposition.

Input: *Model class.* As above.

            Functions. As above.

Output: *Skeletal model.* The structural framework within which the design elements will be placed to form the detailed design.

Method: Heuristic selection, unification, etc. with discrepancy measurement.

Knowledge: Knowledge describing possible skeletal models.

Compose

Brings together the design elements and the skeletal model in order to form the detailed design.

Input: *Design elements.* As above.

            Skeletal model. As above.

Output: *Detailed design.* The skeletal model with the design elements placed within it in an appropriate arrangement.

Method: Rule-based construction, constraint satisfaction, etc.

Knowledge: Composition rules, constraints, etc.

Task Structure

This task can be driven in two basic ways: (1) by the form of the functional decomposition of the conceptual model; or (2) by the class of the conceptual model (or rather, the system it relates to). If the former, the functional breakdown controls the selection of an appropriate skeletal model or 'implementation framework'; if the latter, the type of system under consideration will control how the functions are transformed into design elements. In practice, design tasks usually involve elements of both. The two basic Task Structures are:

> /* Functional decomposition-driven */
> *Incremental Design (+conceptual model, −detailed design) by*
>   *UNTIL detailed enough DO*
>   *(decompose (+conceptual model, −functions) :*
>   *classify (+conceptual model, −model class))*
>   *(transform (+functions, −design elements) :*
>   *select (+model class, + functions, −skeletal model))*
>   *compose (+design elements, +skeletal model, −detailed design)*

> /* Conceptual model class-driven */
> *Incremental Design (+conceptual model, −detailed design) by*
>   *UNTIL detailed enough DO*
>   *(decompose (+conceptual model, −functions) :*
>   *classify (+conceptual model, −model class))*
>   *(transform (+functions, +model class, −design elements) :*
>   *select (+model class, −skeletal model))*
>   *compose (+design elements, +skeletal model, −detailed design)*

Strategies

As for other tasks with two basic strategies (in this case, functional decomposition-driven versus conceptual model class-driven), strategic knowledge can describe if and how these two approaches are mixed in the application of the task. It will also describe whether or not inferences are carried out in parallel.

Example

Again, software design can be used as an example of this task (see the generic design task in Section 12.6.1) and, in particular, KADS. We can roughly map a simple approach to the KADS KBS Design stage onto this task as follows:

1. A conceptual model for a software system is presented (perhaps as the result of performing the second step in the Generic Design task). First, decompose this into functions, e.g. in KADS KBS Design terms, a global design is decomposed into a functional design model of the KBS sub-system.
2. Meanwhile, classify the type of global design to result in a KBS design framework (e.g. a type of implementation environment), assuming a one-to-one mapping of such frameworks to types of global design.

3. Transform the KBS functional design model into a set of design elements, i.e. this is essentially the behavioural design step in KADS. It could also use the KBS design framework as an input.

4. Meanwhile, select the implementation framework, or a detailed description of the implementation framework's capabilities, on the basis of the KBS design framework. It could use the KBS functional design model as an input.

5. Finally, compose the detailed design by mapping the design elements onto the implementation framework to form a physical architecture for the KBS sub-system.

12.6.2 System Synthesis – Configuration

The **Configuration** task is concerned with assembling the elements of a system together such that spatial or logical constraints are not violated. Configuration can be interpreted as a simple case of design. The basic structure of the design will already be known, only the details have to be filled in, e.g. components placed in an empty or partially filled framework.

Two forms of configuration task have been distinguished: **Simple Configuration** and **Incremental Configuration**. The difference between the two is that Simple Configuration only works when there are no common resources, i.e. a resource that can help satisfy several types of function, such as a power supply card in an electronics rack which supplies power to the other cards.

The following is a relevant extract from the hierarchy of tasks/models shown in Table 12.1:

- SYSTEM SYNTHESIS
  - Design
  - Configuration
    - *Simple Configuration*
    - *Incremental Configuration*
  - Planning
  - Scheduling
  - Modelling

The input/output descriptions for these tasks/models are the same as for Configuration, which was shown in Figure 12.25, p. 328.

GTM

System Synthesis – Simple Configuration

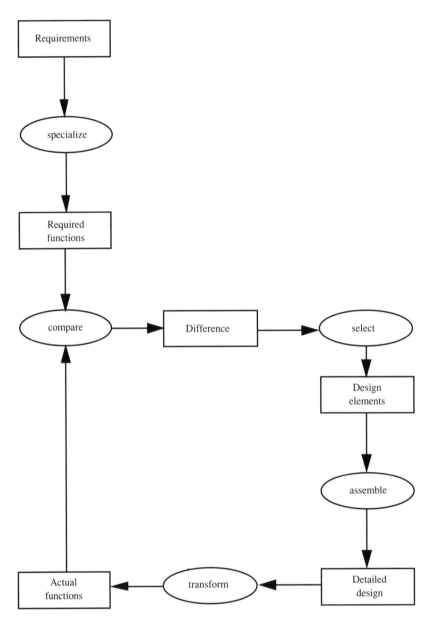

Figure 12.30
Inference Structure for
Simple Configuration

Inference Structure
See Figure 12.30.

Inference Types and Domain roles

Specialize

Given a set of requirements which may only be partially described, derive the full set of implicit functions that the system must perform. This may be a trivial task if the set of requirements is very detailed and specific.

Input:	*Requirements.* A set of demands which may be only partially specified.
Output:	*Required functions.* These are required demands expressed as a sct of concept instances. All attributes of each demand have values.
Method:	Rule-based specialization, hierarchical specialization.
Knowledge:	(None defined.)

Compare

The required and actual functionality are compared and a difference is derived. This difference represents a set of functions which have not yet been met by the detailed design.

Input:	*Required functions.* As above.
	Actual functions. This is the set of functions which can be supported by the detailed design model.
Output:	*Difference.* A difference set is created which contains the functions that appear in the required functions but not in the actual functions set. This difference represents the functions that are not supported by the present detailed design.
Method:	Function matching.
Knowledge:	Comparison criteria.

Select

A set of design elements is selected which satisfies a function contained within the difference set. These design elements represent the units which are required that, when assembled, will perform the required function.

Input:	*Difference.* As above.
Output:	*Design elements.* A set of units that represent the basic building blocks of the system and when combined with other units will perform a particular function.
Method:	Rule-based selection, unification, etc.
Knowledge:	Selection criteria.

Assemble

This describes the satisfaction of physical constraints when allocating the design elements to physical positions within a system.

Input:	*Design elements.* As above.

Output: *Detailed design.* A fully configured system that meets the initial requirements and satisfies both the configuration and physical constraints.

Method: Rule-based assembly, constraint satisfaction.

Knowledge: Construction rules.

Transform

The functionality that can be supported by the detailed design derived. This can consist of either mapping the detailed design into system characteristics (using the inference type instantiate) and then inferring the actual functionality by comparing the characteristics to functionality (using the inference type match) or selecting key elements from the detailed design and assembling them to form functional units.

Input: *Design elements.* As above.

Output: *Actual functions.* These are actual demands expressed as a set of concept instances. All attributes of each demand have values. These demands represent the actual functions that are met by a set of design elements.

Method: Instantiation plus matching; or assembly.

Knowledge: (None defined.)

Task Structure

Simple Configuration can be used in two ways: (1) produce a fully configured system from the requirements – this is called a 'nominate' procedure; or (2) given an existing configuration, verify that it meets the requirements – this is called a 'verify' procedure. A mixture is also possible, with only a small difference from the basic nominate procedure. The Task Structures for these can be summarized in the form of dependency graphs, supplemented by pseudo-code as follows (see Figures 12.31 and 12.32):

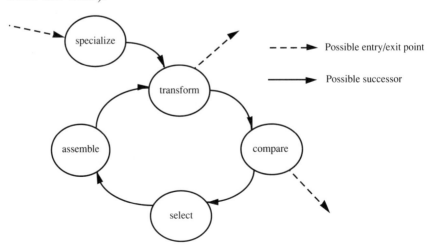

Figure 12.31 Task Structure for Simple Configuration (Nominate)

/* Nominate & Verify/Nominate */
Simple Configuration (+requirements, +detailed design, −difference) by
    specialize (+requirements, −required functions)
    transform (+detailed design, −actual functions)
    compare (+required functions, +actual functions, −difference)
    UNTIL no difference OR select fails DO
       select (+difference, −design elements)
       assemble (+design elements, −detailed design)
       transform (+detailed design, −actual functions)
       compare (+required functions, +actual functions, −difference)

For just a pure 'nominate' procedure, the above is used but omitting the initial 'transform (+detailed design, −actual functions)'. Remember that a partial design may already exist on entry to the task (for verification) hence the '+detailed design' in the first line.

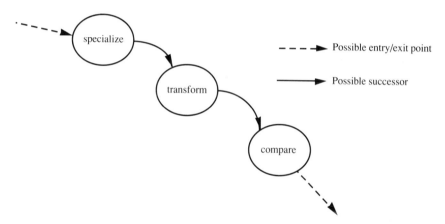

Figure 12.32 Task Structure for Simple Configuration (Verify)

/* Verify */
Simple Configuration (+requirements, +detailed design, −difference) by
    specialize (+requirements, −required functions)
    transform (+detailed design, −actual functions)
    compare (+required functions, +actual functions, −difference)

Strategies

Strategic knowledge for Simple Configuration will be concerned with specifying whether a pure nominate, pure verify or some mixture of the two is required. It could also be concerned with the control of the potential overlapping of inferences in the nominate and nominate/verify tasks, i.e. when 'specialize' is performed, compared with the main loop of the task.

Example

Typical applications of Simple Configuration might be in the selection and assembly of optional car components according to customer requirements, placing printed circuit cards in an electronics rack, or building a modular PC-compatible computer. Taking the last case, the task proceeds as follows:

1. A PC specification is presented. This states requirements such as 'the machine must have a fast processor, large hard disk capacity, fast networking, and high-resolution graphics'. First, specialize these requirements into required functions, i.e. for the examples listed, 486 processor with 33 MHz clock, 200 MB disk, Ethernet capability, VGA graphics, etc. In addition, defaults are also determined, resulting in additional required functions such as PC-compatible, 200 W power supply, real-time clock, and serial and parallel ports.

2. Take what we have at the moment in the current detailed design (which at the start of the configuration could be empty) and transform it into the actual functions that that design can perform (which could be none, initially).

3. Compare these actual functions with the required functions we determined in step 1, resulting in a difference set specifying the functions yet to be incorporated into the detailed design. In this case, let us assume that all the required functions are yet to be met.

4. Select design elements, i.e. real-world components that meet these required functions, one at a time, e.g. select an Intel 486 33 MHz processor, a Seagate hard disk model number 1234, a Novell Ethernet card type A, a Paradise VGA card version 1, a HiPower power supply, etc.[5]

5. Assemble these design elements, one by one, into a new detailed design based on the existing detailed design (which first time around may mean building a completely new design).

6. Transform this updated detailed design into its actual functions each time a new design element is added. Compare the updated actual functions with the original required functions derived in step 1. If the difference is zero, i.e. there are no required functions that are not met by the actual functions, then stop with a working configuration. Otherwise there are still unsatisfied required functions, so keep going by returning to step 4. If the selection in step 4 fails, then stop with an incomplete configuration.

Although it *partially* solves the PC configuration problem, the 'common resources' issue with this task, as mentioned earlier in this section, can be highlighted using the above example. In the case of the required functions 'parallel port', 'serial port', and 'real-time clock', it is possible to find a single design element in the domain, a multi-function card, that satisfies all these functions. However, because the task tries to select design elements for each function individually, it cannot take into account the fact that a multi-function card selected to meet the 'parallel port' function will also meet other required functions. Hence, additional design elements will be selected and a detailed design will result which will have unused spare capacity (in this case, three partially used multi-function cards!). The incremental configuration task described next handles this type of problem.

System Synthesis – Incremental Configuration

GTM

Inference Structure
See Figure 12.33.

Domain Roles
Requirements
   Functional requirements on the system to be configured.
Element demands and constraints
   The requirements broken down into resources required per element (component of the system) and the constraints on how they can be arranged within the system.
Current detailed design
   The present state of the configuration; during problem solving, this represents where the result of the previous iteration is fed back to.
Current design elements
   The design elements making up the current detailed design.
Grouping context
   A relevant level of abstraction within the context of the system, such as a functional area or sub-system.
Required design elements and constraints
   Design elements that are needed to meet the element demands, plus the constraints associated with those elements.
Relevant design elements
   The subset of the current design elements that form part of the current grouping context.
Additional required design elements
   Extra design elements that are required to meet the requirements on the system.
New detailed design
   The result of one iteration of the task, representing an increment towards a fully configured system.

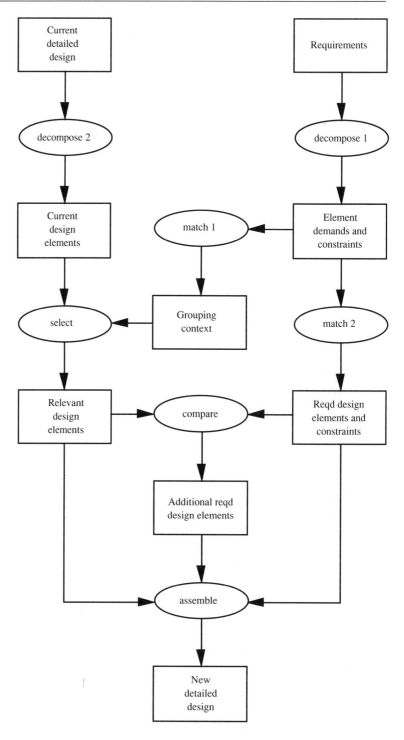

Figure 12.33
Inference Structure for
Incremental
Configuration

Inference Types

Decompose 1

Decomposes requirements into element demands and associated constraints. (This step is unnecessary if the requirements are supplied to the task in a pre-decomposed form.)

    Method: Heuristic decomposition, hierarchical decomposition, etc.

    Knowledge: Heuristics, construction rules, etc.

Match 1

Matches element demands and constraints to determine a grouping context.

    Method: Heuristic match, unification, etc.

    Knowledge: Match criteria, knowledge of grouping contexts in the system.

Match 2

Matches element demands and constraints to determine a full set of design elements (and constraints on them) which will meet the demands.

    Method: Heuristic match, unification, etc.

    Knowledge: Match criteria, knowledge of available design elements for use in the system.

Decompose 2

Decomposes the current detailed design (intermediate configuration) into its constituent design elements.

    Method: Heuristic decomposition, hierarchical decomposition, etc.

    Knowledge: Heuristics, construction rules, etc.

Select

Selects the relevant design elements from the total set making up the current detailed design, using the grouping context as selection criteria.

    Method: Rule-based selection, hierarchical selection, unification, etc.

    Knowledge: None.

Compare

Compares the required design elements with the existing relevant design elements in order to determine if any more elements are required.

    Method: Attribute matching.

    Knowledge: Comparison criteria.

Assemble

Assembles the constraints arising from the required design elements, together with the current (relevant) design elements and any additional design elements as determined by the compare.

Method: Constraint satisfaction, rule-based assembly.

Knowledge: Construction rules.

Task Structure

Incremental Configuration proceeds by iterating over a number of 'grouping contexts' defined in the system, and incrementally increasing the coverage of the configuration. Each iteration starts with the current set of requirements and the current level of design. Each iteration ends with producing a new detailed design, which represents a step towards a full configuration. One option for the Task Structure is as follows:

> *Incremental Configuration*
>
>   *(+current detailed design, +requirements, −new detailed design) by*
>   *REPEAT*
>   *decompose 1 (+requirements, −element demands & constraints)*
>   *match 1 (+element demands & constraints, −grouping context)*
>   *match 2 (+element demands & constraints, −required design elements & constraints)*
>   *decompose 2 (+current detailed design, −current design elements)*
>   *select (+current design elements, +grouping context, −relevant design elements)*
>   *compare (+required design elements & constraints, +relevant design elements, −additional required design elements)*
>   *assemble (+constraints (from required design elements), +relevant design elements, +additional required design elements, −new detailed design)*
>   *UNTIL configured at the required level*

Clearly there is room for parallelism in the task, and pipelining across levels of the iterative operation. For example, both decomposes may operate in parallel, as can the two matches, and so on. Pipelining is achieved by starting the next level of iteration before the previous one has been completed. Such techniques are commonly possible across many of the synthesis Generic Task Models.

Strategies

There are a few alternative Task Structures for Incremental Configuration, which can be selected from during problem solving using strategic knowledge. These alternatives mostly centre on the ordering of the matches and decompositions.

Example

Typical applications of Incremental configuration might be in domains similar to that for Simple Configuration (see p. 341), but where the configuration problem involves resources which can realize more than one function – the so-called 'common resources' problem mentioned for Simple Configuration. Thus, continuing the theme of building a modular PC-compatible computer used in the Simple Configuration example, the task proceeds as follows:

1. A PC specification is presented, as before. This states requirements such as 'the machine must have a fast processor, large hard disk capacity, fast networking, and high-resolution graphics'. First, decompose this single specification statement into its constituents and the constraints between them, i.e. 'fast processor', 'large hard disk capacity', fast networking', 'high-resolution graphics' are the separate requirements; 'all functions should be on separate cards' and 'all cards must use the EISA bus standard' are examples of constraints.
2. Match the required resources onto related groups of functionality, resource types, etc. These groups ('grouping contexts') will be inherent to and derived from the architecture of the system being configured, so in the PC case, potential groups would be: processor, memory, disks, ports, etc.
3. Match the required resources and their associated constraints onto design elements, i.e. real-world components, that meet these required functions, selecting one at a time (e.g. Intel 486 33 MHz processor, etc. – see examples listed for Simple Configuration, step 4).
4. Decompose the current detailed design we have (which at the start will be empty, but during the iteration will be the increasingly configured system) into its design elements.
5. Select from these current design elements, on the basis of a particular grouping context, a set of related current design elements. This is done because it is sensible to configure sub-systems of related design elements. Note that some design elements may fall into more than one grouping, which is how the common resources problem is addressed. Thus, in the PC example we could select all the current I/O port-related design elements (for grouping context = I/O ports).
6. Compare the subset of current design elements just selected with the actual required design elements obtained in step 3, resulting in a difference which specifies the additional design elements required.
7. Assemble these additional design elements together with the current grouping context's existing design elements, taking into account the

constraints associated with the new design elements, to form the new detailed design.

8. Keep going until the system is configured at the right level of detail and coverage of grouping contexts.

GTM

12.6.3   *System Synthesis – Planning*

The **Planning** task is concerned with taking an initial state and determining the actions required to meet a final goal (which may involve sub-goals), within a set of constraints. Although sometimes viewed as a sub-task of design, the planning task has a Generic Task Model of its own. The output of the task is a refined version of the original plan (initial state → goal state) with some or all of its actions decomposed – but still captured in the same knowledge structure (the 'plan'). Optionally, a resource allocation can be output.

Inference Structure
See Figure 12.34.

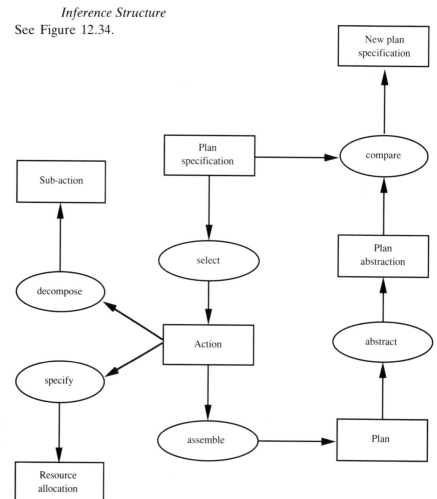

Figure 12.34
Inference Structure for
Planning

Inference Types and Domain Roles

Select

On the basis of the requirements in the specification, select an action which is appropriate.

Input: *Plan specification.* (1) A pair of partial descriptions of the world representing those features that need to be different as a result of plan execution. (2) A set of actions which must be performed and constraints on them (such as deadlines) which must be satisfied.

Output: *Action.* Some behaviour that changes features of the world.

Method: Structure matching and heuristic association between actions and types of plan they are useful for.

Knowledge: Knowledge about the effects of actions and the contexts in which they can take place.

Decompose

Break down an action into two or more sub-actions which represent a more detailed description of the behaviour required.

Input: *Action.* As above.

Output: *Sub-action.* A more detailed action.

Method: Heuristic decomposition, hierarchical decomposition, etc.

Knowledge: Knowledge about alternative ways that actions can be broken down and temporal relations between sub-actions.

Specify

Satisfy the resource requirements of an action by selecting resources or reducing the set of resource options. The former represents an instantiation of the action with respect to resources, the latter a refinement of the action description.

Input: *Action.* As above.

Output: *Resource allocation.* Some agent or other object required to perform the action. This may be a set of options one of which must be used.

Method: Heuristic match, direct association, etc.

Knowledge: Resource requirements of actions. Availability of resources.

Assemble

Satisfy temporal constraints holding between actions by assigning an ordering on their execution. Time stamping of actions represents the *instantiation* of actions with respect to time. Assigning partial orderings or ranges of time values represents the *refinement* of actions with respect to time.

Input: *Action.* As above.

Output: *Plan.* A set of actions which are (possibly partially) ordered and (possibly partially) resourced and which may also be time-stamped.

Method: Constraint satisfaction.

Knowledge: Precedence constraints holding between actions, constraints arising from shared resources.

Abstract

Given a plan or partial plan identify the effects of executing it.

Input: *Plan.* As above.

Output: *Plan abstraction.* A set of partial state descriptions indicating what will have changed at the end of plan execution.

Method: Identification of total effects of plan, possibly by simulation.

Knowledge: None.

Compare

Given a candidate plan and its requirements, identify outstanding requirements that would remain after its execution.

Input: *Plan abstraction.* As above.

              Plan specification. As above.

Output: *New plan specification.* Any outstanding discrepancies are new problems for which plans must be derived. Therefore the output can be used as an input for the *Select* inference type.

Method: Structure matching.

Knowledge: None.

Task Structure

The Planning Inference Structure described above is particularly generic, covering a wide variety of specific planning techniques. Figure 12.35 illustrates the valid sequences of inferences as a dependency graph. The following are five specific approaches to planning based on this dependency graph:

1. *Island-driving* – Island-driving represents a bottom-up approach to problem solving that is appropriate when dealing with uncertain or loosely specified problems. In planning it is realized as the grouping

of primitive actions into appropriate clusters. Once such 'islands' are established, the search proceeds by attempting to link the islands in the best possible way. This tends to occur when a human problem solver attempts to schedule a set of errands. Useful groups of errands which are located close to each other are identified and become temporally fixed, and planning proceeds by attempting to incorporate further useful errands while navigating between the islands. The Task Structure shown in Figure 12.36 reflects this approach. The establishing of islands is performed by selecting and assembling groups of actions. Once this is done the consequences on the initial requirements drives the search for more islands.

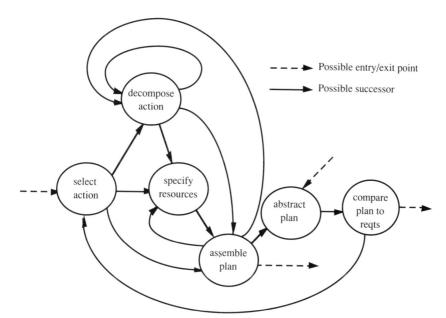

Figure 12.35 General Task Structure for Planning

2. *Incremental non-hierarchical planning* – This approach is quite restricted and simple. It is suitable only for simple problems for which there is a limited number of possible actions and states of the world and for which good heuristics as to the progress of a plan exist. An example is the well-known 'Cannibals and Missionaries' problem. This approach follows the same model as island-driving but the selection of actions is restricted to those that can follow on from the action previously selected. For this case 'assembly' consists only of the addition of the selected action. The task can be driven in either a forwards or backwards direction. The Task Structure shown for island-driving in Figure 12.36 also fits this approach.

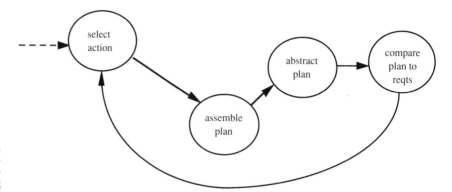

Figure 12.36 Task Structure for island-driving and non-hierarchical planning

3. *Action refinement* – In action refinement very abstract actions are first incrementally refined until a complete set of ordered detailed actions is arrived at (Figure 12.37). Once this is done, resources may be specified and the plan assembled. Each level of refinement produces an abstract plan which satisfies constraints that are formulated and propagated at each refinement. This is a deterministic approach to planning and is reflected in the absence of the use of 'abstract-compare' inferences. A precondition of its effective use is a very detailed knowledge of types of actions in the domain and their resource requirements.

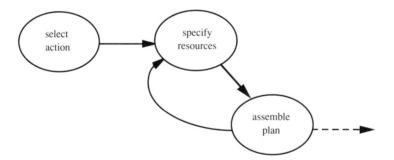

4. *Action breakdown* – In action breakdown, each action is decomposed into sub-actions, which are then immediately assembled into the plan (Figure 12.38). Implicit in this approach is the use of some kind of 'consists-of' structure as a guide for the decomposition of actions. This may be represented explicitly as a hierarchical structure of activities, or alternatively the decomposition may be inferred from structural relations between plan objects. Both action refinement and action breakdown can be thought of as 'knowledge-intensive' approaches, requiring detailed domain-specific knowledge about how

Figure 12.37 Task Structure for Action Refinement

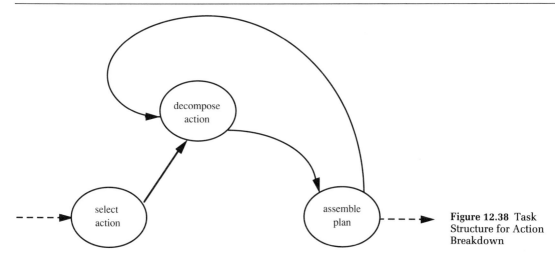

Figure 12.38 Task Structure for Action Breakdown

actions interact and break down. The main difference between action refinement and action breakdown is that in the case of the former, the complete decomposition of actions is done in one go, followed by the assembly of the complete plan; in action breakdown, decomposition and assembly is done on the fly.

5. *Pure scheduling* – In this structure the entry point is a set of actions to be scheduled (Figure 12.39). From the problem-solving perspective the goals that these actions achieve is of no importance. Problem solving is focused on temporal constraints holding between these actions. The specification of resources would in some cases be omitted if there was no choice as to which resource actions require. As the assemble inference is common to all the task structures it can be seen that all the preceding planning approaches must address the ordering of actions and thus embody some type of scheduling. (Scheduling is considered in more detail in its own Generic Task Model in Section 12.6.4.)

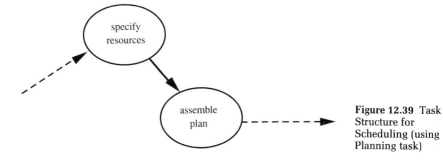

Figure 12.39 Task Structure for Scheduling (using Planning task)

Strategies

The Strategy Layer will be the planning of planning, so-called 'meta-planning'. A meta-planning approach considers the use of problem features at the Strategy Layer. The concerns of meta-planning are the identification of and resolution of conflict between the goals that the plan is intended to achieve. Where such defects in a plan arise, the best resolution can often only be identified with reference to the relative importance of meta-goals such as 'minimize resource consumption' or 'achieve as many goals as possible'. While it is possible to reference these meta-goals dynamically as problems arise, an alternative is to use them to define a strategy for the problem solving initially.

Example

The applications of planning are very diverse. A simple example is the planning of a shopping trip. We will show how the five approaches described under the Task Structure above can be used in this domain. Each one is self-contained.

In each case, assume that a plan to go shopping has been presented. This states two things: (1) rough descriptions of the world before the plan is enacted and then afterwards (e.g. 'the freezer is bare' and 'the freezer is full'; (2) an initial set of actions and constraints (e.g. 'go to the frozen-food shop and buy food' and 'go when the shop is open'). For each approach, the task proceeds as follows:

1. In island-driving, suitable 'islands' or groups of actions in the shopping trip domain are, for example, the actions associated with travelling to and from the shop (by car, say), or the actual process of selecting goods and purchasing them. Once an initial list of such groups has been identified, their temporal dependencies can be checked to form an outline plan or set of sub-plans – one has to get to the shop first before buying anything, for example. Then to refine the plan, further groups are identified that lie between the groups already defined and more detailed planning is achieved by continually filling in the gaps, so to speak. The task follows a sequence of: select an action (e.g. 'travel to the shop by car'), assemble this action with the current working set of actions (e.g. add it to 'select and purchase goods'), abstract the current working set to define what achieves (e.g. 'getting to the shops and getting goods'), match that with the the original requirements of the plan to see if the plan is refined enough (e.g. compare 'getting to the shops and getting goods' with 'the freezer is bare' and 'the freezer is full' – the task obviously has some way to go yet.)

2. In incremental non-hierarchical planning all the possible actions are known beforehand. Shopping is a good example, because often all the actions are familiar from previous experience – e.g. often travelling actions are habitual, as is the choice of shops and even what to buy. The task follows a sequence of (using backwards reasoning): the goal is having a full freezer back at home; the best possible previous action to this is travelling home from the shop (although other actions one could choose in a blind search are: travelling to the shops, buying the food, etc.); the best possible previous action to this is buying the food from the shop (but another state one could choose is: travelling to the shop, etc.); and so on.

3. In action refinement, very abstract actions, such as 'go to the shop' are fully decomposed into sub-actions, such as 'travel by car to the town', 'park the car', 'walk to the shop', etc.; 'travel by car to the town' is broken down into 'get in the car', 'drive to the town', 'park the car', etc. The actions are all fully decomposed. Given this set of actions, resources required by each action can be specified and the action/resource pair assembled into the plan. The task follows a sequence of: get fully decomposed action set (e.g. as just listed), select an action (e.g. 'go to the shop'), specify any resource requirements (e.g. 'mode of transport'), assemble this action/resource with the current working set, then go back to specifying the resources for the next action. Assembly is thus done in a batch.

4. In action breakdown, a *consists-of* structure of actions is used, e.g. 'go to the shop' consists of 'travel by car to the town', 'park the car', 'walk to the shop', etc.; 'travel by car to the town' consists of 'get in the car', 'drive to the town', 'park the car', etc. Using such a structure, appropriate orderings of actions can be selected. The task follows a sequence of: select an action (e.g. 'go to the shop'), decompose it one level and choose a sub-action (e.g. 'travel by car to the town'), assemble this sub-action with the current working set, then go back to decompose again. Assembly is thus done per action.

5. In pure scheduling, all that is done is to examine the constraints of how the actions in an existing plan can be ordered, which in this task is handled entirely within the assemble inference, e.g. assembling the actions 'travel by car to the town' and 'park the car' would imply discovering that the former should precede the latter. Specification of resource requirements for actions is simply considering what resources an action needs to perform its operation, e.g. travelling to the town by car requires a car, petrol, a driver, etc.

12.6.4   System Synthesis – Scheduling

The **Scheduling** task takes a plan and determines the temporal ordering of the groups of actions within that plan, according to a set of minimizing constraints, e.g. lowest cost, shortest time, etc. Scheduling can be viewed as a simple form of planning. Like configuration, a basic or initial plan will be given, but the details have to be worked out, e.g. departure/arrival times within a partly planned journey. The output of the task is the original plan, but with some or all of its time variables instantiated per action.

Inference Structure
See Figure 12.40.

Inference Types and Domain Roles
Select 1
Selects a variable that takes part in the constraint or has an effect on the constraint.

Input: *Plan.* A set of actions, which are possibly partially ordered, and resources which could be time-stamped.
              Parameter. Specifies a variable that takes part in the constraint under consideration.
Output: *Select variable.* The variable that takes part in a constraint.
Method: Direct association.
Knowledge: Variable range.

Select 2
The selection of a constraint.

Input: *Requirement.* For example, a deadline.
              Select   As above.
Output: *Constraint.* A formula which specifies the conditions under which a valid solution exists.
Method: Dependency Search, ordering, tree search.
Knowledge: Dependency graph, priority hierarchy, branch and bound.

Decompose
The constraint is decomposed into its variables which have a mapping to values in the plan.

Input: *Constraint.* As above.
Output: *Parameter.* As above.
Method: Decompose according to knowledge regarding the formal system used to express the constraints.
Knowledge: Constraint formulae and relations.

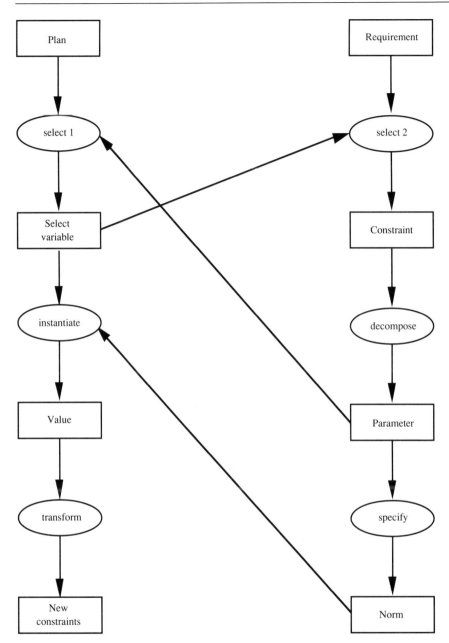

Figure 12.40
Inference Structure for
Scheduling

Specify

The possible value range of the variable in the constraint.

    Input: *Parameter*. As above.

    Output: *Norm*. The range of values that can be assigned to the
                    variable specified by the parameter.

Method: Range evaluation.
Knowledge: Constraint formulae and relations.

Instantiate
Assign a value to a variable within the range specified by the norm.
Input: *Variable value*. As above.
            Norm   As above.
Output: *Value*. Either a limiting of the range of the variable, or a distinct value.
Method: Pattern matching or numeric calculation.
Knowledge: Constraint formulae and relations.

Transform
Propagate the value assigned to the variable to other constraints and formulas.
Input: *Value*. As above.
Output: *New constraints*. The new constraints given a partially worked out schedule.
Method: Constraint propagation.
Knowledge: Dependency graph.

Task Structure
Scheduling can either be data-driven or constraint-driven. The appropriate Task Structures for these can be summarized in Figures 12.41 and 12.42. The control structures over these are simply sequences along the dependencies until the instantiate fails, thus indicating completion.

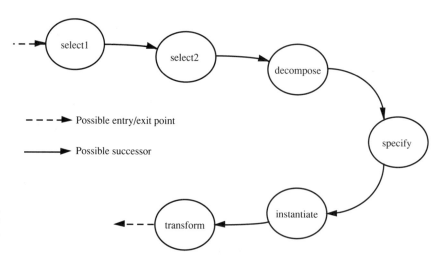

Figure 12.41 Task Structure for Scheduling (data-driven)

/* Data-driven */
Scheduling (+plan, +requirement) by
   REPEAT
      select 1 (+plan, −select variable)
      select 2 (+requirement, +select variable, −constraint)
      decompose (+constraint, −parameter)
      specify (+parameter, −norm)
      instantiate (+select variable, +norm, −value)
      transform (+value, −new constraints)
      requirement ← new constraints
   UNTIL instantiate fails

/* Constraint-driven */
Scheduling (+plan, +requirement) by
   REPEAT
      select 2 (+requirement, −constraint)
      decompose (+constraint, −parameter)
      select 1 (+plan, +parameter, −select variable)
      specify (+parameter, −norm)
      instantiate (+select variable, +norm, −value)
      transform (+value, −new constraints)
      requirement ← new constraints
   UNTIL instantiate fails

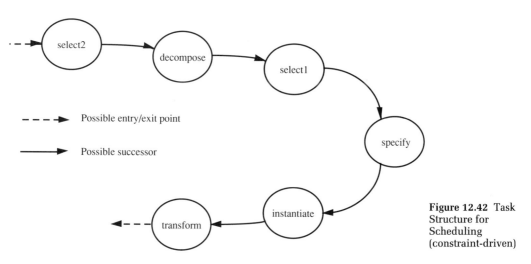

- - - →   Possible entry/exit point

——→   Possible successor

Figure 12.42 Task Structure for Scheduling (constraint-driven)

Strategies

Strategic knowledge for Scheduling will take into account the selection of a data-driven or constraint-driven approach, or some mixture of the two.

Example

A simple example of the use of Scheduling is in the domain of a shopping trip, as we used in planning (see Section 12.6.3). The task proceeds as follows (constraint-driven):

1. A partial (i.e. not fully scheduled) plan to go shopping has been presented (perhaps as the result of using the planning task). First, select from the requirements associated with this plan (e.g. the shop must be open), constraints (e.g. must get to shop after opening time and before closing time).

2. Decompose the constraints into parameters, e.g. 'opening time' and 'closing time'.

3. Select appropriate time variables from the plan on the basis of these parameters, e.g. 'departure time' and 'shopping time'.

4. Specify the expected (or 'normative') ranges of values of the parameters, e.g. 'opening time = about 9 am' and 'closing time = about 5:30 pm'.

5. Instantiate the time variables taken from the plan with values that are within the required ranges just specified, e.g. 'departure time = after 9 am' and 'shopping time = 5:30 pm minus start_time'; alternatively, these could be even more specific, such as 'departure time = 10 am', etc. (The task could iterate around choosing such particular values within the ranges specified by the norms, perhaps even refining the norm ranges each time, until an appropriate set of values is arrived at.)

6. Transform these new values into a form representing new constraints (e.g. 'must leave after 9 am' and 'must restrict how long we shop for') and re-start the task to look at these and the remaining constraints and requirements. The new constraints may also impact the next level of requirements, e.g. the newly assigned departure time may affect when to get up in the morning. Stop the task completely when no more variables can be instantiated, i.e. all the time variables in the plan have been instantiated and the schedule is complete.

12.6.5   *System Synthesis – Modelling*

Modelling is similar to the design task in many ways. The difference is the input modelling used: it involves much stronger constraints than most design tasks and it has to satisfy guidelines from the object to be modelled. Thus, the method of evaluating a solution will be stricter for a modelling task. However, no Generic Task Models have been developed that are specific to Modelling at the time of writing.

Notes

1. There are some models covered in the library that only have simple descriptions in the current state of the art. These are in plain type.
2. Note there is not necessarily a one-to-one correspondence. For example, there may be Domain Roles in a model that are only outputs, but which do not correspond with an output of the task shown below. This is because the models sometimes show possible intermediate outputs which are not shown. Likewise, not all optional inputs are shown.
3. Be careful! Some of the input Domain Roles are therefore also used as outputs. This occurs primarily with the following GTMs: Simple Configuration, and Planning and Scheduling. However, this sort of 'side effect' techique can be found useful in other tasks.
4. If one replaces the *consists-of* structure used by systematic diagnosis tasks with an *is-a* structure, one effectively gets the Systematic Refinement task. This is how a diagnosis task may be used for classification and vice versa.
5. Inference Types can thus in some senses be viewed as degenerate problem-solving tasks – see also 'verify' as a manifestation of the Verification task as an Inference Type, as used in Mixed Mode Diagnosis, on p. 280.
6. N.B. Although some of these manufacturers exist, some of the products certainly do not. They are simply examples of what we mean by design elements – specific components.

13 Library of problem-solving methods and knowledge representations

This chapter presents a basic set of 'problem-solving methods' and knowledge representations. These are used during behavioural design of the KBS sub-system in KADS, in the KBS Design activity 'Assign Design Methods' (see Section 7.2.3). Problem-solving methods are used to realize Inference and Composite Problem-Solving Functions; knowledge representations are used to describe the contents of Domain Model items. Also in this chapter, combinations of methods and representations are presented which can support the whole of KBS Design – particularly via the KBS Design Framework (see Section 7.2.1), as well as in the 'Assign Design Methods' activity. These combinations are termed problem-solving 'paradigms'. Thus, the three main parts to this chapter are guides to:

- *Suggested problem-solving methods grouped by Inference Type* – offering several options for realizing an inference step.
- *General knowledge representations* – concentrating particularly on the representations used or referenced elsewhere in this book.
- *Further methods and representations in combination*, grouped by 'paradigm' – offering more options for realizing an inference step and its associated knowledge.

For reasons of size, this library can only contain summary descriptions. Its contents are also neither exhaustive nor exclusive. Pointers to more complete descriptions of problem-solving methods and knowledge representations can be found in the Bibliography ('Problem-solving methods and knowledge representation'). The KBS developer should have a good selection of such texts to hand when embarking on the implementation of a non-trivial system. In addition, some knowledge of problem-solving methods and knowledge representations is assumed of the reader – this is a 'memory jogger' library, not a chapter of in-depth or rigorous explanations.

13.1   Problem-solving methods grouped by Inference Type

Essentially, problem-solving methods are computational approaches to reasoning. In a system built using KADS they map onto (parts of) the required problem-solving behaviour, as described by the Expertise Model. One way to classify them is by the Inference Type that they can be used to realize most directly.[1] This allows the designer to look at the Inference Types, and to choose corresponding methods from this classification. There is at least one method described below for every Inference Type in the library presented in Section 11.2.

Figure 13.1 is based on the hierarchical classification of Inference Types shown in Figure 11.2. The same breakdown is used to order the presentation of the problem-solving methods in this section as was used in Section 11.2 for the Inference Types.

```
Methods for Inference Types
    Concept Manipulation
        Generate Concept
            Instantiate Methods
            Generalize Methods
            Classify (Identify) Methods
        Change Concept
            Abstract Methods
            Specialize (Refine, Specify) Methods
            Assign_Value (Change_Value) Methods
                Compute (Evaluate) Methods
        Distinguish Between Concepts
            Compare Methods
                Confirm Methods
        Filter, or Home-in on Concepts
            Select Methods
        Associate Concepts
            Match (Associate, Relate, Map) Methods
    Structure Manipulation
        Build or Destroy Structure
            Assemble (Aggregate, Compose, Augment) Methods
            Decompose Methods
        Re-arrange Structure
            Transform Methods
            Sort Methods
            Parse Methods
```

Figure 13.1 A hierarchy of methods for Inference Types

13.1.1   Methods for Concept Manipulation: Generate Concept

Instantiate

Instantiation may be directly supported by an implementation environment, e.g. Prolog, or by instance creation in an object-oriented programming language.

- Sometimes the required instantiation may follow implicitly from a *numerical calculation* or other *computation* in such an environment.
- It can also involve the *direct manipulation* of structures with attributes, such as frames, and individually filling the attribute slots with values.

Where instantiation appears to require more complex methods, such as *pattern matching* or *searching over a hierarchy*, it is likely that instantiation is only one *part* of the required inference. Either another choice of Inference Type or an additional Inference Type as well as 'instantiate' may be needed.

Generalize

Generalization methods can be characterized as using *inductive* or *'learning'* mechanisms – in contrast to the 'classify' and 'abstract' methods, which are essentially deductive. Inductive problem-solving methods are at a less well-evolved stage of development than deductive ones and are the focus of extensive research at the time of writing. Therefore, there are many different examples of such methods. Some general pointers are given below. (Note that the realization of 'generalize' inferences may well be costly in terms of processing time and require extensive experimental prototyping.)

Genetic learning – These algorithms facilitate machine learning, based on a simplified view of the role of *genetic inheritance* within the evolutionary process in biology. Learning occurs through the growth of structures of knowledge that are in competition with each other. Over time, each set of structures produced is called a 'generation'. The structures are tested in the domain, and each structure is graded according to an evaluation of its relative performance within its generation. New structures are produced by combining existing structures from the previous generation. This is done on a probabilistic basis, favouring those that are found to be successful. Operators are used in the generation process which are based loosely on those types of operators found in biological systems, such as in the transformations of DNA during reproduction. The 'generate-test-generate-test...' process repeats until a solution results which is deemed 'acceptable'. A drawback to this method is the lack of any readily available explanation of the reasoning process to be fed back to the user.

Neural learning – This approach is also based on a biological system – modelling brain mechanisms. It is often implemented in the form of the so-called '*neural network*'.[2] The most beneficial application areas are likely to be those where generalization is performed over imprecise data, e.g. pattern recognition in vision systems and speech recognition. This is an area of considerable research. Like the genetic learning method, a current drawback is the lack of explanatory feedback to the user.

Analytic learning – These techniques can be used to derive *evaluation functions* for nodes in a tree search. The algorithm takes as its input a set of nodes in the search space, a set of heuristics for evaluating nodes and a set of node successors divided into good and bad choices. The evaluation function derived contains weightings for each heuristic, based on their performance in evaluating successors against an idealized function yielding '0' for bad choices and '1' for good. As with the genetic and neural approaches, no useful explanations can be provided to the user.

Symbolic learning – These methods, such as '*explanation-based learning*', '*similarity-based learning*' ('*reasoning by analogy*') and '*incremental learning*', have the common goal of inducing general statements from a set of specific ones. For example, explanation-based learning requires a trace of specific explanations to generalize (as opposed to a set of test cases). On the basis of known relations in the base set of facts, new relations are hypothesized and tested. The incremental approach is distinguished by testing new facts against the current set of induced statements and consequently modifying the set.

Classify (identify)

Five alternative methods for classification inferences have been identified below. The simpler methods (table look-up, decision tree, and simple rule-based) are usually appropriate when the features of the input to the inference map directly to the features of the desired output. Otherwise some form of abstraction of the features of the input must take place (see 'abstract' methods) prior to performing the tests for membership of the output class.

Table look-up – This method consists of two parts. First, relevant features of the input are extracted and matched against those of a candidate concept. This yields a vector of truth values for concept features. This vector is referenced in a table of all possible vectors for the concept. For each vector a probability is assigned, indicating the likelihood that the input is described by the concept. To produce a solution, either the highest probability one is output or, optionally, the whole set may be produced.

Decision tree – Concepts are organized into a *tree structure* where each non-terminal node marks a test on features of the input. The result of a test will point to a branch to be followed to the next node down. The algorithm works down the tree, applying the test at each node and following the resulting route to the next node. Leaf (terminal) nodes in the tree are the concepts that are returned as solutions.

Rule-based classification – There are two alternative rule-based approaches to classification. The first uses a flat set of rules which provide a direct mapping between features of the input and possible output concepts. This is suitable for very simple cases. The second approach uses two types of rule: first, rules that map from input features to more abstract output concept-level features; second, mappings from these features to the possible output concepts. This approach is appropriate for realizing a pair of inferences 'abstract' followed by 'classify' (see 'Abstract' methods). Classification using '*heuristic association*' is usually a form of rule-based classification. (See also rule-based methods in Section 13.3.)

Structured matching – This combines the approaches of decision trees and table-lookup in order to handle feature abstraction. Possible outputs are represented within '*abstraction trees*', with leaf nodes representing features of the input. At each intermediate level disjunct groups of abstract features are clustered. For each cluster, a look-up table (see above) is defined matching features of the input to the abstract features. Classification proceeds by descending the tree and performing a look-up test on the input at each level. Search is cut off at nodes for which a local probability threshold is exceeded. It continues until either all routes are closed (in which case classification has failed for this concept), or until a successful match is performed at the leaf level. As only one successful match is required to classify successfully, a depth-first traversal is most appropriate for this approach.

Hierarchical refinement – This approach may exploit the rich and flexible representation systems provided by tools such as ART and KEE, but it is also possible to build the method from more basic building blocks. Possible output concepts are organized into a *taxonomic (classification) hierarchy*. At the highest level is the most abstract possible concept, 'thing' or 'object', i.e. a class into which everything falls. Beneath this, concepts are specializations of their 'parent' concepts, where the 'children' inherit attributes or other characteristics from their parents. The specialization may take several forms:

- New attributes are introduced.
- Values for attributes are restricted.
- A structural description involving the concept is introduced or specialized.
- A structural description defines a relationship between nodes in the hierarchy.

Each node therefore has at least one feature which distinguishes it from its siblings. Classification entails finding the most specific concept in the hierarchy for which attributes agree best with the features of the input. This will proceed by descending the hierarchy and finding at each level the node whose attributes, value restrictions and structural descriptions are in closest agreement with the input. Classification can also be envisaged over a general *graph*, as opposed to a pure hierarchy.

13.1.2 Methods for Concept Manipulation: Change Concept

Abstract

Abstraction methods can be seen as complementary to specialization methods (cf. 'specialize'). Both can be realized using *production rules* or *navigating over graphs* such as hierarchies. They are distinguished by different control regimes in that abstraction can be thought of working in the 'opposite direction' to specialization (and vice versa). As with 'classify' methods, this inference is often a precursor to classification. However, in the general case, abstraction is necessary where specific data need to be expressed in an abstract way if the data is to be interpreted. Other forms of abstraction are '*definitional*' and '*qualitative*'. The first is usually meant as a form of rule-based abstraction, where the rules 'define' what is meant by 'abstract'. The second is simply used to emphasize qualitative reasoning.

Rule-based abstraction – Rules express a relation between a set of specific features in the antecedents and at least one abstract feature in the consequence. Conditions (antecedents) and conclusions (consequences) are usually strings representing logical expressions. For example, specific features might appear on the left-hand side of the rules and more general ones on the right. There may be intermediate-level features expressed by some rules, so abstraction may require the firing of sequences of related rules; or rules might be 'flat', with each rule representing one complete abstraction. Abstraction could then be driven in a forward direction, for example, with evaluation of the antecedents first (forward chaining). Without a more complex strategy, all rules are fired in simple sequence until no more are applicable or the abstraction is found. Alternatively, abstraction may proceed by processing specialization rules in reverse, by backward chaining, say – see 'Rule-Based Specialization'. (Other variations of rule-based processing for abstraction are possible.) Abstraction using '*direct/heuristic association*', or just '*heuristic abstraction*', is generally a form of rule-based abstraction. (See also rule-based methods in Section 13.3.)

Hierarchical abstraction – Cf. Hierarchical Refinement described under 'classify'. Possible output concepts are organized into a hierarchy. At the highest level is the most abstract possible concept, 'thing' or 'object', i.e. a class into which everything falls. Beneath this concepts are specializations of their parent concepts. The specialization may take several forms, as with 'Hierarchical Specialization'. Abstraction may entail starting at a leaf node or an intermediate node, and navigating up the tree to a more abstract node. This navigation may step one link, or more, depending upon the type of abstraction required. A test may be applied to stop the abstraction at the right level. The same hierarchy may equally be used by an analogous, but inverse, specialization inference (cf. 'Specialize'). Abstraction can also be envisaged over a general graph, as opposed to a pure hierarchy. Abstraction by '*inheritance*' may use this process over an inheritance graph.

Specialize (refine, specify)

Specialization methods can be seen as complementary to abstraction methods. Both can be realized using *production rules* or *navigating over graphs* such as hierarchies. They are distinguished by the different control regimes, in that they operate in opposite directions for abstraction compared with specialization (cf. 'Abstract').

Rule-based specialization – This is analogous to 'Rule-Based Abstraction'. Rule-based specialization can take the form either of using the same rules as in rule-based abstraction, but run in reverse (backward chaining); or specific specialization rules may be written, to be evaluated using forward chaining. These are completely analogous to the forward chain rules for rule-based abstraction, but the consequence now forms a specialization or a step towards a specialization, with more general features on the left-hand side. Specialization using '*direct/heuristic association*', or just '*heuristic specialization*', is generally a form of rule-based specialization.

Hierarchical specialization – This is analogous to 'Hierarchical Abstraction'. The same hierarchy or graph may be used as for abstraction. The only difference is in the direction of navigation: in specialization, the hierarchy, say, is navigated away from the root. Again, specialization can also be envisaged over a general graph, as opposed to a pure hierarchy. '*Specialization by inheritance*' may use this process.

Assign_value (change_value)

Assignment of values is sometimes like 'instantiate', in terms of the underlying method. It may be directly supported by an implementation environment or may require the explicit manipulation of knowledge structures – where the *structure* is not changed but its contents are. Sometimes the required assignment of value(s) may follow implicitly from a *numerical calculation* or other *computation* in such an environment (cf. 'instantiate').

The apparently trivial assignment of values is more interesting where *probabilities* (or, more generally, 'uncertainty ratings') must be associated with values to support *uncertainty*. There are many different ways of implementing probabilities within the inference process, and further discussion is beyond the scope of this book (see Ng and Abramson, 1990, in the Bibliography, 'Problem-solving methods and knowledge representation'). If implemented, associating probabilities with values may have an influence on other methods (and, by implication, Inference Types) apart from 'assign_value', of course.

Compute (evaluate)

Computation is like 'instantiate' in that it is often directly supplied by an implementation environment, at least in a basic form. Also, compute is a specialization of 'assign_value' (cf.). However, in the general case, the computation or expression evaluation method may be extremely diverse and complex, depending upon the domain knowledge concerned. An important specific example, though, is the application of statistical methods. Compute may involve the *direct manipulation* of knowledge structures, and specially built expression *interpreters*, etc. Uncertainty implemented in the system can also make computation complex (see Ng and Abramson, 1990).

13.1.3 Methods for Concept Manipulation: Distinguish Between Concepts

Compare

In the general case, comparison methods are varied and domain-specific, although some basic comparison methods are provided by the various implementation platforms. One very general way of breaking down comparison is into three sequential steps:

1. *Feature matching*: First, comparison is made for similar features across the inputs, according to some control criteria (knowledge) specifying which features to examine (e.g. using '*attribute matching*' or '*structure matching*'); each feature is then examined in turn, and a check made for similarity according to the control criteria. Depending on the precise behaviour required, this operation could run to completion or could be stopped as soon as a difference is found.

2. *Computing differences*: Second, any detected differences across the examined features can be measured – for example, in a numerical case the values can be subtracted; qualitative differences are trickier but possible to calculate.

3. *Classification*: Third, the differences and similarities are compiled or converted into some result – an overall difference value or '*discrepancy class*', for example.

Note that the comparison criteria control knowledge may have to supply the following details: which features to compare; how to compare them for similarity; how to calculate differences; and how to calculate an overall result of the comparison.

Apart from this general description, a much simpler form of comparison can be envisaged centred on the humble IF-THEN-ELSE or CASE statements of conventional programming languages; in a more knowledge-based sense, comparisons can also be made using heuristics or other rules.

Confirm

Confirmation is used to check whether some assertion about a newly derived hypothesis is true. For example, a hypothesis may need to be checked to see if it is the only thing left. The following are some scenarios for confirmation methods:

- Confirmation could be used to check that the navigation of a hierarchy has reached a *leaf node*. In a more general case it should be able to check for any position within a hierarchy or a graph. This can be achieved using an *index* over the hierarchy or graph. The index could contain a list of the current leaf nodes, for example.
- Confirmation may be achieved by dynamically searching over a knowledge structure over which the hypothesis holds, to confirm a position in that structure. Every time the confirmation is requested, the structure will be researched. (Cf. just looking up positions in an index.)
- Confirmation could check that only *one conclusion* has been found during some problem solving. Again, this can be realized by confirm maintaining a list, this time of conclusion values. Confirm can then easily perform its task by examining the contents of this list when called.
- Confirmation could check the *unique truth* (say) of a general proposition; or that *all true* (say) propositions have been found in a knowledge base. Such confirmations may be performed by *exhaustive evaluation* over a knowledge base, where this is feasible. Alternatively, it may be possible to make available a special set of confirmation rules/heuristics and test these.

(Note that confirmation may also be realized by following a 'verification' task – see Section 12.4.2.)

13.1.4 *Methods for Concept Manipulation: Filter, or Home-in on Concepts*

Select

Selection can take many varied forms according to the domain requirements. However, the general principle is of searching over some collection of objects in order to find one or more of those object(s) on the basis of some control criteria (knowledge); then grouping or extracting those object(s). Thus, the central issue of the method is a *test*. (This makes it very like a 'match' inference – cf.) Different forms of implementing the test part of the method are:

- By using a *rule or rule-set* of some kind (ranging from a simple IF-THEN statement to a full-blown set of heuristics).
- By using '*generate-and-test*', where the collection is searched using an iterative approach.
- By using *unification*, which is where one object is bound to another based on the form and/or content of the object. Unification for selection is particularly useful in environments where it is built-in, such as Prolog.
- By using *decision trees*; and, in principle, it is possible to envisage a whole classification inference behind the test – see 'Classify'.

Specific forms of selection are:

- Selection by '*direct/heuristic association*' and '*(heuristic) matching*' – which are generally rule-based;
- Selection by '*(various types of) searching*' – is generally analogous to the use of decision trees, as in tree-searching, but can mean any of the methods;
- Selection by '*constraint satisfaction*' – can refer to a method supported by constraint handling provided by the implementation platform.

The extraction of the object(s) following the execution of the test to search for them is too knowledge structure-dependent to discuss, but will follow from the knowledge representation used in the input. In some cases an implicit decomposition of the input is required – see 'Decompose'. Similarly, some forms of decompose require an implicit selection.

13.1.5   *Methods for Concept Manipulation: Associate Concepts*

Match (associate, relate, map)

Matching is very like selection, in terms of method. In particular, it is based on the central idea of a test. (Cf. 'Select'.) For example, the simple case where the match is based on *heuristic rules* associating pairs of concepts is frequently used. It works by looking at the left-hand side (say) of some expression, and where there is a match with the input to the inference according to the control criteria, the right-hand side (say) of the expression is output (or added to the output collection). Likewise, *unification* is a popular choice of matching method. In general, though, the same methods described for the *test aspect of 'select'* may be used. Where matching differs is that the output of a match is the result of the test; in selection, a further step is required. (See 'Select'.) Specific forms of matching are (these are generally simple rule-based variations of the same form):

- 'Heuristic match(ing)';
- Matching by 'direct/heuristic association'.

13.1.6 Methods for Structure Manipulation: Build or Destroy Structure

Assemble (aggregate, compose, augment)

Assembly is about generating a structure from a set of components. It is the opposite of decomposition – cf. 'Decompose'. The most frequently encountered form of assembly is in building *knowledge structures* such as hierarchies and graphs. These structures can be assembled using a set of *construction rules*, defining the ordering of, partial ordering of or relationships between nodes within the hierarchy. (Cf. parsing and sorting.) *Constraint satisfaction* approaches are sometimes used to support this inference. Relations holding between component items are represented as constraints holding over variables representing the component's 'position' in the structure. The goal is to generate values for these variables such that all the constraints are satisfied. Note that assembly (and decomposition) inevitably involves the *direct manipulation* of structures, as opposed to just their contents. Apart from the above points, assembly is too general to give specific guidelines for methods, as its details depend on the structure being built.

Decompose

Decomposition is about breaking down a (knowledge) structure to gather a set of components. It is the opposite of assembly – cf. 'Assemble'. However, the core methods used have more in common with selection – cf. 'Select'. There are two forms of decomposition connected with selection:

- The first is where a selection from a structure requires an *implicit decomposition*.
- The second is where a decomposition from a structure results in a single or isolated collection of objects, which requires an *implicit selection*.

The selections involved in these operations could use the methods outlined for 'select'. The actual decomposition of a structure might require knowledge of how the structure is put together – *construction rules*, such as those used to 'assemble' the structure, might be used in reverse to break down the structure. Alternatively, new or specific '*decomposition rules*' might be used, which specify valid decompositions of the structure. (These could be like 'inverse assembly rules'.)

Specific forms of decomposition are:

- Decomposition by '*direct/heuristic association*' and '*(heuristic) matching*' – which are generally rule-based.
- Decomposition by navigation of a *part-of* hierarchy or other graph, '*hierarchical decomposition*'.

13.1.7   Methods for Structure Manipulation: Re-arrange Structure

Transform

Transformation takes a structural description as input and produces a new structure. Often this is best realized by a pair of '*decompose-assemble*' methods, but may be as complicated as to require a full-blown 'modification' task (see Section 12.5). One exception is the use of parsing methods – see 'Parse'. Transformation may also rely on the use of specific collections of rules, such as *definitional rules* for a new structure, or (structure-building) *construction rules*. *Default reasoning* may also apply. Special techniques such as *constraint propagation* can be used to help realize the inference. Otherwise, structure manipulation by transformation is simply too general to discuss without reference to a specific domain or knowledge structures.

Parse

Parsing takes an input structure as a flat string and produces a parse tree in which sub-strings are classified. There are two main methods used to do this, based on two different sorts of control knowledge, or '*grammar*'.

Rule-based grammars – Two design elements are needed for any parsing method: a grammar (a data structure) and a parsing algorithm. Grammars can be further decomposed into a set of rules representing how non-terminals can decompose to sequences of terminals and non-terminals, and a lexicon representing which classes of terminals a string can belong to. These methods are widely described in the literature.

Deterministic finite state grammars – Finite state grammars provide a convenient and efficient means of parsing programming languages and very small subsets of natural languages. The grammar is represented as a set of states linked by arcs indicating possible transitions from state to state – a form of finite-state machine known as an '*augmented transition network*' (ATN) (see 'Parsing methods' in Section 13.3). These transitions are marked with the inputs required to make the transition. The algorithm traverses the network by reading off inputs and following the required transition. These methods are widely described in the literature.

Sort

The sorting process is perhaps the most widely discussed computational approach in the field of computing. There are numerous methods described for this process in the literature. Note that sorting from an unstructured collection of objects requires an implicit assembly – see 'Assemble'.

Table 13.1 summarizes the Inference Types shown in Figure 11.2, alongside the associated methods described above.

Table 13.1 Summary of Inference Types and corresponding problem-solving methods

Inference Type	Methods
Instantiate	Attribute filling, Direct manipulation of structures, Implicitly through computation.
Generalize	Inductive reasoning, including: Genetic learning, Neural learning, Analytic learning, Symbolic learning.
Classify (identify)	Table look-up, Decision tree, Rule-based classification (Heuristic association), Structured Matching, Hierarchical refinement.
Abstract	Rule-based abstraction (Definitional abstraction, Direct association, Heuristic association, Heuristic abstraction), Qualitative abstraction, Hierarchical abstraction (Abstraction by inheritance).
Specialize (refine)	Rule-based specialization (Definitional specialization, Direct association, Heuristic association, Heuristic specialization), Qualitative specialization, Hierarchical specialization (Specialization by inheritance).
Assign_value (change_value)	Value filling, Direct manipulation of contents of structures, Implicitly through computation.
Compute (evaluate)	Direct manipulation of structures, Interpreters.

Inference Type	Methods
Compare	(Feature-matching + Computing differences + Classification), Rule-based comparison, Heuristic comparison.
Confirm	Indexing, Exhaustive evaluation, Rule-based confirmation, Verification task.
Select	(Searching + Grouping (+ Decomposition)), Rule-based selection (Direct association, Heuristic association, Heuristic matching), Generate-and-test, Unification, Decision trees, Constraint satisfaction.
Match (associate, relate, map)	Rule-based association (Direct association, Heuristic association, Heuristic matching), Unification.
Assemble (aggregate, compose, augment)	Rule-based construction, Constraint satisfaction, Direct manipulation of structures.
Decompose	Selection-based decomposition, Rule-based decomposition (Direct association, Heuristic association, Heuristic matching), Inverse construction, Unification, Decision trees, Constraint satisfaction, Hierarchical decomposition.
Transform	Decompose-Assemble methods, Modification tasks, Rule-based transformation, Default reasoning, Constraint propagation.
Parse	Rule-based grammars, Deterministic finite state grammars
Sort	There are many forms of sorting methods available from conventional computing. (May also require implicit Assemble.)

13.2   Knowledge representations

The purpose of this section is to summarize some knowledge representations that are found useful in building KBSs. In particular, it includes summary descriptions of the knowledge representations mentioned throughout this book. Knowledge representations have been discussed in the context of the Expertise and Generic Task Models, and in Behavioural Design. This section concentrates on knowledge representations to be used in the actual implementation of systems.

There are at least eight questions to consider when selecting an appropriate form in which to represent knowledge:

1. Can it comprehensively represent all the knowledge required? Concisely? If not, can it be supplemented by and interworked with another representation?

2. Can it support the required structure of the knowledge, as well as the basic contents?
3. Can it be easily maintained by the class of agent assigned to maintenance?
4. Can it support efficient execution of the problem-solving method?
5. Can it easily be mapped onto the chosen or available implementation platforms?
6. Can it support reasoning with an incomplete knowledge base, if required?
7. Can it support uncertainty, or other forms of modal logic, if required?
8. Can it avoid or minimize the dangers of paradoxes and self-references?

The main points are that knowledge representations should first be chosen with care for close correspondence with the form(s) of knowledge in the problem domain; second, though, the designer should take care not to compromise the constraints on the design. Typically, a good match of knowledge representation to a problem domain may not result in the most efficient production of a solution, perhaps potentially breaking a technical constraint. Thus, a good correspondence of knowledge representation from domain to system may benefit maintenance, for example; but a different knowledge representation may result in increased performance.

However, it is all these factors that make a usable library of representations hard to construct. We have therefore concentrated on summarizing the representations that we have mentioned in this book. There are five types, listed below under the following categories:

- *Networks* – including: hierarchies, graphs, semantic nets.
- *Rules* – including: production rules, meta-rules, heuristics.
- *Logic* – including: algebraic logics, first-order logic, modal logics, etc.
- *Frames* – including: attribute-values, slots, defaults, daemons, objects.
- *Others* – including: pseudo-code, problem-oriented languages, tables, lists.

13.2.1 *Network representations*

These include *hierarchies* (trees), *graphs* and *semantic nets* (networks). In the general case, they are a network of nodes joined by links. The nodes represent concepts or other knowledge entities (such as 'man', 'woman', 'John', 'Jane', 'husband', 'wife', etc.); the links represent relations (such as *is-a*, *is-married-to*, *can-marry*, etc.). A classification of networks in order of increasing specialization is as follows:

Type of network	Topology	Semantics of links
Semantic net	General graph	Mixture of relationships
Graph	General graph	Single relationship
Hierarchy	Tree	Single relationship

Particularly important hierarchies (or graphs) in KADS are '*is-a*' forms (cf. classification or inheritance hierarchies); and '*consists-of*' and '*part-of*' forms (as used in assembly, decomposition and transformation; and tasks such as diagnosis). Particularly important graphs are '*dependency graphs*' (as used in the Task layer descriptions of Generic Task Models and Expertise Models), '*OR*' and '*AND/OR*' graphs/hierarchies (as used in state-space searching problem-solving methods).

Graphs and hierarchies have similarities to frame representations and entity-relationship models in conventional software development. Frames may be stored at the nodes. Procedural knowledge may be attached to nodes in the network, as can be done with frames (see 'Frame representations').

- *Advantages* of network-based representations include: modularity and coherency; graphical, therefore easy to draw and understand (in principle).
- *Disadvantages* are that: they are relatively unexpressive (it takes a lot to say much), and complex facts, concepts and relationships are hard to represent; searches may have to be supplemented by indexing for efficiency; and exceptions, defaults and incorrect or incomplete information are difficult to implement.

13.2.2   *Rule-based representations*

Rules are perhaps the most familiar and accessible form of knowledge representation. They are also apparently a very 'natural' way of expressing many forms of knowledge – although they do have limitations. The most common form is the IF/THEN *production rule*. (In forward chaining, for example, satisfaction of the antecedents (IF part) gives rise to the evaluation of the consequents (THEN part).) Where more than one rule matches the current set of antecedents, '*conflict resolution*' is required to determine which consequences should be executed (e.g. using the RETE algorithm). '*Meta-rules*' may be used to determine the execution of other rules. Often the ordering of rules is significant in certain implementation platforms.

- *Advantages* of production rule-based representations include: a natural fine-grain modularity (at the single rule level) – allows for easy maintenance of the knowledge base, in principle; the possibility of firing single rules in isolation; explanations can be easily generated (in principle); simple forward/backward chaining reasoning is often similar to equivalent human problem solving, and only a single control regime is required; large rule-based systems can be constructed successfully.

- *Disadvantages* are that: control knowledge is often intermixed with domain knowledge – e.g. ordering of rules may be significant, or context knowledge has to be recorded as an explicit antecedent in each rule, etc.; rule bases have no intrinsic structure, and there may be many interdependencies between rules, so large knowledge bases are hard to maintain and debug; not all human problem-solving processes can be represented; rules do not address well the representation of basic domain facts, concepts and relationships; the 'match-select-fire' process of rule-based processing is inherently computationally inefficient; and exhaustive testing is effectively impossible by static analysis.

Note that rules are often used to supplement network- and frame-based representation schemes. For more on rules, see also rule-based methods in Section 13.3.

13.2.2   *Logic representations*

Using mathematical logic as a basis to represent knowledge has the advantage of having an off-the-shelf and well-understood means of formal evaluation and proof (in general). The basic idea is to apply a formally defined symbolic notation (an algebra) to the specification of statements that are true and to be able to draw conclusions, in the form of new statements, from only the statements already known. There are many forms of logic-based representations, including 'first-order (predicate) logic', developments of first-order logic based on its limitations, and others.

The basic elements of *first-order predicate logic* are: *Propositions*, which may be TRUE or FALSE; *Connectives*, which may be AND, OR, NOT and IMPLIES (so-called *'propositional logic'* consists of only connectives and propositions); *Quantification*, which may be FOR_ALL and THERE_EXISTS; and *Predicates*, which are sets of objects for which a certain property is true. Representing knowledge in first-order logic involves combining these elements into statements.

- The *limitations* of first-order logic include:
  – restriction to deductive reasoning (no induction is possible);

– the lack of handling 'intension' – qualities implied by a concept as opposed to the set of objects it describes (so-called '*modal logics*' address this);

– *monotonicity* – new axioms cannot invalidate previous conclusions, or put another way, one cannot 'un-assert' existing facts (this has given rise to '*non-monotonic logics*', *default reasoning*, *truth maintenance* (using Truth Maintenance Systems, such as JTMS, LTMS or ATMS – justification-based, logic-based and assumption-based, respectively), and '*temporal logics*', to handle the problems this causes when reasoning about time and other factors, e.g. beliefs);

– limited truth and falsehood (addressed by '*multi-valued*', '*uncertain*' and '*fuzzy logics*';

– no meta-propositions (propositions about propositions are allowed in *higher-order logics*, such as second-order; and alternatively, using 'modal logics').

13.2.4   *Frame representations*

Frames, also called schemata, are a simple means of representing objects in a structure. There are similarities with hierarchies and graphs. The idea is that a frame represents an *object*, and has a set of associated '*slots*', which can hold *values* of the *attributes* of that object. *Relationships* holding between objects are represented by links between frames or by separate 'relationship' objects.

Some resemblance to the frame representation found in entity-relationship modelling in conventional software development may be found; there are also parallel object-oriented techniques. *Default ('common sense') reasoning* and *inheritance* is often applied to frames, but there have been problems identified where default values need to be cancellable under certain conditions (also called '*exception handling*'). *Procedural knowledge* may be attached to frames in several ways: for example, functions may be attached to slots; alternatively, '*daemons*' may be attached to slots and fired up whenever their slot is updated and/or accessed. Reconstructing unstructured production rule knowledge bases using frame systems has been found to result in significant improvements in comprehensibility and ease of maintenance.

• *Advantages* of frame-based representations include: greater efficiency of execution than rules (no 'match-select-fire' cycle); convenient for representing hierarchies (slots can themselves be frames); good for representing basic domain facts, concepts and relationships; slots can be left unfilled.

- *Disadvantages* are that: the precise organization and structure of frames may be hard to select to achieve the required performance; complex facts, concepts and relationships are difficult to represent; and relatively hard to design, as there are many components to the representation – frames, slots, and organization are all non-trivial.

13.2.5 *Other representations*

There are three other groups of knowledge representation used in this book:

Tables and lists – These are straightforward but important simple representations. They are widely used in the systems built using KADS, as in most computer systems using a basically *von Neumann architecture*. Tables may have similarities with *arrays* and *database tables* in conventional software. Lists are likewise familiar from conventional computing.

Pseudo-code – This is not proposed as a directly implementable representation – although it is possible to envisage a formalization of pseudo-code used during Analysis into some specific language. An example of such a formalization is a *'problem-oriented language'* (POL). A POL is like a high-level specialized programming language but geared to a particular problem domain. Pseudo-code is typically used in KADS for representing control knowledge, such as in the Task and Strategy layers of the Expertise and Generic Task Models. There are potentially many variations, depending upon the origins of the writer and the requirements of the task in hand. For example, *imperative (procedural)*, or *declarative*, or even *applicative (functional)* code may be used. The style of the pseudo-code may be based on an existing programming language or it may be more rooted in natural language. Problem-oriented languages are naturally highly domain-specific.

Domain-modelling language (DML) – Finally, there is the DML as supplied by KADS. This is a general-purpose 'fall-back' notation for describing Domain Structures in the Domain layer of an Expertise Model (primarily), where a more (domain-) specific notation is not available. See Section 4.3.2 and the BNF specification of the notation in the Summary of Notations at the end of the book.

13.3   Problem-solving methods grouped by paradigm

Some problem-solving methods are widely applicable across more than one Inference Type, usable for realizing a broad range of Inference Functions. These can be classified according to how the problem is represented,[3] or what particular combination of knowledge structure and processing they based upon. The general term for this classification is 'problem-solving paradigm'. As with the other sections in this chapter, this classification can support Behavioural Design. But in this case it allows the designer to take a broader look at the structure of the problem to be processed in their system (as specified in the Expertise Model/ Functional Design Model), and take a more holistic perspective on the problem-solving process when selecting an appropriate method or combination of methods. This section complements the other two sections in this chapter, but note that there is inevitably some overlap.

Seven groups of problem-solving methods are distinguished below, derived from seven general-purpose ways of solving problems. The groups are not mutually exclusive. In particular, the search algorithms discussed under the state-space search methods may be used by all the other methods. The seven groups of methods are:

- *State-space searching* – problems solved using searches over solution spaces.
- *Rule-based* – problems solved by searching rule-sets.
- *Automatic deduction* – problems solved using highly generic inference algorithms.
- *Constraint satisfaction* – problems solved by satisfying a set of constraints.
- *Structure matching* – problems solved by recognizing patterns.
- *Parsing* – problems solved by grammatic analysis.
- *Model-based* – problems solved using searches over the states of models.

13.3.1   *State-space searching methods*

These methods are some of the most widely used in problem solving, either on their own or in support of other methods. Problem solving is represented in these methods as finding a path between some initial state and a goal state, through a 'space' (or set) of problem/solution states. A typical scenario is where the state space is represented as a graph, such as an *OR-graph* or an *AND/OR-graph*, and the knowledge about the problem is represented as a database of facts and rules. The method supplies a set of operators which can be used to construct new states, together with heuristics for deciding which state to explore next, on the basis of the database of facts and rules. Thus, the application of rules or operators causes the transition from one state to another. At any point in the search there may be several allowable transitions between states. In these cases, heuristics or algorithms may be used for evaluating then selecting or eliminating possible successor nodes to explore, thus reducing the size of the search space.

Several different algorithms for traversing the state space have been derived. Features of the problem will determine which is the most suitable. Figure 13.2 illustrates problem criteria and how they affect the choice of algorithm.

Search algorithms are embedded in the Prolog language (depth-first backward chaining) and in the interpreters of various expert system shells. Other implementation platforms may have their own built-in search algorithms. These algorithms are fundamental to the other groups of methods discussed in this section.

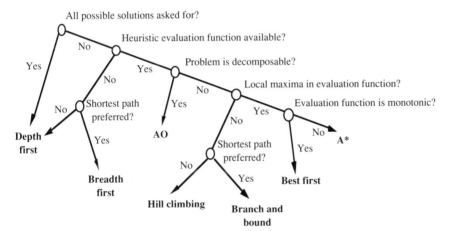

Figure 13.2 Search method selection as determined by problem features

The following summarizes the approaches taken by these algorithms:

Depth-first – At each state, apply any operator, then move on to the successor state. Where failure occurs, backtrack to the last state where another operator is applicable and continue. A key attraction of this algorithm is that it enables a solution to be found without all the branches needing to be expanded.

Breadth first – Apply each available operator at a given state in turn. Prune unproductive branches. Repeat for each successor state yielded until one route successfully terminates. A key attraction of this algorithm is that it avoids being trapped by dead-end branches of the search tree.

Hill climbing – In '*simple hill climbing*' a successor state is selected on the basis of a global evaluation function. In '*steepest-ascent hill climbing*' the successor state selected is the one that yields the highest value for a global evaluation function. It is presupposed in the latter case, therefore, that there are no local 'peaks' in the search space, where a solution has not been found but no improving successors to the current state are available. Problems with such local maxima and other features such as plateaus in the search space may cause either hill climbing algorithm to fail to find a solution. However, this situation can be solved with the special variation of hill climbing called '*simulated annealing*', which allows some downhill moves. Hill climbing can be seen as a variant of the very simple '*generate and test*' algorithm.

Branch and bound – This operates like hill climbing, except that it operates in a breadth-first manner on the set of possible successor states for which the evaluation function is within a certain threshold. It is therefore more suitable for cases in which the evaluation function is sub-optimal.

Best-first search – This is like depth-first search, but an evaluation function is used to select the successor state to explore first, rather than simply selecting at random. On backtracking, the second-best scoring successor will be explored. Best-first search is a way of combining the advantages of both depth-first and breadth-first searching.

A* – This is a variant of best-first search suitable for where there are multiple possible paths to some state and the shortest path is required. (Some might therefore call it a more general case of best-first search.) Where an expansion produces a state that was achieved by another path and the route is shorter than for the original, the evaluation function at that state is reduced and the reduction propagated to any successors produced earlier.

AND/OR (AO) tree search – Where the problem can be decomposed into non-interfering sub-problems each sub-problem is treated separately. The set of sub-problems is represented as 'AND' branches in a tree. 'OR' branches represent possible ways that a (sub)problem can be solved. The search is therefore conducted on an abstraction hierarchy of known possible solutions, rather than generating solutions dynamically. (In the general case the AND/OR structure may be a graph; also, a pure 'OR' graph or hierarchy is possible.) Specific examples of AO tree search algorithms are '*problem reduction*' and '*AO**'.

All the above algorithms can be used with either of two alternative goals:

- Where the *node* being searched for represents the solution; or
- Where the *path* taken by the search represents the solution.

An example of the former is in hierarchical classification (refinement), where a concept is classified on the basis of searching for a node further up in a specialization hierarchy (see methods for 'classify' in Section 13.1). An example of where the path taken by the search is the more important is in route-planning. In such cases *both* the goal state *and* the initial state are given, but a route must be found between the states – these are planning methods.

Planning methods are a special group, realized by search methods such as those summarized above, but also facilitated by special techniques, including: '*means–end analysis*', *least commitment strategy*, *triangle tables*, *meta-planning*, *immediate execution* and *plan boxes*. (In addition, a Generic Task Model is available for the 'planning' task in Section 12.6.3. This can be used to decompose the task into other methods.)

There are many other issues to consider in search methods beyond those briefly mentioned above. For example, a choice can be made between the use of simple *chronological backtracking* or more sophisticated *dependency-directed backtracking*. Further discussion is beyond the scope of this book, but the Bibliography ('Problem solving methods and knowledge representation') contains pointers to excellent sources for in-depth descriptions of state-space searching and other methods.

13.3.2   *Rule-based methods*

A rule is a mapping of a set of conditions (antecedents) onto a set of conclusions (consequences). Rules are a common representation used in problem solving. Often, certainty factors or probabilities are associated with the conclusions asserted, and/or with the antecedents, which can be used for reasoning with uncertainty. A particularly common form of rule is the heuristic, which is used to map direct associations of problem states or features onto new states or (sub-)conclusions, without further justification from the domain. Rules have the advantage of being accessible and comprehensible. A disadvantage is that they do not support the designer in structuring the problem representation – their basic underlying structure is fundamentally flat, and, although richer structures may be constructed, they are not built-in. Also, unless used with care, at least two types of problems can occur when rules are used:

1.   *Control knowledge can easily be mixed with domain knowledge* – Unfortunately, control-level rules are of the same form as domain-level

rules; further, it is possible to mix control-level conditions with domain-level conditions within a single rule. Conditions that are problem-solving control statements, as opposed to domain-level expressions, should be separated, if possible. Control statements are specific to a particular problem-solving task, thus any rule containing them cannot be used flexibly. Maintenance of rule-bases containing control statements will entail not just considering the validity of the rule but also identifying the contexts in which it is valid. It is far better to modularize the knowledge for the types of tasks it is to be used in. However, modularization can be difficult for large rule-bases, where there are many potential interdependencies.

2. *Context may affect the probability associated with a conclusion* – A common problem can occur with the use of probabilities in rules. When a probability is established for a rule it must be ensured that the context in which the rule might be applied will not affect the probability that the conclusion is true. Often knowledge cannot easily be decomposed in this way and dependencies are obscured. Consequently, the quality of the solutions yielded by the system will probably be variable, and the reasons for this may be hard to ascertain unless this factor is taken into account.

Some more problems and other issues relating to rules as a knowledge representation have been described in Section 13.2.

13.3.3   *Automatic deduction methods*

The principle underlying automatic deduction is that a purely declarative formal[4] description of domain facts and relations (the 'logic') can be separated from an inference mechanism (the 'control'). Thus, a problem is solved by presenting the formal declarative problem-statement and context to a general-purpose problem-solving algorithm. Often, the algorithm can be found in an implementation platform. For example, the *'logic programming'* Prolog language provides a 'hidden interpreter' to perform its general-purpose problem-solving capabilities. Some may consider *functional languages*, such as Lisp and ML, to be a form of automatic deduction.

The advantages of this approach are similar those of the rule-based method, including accessibility and comprehensibility. A shared disadvantage is that this approach also does not give rich support to structuring the problem representation, but it has an advantage of conciseness and simplicity in the representation.

However, writing efficient programs is often only feasible with a good understanding of how the interpreter works and by using non-logical expressions (e.g. the 'cut' operator in Prolog). Unfortunately, these tend to pollute the purity of the declarative statement of the problem and its context. The use of these operators re-introduces many of the maintenance problems which the approach seeks to solve. Current implementations also suffer from being not 'logically pure' in other ways, such as the lack of commutativity of the conjunction/disjunction operators in Prolog. (No practical programming language can be pure mathematics, however.) One solution to these problems may lie in the use of a meta-interpreter, if available, in which a purely declarative program is compiled to a more efficient one.

13.3.4   *Constraint satisfaction methods*

In constraint satisfaction a problem is represented as a set of constraints holding over the domains of variables (i.e. the ranges of values that those variables can take). The variables are often associated with the attributes of some object(s). A solution is a set of values for these variables in which all constraints are satisfied. One problem is that because solutions are derived by analytic methods, meaningful justifications for solutions are hard to define. There are a small but increasing number of implementation platforms which have constraint satisfaction methods built in. Different environments have different capabilities in the sorts of built-in constraint satisfaction that they provide. For example, the '*constraint logic programming*' languages CHIP, CLP and Prolog III combine this approach with the automatic deduction approach (all Prolog-based) by providing a built-in interpreter for a set of constraint types.

13.3.5   *Structure-matching methods*

These methods are related to the recognition of patterns in structures and are also commonly known as '*pattern matching*'. They are a very widely used underlying form of method, like searching. (They usually also involve searching.) One specific example is *unification*, as used in logic programming languages like Prolog and functional languages like ML. There may be a set of structure-matching methods provided directly by an implementation platform. For example, these may match structures such as hierarchies or frames. Where structure-matching methods have to be built from scratch, the use of other methods such as rule-based and constraint-based methods, as well as state-space searching, will probably be required.

13.3.6   Parsing methods

This is where the problem is represented as a string and the methods seek to generate a description of the string in terms of the grammatical roles of its parts. It is not just useful for language processing. Knowledge about the problem is expressed as grammar rules or a transition network (e.g. an Augmented Transition Network – ATN[5]). A solution is found if it is possible to completely describe the string in primitive terms of the grammar. Parsing uses various search algorithms as described for state-space searching. A major decision in the design is whether the parsing should be driven by top-down backward chaining, bottom-up forward chaining, or some other strategy (e.g. recursive descent).

13.3.7   Model-based methods

These methods (also called 'model-based reasoning') are based on the representation of some relevant part of the domain (the model) in such a way that the behaviour of the representation (acceptably) accurately reflects the behaviour observed in the real world. Problem solving is achieved by measuring the model and comparing the values produced with those found in the real world, or comparing the model's behaviour itself with that found in the real world. One example of model-based reasoning is 'qualitative reasoning'. (More on qualitative reasoning can be found in the description of the 'prediction' Generic Task Models in section 12.4.6.)

Notes

1. Therefore, note that a problem-solving method described under one Inference Type below does not preclude its use to realize other Inference Types (and vice versa); just that this may be the most appropriate at first. Where a method is especially widely applicable, though, it is described separately in Section 13.3, using the alternative classification by a problem-solving paradigm.
2. As well as generalization, neural networks have also been suggested as being useful implementations of other inferences/problem-solving tasks. For example: classification, correlation (assessment), control, recognition (comparison) and filtering.
3. Note that this is the structure or format of the problem to be solved within the system, *not* the knowledge representation used to support the problem-solving process from a domain perspective.
4. What distinguishes 'automatic deduction' from the whole general declarative nature of KBS is the *formality* of the problem description.
5. An ATN adds to the concept of a simple state transition network the ability to compare the constituent components of the parse structure.

14 Assessing and choosing KBS implementation environments

Implementation environments are the physical platforms upon which actual code is written and executed to make a KBS. They may be used singly or in combination. In particular, KADS is concerned with the implementation environments ultimately used to construct the knowledge-based components of a system, according to the results of KBS Design. Of course, many more sophisticated and realistic systems will usually involve significant non-knowledge-based components, but KADS is not concerned with implementation platform issues for conventional software – except where KBS sub-system(s) have to use such an environment. This chapter summarizes some ideas about how to assess and choose KBS environments with respect to KADS. In particular, three aids to this task are presented:

- A checklist of issues to consider.
- A 'map' for plotting environments, showing relative strengths and weaknesses.
- Two tables for summarizing the relative capabilities of environments.

These aids, particularly the last two, are not 'libraries' like some of the preceding chapters – they are not filled with information usable 'off the shelf'. Instead, they are presented as suggested frameworks for the reader's own tailoring and instantiation. Thus, this chapter is in very much a 'get you started' mould.

Unfortunately, it is not feasible in this book to present a library of pre-assessed environments from which to choose. (Where these have been presented in the past they tend to suffer from such problems as personal opinions and organizational prejudices, incompleteness, and dating very quickly.) The idea here is to present something from which readers can build their own, localized library of environments' capabilities, tailored to their (organization's) specific needs. Where specific environments are mentioned below this is done for the purposes of *illustration only* and should not be taken as a statement of recommendation or otherwise; also, such information may be out of date and/or incorrect.

14.1 The problem of assessing and choosing environments

In KADS terms an implementation environment is an off-the-shelf software system which contains a set of basic problem-solving methods, associated design elements, and knowledge representations. These range from quite general-purpose platforms, such as programming languages, to the classic 'AI' (Artificial Intelligence) environments or toolkits. There are many variables within this definition, such as the number, level, flexibility and extendability of the built-in methods, and more mundane factors such as cost and availability on hardware platforms.

It is the goal of the KBS sub-system(s) designer to produce a physical KBS design which maps straightforwardly onto the implementation environment on which the system will ultimately be delivered. A key aid to doing this is by designing within a 'context' or 'paradigm' that is easily supported by the environment. This may require more explicit definition of higher-level functionality or richness of knowledge representation than the unadorned implementation platform can provide. The definition of this 'paradigm' is the task of the 'Define KBS Design Framework', as described in Section 7.2.1.

The choice of an implementation platform may be affected by many factors. For instance, it may simply be a constraint (requirement) that a certain environment must be used, perhaps because of organizational or business reasons, or performance. Alternatively, the choice may be left more to the designer's discretion, perhaps from a subset of environments for which there is in-house experience, or existing licence agreements. In the case where the selection of an environment is relatively open, the designer may need some help in knowing how to assess environments and choose between them.

14.2 Distinguishing between different environments

Three main types of KBS implementation environment have been distinguished:

- *Shells*: (e.g. EMYCIN, Crystal, Leonardo, XiPlus)
- *Hybrid 'AI' environments*: (e.g. KEE, ART, EGERIA, Kappa, Nexpert Object, Goldworks, LOOPS, Flavors)
- *'AI' languages*: (e.g. Prolog, CHIP,[1] Common Lisp, CLOS)

There is considerable overlap within this classification, especially between the first two types. However, in general, ('expert system') shells are relatively constrained environments, limited in flexibility compared to the alternatives, but having a tightly coupled and well-integrated set of knowledge representations and problem-solving methods. They are good when the methods and representations map straightforwardly onto the problem in hand. Hybrid 'AI' environments (or 'toolkits') are more flexible, generally having a wider portfolio of knowledge representations and problem-solving methods and less constrained ways of interworking them. A significant subset of this class are the Lisp-based environments. 'AI' languages are the most flexible of all, but offer the least support in terms of built-in knowledge representations and problem-solving methods. For example, for all but the simplest of cases, if the design cannot be reduced to depending on a single problem-solving method then a richer set of methods must be built on top of the basic offering(s) in the language.

A fourth common option for implementing KBSs is, of course, conventional programming languages, such as C. It may also be possible to imagine other types, such as object-oriented environments (e.g. Smalltalk), object-oriented languages (e.g. C++), and so on. In addition, there are an increasing number of hybrid conventionally based languages and environments from all sources (e.g. Hypercard). However, these all provide virtually no KBS-specific support, so they cannot be considered further – note that if it is required to use these, the KBS Design Framework will need to be very carefully defined.

Yet another implementation option is the neural network. However, except when used in tandem with other technologies, such as those above, neural nets are best suited to realizing a narrow range of inferences or problem-solving tasks (see the 'generalize' inference in Section 13.1). They are also a complex field in themselves and further discussion is beyond the scope of this book.

14.3 Issues to consider in assessing environments: a checklist

There are many potential questions to ask about a particular implementation environment in order to generally assess its capabilities, or its suitability for use in a particular problem area. The following is a checklist of items to consider:

Problem-solving methods issues
- What different problem-solving methods are built in? (See Sections 13.1 and 13.3.)
- How flexible are the built-in methods/design elements/algorithms (i.e. can they be easily used to build others)?

- Is uncertainty supported? Is fuzzy logic supported?
- Is a TMS (truth maintenance system) supported?
- Is constraint handling supported?
- Are daemons supported?

Knowledge-representation issues
- What different knowledge-representation (KR) formalisms are built-in? (See Section 13.2.)
- How flexible are the built-in KRs (i.e. can they be easily used to build others)?
- Are procedural chunks of knowledge supported? Is there a general-purpose programming language built-in? Does it have a 'standard' syntax?
- How easy are the KRs to write? To read? To edit?
- Is the knowledge base easily partitionable? In arbitrarily defined modules?
- Can control knowledge be easily separated from other knowledge?

Interface issues
- User interface building – does it have built-in capability? If so, what? Is it a (yet another) high-level language? Can you 'draw' interface objects? Can it utilize all the interface primitives in any underlying environment (e.g. Motif, Microsoft Windows, etc.)? Is the resultant interface code portable (with the KBS)?
- Does the user interface building capability conform to a standard (e.g. Motif, Microsoft Windows, etc.)?
- Can it call external functions written in a different language? How good is the performance?
- Is there any provision for inter-process communication? How good is the performance?
- Can it be easily used in conjunction with other KBS platforms?
- Can it be easily used in conjunction with other types of platforms (e.g. database management system, spreadsheets, etc.)?
- Can it be embedded?

Usage issues
- Is a special-purpose knowledge base editor built in? Can you cut and paste between projects? Must the special editor be used? Can a general-purpose text editor be used? Are templates for code/ representations available?
- Is a debugger built in?
- Is the knowledge base interpreted, compiled or incrementally compiled?

- Can standalone executables be generated? What are the licensing issues and cost?
- Does it have provision for revision control/configuration management? Can this be provided easily by interworking with third-party tools such as SCCS or PCMS?
- Is the platform fast enough? In final use? When developing? (More objectively, and if available, how does it perform against a standard set of benchmarks?)
- What are its storage (memory and disk) requirements? In development mode? As a run-time?
- Is garbage collection supported? What sort? How good is the performance?

General issues
- Operating system/machine architecture availability – does it run under the one required?
- Operating system/machine architecture portability – does it run under many? Is the generated code portable? Is cross-development possible?
- Is it a commercially supported product? Is there a phone hot-line? Email address?
- Has it a proven track record? What is the standing of the supplier? The distributor/retailer?
- How much does it cost? Per 'seat'? For development platform versus run-time licences?
- Is there a maintenance agreement? How much does it cost?

Other
- Is an object-oriented paradigm used? How pure is it? How rich is it?
- Is a functional paradigm used? How pure is it? How rich is it?
- Is a logic-based paradigm used? How pure is it? How rich is it?

In the next two sections are suggestions for frameworks which can be used to build a database of information about implementation environments, localized to the reader's particular requirements. Some of the answers to the above issues can be stored for future reference in this way.

14.4 Framework for assessing environments: a map

One way to classify implementation environments is to group them into 'closed' and 'open'. In a **closed** environment, the set of built-in methods and design elements is not readily expandable (e.g. simple shells); in contrast, an **open** environment has the capability to have its repertoire of methods and design elements expanded (e.g. Prolog).

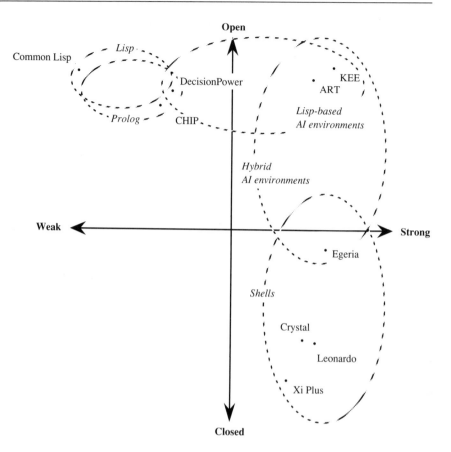

Figure 14.1 A map of implementation environment relative capabilities. (Warning: these examples are for illustrative purposes only, may not necessarily be correct at the time of reading and do not constitute a recommendation.)

Implementation environments can be further specified as being 'weak' or 'strong'. A **strong** environment is relatively rich in built-in problem-solving methods, design elements and knowledge representations (e.g. KEE); a **weak** environment has relatively few (e.g. Prolog).

These two classifications can be viewed as dimensions. If presented as a pair of orthogonal axes, a plot of particular environments may be made on the plane they define. Figure 14.1 shows such a plot, with some example entries. General types of environment are shown as regions and specific products as points.

The resulting graph will be relatively informal in practice, and will reflect the personal experiences or preference and prejudices of the author. However, if readers use the basic idea in their own workplace they can generate a useful local tool. It can help support the selection of environments, or may be used to give an indication of how hard detailed design and coding might be. To aid in the production of such a graph, the following questions could be added to the checklist presented in Section 14.3:

Weak versus strong (weak means that it has few methods and KR support; strong means rich.)

- Rate the platform as a weak or strong environment.
- Compared with others available or previously assessed, rate the degree of weakness or strength on a scale of 1–5 (1 is least strong or least weak; 5 is most).
- (Alternatively, just rate the platform's richness of built-in problem-solving methods and KR support on a scale of 1–10, say; ≤5 would be weak, >5 would be strong.)

Closed versus open (closed means that it has low extendability; open means high.)

- Rate the platform as a closed or open environment.
- Compared with others available or previously assessed, rate the degree of closedness/openness on a scale of 1–5 (1 is least closed or least open; 5 is most).
- (Alternatively, just rate the platform's extendability on a scale of 1–10, say; ≤5 would be closed, >5 would be open.)

14.5 Framework for assessing environments: tables

Another simple way to present the different capabilities of implementation environments is to give them in a table. Again, this could be built up on the basis of answers to questions like those in Section 14.3.

One example is Table 14.1. Its contents concentrate on a specific selection of problem-solving methods, knowledge representations and other features offered in some example platforms. As before, though, the reader should adapt the basic idea for his or her particular requirements and maintain it as a local tool.

Another format is shown in Table 14.2. This time the contents are like a catalogue of problem-solving methods and design elements. This would be especially useful to help Behavioural Design in KADS (see Section 7.2.3). Again, the reader should adapt the basic idea and maintain it as a local tool.

Table 14.1 Implementation environment general capabilities. (Warning: these examples are for illustrative purposes only, may not be correct at the time of reading and do not constitute a recommendation.)

Environment	O/S	F-C	B-C	O-O	C-H	GUI	TMS	Frames	FF	Unc
Leonardo	MSDOS	√	√	√	X	?	X	√	√	√
ICL Decisionpower	UNIX	•	√	•	√	√[a]	•	•	√	•
Crystal	MSDOS	√	?	X	X	?	X	?	?	?
EGERIA	MSDOS/ VME/UNIX	√	√	√	X	√[b]	X	√	√	√
KEE	UNIX (CLisp)	√	√	√	X	√	√	√	√	√
Common Lisp	UNIX	•	•	•	•	X	•	•	√	•
Kappa	UNIX/ MSDOS	?	?	?	?	?	?	?	?	?
Quintus Prolog	UNIX	•	√	•	X	√[a]	•	•	√	•
Xi Plus	MSDOS	√	√	X	X	√[c]	X	X	√	X

Key:

O/S	Operating system	√	Yes
F-C	Forward chaining on rules	X	No
B-C	Backward chaining on rules	•	Not built in, but can be built easily
O-O	Supports object-oriented approach	?	Not known
C-H	Constraint handling		
GUI	Graphical user interface building facility		
TMS	Truth Maintenance System	[a]	Using special graphics sub-system
Frames	Frame-based representation	[b]	Not on UNIX
FF	Foreign function calling facility	[c]	Forms only
Unc	Uncertainty-handling mechanism		

Table 14.2 Implementation environments and associated methods and design elements. (The warning in Table 14.1 also applies here.)

Environment	Methods (problem-solving + others)	Design elements
EMYCIN	Backward search of AND/OR tree Rule-tracing Rule translation	Rules Parameters Contexts Rule interpreter Solution trace
KEE	Hierarchical classification Production system Multiple words database	Frames Production rules Subsumption relations Classifier Database procedures
KES	Backward search Single-world database User interface	Parameters Rule interpreter Database procedures Interface procedures
Prolog	Depth-first backward chaining Single-world database	Rule interpreter Horn clause logic Database procedures Unification
CHIP	Depth-first backward chaining Single-world database Constraint satisfaction	Rule interpreter Horn clause logic Database procedures Constraints Domains Optimization/labelling Clarification

Note

1. 'Constraint Handling in Prolog', originally developed at the European Computer Research Centre.

15 Guided tour of KADS Analysis

This chapter presents a 'guided tour' of the KADS Analysis methods and provides a basic level of detail which is intended to support the day-to-day use of the KADS methods. It can be used as a checklist or as a summary description of Analysis.

Each Analysis activity is described in a separate section, broken down into a number of bullets, so that a sort of 'frame' is built up. There is also

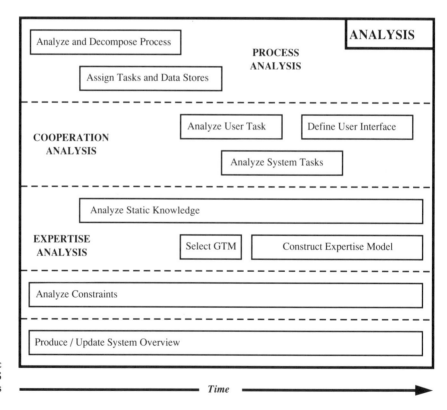

Figure 15.1 Basic 'road map' of KADS Analysis

an introductory comment per stage. For a short overview description of Analysis, see Chapter 3; for a complete description, see Chapter 4; for some background 'theory', see Chapter 5.

The road map diagram shown in Figure 15.1 provides a reminder of the contents of Analysis. The ordering of sections in this chapter is the same as reading this diagram from top to bottom.

15.1   Process Analysis

Process Analysis explores the overall process or context in which the system and user (and any other such agents) are involved. It defines the tasks performed within the context and the stores accessed. Before this stage there is no clear separation between the tasks the system will perform and those the user will carry out. These will need to be allocated to the various system components (internal agents) or external agents.

Process Analysis uses Data Flow Diagrams (DFDs) plus a Process Glossary to describe and decompose the problem. The Process Glossary is like a data dictionary for the DFDs, which can be used to describe both the current view of the organization and also the way in which this will change when the proposed system is in use – the future view.

The process is decomposed to the level at which the various agents (user, KBS, database, etc.) can be distinguished. For the description of the current organizational view, these agents relate to the sources of analysis information, e.g. existing database structures, computerized tasks, manual tasks, expert tasks, etc. For the future view with the proposed system the agents relate to different kinds of user and system component, e.g. tool user, tool administrator, conventional software, KBS software, etc.

Process Analysis thus provides a basis for semi-independent analysis of the various system constituents. The special KADS Expertise Analysis methods can be used to analyse the system's required problem-solving capability in detail while conventional methods, such as SSADM, Yourdon etc., can be used to explore the more conventional system components. Cooperation Analysis will later analyse the interaction between system and user(s) (and any other agents) in detail.

There are two interleaved activities in Process Analysis:

Analyze and Decompose Process – Decomposition of the overall process, as supported by DFDs plus a Process Glossary.
Assign Tasks and Data Stores to Agents – Allocation of the elements identified via process decomposition, to internal system or external user (or other) agents.

The activities are interleaved in that the inability to achieve a unique agent assignment at a particular level of process decomposition suggests the need for further decomposition. The results of these activities are a Process Decomposition and Process Distribution respectively, collectively termed the Process Model.

15.1.1   Analyze and Decompose Process

Aims

- To decompose the overall process into problem-solving tasks requiring expertise, other tasks (it does not matter which are which yet), and data/knowledge stores.
- To take this decomposition to a level at which unique agent assignment is possible, i.e. a task is performed by a single agent; a store is owned by a single agent.

What do I need?

- The defined ('scoped') part of the client environment where the proposed system is to be placed – also an input to Environmental Constraints (see Section 15.4.1).
- The initial System Overview (if available).
- The results of any pre-analysis phase.

What do I produce?

- The Process Decomposition – a hierarchical breakdown of the process into tasks and data/knowledge stores.
- The Process Glossary describing the logical structure of the information ('data') in the flows and stores shown in the Process Decomposition – like a data dictionary.

When should I do it?

- As soon as Analysis starts.

Tasks

- Describe and decompose the organizational or system context by identifying the constituent tasks, data/knowledge stores and data flows within the process.
- Describe the structure of the data which flows into or out of this context, between tasks and stores.

Techniques

- Talk to experts, users, and others in the domain; read relevant domain literature.
- Knowledge acquisition (introspection, self-report, written material etc.) – see Chapter 10.
- Conventional data flow diagramming.

Tools

- There are no KADS-specific tools to support the construction of the Process Decomposition. Data Flow Diagrams are, however, supported by many existing conventional CASE tools.
- General-purpose drawing tools, such as MacDraw, etc., may also be useful in producing the diagrams.
- Consider drafting the diagrams using yellow sticky notes (for tasks and stores) on a large piece of paper or surface, connected by pencilled lines.

Representation

- Data Flow Diagrams (DFDs) – use any reasonable standard notation.
- Backus-Naur Form (BNF) may be used for the Process Glossary.

QA checklist

- All decompositions are consistent where a task, data store or data flow occurs on more than one level in the hierarchical structure.
- All decompositions are correct – check with a domain expert/user.
- The decomposition is complete. No tasks are omitted in any single level of decomposition – check with a domain expert/user.
- The names given to the tasks, data stores and data flows are unambiguous and concur with the client's view – check with a domain expert/user.
- There is an entry in the Process Glossary for each data store and data flow depicted in the Process Decomposition.

Tips and comments[1]

Remember that there are two contexts for which to produce a Process Decomposition: current and future. The basic approach used in this activity is to identify and describe what tasks and data/knowledge stores are used in the existing organizational context, and then to prescribe the changes which will be needed in order for the projected system and user(s) (and other agents) to cooperate. The system's objectives and purpose will need to be known to support the future view. This is a first attempt, and may be refined by later analysis, especially following

Analyze User Task(s) and/or user interface prototyping – do not be afraid of returning to this activity to adjust the decomposition. Accept that the DFDs will be produced iteratively.

The DFDs will generally take quite a lot of work to produce. One reason for this is that, at the start of a development no single individual will understand how the whole system will work in its future organizational environment. In addition, when modelling the current situation the task of transforming a user or domain expert's view of their process into DFDs is not always easy, as it imposes a formality on what may be quite a poorly defined process. (This is especially a problem when conflicting views of the process are given by different interviewees.)

It is a bad idea to produce DFDs on a CASE tool or otherwise 'pretty them up' when showing them to managers, users, experts, etc. for review – early on, at least. Produce hand-drawn ones first. This is because many people assume that a document that looks good is somehow more likely to be correct, and the DFD authors will receive less critical review – especially from those who are the most important: the members of the client organization. It is crucial that the *contents* of the DFDs are high-quality, as much of the rest of the development will rest on their correctness.

Example
See p. 36.

15.1.2   *Assign Tasks and Data Stores to Agents*

Aims

- To assign the tasks and data stores identified in the Process Decomposition to agents (KBS, user, database, etc.), to show who does what and who stores what.

What do I need?

- The Process Decomposition, which may be partially complete.
- The initial System Overview – particularly System Objectives and Functions.
- Knowledge of KBS applicability and feasibility (see Appendix 1).
- Knowledge of the capabilities of user(s) and other agents.

What do I produce?

- The Process Distribution – a Process Decomposition augmented with agent assignments (ownerships) for tasks and stores.

When should I do it?

- As soon as the Process Decomposition is complete or at a level of detail where further decomposition requires decisions on agent assignments.

Tasks

- Identify tasks which can be carried out only by one agent by matching each task against the capabilities of the possible agents to perform it.
- Identify which agents to use in the distribution.
- Decide which agents perform which tasks and which agents own which data stores.
- Carry out further decomposition of the process for tasks and/or data stores that cannot be uniquely assigned to agents at the current level.

Techniques

- Assign agents on the basis of the aims of the system and capabilities of agents.
- Use knowledge of which tasks are suitable for KBS applications.
- Distinguish conventional data stores from 'knowledge' stores by looking at their contents and associated flows.
- Consider end-user capabilities, and the capabilities of any other agents.

Tools

- Criteria for KBS applicability (see Appendix 1).
- General-purpose drawing tools, such as MacDraw, etc., may be useful in producing the augmented diagrams. CASE tools may need to be 'stretched' to annotate the basic DFDs, e.g. by using a general text-annotation mechanism built into the tool, for this specific purpose. Use pencil and paper first, though!

Representation

- Data Flow Diagrams (DFDs) augmented with agent assignments as annotations.

QA checklist

- The system is correctly bounded, i.e. the set of system responsibilities is consistent with client expectations – check with System Overview.
- All tasks and data stores are correctly assigned – external agents should be checked with domain experts; internal agents can be checked within the project team.

- Assignments are consistent. No sub-task of a task assigned to agent X is assigned to agent Y.
- All joint assignments are resolved.
- No tasks or data stores are unassigned.

Tips and comments
The basic approach used in this activity is to add agent assignments to the Process Decomposition produced by the preceding activity. Process Distribution will still have the two contexts, current and future. However, the current process will obviously not have any internal agents to assign; it only holds external agents, in general. Thus, in many cases the amount of work in producing the distribution for the two situations is reduced, because the future situation will inherit the external agent assignments from the current situation. (But of course, this may not always be the case.)

In building the Process Distribution, there will usually be only one reasonable distribution of agents over tasks and data stores. However, in more complex cases the Process Distribution may give alternatives: it may represent a 'space' of possible agent distributions. If this is the case it will be the job of further analysis (such as Constraints Analysis, or redefinition of the System Objectives) to decide which of the possible distributions is suitable for the application.

Example
See Section 4.1.2.

15.2   Cooperation Analysis

Cooperation Analysis takes the results from Process Analysis and analyses the system and its boundaries in more detail. It examines the required high-level dynamic behaviour of the system. Of particular importance at this stage is the analysis and specification of the relationship between the system and user(s) as they work together on the tasks identified in Process Analysis. More complex systems may have other agents for the system to cooperate with, which will need analysing.

Cooperation Analysis models the cooperation between agents at two levels: across the system boundary and within the system. Cooperation Analysis specifies no preferred notations, but typically for dynamic behaviour, State Transition Diagrams (STDs) are a popular choice for modelling the user–system interaction. For modelling cooperation between agents within the system boundary, pseudo-code is a popular choice.

As well as modelling the dynamics of cooperation between internal and external agents, Cooperation Analysis is also concerned with specifying the interfaces between external and internal agents. In particular, this means the user–system interface. These activities are all supported and tested by user analysis techniques, including user interface prototyping.

There are three activities in Cooperation Analysis:

Analyze User Task(s) – Identifies and describes the logic of the user task and the points at which information is transferred to or from the system.

Analyze System Task(s) – Takes the results of Process Analysis and analysis of the user task and defines the information flows between the internal system agents.

Specify User Interface(s) – Defines the medium for information transfer between user and system, and the way in which this information is to be represented.

These activities may be extended with analogous activities to analyse other external agents and their interfaces with the system, where such agents are present.

The results of these activities are a User Task Model, a System Task Model, a User Interface Specification, (and optionally, a User Model may also be produced, representing a definition of the classes of user of the system), collectively termed the Cooperation Model.

15.2.1   *Analyze User Task(s)*

Aims

- To identify and record the logic of the user task(s).
- To identify and record information exchange between the system and the user (and by analogy, the system's external agents).

What do I need?

- Process Model:
  - Process Decomposition (complete).
  - Process Distribution – at least with tasks assigned to user(s) and other external system agents.

What do I produce?

- User Task Model(s).

When should I do it?

- As soon as the Process Decomposition is complete and the Process

Distribution distinguishes user (and other external agent) tasks from system tasks.

Tasks

- Identify the logic of the user task(s) by analyzing what activities are carried out, how they are related, and how information flows as the prospective system and user cooperate; identify the 'states' of the user.
- Identify whether system or user takes responsibility for initiating information flows, to distinguish who 'owns' each flow – these will relate to events (actions).
- Identify whether these actions trigger control flows or data flows.
- Cross-reference actions associated with data flows to tasks in the Process Decomposition according to who owns the flow.
- [Optionally] produce a User Model describing the characteristics of each class of user of the system (see p. 56)
- [Optionally] produce a Task Model/Agent Model for any other external system agents.

Techniques

- User analysis – including user/expert dialogues and walkthroughs.
- Prototyping, Mock-ups, 'Wizard-of-Oz' technique.

Tools

- There are no specific tools to support this activity. KADS does not prescribe a specific representation, so general-purpose drawing tools such as MacDraw may be used. CASE tools may provide support for producing certain applicable notations.
- Consider drafting the diagrams using yellow sticky notes (for states) on a large piece of paper or surface, connected by pencilled lines and annotated with events (actions).

Representation

- State Transition Diagrams (STDs) can be used to describe the logic of the user task(s). They should cross-reference the tasks in the Process Model, by marking (data flow) actions with the associated task. If the user task is simple, then pseudo-code or JSD could provide an alternative representation. Role Activity Diagrams may be useful for complex, relatively unstructured user tasks.
- Initiatives for information flow should be described in terms of the agent responsible for initiating the flow, e.g. 'USER: enter name', 'SYSTEM: provide information'.
- Actions associated with control flows should be distinguished from

data flows, e.g. by marking control actions with a label such as in: 'USER: request quit system (C)'.

QA checklist

- The model must cover all pertinent user activities – check with user(s).
- All system activities in response to user events must be mappable onto tasks within the Process Model (otherwise the Process Model should be updated).
- All system actions which affect the user(s) should be described (check by cross-referencing to the Process Model).
- All user states should be complete with respect to the events which can occur in them.
- Each user or system action should include an indication of the associated information flow(s).
- Actions associated with data flows should be distinguishable from those with control flow(s).

Tips and comments

There are various strategies which can be applied in this activity: the analyst can search for events in the domain directly; alternatively, each information flow in the Process Decomposition could be examined to see what event it maps onto. Events might be elicited by examining what activities or operations in the domain cause instances of relationships between agents to be created or deleted. A draft User Task Model may be constructed prior to the Process Decomposition and may be refined during this activity. This activity concentrates on the user–system relationship, but the methods can, in principle, be used to analyze inter-system relationships and other people-system relationships (i.e. between the system and other external agents).

Many of the general tips noted in Section 15.1.1 will also apply to this activity. For example, like the Process Decomposition DFDs, the User Task Model will be built up by a process of iterative refinement as increased understanding is gained.

Example

See p. 54.

15.2.2   *Analyze System Task(s)*

Aims

- To identify and record the logic of the system task(s).
- To identify and record information exchange between internal system agents.

What do I need?

- Process Model (complete).
- User Task Model (draft).
- System Overview (list of system functions).

What do I produce?

- System Task Model.

When should I do it?

- As soon as the Process Model is complete and 'Analyze User Tasks' has identified all events which trigger information flows between user(s) and system.

Tasks

- Identify the logic of the system task(s) by taking each trigger event in the User Task Model and describing the system actions in terms of the flow of control between system agents.
- Cross-reference system actions to tasks in the Process Decomposition.
- Check against the System Overview to ensure that all the desired system functions are covered within the System Task Model.

Techniques

- The main technique is to create a mapping between the User Task Model and the Process Model, by expanding on the SYSTEM actions in the User Task Model using the full range of internal agents specified in the Process Distribution.

Tools

- There are no specific tools to support this activity. KADS does not prescribe a specific representation, so general-purpose drawing tools such as MacDraw may be used. CASE tools may provide support for producing certain applicable notations.
- Using pseudo-code may only require word-processing.

Representation

- State Transition Diagrams (STDs) can be used to describe the logic of the system task(s). This should cross-reference the tasks in the Process Model. Other state-transition notations, including pseudo-code, can also be used.
- Initiatives for information flow should be described in terms of the

internal system agent that initiates the flow, e.g. 'KBS: solve problem', 'DBMNGR: store result'.

- Actions associated with control flows should be distinguished from data flows, e.g. by marking control actions with a label such as in: 'SYSTEM: quit system (C)'.
- Cross-reference the User Task Model by indicating which external event drives which sequence of internal system actions.

QA checklist

- The model must cover all the user activities described in the User Task Model.
- All agent activities in response to user events must be mappable onto tasks assigned to the same agent within the Process Distribution (otherwise the Process Model should be updated).
- Each agent action should include an indication of the associated information flow(s).
- Actions associated with data flows should be distinguishable from those with control flow(s).

Tips and comments

Remember, the System and User Task Models document the dynamic behaviour of the future system and are therefore complementary to the parts of the Process Model that document the possible information flows in the future situation. The User Task Model documents from the point of view of the user (or other external agents); the System Task Model shifts the perspective to the point of view of the system, but is still driven by the original user-view. The main approach to this activity is to take the User Task Model STDs and explode the 'SYSTEM' actions to correspond fully with all the detail of the Process Model.

A detailed System Task Analysis may unearth problems with or omissions from the Process Model. The analyst has the option to go back and refine the Process Model if this is felt to be necessary.

Note that the 'SYSTEM' agent as used in the System Task Model is used as a shorthand to mean the 'non-KBS parts of the proposed system', as also used in the full decompositions in the Process Model. It is *not* the same as 'SYSTEM' in the User Task Model, which there represents the *whole* future system.

Example
See p. 60.

15.2.3   *Define User Interface(s)*

Aims

- To define the logical medium for information transfer between user(s) and system.
- To specify the way in which the user interface(s) should be constructed in order to facilitate the desired information transfer.

What do I need?

- Process Model (complete).
- User Task Model(s) (complete).
- User Model, if available.

What do I produce?

- User Interface Specification:
  - Decomposition of the user interface into its constituent parts.
  - Description of the system facilities associated with each user interface component.
  - Guidelines or requirements for user interface implementation.

When should I do it?

- Ideally, the production of the User Interface Specification follows on naturally from user task analysis. However, user interface prototyping may provide the information necessary for this activity independently of a detailed user task analysis.

Tasks

User interface specification is inherently an unstructured task. See p. 64 for one example approach.

Techniques

- Interviews with prospective system users.
- Prototyping, mock-ups, 'Wizard-of-Oz' technique.

Tools

- General-purpose drawing tools can be used to represent screen layouts.
- Outlining tools could be helpful to define the user interface composition.
- Consider drafting the interface on paper, perhaps using yellow sticky notes for windows and dialogues (if using a graphical paradigm), stuck on sheets of A4 paper for screens, etc.

Representation

- *Consists-of* hierarchies for user interface composition.
- Schematic diagrams for logical user interface layout.

QA checklist
There are no firm rules to support user interface specification. See Section 4.2.3 for some guidelines. The following checks may be employed to ensure completeness and correctness of the resultant specification:

- Ensure that every state in the User Task Model maps onto a recognizable state of the user interface.
- Ensure that every user event in the User Task Model is supported by a corresponding user interface component.
- Ensure that every system response to the user(s) is supported by one or more user interface components.
- Involve the user(s) in the interface specification activity – the user provides the ultimate check that the interface is acceptable.

Tips and comments
There are no golden rules or short-cuts to defining what constitutes a good user interface specification. Many guidelines are available and can be found in texts on this subject. However, the analyst should bear in mind that the ultimate choice as to what comprises an acceptable user interface should rest with the user – except that users must also be fully informed of the implications of their decisions where these conflict with different recommendations from the analyst. Be careful with different classes of user with a single user interface – different classes of user may prefer conflicting styles of interaction or variations in detailed functionality.

Example
See p. 64.

15.3 Expertise Analysis

Expertise Analysis aims to produce a model of the problem-solving activities that the system must perform: the Expertise Model. This model is built by a process of incremental knowledge acquisition. The engineer takes the human expert's behaviour as the basis for constructing the expertise model, and refines the model as analysis proceeds. The situation is more complex when there is more than one existing expert, or none, but the principle is the same.

Previous and parallel analysis (Process and Cooperation Analysis) is concerned only with the general identification and assignment of tasks;

Expertise Analysis is concerned with the detail of the expert problem-solving (system) tasks and knowledge.

There are three activities within Expertise Analysis:

Analyze Static Knowledge – Identifies and describes basic facts, concepts and relationships that exist in the domain of the required problem-solving behaviour, and that will form the Domain layer of the Expertise Model.

Select/Construct Initial Generic Task Model(s) – Matches the required problem-solving task(s) onto a Generic Task Model as closely as possible, or builds a suitable new one.

Construct Expertise Model – Uses the Generic Task Model(s) to drive the knowledge-acquisition process, and on the basis of the contents of that model, gradually builds up the Expertise Model's Inference, Task and Strategy layers for the required problem-solving task(s); links the Domain layer to the other layers.

'Construct Expertise Model', can be further split up into the explicit construction of the Inference layer, the Task layer and the Strategy layer. A description of the KADS four-layer Expertise Model can be found in Section 4.3.1.

15.3.1   Analyze Static Knowledge

Aims

- To identify, organize and describe basic domain concepts and relations.

What do I need?

- Background domain knowledge, in the form of reference books and other documents.
- Constraints Document (draft).
- Process Model (draft).

What do I produce?

- The components of the Domain layer of the Expertise Model – a set of Domain Structures.

When should I do it?

- After interviewers have familiarized themselves with basic domain terms and the basic process used within the domain.
- As soon as other Analysis interviewing starts.

Tasks

- Read background material and abstract relevant static knowledge.
- Interview experts and other domain personnel, and (optionally) transcribe the dialogue.
- Identify domain terms from interviews and source material (especially from the existing Process Glossary as it relates to the KBS system aspects).
- Identify structures of domain concepts and relationships, either using existing structures in the domain or by invention.
- Represent the concepts and their relationships in an appropriate form, e.g. frames, rules, semantic networks, *consists-of* and/or *is-a* hierarchies, etc.
- Re-interview people and refine the Domain Structures by review, as necessary.
- Update the Domain Structures throughout Expertise Analysis as the understanding of the static knowledge becomes clearer.

Techniques

- Knowledge acquisition (focused interview, structured interview) – see Chapter 10.
- Review of interview transcripts ('protocol analysis').
- Prototyping: validating the choice of knowledge-representation formalism.

Tools

- Ordinary word processors may be used to document the Domain Structures.
- Outliners may be useful to document hierarchies.
- KBS toolkits with knowledge-representation tools, such as KEE, or general-purpose drawing tools, such as MacDraw, may be used as alternatives. Entity-Relationship Diagram (ERD) editors in CASE tools may also be useful.

Representation

- A set of concepts and relationships, organized into Domain Structures and expressed in a formalism appropriate to the characteristics of the domain. The KADS Domain Modelling Language (DML) may be used for this purpose (for the DML see Section 4.3.2 and the Summary of Notations; see Section 13.3 for other knowledge-representation techniques).

QA checklist

- All domain terms needed are defined. This is best checked with a domain expert, but as an additional guide ensure that all Domain Roles and support knowledge used within the Expertise Model are described by Domain Structures (see p. 423).
- The definitions are correct – check with a domain expert.
- The formalism(s) used are appropriate for describing the domain.
- All terms are used consistently, e.g. the types of *is-a* relation used are clear.
- Attributes and relations are specified as holding on concepts of the right level of abstraction, e.g. *mortal(humans)* not *mortal(englishmen)*.

Tips and comments

This activity proceeds step-wise, i.e. it is not performed once at the start of Expertise Analysis and then left. Other Analysis activities will require further knowledge acquisition, which in turn may lead to revisions of the Domain Structures. Thus, from a practical and efficiency point of view, an Analysis interview may serve more than one purpose, e.g. the knowledge engineer may elicit information about both the static domain knowledge and the problem-solving strategies, in one interview. In many cases, the knowledge engineer can rely on eliciting much of the static knowledge required as a side-effect of other interviews in this way.

Apart from the tasks and techniques mentioned above, other sources of static domain knowledge for this activity may arise from considering:

- The way problems and solutions are structured.
- The way support data are structured.
- In association with other activities in Expertise Analysis:
  - What Inference Types support the problem-solving task? What support knowledge do they require?
  - What goals are being attempted? What is the static knowledge component of what is being determined?
  - What strategies are being used in problem solving? What knowledge structures are used to support them?

Representing static knowledge is a skill that greatly benefits from an appreciation of many different types of knowledge representation and experience in using them.

Example

See Section 4.3.2.

15.3.2   Select/Construct Initial Generic Task Model(s)

Aims

- To identify the generic problem-solving task(s) that the system must perform.
- To select or build a template(s) in the form of a Generic Task Model (GTM) for further analysis, matching the generic problem-solving task(s).

What do I need?

- The Generic Task Model Library (GTML) – see Chapter 12.
- Process Model (complete).
- Domain Structures from 'Analyze Static Knowledge' (draft).

What do I produce?

- A Generic Task Model per problem-solving task – either selected directly from the library or created to suit the requirements of the particular expert task and perhaps based on fragments from existing models.

When should I do it?

- As soon as a reasonable estimate can be made of the problem-solving capability of the system – normally by identifying the tasks from Process Analysis which are to be supported by KBS functionality ('KBS tasks').
- Whenever further analysis indicates a change to the problem-solving nature of the system.

Tasks

- Identify problem-solving tasks in the Process Model, i.e. tasks in the Process Distribution owned by internal KBS agents.
- Match the characteristics of the tasks with those represented by models in the GTML.
- Select models or fragments of models from the GTML to create a Generic Task Model per problem-solving task.
- Use the Generic Task Model(s) to drive further knowledge acquisition by comparing and contrasting the task represented by the Generic Task Model(s) with the actual tasks in or required by the domain.

Techniques

- Analyze input/output behaviour of each KBS task in the Process Decomposition.

- Identify any additional knowledge needed to support the task.
- Identify key types of inference required to support the task.
- Identify relevant (comparable) tasks or task fragments in the GTML.
- Match all these elements onto models or model fragments in the GTML.
- Match the Domain Roles in the GTML tasks or task fragments against the contents of the draft Domain Structures.
- Prototyping – to verify the similarity between the GTM and that required by the proposed system, by operationalizing the model to make its behaviour more visible.

Tools

- The Generic Task Model Library (GTML) – see Chapter 12.

Representation

- Use the representation in the model selected from the library as a starting point. This will be consistent with the representation of the Inference, Task and Strategy Layers, as the Expertise Model is built up. The selected model will also provide guidelines as to the nature and likely content of the knowledge in the Domain Structures which will be needed to support the problem-solving task(s). Also, see Section 4.3.1 for comments on representing the layers of such models.

QA checklist

- The input–output relations for the chosen or constructed GTM should match those described for the task within the Process Model.
- (The GTM will be continually revised during 'Construct Expertise Model'. When complete, it should be consistent with the Inference, Task and Strategy Layers of the Expertise Model; thus, the other checklists to be used are those provided for the Inference, Task and Strategy Layers respectively, in Section 15.3.3.)

Tips and comments

The selection of the initial Generic Task Model will often be based on an educated guess as to the problem-solving nature of the finished system. The knowledge engineer will base this on an understanding of the tasks the system must perform (ultimately from the Process Model), a knowledge of previous projects, and a familiarity with the Generic Task Model Library. The last is especially important with respect to getting the best from KADS.

There will be cases where the task does not map easily onto any of the models in the Generic Task Model Library. In such cases the knowledge engineer will have to construct a new Generic Task Model, possibly using fragments of existing ones. More details on this may be found in Section 4.3.3.

Knowledge engineers should be *pragmatic* with the models in the library – they should be very prepared to change aspects of the models to suit their domain requirements. Generic Task Models are *tools for thinking*, not definitive statements of rigorous truth. In most cases it should not be expected to use a model straight from the library. It is rare to meet a problem domain that embodies a simple implementation of a generic task, where this would be possible.

Useful information on Generic Task Models and their relationships to Expertise Models will be found on p. 78; see also Chapter 12.

Example
See Section 4.3.3.

15.3.3 *Construct Expertise Model*

Aims

- To refine (and reselect as necessary) the Inference, Task and Strategy layers of the chosen Generic Task Model(s), with the objective of making the problem-solving task represented by the model the same as that required by the system.
- To link the Domain Structures produced by 'Analyze Static Knowledge' to the refined Generic Task Model(s), in order to form the Domain layer and so complete the Expertise Model.

What do I need?

- Generic Task Model(s).
- Process Model (complete).
- Cooperation Model (draft).
- Domain Structures from 'Analyze Static Knowledge' (draft/completed).

What do I produce?

- Refined Generic Task Model(s).
- The Inference layer of the final Expertise Model.
- The Task layer of the final Expertise Model.
- The Strategy layer of the final Expertise Model.
- The completed Expertise Model = the above three layers + Domain layer.

When should I do it?

- As soon as the first Generic Task Model is chosen.

Tasks

- Construct Inference Layer – (see p. 423).
- Construct Task Layer – (see p. 425).
- Construct Strategy Layer – (see p. 426).
- Form the Expertise Model by bringing these three layers together with the Domain layer.

Techniques

- See pp. 423–6 for relevant techniques.
- Prototyping may be employed at most stages of Expertise Model construction as a means of verifying work done so far, and exploring possible solutions.

Tools

- See pp. 423–6 for relevant tools.

Representation

- See pp. 423–6 for details of representation methods.

QA checklist

- See pp. 423–6 for details of relevant quality checks.

Tips and comments
The bulk of 'Construct Expertise Model' activity has been described in terms of three sub-activities: 'Construct Inference Layer', 'Construct Task Layer' and 'Construct Strategy Layer', as presented below. This is because the tools, techniques, representation issues, etc. differ widely for these sub-tasks. Note that they are richly iterative in nature.

The only task to perform outside of the construction of these layers is in bringing the layers together with the Domain Structures to form the complete four-layer Expertise Model. Essentially, this means ensuring that the layers are mutually consistent and linked by the same terminology. In particular, it will involve making sure that the Inference layer uses Domain Roles, Inference Types and any support knowledge that map onto Domain Structures. When the latter is the case, the Domain Structures can be said to form the Domain layer of the Expertise Model.

For complex Expertise Models representing more than one problem-solving task, bringing the layers together may be more involved. See

p. 64. The knowledge engineer should be familiar with the KADS four-layer model; details of this may be found in Section 4.3.1.

Example

- See pp. 423–6 for pointers to examples per layer.

Construct Inference Layer

Aims

- Identify all inferences possible using the relevant domain knowledge, as required by the knowledge-based ('KBS' or 'K', etc.) tasks in the Process Model.
- Construct one or more Inference Structures expressing these inferences.

What do I need?

- Generic Task Model(s).
- Process Model (complete).
- Domain Structures (drafts).

What do I produce?

- An Inference Structure(s).
- Descriptions of the Inference Types and Domain Roles contained in the structure.

When should I do it?

- After the selection of the Generic Task Model(s).
- After initial work has been done on the Domain Structures.

Tasks

- Refine Inference Types and Domain Roles in the Inference Structure of the Generic Task Model(s) to match the required problem-solving behaviour.
- Bring Inference Structure fragments together to form one or more composite Inference Structures which express the desired problem-solving capability.

Techniques

- Knowledge acquisition (structured interview and/or self-report) to elicit information on the inferences the expert uses – see Chapter 10.
- Refine and populate the Inference Structure from the results of elicitation.

Tools

- The KADS classifications of Inference Types and Domain Roles (Sections 11.1.1 and 11.2.1 respectively).
- General-purpose drawing tools such as MacDraw may be used to draw Inference Structures; DFD editors in CASE tools could be adapted to do so.
- Inference Types and Domain Roles can be documented in frames using a word processor.

Representation

- The simplified diagrammatical convention for expressing Inference Structures is as follows (see p. 72 for more detail):
  - Domain Roles are labelled rectangles.
  - Inference Types are labelled ellipses.
  - Possible inferences are shown with one-way arrows.
- Describe Inference Types and Domain Roles using the frame notation suggested on p. 86.

QA checklist

- Domain bindings are correct, i.e. Domain Roles map onto elements in the Domain Structures produced by 'Analyze Static Knowledge'; Inference Types are able to process such knowledge, and any support knowledge required by them is also provided in the Domain Structures.
- Domain Roles all describe some part of the Domain Layer.
- Inference Types all reference some part of the Domain Layer.
- The Inference Structure is well formed according to the diagramming conventions (see p. 72 for details of these).

Tips and comments

Remember: Inference Structures document potential inferences ('inference steps'). However, they do not say *when* these inferences should occur. (The 'when' is handled by the Task Layer.) *Inference Types* are descriptions of the way domain knowledge may be used in making inferences. *Domain Roles* describe the role that 'packets' of domain knowledge may play in inference. A particular domain concept may, therefore, effectively appear more than once in an Inference Structure, depending on the roles it is playing. Where this occurs, a different Domain Role will be used in each case, even though the underlying domain concept is the same. For further detail on Inference Structures, see p. 72.

Example
See p. 93.

Construct Task Layer

√

Aims

- Identify the order in which inferences in the Inference Layer are performed.
- Construct one or more Task Structures expressing these orderings.

What do I need?

- Generic Task Model(s).
- Process Model (complete).
- Inference Layer (draft).
- Cooperation Model (draft).

What do I produce?

- A Task Structure(s) showing the sequencing (ordering) of inferences.

When should I do it?

- As soon as the Inference Layer is in a reasonable draft form.

Tasks

- Refine the Task Structure(s) from the Generic Task Model(s) to match the required problem-solving behaviour.
- Alternatively, construct a Task Structure(s) specific to the tasks to be carried out, as defined by the requirements within the System Task Model.

Techniques

- Knowledge acquisition (self-report and/or introspection) to elicit how the inferences specified at the Inference layer are used – see Chapter 10.
- Refine the Task Structure from the results of elicitation.

Tools

- There are no specific tools to support documentation of task structures. Where pseudo-code is used, word processing is adequate; although if a very high-level language tool is available, it might be possible to operationalize Task Structures. Diagrammatic representations can be produced using general-purpose drawing tools such as MacDraw.

Representation

- Usually one of: Procedural pseudo-code; Declarative 'meta-rules'; Dependency diagram.

QA checklist

- The Task Structure reflects the sequences of inferences used to achieve goals – best checked with a domain expert.
- All (inference) steps specified are described by Inference Types in the Inference Layer.
- If the notation applies, all parameters to inference steps are described by Domain Roles in the Inference Layer or data shown in the System Task Model.
- All sequences obey input/output dependencies between inferences.

Tips and comments

In order to construct the Task Layer the knowledge engineer should elicit information concerning not *what* the knowledge or inferences are but *how* the inferences are used. The chosen Generic Task Model may give some help as to typical Task Structures for the task concerned – these may be utilized as a starting point for knowledge acquisition.

The usual way of representing Task Structures is to use procedural pseudo-code. This is fine where the Task Structure is fairly simple, but in more complex cases pseudo-code may obscure some dependencies between inferences. An alternative is a dependency diagram (between Inference Types). Examples of this can be seen in the Task Structure for the 'planning' Generic Task Model (see Section 12.6.3).

Example

See p. 97.

Construct Strategy Layer

Aims

- Identify control knowledge for selecting, sequencing or configuring Task Structures within the KBS parts of the proposed system.

What do I need?

- Domain Structures from 'Analyze Static Knowledge'.
- Inference Layer.

- Task Layer (draft).
- Cooperation Model (complete).
- Process Model (complete).

What do I produce?
Examples:

- A means of configuring Task Structures at the Task Layer (i.e. flexible problem solving).
- A means of controlling execution of Task Structures according to the state of problem solving or mode of KBS operation.
- A means of choosing between alternative Task Structures (alternative strategies).

When should I do it?

- As soon as the inputs described above are ready.

Tasks

- Identify control knowledge for the entire KBS by examining the overall problem-solving process required.

Techniques

- Knowledge acquisition (self-report, introspection, user–expert dialogues) – see Chapter 10.

Tools

- Knowledge of types of strategic knowledge (see p. 77).
- There are no specific tools to support documentation of strategic knowledge. Where it is produced, it uses similar notations to the Task Layer – see p. 425.

Representation

- Procedural pseudo-code or further 'meta-rules' to the Task Layer.

QA checklist

- The alternative ways of achieving goals which are specified should correspond to the expert's problem-solving strategies – best checked with the domain expert and users.
- All tasks for all strategies are described at the task layer and all trigger points and consequent interactions are described in the Cooperation Model (User and System Task Models).

Tips and comments
The Strategy Layer considers three issues:

1. For flexible problem-solving, the Task Structures in the Task Layer may not be fixed in advance but may need to be constructed dynamically according to the state of problem solving and input data – this would imply some kind of planning task prior to problem solving proper.
2. The way in which a Task Structure is executed may depend in some way on the state of problem solving or the mode of KBS operation. For example, a tutoring system might need to operate either in pure problem-solving mode or in teaching mode, with differences between the Task Structure required in each case.
3. A Task Structure may need to be selected from alternatives according to the input data or state of problem solving. Many of the KADS Generic Task Models provide alternative task structures to cope with different strategies.

Although the above sounds complex, in most KADS projects to date there has been little strategic knowledge to capture, and so it is quite manageable. In the simplest case there is simply a one-to-one mapping between trigger events documented in the Cooperation Model and the invocation of Task Structures. However, it is still useful to make this explicit.

KADS provides two techniques for integrating the elements of the System Task Model with those of the Task Layer:

1. Combine the Task Layer and the System Task Model into one structure (this gives high-level, rigid control).
2. Use the Strategy Layer to specify the relationship between the User Task(s) and the problem solver, by providing links between system events and task structure invocations.

Note that strategic knowledge is relatively domain-dependent, and so the guidance that can be supplied by Generic Task Models is limited. (See Section 12.1.1.)

Example
See p. 99.

15.4   Constraints Analysis

Constraints Analysis aims to ensure that all externally arising non-functional (primarily) requirements and constraints on the future system are recorded. (The key functional requirements are placed in the System Overview – see Section 15.5.) This information is used to constrain the system's development throughout Analysis and then later, in Design.

Constraints Analysis is a 'maintenance-type' activity, following on from similar work carried out in development phases preceding Analysis (e.g. in a feasibility study). It keeps a record of the constraints on the system which are determined during Analysis and should be performed as a background task throughout Analysis.

In some ways, this activity can be seen as an insurance policy. It helps to protect the development against changing requirements, and ensures that a sufficiently detailed and broad analysis of external constraints is effected. Because of this nature, different projects will require different amounts of Constraints Analysis. It is therefore presented as a 'checklist' of documents to produce, covering three areas that the analyst needs to consider.

Constraints Analysis can be divided into three sub-activities, focusing on three areas of external constraints and requirements. However, Because these are all analyzed in the same basic, conventional way they are grouped together for description in this section. The three sub-activities within Constraints Analysis are:

Analyze Environmental Constraints – Identifies and describes factors arising from organizational issues and the contexts with which the system being developed is concerned or will pass through.
Analyze Technical Constraints – Identifies and describes system-specific factors.
Analyze Policy Constraints – Identifies and describes procedural and standards factors.

Each of these covers a diverse range of areas to consider for which constraints arise. The consolidation of the documentation of all these factors is termed the Constraints Document.

15.4.1   *Analyze Constraints*

Aims

- To maintain and update a record of external constraints and other requirements.
- To identify and record new external constraints.

What do I need?

- Record of constraints and other requirements obtained in phases preceding Analysis.

- General domain documentation.
- Interview transcripts produced by other Analysis activities.

What do I produce?

- Constraints Document (see Section 4.4 for full details):
  - *Environmental Constraints*
    - Existing (Client) Environment
      - Model of present situation/system
      - Functioning objectives of user organization
      - Functioning problems of user organization
    - Development (Developer) Environment
      - Development environment requirements
      - Testing and validation procedures
    - Operational (Client) Environment
      - Operational environment requirements
      - Organizational consequences
      - Installation requirements
      - Acceptance procedures
      - Expected future enhancements
      - Maintenance procedures
  - *Technical Constraints*
    - General Technical Constraints
    - Knowledge Base and Other Storage Constraints
    - Database Constraints
    - User Interface Constraints
    - Communications Constraints
    - Hardware Constraints
  - *Policy Constraints*
    - Standards
    - Laws
    - Other Policies and Procedural Constraints.

When should I do it?

- As soon as Analysis is started, and continued (at least) until Analysis is completed.

Tasks

- Identify constraints as they become known throughout Analysis phase.
- Identify constraints arising from results of other Analysis activities.
- Record constraints in the document structure detailed in Section 4.4.
- Use that document structure as a checklist to ensure that all areas are covered.

- Supplement that basic structure with special constraints or requirements as needed.

Techniques

- Direct acquisition using focused interview and/or structured interviews – see Chapter 10.
- Reviewing interview transcripts produced in other activities ('protocol analysis').
- Reading relevant domain documentation.

Tools

- The Constraints Document structure (see Section 4.4.1 and above) as a checklist.
- Word processing can be used for producing the Constraints Document; special-purpose requirements engineering tools which support automatic cross-referencing and traceability are better (e.g. RqT or RTM), but are not KADS-specific.

Representation

- Free text: constraints should be recorded in categorized 'documents' – these can range in size from a number of pages to just a single paragraph. Use text, bullets and graphics freely.

QA checklist

- Use the document structure in Section 4.4.1 and above as a checklist.
- The analyst should ensure that all types of constraints have been considered, indicating explicitly where any type of constraint is 'not applicable'.
- As with the rest of the system documentation, the Constraints Document should be clear, unambiguous, consistent, comprehensive and make no assumptions (or clearly document any). A high-quality document is especially important as it needs to be referred to throughout the rest of the development.

Tips and comments

Use the document structure in Section 4.4.1 and above as a guide to this activity. Go through it as often as required throughout the development, to ensure that by the end of Analysis you have an up-to-date record of all the external constraints on the system being developed.

There are two major problem areas with this activity: the quantity of information and the potential for change. These can only be addressed by regular attendance to the activity.

Example
See Section 4.4.

15.5   System Overview

The objective of the System Overview is to ensure that a comprehensive but concise summary of the complete system's objectives and functionality is kept up to date throughout the Analysis phase. It maintains a view of 'the big picture', if you like. This information is used to preserve a focused context for the other, more detailed Analysis activities. In particular, though, it can greatly aid communication within the project team, and with the client, users and management. It is also where the main functional requirements of the system are captured and held. (Non-functional requirements go in the Constraints Document – see Section 15.4.)

Like Constraints Analysis, the System Overview is generally a 'maintenance-type' activity, furthering similar work done in development phases preceding Analysis (e.g. in a feasibility study). It keeps a record of the future system's objectives and functionality first recorded in the pre-Analysis phases. Again, it should be performed as a background task throughout Analysis.

The 'Produce/Update System Overview' activity is presented as a 'checklist' of four documents to produce, covering the areas required to provide a comprehensive overview. They are all produced using the same general techniques, but can be mapped onto four sub-activities. The four sub-activities within Produce/Update System Overview are:

Objectives of prospective system – Defines the aims of the future system.
System functions – Lists the key functionality in the future system.
Provisional system structure – Shows a schematic overview of the system and its context.
Provisional information requirements – Lists the information flowing in and around the system and its context.

A single consolidation is produced from these: the System Overview Document itself.

15.5.1   *Produce/Update System Overview*

Aims

- To produce and maintain an overview of the future system's objectives, functions, prospective structure and information flows.

What do I need?

- Record of objectives, functions, etc. defined in phases preceding Analysis.
- Project management records, e.g. contracts, etc.

What do I produce?

- System Overview Document (see Section 4.5.2 for full details):
  - Objectives of prospective system
  - System functions
  - Provisional system structure
  - Provisional information requirements

When should I do it?

- As soon as Analysis is started, and continued (at least) until Analysis is completed.

Tasks

- Identify changes in objectives as they become known throughout the development.
- Record functionality as it becomes decided in other parts of Analysis.
- Draw up a rough sketch of the system's logical architecture and its future context in the client organization using the results of other parts of Analysis, e.g. Process Analysis.
- Determine the input/outputs of the components noted in the previous structure, also using other parts of Analysis, e.g. Process Analysis.

Techniques

- Abstract the results of the more focused parts of Analysis, such as Process Analysis, Expertise Analysis and Cooperation Analysis.
- Also use project management material as a source of information.

Tools

- The System Overview Document structure (see above) as a checklist.
- Word processing can be used for producing the System Overview Document, supplemented by general-purpose drawing tools such as MacDraw.

Representation

- Free text: the System Overview can be recorded in the four categorized 'documents' – these can range in size from a number of pages to just a single paragraph. Use text, bullets and graphics freely.

QA checklist

- Use the document structure above as a checklist. Go through it as often as required throughout the development, to ensure that by the end of Analysis you have an up-to-date record of all System Overview topics.
- As with the rest of the system documentation, the System Overview should be clear, unambiguous, consistent, comprehensive and make no assumptions (or clearly document any). This is especially important in this case, as the System Overview represents the reference point for the whole system – it is the 'system definition'.

Tips and comments

The Provisional System Structure and its associated Information Requirements should not be thought of as a 'first stab' at design, at least in the first instance. These, and the other two documents, are primarily to aid communication with people outside of the development team, e.g. consider what steps are necessary to make the Process Model easily comprehensible to non-project team members.

Think of the System Overview as an external communication aid as well as a 'reminder' to the development team as to what exactly the system is they are trying to build. This is especially useful in the event of team personnel changes.

Example

See Section 4.5.2.

Note

1. Some of this advice is generally applicable (or can be generalized) across Analysis and will not be repeated, to save duplication.

16 Guided tour of KADS Design

This chapter presents a 'guided tour' of the KADS Design methods. It provides a basic level of detail which is intended to support the day-to-day use of the KADS methods. It can be used as a checklist or as a summary description of Design.

Each Design activity is described in a separate section, broken down into a number of bullets, so that a sort of 'frame' is built up. There is also an introductory comment per stage. For a short overview description of Design, see Chapter 6; for a complete description, see Chapter 7; for some background 'theory', see Chapter 8.

The road map diagram shown in Figure 16.1 provides a reminder of the

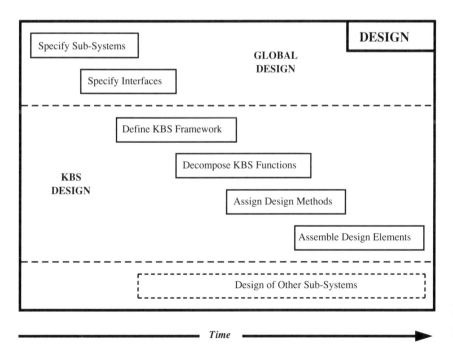

Figure 16.1 Basic 'road map' of KADS Design

contents of Design. The ordering of sections in this chapter is the same as reading this diagram from top to bottom.

16.1   Global Design

The aim of Global Design is to divide the system into a set of sub-systems, define the functions within each sub-system and specify the interfaces between sub-systems. This allows further design to be carried out on each sub-system relatively independently. For example, database design can proceed independently of KBS design. In KADS, the most important functional aspects of a system are within the KBS component. KADS therefore emphasizes these system aspects and provides methods to design them as an independent sub-system.

The Provisional System Structure, produced within the System Overview part of KADS Analysis, may be seen as a first attempt at defining a System Architecture. However, in Analysis, the emphasis is upon describing, rather than designing, the system. So the Provisional System Structure is oriented towards the customer's rather than the designer's view of the system. Nevertheless, it should be seen as a valuable input to Global Design, along with the more formal results of Analysis.

There are two activities in Global Design:

Specify Sub-Systems – Decomposes the functions which the system must support into a set of discrete components.

Specify Sub-System Interfaces – Defines what information flows between sub-systems and how the information flow is controlled.

The output from Global Design is the Global System Architecture.

16.1.1   *Specify Sub-Systems*

Aims

- To split the system into a set of discrete units to support independent sub-system design and implementation.
- To define the functions which each sub-system will support.

What do I need?

- Process Model (complete).
- Cooperation Model (complete).

What do I produce?

- A specification of the overall system architecture, including sub-system definitions.

When should I do it?

- This activity follows on from the analysis of system functions and interfaces carried out within Process and Cooperation Analysis. It is the first activity in design.

Tasks

- Identify (cross-reference) the functions which the system must realize.
- Group the functions into sub-systems.
- Illustrate how these sub-systems fit together to form the system architecture.

Techniques

- Identification of functions from Process and Cooperation Analysis.
- Grouping of functions according to type, sequence, associated agent, etc.
- Production of system architecture diagram.

Tools

- General-purpose drawing tools may be used to illustrate the System Architecture.
- A CASE tool which supports a notation such as structure charts may also be useful.

Representation

- The System Architecture is described in terms of two basic relations: *consists-of* to identify sub-systems and embedded functions; and *input–output* to identify that information or control must be moved between sub-systems. The representation may be schematic in terms of boxes connected by arrows; or more formal, such as structure charts.

QA checklist

- Each task and data-store from the Process Model must be allocated to a sub-system.
- Each system function within the System Task Model must be allocated to a sub-system.
- Each system function allocated to a sub-system in the Global System

Architecture should be described and cross-referenced to either the Process Model or the System Task Model.

- The elements from within the Expertise Model must be allocated to one or more sub-systems. Unless the Technical Constraints dictate otherwise, all KBS functions should reside within a single sub-system.
- The number of input–output relations between sub-systems should not be excessive given the number of sub-systems.

Tips and comments

There is no single, logical method which will achieve Global Design given the results of KADS Analysis. A number of guidelines are offered below, but the system designer is left to decide when and if it is appropriate to use each of them:

- The Process Decomposition may be used to break down the system into a set of functions.
- The Process Distribution can provide guidance on how to group functions. For example, the system KBS functions often need to be grouped together into a single sub-system as they are dependent upon a special implementation environment.
- The System Task Model can be used to explore the interconnections between system functions. The principles of maximizing cohesion and minimizing coupling may be employed to find sensible groupings.
- Separation of external system interfaces into separate sub-systems is a good principle. For example, the User Interface can usually be separated from the main system functionality and implemented independently.
- A decision should be taken about whether to provide global or local system control. If system control is to be global then the System Task Model describes the required control functions.
- Constraints Analysis results can have an impact upon Global Design. For example, functions may need to be grouped according to location, hardware platform, performance criteria, etc.

Example
See p. 138

16.1.2   *Specify Sub-System Interfaces*

Aims

- To define what information flows between sub-systems.
- To define how the information flows are controlled.

What do I need?

- Process Model (complete).
- Cooperation Model (complete).
- Sub-System Definitions (draft).

What do I produce?

- A specification of the sub-system interfaces.

When should I do it?

- This activity follows on from, and can be interleaved with, the specification of sub-systems.

Tasks

- Identify (cross-reference) the information flows between sub-systems.
- Define the control aspects of information flows.

Techniques

- Identification of information and control flows from Process and Cooperation Analysis plus sub-system definitions.

Tools

- No special-purpose tools are required or available, apart from a word-processor and/or drawing package.

Representation

- Free-format text or loose tables/frames.

QA checklist

- Each input–output relation between sub-systems should be expanded into one or more sub-system interface definitions.
- Each information or control flow should be documented to include the information specified on p. 141.

Tips and comments
A comprehensive but time-consuming way to ensure the completeness and correctness of this activity is to draw up a matrix of the functions identified within each sub-system. Mark which functions need to communicate with each other by reference to the Process and System Task Models. If two functions are in separate sub-systems, but need to communicate, then a sub-system interface definition is required.

Example
See p. 141.

16.2   KBS Design

The aim of KBS Design is to design the problem-solving parts of the system, once these have been identified and grouped into an independent sub-system. Since the problem-solving part of the system has been captured during Analysis in the form of the Expertise Model, the most natural way to achieve KBS Design in KADS is to map the layers of the Expertise Model directly onto a physical sub-system architecture. However, this is rarely directly possible in practice. The KBS sub-system may need to realize additional functions, such as explanation and support facilities, which are not part of the Expertise Model. Furthermore, if the KBS sub-system is to be implemented using a KBS shell or toolkit then this is unlikely, in general, to provide direct support for each element of the Expertise Model.

KADS seeks to assist a KBS designer in selecting the most appropriate design framework, identifying the functions which must be realized in the context of this framework, mapping these functions onto computational methods and knowledge representations, identifying the component design elements of the methods, and finally, composing these design elements into a physical KBS sub-system architecture. There are four activities in KBS Design:

- *Define KBS Design Framework* Identifies the general technique or architecture which will be used to support the KBS sub-system design.
- *Decompose KBS Functions* Identifies and decomposes the functions which are needed to realize the KBS sub-system.
- *Assign Design Methods* Selects problem-solving methods which realize the desired functions and maps these onto design elements via computational methods and knowledge representations.
- *Assemble Design Elements* Composes the selected design elements into a physical KBS sub-system architecture.

The output from KBS Design is the combination of the results from these activities, forming a comprehensive design of the KBS sub-system(s). The complete system's design may involve the design of other, non-KBS sub-systems to complement this one.

16.2.1   *Define KBS Design Framework*

Aims

- To choose a framework in which to carry out KBS design. This could be a general problem-solving technique, such as constraint-based logic or blackboard reasoning. Alternatively, it could be related to the chosen or dictated implementation environment, e.g. frame- or rule-based.

What do I need?

- Global System Architecture (defining bounds of KBS sub-system).
- Expertise Model (complete).
- Technical Constraints (chosen/pre-defined KBS implementation environment).

What do I produce?

- A description of the general technique or environment which is to be used.

When should I do it?

- This activity follows on from Global Design. It is the first activity in KBS design.

Tasks

- Identify the problem-solving frameworks offered by chosen or pre-defined environments.
- Identify any frameworks which are well suited to the required problem-solving capability of the KBS sub-system.
- Resolve any inconsistencies and chose the most appropriate framework or environment.

Techniques

- Identifying general characteristics of the implementation environment (if given).
- Identifying general characteristics of the Expertise Model.
- Choosing a framework to match the pre-specified environment and/or the Expertise Model.

Tools

- The KADS Generic Task Model Library (Chapter 12) and Problem-Solving Method Library (Chapter 13) may be helpful in characterizing the Expertise Model.
- Environment feature guidelines (see Chapter 14 for ideas).
- A word-processor can be used to document the framework description.

Representation

- Free-format text.

QA checklist

- If an implementation environment has been chosen or stipulated then this should provide a reasonably good match against the characteristics of the required problem-solving capability.
- The chosen KBS Design Framework must be consistent with the general characteristics of the Expertise Model.
- The KBS Design Framework and implementation environment should be consistent with the contents of the Constraints Documents from Analysis.

Tips and comments

KADS Generic Tasks often map directly onto problem-solving frameworks. Heuristic Classification, for example, can be supported by a rule-based approach provided that the implementation supports meta-rules to realize control over the inference steps. Similarly, synthesis tasks such as 'planning' and 'scheduling' can often be implemented within a constraint-based framework.

The significance of this activity will vary with the suitability of, and tightness of constraints on the implementation platform. Where an inappropriate tool is imposed on the design, the success of the project may be jeopardized. Other problems can arise as a consequence of needing to develop design elements from very low-level (relatively speaking) languages, as this may result in an excessive burden on resources.

Example

See p. 145.

16.2.2   Decompose KBS Functions (Functional Design)

Aims

- To decompose the functions which must be supported by the KBS sub-system and analyze their interrelations in terms of input–output.

What do I need?

- Expertise Model (complete).
- KBS Sub-System Specification from the Global System Architecture (complete).

What do I produce?

- Functional Design Model, consisting of:
  - A hierarchical decomposition of problem-solving functional blocks,

terminating with primitive inference functions and domain layer elements.

- [Optionally] a structure chart showing input/output between functional blocks in the hierarchy and with other functional blocks.
- Specifications for Task or Inference functions, Control functions, Support Functions and Domain Knowledge.

When should I do it?

- This activity can start as soon as Global Design is complete. It is not strictly necessary to have the KBS Design Framework in place before commencing this activity, although the framework can be helpful when decomposing inference steps.

Tasks

- Decompose the KBS functions in the KBS Sub-System Specification, using the Expertise Model to guide decomposition.
- [Optionally] identify input–output relations.
- Write Inference, Composite Problem–Solving (Task), Strategic Control and Support function specifications.
- Write Domain/Data Model specifications.

Techniques

- Hierarchical decomposition of functions, guided by the Expertise Model structure.
- Prototyping by functional control simulation with 'black box' inference procedures.

Tools

- General-purpose drawing and word-processing tools.
- Design Description Language (DDL) frames for specifications – see Section 7.2.2.

Representation

- *Consists-of* hierarchy of functional blocks; label the different types of functions.
- [Optional] Structure chart illustrating input/output relations.
- Design Description Language (DDL) frames.

QA checklist

The Functional Design Model is checked against the Analysis input from which it is specified. The following should be ensured:

- All Inference Types have corresponding functional blocks at some level of decomposition.

- I/O dependencies between functional blocks are consistent with those described in the Process Model and the Sub-System Interface Specifications.
- All functions defined to reside within the KBS sub-system have corresponding functional blocks.
- The Domain Model is consistent with the Domain layer of the Expertise Model.
- Any component of the Domain model is represented only once.
- Function blocks are specified for all inference, strategic control and support functions.

Tips and comments
The goal of Functional Design is to specify all the functions to be performed by the KBS sub-system. Functions are represented as functional blocks, between which input/output relations are defined. These blocks are arranged in a *consists-of* hierarchy, in which the highest node represents the full KBS sub-system. Beneath this, blocks are separated according to the type of functionality they address. A standard separation at level one is between the following types (with typical labels shown in parentheses):

- Problem-solving (P) – Functions that perform expert tasks.
- Domain Model (K) – Knowledge storage.
- Data Model (D) – Data storage.
- Strategic control (C) – (Optional higher-level overall KBS control).
- Support functions (S) – (Other functions such as explanation).

The DDL frames to use for these functions are as follows:

- Problem-solving (P) – Composite PS Function or Inference Function frames.
- Domain Model (K) – Domain/Data Model frames.
- Data Model (D) – Domain/Data Model frames.
- Strategic control (C) – Strategic Control/Support Function Block frames.
- Support functions (S) – Strategic Control/Support Function Block frames.

Inference types in the Expertise Model are usually mapped directly onto Inference Functions. This will lead to a good level of consistency between the structure of the Design and Analysis models. However, where groups of inferences are always used in the same order, or where all the inferences in a task are closely related within the chosen KBS Design Framework, it may be more convenient to group them into a higher-level function, known as a Composite Problem-Solver (PS) Function (or task). Conversely, when inference types are complex it may be appropriate to decompose them into smaller supporting functional blocks.

Inference functions will often require two distinct types of input: first, the data that populate the input domain roles; second, the domain knowledge required to perform the inference. Support knowledge for an inference function should be considered together with the inference type which it supports. Input and output domain roles may be considered independently.

Example
See p. 152.

16.2.3   *Assign Design Methods (Behavioural Design)*

Aims

- To find an appropriate and feasible computational approach for each Problem-Solving Function Block specified in the Functional Model.
- To choose a suitable representation for each Domain Model component.
- To identify the Design Elements that will need to be included in the Physical Design – including those elements which will support the computational methods and domain knowledge.

What do I need?

- Problem-Solving Function Block descriptions.
- Domain Model descriptions.
- KBS Design Framework.
- Technical Constraints.

What do I produce?

- Behavioural Design Model, consisting of:
  - A set of descriptions of methods, listing the Design Elements required to realize them.
  - A set of knowledge/data representations which will be used to support these methods.
  - [Optionally] a diagrammatic representation of the relationships between inference functions, methods and design elements.
  - Finished slots in Problem-Solving Function Block descriptions and Domain Model descriptions, plus (optionally) their own method frames for Inference Function and Composite PS Function blocks.

When should I do it?

- Once (some) Function Blocks have been identified and documented by 'Decompose KBS Functions'.

Tasks

- For each Problem-Solving Function Block, identify an appropriate and feasible computational method; map this onto Design Elements.
- For Domain Model elements, identify and select a suitable (knowledge) representation – note that support knowledge elements will be constrained by choices made for associated Problem Solving Function Blocks.

Techniques

- Investigation of the type of problem-solving function and the type of inputs and outputs.
- Investigation of suitable problem-solving methods and associated design elements – see Sections 13.1 and 13.3.
- Knowledge-representation techniques – see Section 13.2.
- Conventional software design techniques should normally be used for Strategic Control and Support Function blocks.

Tools

- General-purpose drawing and word-processing tools.
- The KADS Problem-Solving Methods Library – see Chapter 13.

Representation

- Augmented Problem-Solving Function Block descriptions.
- Augmented Domain Model descriptions.
- DDL frames for Inference Methods.
- [Optional] Diagrammatic binding of Design Elements to inference functions (see p. 166).

QA checklist
The Behavioural Design results are checked against the Functional Model input from which they are specified. The following should be ensured:

- All Function Block frames have their 'realized-by' slots filled.
- All methods realizing functions are specified to a level where Design Elements can be identified.
- All Domain Model description frames have their 'representation' slots filled.
- All algorithms and data structures required to achieve design methods are identified as Design Elements.

Tips and comments

Following Functional Design and its specification of the Functional Model, the designer must address the problem of how best to realize the problem-solving functions arrived at. This part of the design process is known as *Behavioural Design*. This can be viewed as a prerequisite for assembling the Physical Model. The goal of Behavioural Design is to find an appropriate computational approach for realizing the required KBS functionality. The choices made will lead to a set of *design elements* being specified. It is these elements that will be assembled into the Physical Model in Physical Design.

During Behavioural Design considerations must be made not only about the suitability of a proposed approach but also its feasibility within the context of the chosen KBS Design Framework.

Design elements can be either algorithms or data structures. A method will usually be realized by a single algorithm and at least one data structure. More than one inference function can be realized by the same method and methods may use common design elements, even if the inferences are not related by input/output.

The Problem-Solving Methods Library in Chapter 13 presents methods grouped by Inference Types, as one classification (Section 13.1). While for some types fairly detailed criteria for selecting methods are given, for others there are little or none, due to the difficulty of providing a useful general description for certain Inference Types. The alternative grouping of methods by paradigm provides a closer link to the types of methods supported by implementation environments (Section 13.3).

Design of inference functions cannot take place independently of choice of knowledge representation. The choice of method will often constrain choice of knowledge representation and vice versa (Section 13.2). There will always be a tension in design between these two activities and ultimately the choice of emphasis must rest with the designer.

Example
See p. 166.

16.2.4   *Assemble Design Elements (Physical Design)*

Aims

- To assemble the Design Elements arrived at through method selection in Behavioural Design into physical code modules.
- To assemble the modules into an architecture for the KBS sub-system.

What do I need?

- Design Elements (algorithms and knowledge) obtained from the Behavioural Design Model.
- A description of the implementation environment facilities (KBS Design Framework).
- Technical Constraints.

What do I produce?

- Physical Design Model, consisting of:
  - A diagrammatic representation of modules and their access relationships.
  - For each module, a specification which includes:
    - a description of the module.
    - a list of Design Elements realized by the module.
    - the access ports: indicating from where the module is accessed and which others it accesses.
    - a description of all algorithms and data structures local to the module.

When should I do it?

- When Design Elements have been specified for (some) Function Blocks.

Tasks

- Group Design Elements according to type, similarity, interrelatedness, etc.
- Simply go through each module in turn and produce the items required.

Techniques

- Classic good design heuristics, e.g. minimize coupling, maximize coherence.
- Designing for re-usability, e.g. separation of domain knowledge from inference.

Tools

- General-purpose drawing and word-processing tools.

Representation

- Module specification frames (not part of KADS, but an example appears on p. 173).
- Diagram showing interfaces between modules.

QA checklist

The Physical Design results are checked against the inputs from which they are specified. The following should be ensured:

- All parts of the Functional Model have been realized within the physical design.
- All Design Elements have been implemented in some module.
- Where possible, there is a strong mapping between the Functional and Physical models.
- The design is at the level of detail where implementation can proceed without any further major design decisions.

Tips and comments

As far as possible, the KBS sub-system physical architecture should reflect the structure of the Functional Design Model. This provides a good basis for maintenance of the system and coherent documentation. However, where functions are realized by common Design Elements, it is often appropriate to group them into the same modules.

The tasks noted above are stated simplistically – in reality, there will be more of an evolutionary flavour to module assembly, and also parallel work done. All the activities within KBS Design will be interleaved to some degree. Unfortunately, like much of design, it is extremely difficult to describe how humans go about designing in practice. However, if one *starts* in the step-by-step, serial manner, this will soon develop into the more natural approach.

Example

See p. 173.

Part IV
Additional information

This part of the book contains appendices that provide information peripheral to KADS as it is described in the book but which may help to set the methods in a wider context.

Appendix 1's objectives

- To present a summary view of how KADS techniques can be used to support the pre-analysis phase of development and what that phase should produce.

Appendix 2's objectives

- To present a summary view of the relationship between KADS and conventional structured methods.

Appendix 3's objectives

- To present a summary view of the relationship between KADS and object-oriented methods.

Appendix 4's objectives

- To present a summary view of the relationship between KADS as presented in this book, the original ESPRIT I results, the ESPRIT II KADS project, and other related work.

Appendix 1   Pre-analysis phases and KADS

This appendix summarizes the ways KADS can be used to help in the phase(s) of KBS development that precede KADS Analysis. As was first shown in Figure 2.3, and highlighted in Figure A1.1, pre-analysis maps onto the 'Feasibility Study' phase of the 'V' model software development lifecycle. (See Appendix 2 for descriptions of the other phases.) KADS does not fully support this phase, but can aid it in various ways.

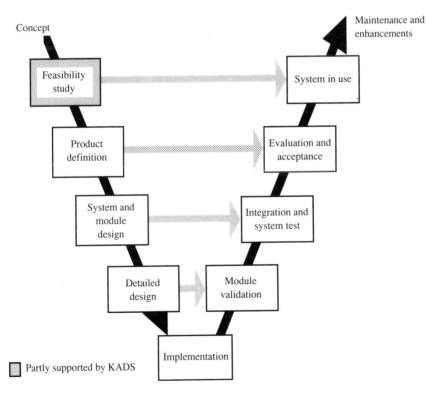

Figure A1.1 KADS support for pre-analysis in the 'V' model lifecycle

A1.1   What is the pre-analysis phase?

Pre-analysis is the phase of development that precedes detailed requirements analysis. It may include a project definition, a scoping exercise, business case analysis, feasibility study, option generation and analysis, etc. It is where an original idea for a piece of software is taken and studied enough to determine whether a full-blown development is worth starting or not. There will be many different approaches to and contents of this phase, depending on the type of organization(s) involved and other parts of the project context. The 'Feasibility Study' box shown in Figure A1.1 covers all the pre-analysis activities listed for the purposes of this book.

Pre-analysis is partly undertaken by consultation with client representatives, future users and system administrators, and other information sources in the domain, and by cross-referencing the information thus elicited with the project's business case and technical feasibility of the software. In the realm of KBS technology, though, it will also involve considering which parts of the software are potentially knowledge-based. KADS can help in performing this latter activity.

Figure A1.2 shows an attempt at drawing a generic process diagram for pre-analysis. (Note, however, that it is still just *one* view – the precise contents of pre-analysis varies greatly between organizations.) The figure contains some terms used within KADS, which will be described below, but we will not consider all the tasks shown.

A *scoping study* is where the whole possible context of the future system is trimmed down to determine the actual parts of the organization that the system will have to work with and within. A *feasibility study* takes a more formalized description of the result of the scoping study in the form of a process/data model, and uses business considerations to determine which solution option(s) should be followed up with a full-blown requirements analysis. The result of a feasibility study in Figure A1.2 can be used as the first version of a System Overview (see Section 4.5) – providing a natural link to KADS Analysis.

In performing a scoping study or feasibility study there are three sets of issues to consider:

- *Issues concerning the tasks involved*
  - Types of KBS tasks.
  - Nature of tasks (size, complexity, stability, whether well defined or not, decomposability).
  - Nature of solutions (single/multiple solutions required, speed of production, level of interaction needed).
- *Issues concerning the knowledge involved*
  -    Type (heuristic, common sense, skill, etc.).

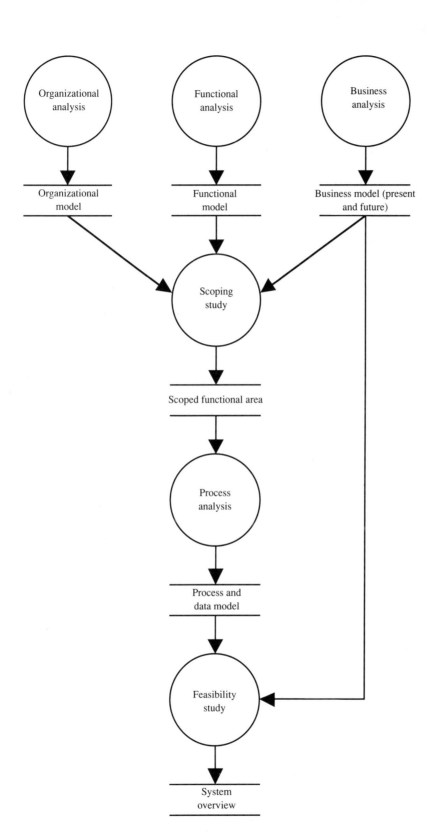

Figure A1.2 Possible generic process for pre-analysis. Note that the 'Feasibility Study' box shown here is *not* the same as that in figure A1.1 – the whole process would fit into the 'Feasibility Study' box in figure A1.1

    – Nature (size, completeness, diversity, accuracy).
    – Availability of test cases.
- *Issues concerning the expert(s) involved*
–   Availability, experience, reputation, motivation.
    – Single/multiple, problem-solving approach.

KADS can help in addressing some of these issues.

(Note: there may be existing in-house or published methodologies that can be applied to these early activities in system development. For example, Checkland's 'Soft Systems' methodology can be usefully applied in scoping studies – see Checkland (1981) in the Bibliography, 'Documents about conventional software engineering'.)

A1.2   How can KADS help the pre-analysis phase?

KADS can help pre-analysis in the following ways:

- Identifying areas of the proposed system concept that may be knowledge-based.
- Making initial assessments of the technical feasibility of KBS in such areas.

As with the whole pre-analysis phase, these activities may be performed for different purposes depending upon their context. For example, the first may be carried out perhaps to gauge whether a KBS approach may be needed in any subsequent development, which may influence the decision whether or not to proceed with a system option. Alternatively, it may be undertaken with a view to eliciting as many KBS opportunities as possible. There are many other possibilities for applications of these activities.

Below we consider identifying KBS solutions and opportunities. Assessment of the feasibility of identified opportunities will be based on such identification, and will not be dealt with separately. For example, if a KBS opportunity is identified on the basis of mapping onto a well-established Generic Task Model, and for which previous in-house experience of implementation exists, this suggests few technical problems in subsequent development. Alternatively, if a less well-defined model exists for the task, or even if no model in the library seems to fit, then greater risk is suggested.

A1.2.1 · Identifying KBS solutions and opportunities without KADS

The scoping study task in Figure A1.2 may include the need to identify opportunities for applying KBS technology. The feasibility study task may involve the identification of potential KBS solutions. These activities will often ultimately depend upon the judgement of experienced KBS developers. This is probably unavoidable. However, the following points attempt to summarize the reasons why someone *might* choose a KBS solution over a more conventional one, and may be useful to those less experienced with such systems.

A KBS may be appropriate where one or more of the following are true:

- Knowledge is expressed and/or used – rules, relationships, assumptions, etc.
- Facts in the domain may have qualifiable degrees of certainty.
- The amount of knowledge to be consulted is large.
- An exhaustive check of all possibilities must be explored.
- Rules exist in some domain, or other concept-connecting relations, apart from plain facts.
- Little 'world knowledge', common sense or manual dexterity is required.
- A step-by-step deduction or diagnosis is needed.
- There is no established theory, just heuristics (i.e. 'rules of thumb').
- Established human experts for the domain exist.
- Human expertise needed is scarce, for whatever reason.
- The processing required is not *purely* based on numerical calculation, or does not *only* require the application of a standard formula or other algorithm (but may do in parts, though).
- The task can be viewed as a mapping from a problem description to a solution of some kind.
- The task involves qualitative values and judgements, as opposed to purely quantitative ones.

More thorough checklists have been published. In particular, we have found that Laufmann *et al.* (1990) (see Bibliography, 'Other relevant KBS topics') describes a very comprehensive approach, and recommend readers compare this with their current methods.

A1.2.2   Identifying KBS solutions and opportunities with KADS

The structure of some of the KADS objects and methods themselves can help to identify prospective KBS solutions. *This would be done in conjunction with the considerations outlined above.* Consider the following (although note that care must be exercized here in order to avoid a self-fulfilling prophecy):

- Where the domain/problem is seen to very easily fit the four-layer Expertise Model structure.
- Where the problem to be solved clearly matches an existing Generic Task Model in the library (Chapter 12).
- Where the problem-solving tasks in the domain seem to map onto Generic Tasks as described in the KADS classification (Table 12.1 and Figure 12.2).
- Where the types of 'inferences' required in the domain map directly onto parts of the KADS Inference Types (Section 11.1).
- Similarly for Domain Roles (Section 11.2).

For example, in the identification of problem-solving tasks found in some potential system context, to search for possible KBS applications, one can:

- Identify keywords (verbs and nouns) used in the domain which include or map onto:
  'Identification', 'Diagnosis', 'Verification', 'Correlation', 'Assessment', 'Monitoring', 'Classification', 'Prediction', 'Repair', 'Remedy', 'Control', 'Maintenance', 'Design', 'Configuration', 'Planning', 'Scheduling', 'Modelling', etc.

A1.3   What does KADS need from the pre-analysis phase?

If full-blown development of a system starts with KADS Analysis, some inputs are required that should or could be produced by pre-analysis. Even if no formal pre-analysis phase seems to take place, the items classified 'vital' are required before Analysis can start.

The following items are *vital* outputs of pre-analysis for input to KADS Analysis:

- Solution option that is deemed technically feasible and financially justifiable.

- Solution option that contains KBS functionality, i.e. 'problem-solving' behaviour.
- Scoped functional area for the future system.
- Provisional system objectives.
- Provisional system functions.

The following items are *useful* outputs of pre-analysis for input to KADS Analysis:

- Provisional Process/Data model, perhaps including initial Process Distribution.
- Initial System Overview.
- Initial list of Constraints.

Appendix 2   Conventional structured methods and KADS

This appendix summarizes some of the issues concerning KADS in relation to structured software development methods for conventional software. A major thrust in the field at the time of writing is in *'methods integration'*. This addresses how KBS-specific methods can be made to work in conjunction with conventional structured methods. This is needed because KBS is increasingly being recognized as a practical and useful technology to be added to the current portfolio for building software solutions, and not so much a specialized research backwater. The UK government standard methodology SSADM is used as an example for comparison with KADS; other structured methods such as SA/SD and the many proprietary methods could be compared in the same way. The aim is to start to show how KADS could be used alongside such methods and vice versa.

First, we clarify that the 'V' model lifecycle first shown in Figure 2.3 covers the phases of development found in both conventional and KBS development. Following a summary description of each phase of the lifecycle, a résumé of SSADM is presented. Then KADS is described in the same format, and comparisons and links are made between the two. At the end of the appendix some general comments are made with respect to KADS and current issues in conventional software development.

A2.1   A simple general software development lifecycle

Figure A2.1 shows the 'V' model software development *lifecycle* (or process) used before in this book, which is just one of many particular versions of this shape of lifecycle. There are, of course, many completely different lifecycles in software engineering, using shapes ranging from the simple waterfall, through an 'X' shape, to the spiral model. Some are just illustrative; some are used as practical guides to project planning, such as the modern risk-driven lifecycles. The definitive practical lifecycle has yet

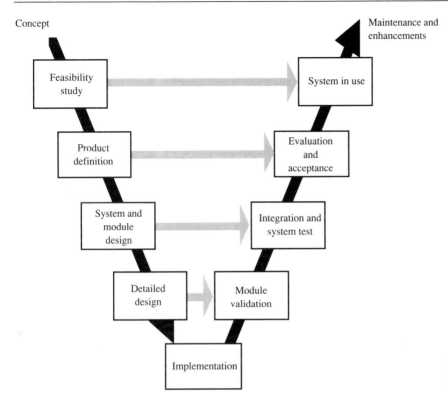

Figure A2.1 A basic software product development lifecycle

to be produced. The 'V' model is used in this book because it is familiar and simple for illustrative purposes.[1]

The 'V' model describes the phases of product development from an original product concept, through to the successful use of the final product as a working computer system. The boxes in Figure A2.1 represent the different *phases* of development – major partitions of the overall development of a piece of software. The basic 'V'-shaped arrows represent the progression of the development of the software. The horizontal (left to right) arrows represent relationships which mean that the results of the left-hand side phases are used to help define the contents and scope of the phases on the right-hand side.

The following sub-sections summarize the contents of the key phases and features of the 'V' model lifecycle. KBS-specific comments are made as needed.

A2.1.1   Feasibility Study phase – 'Pre-analysis'

The *Feasibility Study phase* is that part of the lifecycle where an original concept for a piece of software is taken and studied sufficiently to determine whether or not a full-blown development is worth starting. This phase, called 'pre-analysis', was described in overview in Appendix 1, Section A1.1.

A2.1.2   Product Definition phase – 'Analysis'

The *Product Definition* phase is that part of the lifecycle where a feasible product concept, together with the results of studying the feasibility of that concept, is analyzed in depth, in order to fully define the software to be built. As for the Feasibility Study phase, this is done by consultation with client representatives, future users and system administrators, and other information sources in the domain. Here, however, the consultation and analysis is in complete detail. Real-world requirements arising from the problem domain are captured, analyzed and translated into an abstract form and documented. The documentation is a specification for the software. The requirements specification defines what the software will do, and the context in which it will do it – the required behaviour of the future system. It will also include a description of the constraints on the development of the software. The Product Definition phase is also known as the requirements analysis (and capture), system analysis, or just analysis phase – but it corresponds to KADS's *Analysis phase*.

Analysis for KBSs needs to represent or model the required problem-solving or reasoning behaviour of the future system – this is not covered by conventional software development techniques. In addition, KBS developments, especially embedded KBS, may require particularly complex cooperative behaviour, either with their user(s) and/or other systems. KADS Analysis has special modelling techniques to address both of these issues. Otherwise, as for conventional software, the functional and non-functional requirements on the future KBS still have to be captured and analyzed – so that they may be understood by the developers (plus client and users) and well documented.

A2.1.3   System and Module Design – 'Design'

The *System and Module Design* phase is that part of the lifecycle where a requirements specification, judged sufficiently complete to continue, is taken and, together with the known constraints on the system's development, is transformed into a definition of the software. This software definition is described in terms of how the system will be implemented in modules of code ('module-level design') and an overall architecture for arranging those modules ('system-level design'). Modules are precisely defined functional blocks; the Architecture is a structure into which those modules will fit. (Note that the architecture can define the software's partitioning at both the hardware and software levels.)

Like the Product Definition phase, the result of this phase is a specification. But the design specification, while abstract, is described in terms that will be much more readily transformable into code – translatable, even. The design specification defines how the software will provide its required behaviour – including the required algorithms and data structures; or in knowledge-based terminology, inference processes and knowledge representations. This level of design is notoriously creative in nature,[2] although it is possible to provide some guidance. The System and Module Design phase is sometimes split into two or more phases – but it corresponds to KADS's *Design* phase.

Design for KBSs needs to cope with the transformation from a specialized model of the required problem-solving behaviour of the system into modules of program code, via new or known reasoning algorithms and knowledge representations – this is not handled well by conventional software development techniques. In addition, it would be inappropriate to design an entire system using KBS design techniques, as all but the simplest KBSs are not wholly knowledge-based. Therefore, the design phase needs to be able to separate KBS sub-system(s) design from the design of the other system modules. KADS Design has been developed to address both these issues.

However, as for conventional software, on the basis of a documented understanding of what the system must do (how it must behave), and the constraints upon that required behaviour (both from the Product Definition phase), a transformed description of the KBS to be built must be produced which can be readily translated into code.

Note that the apparently clear split between the Analysis and Design phases is not generally realizable in real developments. This can arise from human factors such as the natural tendency to move to and from Analysis- and Design-type considerations while in one or the other phase. It can also arise from real-world constraints in developing software, such as when the inputs to the start of a project are not a well-defined product concept or there are special hardware, software, people or organization constraints.

A2.1.4   *Maintenance and Enhancements phase – 'Post-Initial Development'*

The *Maintenance and Enhancements* post-development phase is often poorly understood in terms of its position in the lifecycle. The problem stems from the fact that the full software development lifecycle, such as that shown in Figure A2.1, is actually a *new* software development lifecycle – a lifecycle for a wholly new system. This is an idealistic situation. 'Maintenance-type' and 'enhancement-type' developments are much more common. But do they need some sort of lifecycle to themselves?

Maintenance is the activity primarily concerned with small changes to an existing system. Enhancements are generally larger in nature, and may represent additions of whole new sub-systems to an existing system. One can use the *same* general software development lifecycle, like that in Figure A2.1, to illustrate maintenance and enhancement projects – they simply correspond to *subsets* of the complete development lifecycle. A realistic system complete lifecycle will include many iterations around (parts of) the basic development lifecycle, as it is maintained and enhanced.

Maintenance-type developments generally start at the Product Definition phase, but could start as late as the System and Module definition phase. Enhancement projects may start at the Product Definition phase, or earlier. (This applies to properly managed commercially developed systems, where even small bug-fixes should be carefully documented. Less stringently managed systems may not have to bother considering small changes to an existing system in terms of phases.) The other special characteristic of such developments is that a major input to the requirements on the development (in KADS terms, the Constraints) will be the existing system's Analysis and Design documentation.

In KBSs, maintenance and enhancements are particularly interesting, as the maintenance of knowledge in a system is potentially difficult and may be more frequently required than information changes in conventional systems. In KADS, although not specifically covered in this book, maintenance and enhancement projects may be facilitated by basing such development on a full KADS Analysis and Design of the existing system. The clear documentation and separation of concerns will help updates to be made. Where the system was not built using KADS originally, reverse engineering may be used to produce KADS Analysis and Design models.

A2.1.5   *Pre-implementation's influences on post-implementation – 'Cross-links'*

Figure A2.1 shows arrows pointing from left to right across the two halves of the lifecycle. These *cross-links* represent how the phases on the left-hand side will influence the way the corresponding right-hand side phases are performed. For example, the pre-implementation phases can be used to define the test definitions that must be executed in the post-implementation phases. The same relationships can be exploited in KBS development as with conventional software.

For example, using KADS Analysis activities in a Product Definition phase can help to define the test acceptance criteria for Evaluation and Acceptance. Likewise, performing KADS Design activities in a System and Module Design phase will help to define the test acceptance criteria for the Integration and System Test phase.

A2.2   A comparison of SSADM and KADS

The use of a structured methodology to support the software development is now quite standard practice in the industry. It gives benefits such as improving controllability, maintainability and document standardization. Two possible methodologies to consider for use on a project are SSADM and KADS.

SSADM is increasingly becoming one of the industry-standard methodologies for the development of conventional, data processing (DP) type applications. KADS is a newer methodology (or at least its origins are much more recent), specially devised to support the development of KBS applications. It also seems likely to become an industry standard. The following sections summarize the contents and approach of these two methodologies, and a comparative conclusion is presented at the end.

A2.2.1   SSADM

SSADM (Structured Systems Analysis and Design Method) is a modern conventional systems methodology. It prescribes how the development of a system can be conducted, and is particularly suitable for medium or large DP systems – conventional computer programs with a substantial database element(s). In the familiar way, it breaks down a development project into phases, which are in turn broken down into stages, and then steps. Each step has a list of tasks to perform, and a list of inputs and outputs. Associated with these components is an overall structure and procedure – the development lifecycle.

Three further important distinctive characteristics of SSADM are:

- It takes a data-driven approach to development.
- It separates logical and physical aspects of the development.
- It supports cross-checking between differing data views taken during development.

The basic phases of development that SSADM supports are 'Systems

Analysis' and 'Systems Design'. There is also an optional phase which can precede Systems Analysis, called 'Feasibility Study'. This is a relatively recent addition to the methodology. There is a trend towards additions to the methodology like this one, as it is enhanced over the years, e.g. 'Maintenance SSADM' (to support system maintenance) and 'Micro SSADM' (a cut-down version for small systems). However, we shall ignore this phase in this description. The following breakdown gives an overview of the main phases, their component stages and steps (note phase 1 is the Feasibility Study):

+ *SSADM*
    + *Phase 2 – Systems Analysis*
        + Stage 1 – Analysis of systems operations and current problems
            - Step 110 – Initiate analysis
            - Step 120 – Investigate current systems
            - Step 125 – Investigate system data structure
            - Step 140 – Develop problem/requirement list
            - Step 150 – Review investigation results
        + Stage 2 – Specification of requirements
            - Step 200 – Define logical system
            - Step 205 – Define audit security and control requirements
            - Step 210 – Define and consolidate user requirements
            - Step 220 – Identify and select from business system options
            - Step 230 – Further define chosen option
            - Step 240 – Create required data structure
            - Step 250 – Investigate detailed system logic
            - Step 260 – Review required system specification
        + Stage 3 – Selection of technical options
            - Step 310 – Create technical options
            - Step 320 – User selects from technical options
            - Step 330 – Complete and review required system specification
            - Step 340 – Define performance objectives
    + *Phase 3 – Systems Design*
        + Stage 4 – Data design
            - Step 410 – Conduct relational data analysis
            - Step 420 – Create detailed logical data design
        + Stage 5 – Process design
            - Step 510 – Define logical enquiry processing
            - Step 520 – Define logical update processing
            - Step 530 – Validate and review logical system design

+ Stage 6 – Physical design
  - Step 610 – Create first cut physical data design
  - Step 620 – Create program specifications for major transactions
  - Step 630 – Create performance productions and tune design
  - Step 640 – Create file/database definitions
  - Step 650 – Create remaining program specifications
  - Step 660 – Create system test plans
  - Step 670 – Create operating instructions
  - Step 680 – Create implementation plans
  - Step 690 – Define manual procedures

To support each step's list of tasks, there are a number of standard SSADM techniques usually considered part of the methodology itself. These techniques include:

- Dataflow diagrams
- Logical data structuring
- User options
- Entity life histories
- Dialogue design
- Relational data analysis
- Composite logical data design
- Process outlines
- First cut data design
- First cut program design
- Physical design control

Complementing these, there are other activities and techniques undertaken within projects which are generally not considered part of SSADM but are required nonetheless. These include the activities of estimating, planning, and quality assurance, and generic techniques such as interviewing.

A2.2.2   KADS

KADS is a collection of methods that describe a modern structured approach to key areas of the development of KBSs. In particular, the KADS methods concentrate on the Analysis and Design phases of development, equivalent to SSADM's System Analysis and System Design phases, respectively.

Like any structured methodology, use of the methods will provide benefits, including better control of the development resulting in a more maintainable final system. This is novel in the field of KBS, where an unstructured iterative or evolutionary approach to development has been the norm.

Like SSADM, KADS breaks down a development project into phases, which are in turn broken down further, into activities and sub-activities. Likewise, each activity has a list of tasks to perform, and a list of inputs and outputs. Again, associated with these components is an overall structure and procedure – although this is much less prescriptive than the lifecycle of SSADM. In KADS, because of the much more difficult nature of KBS, the sequencing of activities, especially lower-level ones, is necessarily left much more to the analyst or designer. Normative support is still provided, but it is recognized that in practice, procedures may vary.

KADS covers the following areas:

- Structured model-driven activities for Analysis and Design.
- Definitions and frameworks for the results produced by activities.
- Advice and guidance for tools and techniques to support activities in KBS development.
- Techniques and checklists for quality assessment and control (QAC).
- Identified prototyping opportunities.

KADS is founded on modelling. Models in KADS are structured descriptions of observed or required behaviour. KBS development is viewed as consisting of a series of modelling tasks – where the ultimate output of the development is an operational model, i.e. an implemented system. There are seven key models. The Analysis models are: Process Model, Expertise Model and Cooperation Model. The Design models are: Global System Architecture, Functional Model, Behavioural Model and Physical Model. A document framework for recording more general requirements and constraints is also provided, so that any non-KBS-specific areas which still impact on the development are covered.

The following breakdown gives an overview of the main phases and their component activities:

+ *KADS*
   + *Analysis Activities*
      + Process Analysis
         – Analyze and Decompose Process
         – Assign Tasks and Data Stores to Agents
      + Cooperation Analysis
         – Analyze User Tasks
         – Analyze System Tasks

- Define User Interface(s)
+ Expertise Analysis
    - Analyze Static Knowledge
    - Select Initial Generic Task Model(s)
    - Construct Expertise Model
+ Constraints Analysis
    - Analyze Environmental Constraints
    - Analyze Technical Constraints
    - Analyze Policy Constraints
+ System Overview
    - Produce/Update System Overview
+ *Design Activities*
    + Global Design
        - Specify Sub-Systems
        - Specify Sub-System Interfaces
    + KBS Design
        - Define KBS Design Framework
        - Decompose KBS Functions (Functional Design)
        - Assign Design Methods (Behavioural Design)
        - Assemble Design Elements (Physical Design)
    + Design of Other Sub-Systems

Like SSADM, there are a number of associated supporting techniques. These include the activities of knowledge acquisition, estimating, planning, and quality assurance, and generic techniques such as interviewing. Both SSADM and KADS provide similar levels of support in this respect.

A2.2.3   *Comparative conclusions*

Both SSADM and KADS provide similar levels of support to system development. SSADM is more widely known in the software industry, and perhaps more widely applicable. It is also probably more mature, although this is often overestimated. SSADM is especially suited to the development of conventional DP systems. It is an industry-standard methodology in the UK. KADS is specially targeted at KBS development, although it is flexibly suitable for systems with small or large KBS elements. KADS has 'hooks' for allowing the application of non-KBS development methods in certain areas of the development: External agent and agent task analysis, Constraints Analysis and non-KBS sub-system design. KADS is a *de facto* European standard methodology. Both methods are based on the fundamental triad of static/dynamic/

process views of the system during analysis and design; both rely heavily on functional decomposition; both methods have a hierarchical structure of activities and interrelated results. These latter factors, together with KADS's purpose-built hooks, encourage the possibility of interworking between the methods.

A2.3   Current issues in conventional software and KADS

This section summarizes some current conventional (i.e. non-KBS) software issues and their relation to KADS:

Object-oriented methods – This approach to software development is seeing a marked increase in popularity at the time of writing. This is partly because of the importance of the potential for 're-use' in software production as costs escalate. Some comments about KADS with respect to Objected-Oriented (OO) approaches are made in Appendix 3.

Formal methods – The application of mathematical techniques to software development is seeing a much more pragmatic approach at the time of writing. The ESPRIT-II project furthering KADS research is working on introducing formal techniques to KADS – see Appendix 4.

CASE – Computer-Aided Software Engineering tools are frequently seen as indispensable to the application of structured methods. The KADS ESPRIT-II project is addressing the lack of a commercially available and supported KADS-specific CASE tool – see Appendix 4. In addition, the possible adaptation of conventional software CASE tools for use with KADS has been described in Section 9.7.

ISO 9000 – This is the international standard for quality management and assurance in production, which is being increasingly adopted by the software industry, as in many others. (It is also known as BS 5750 in the UK.) ISO 9000–3 describes quality management and assurance guidelines for the application of the standard to the development, supply and maintenance of software. (This is BS 5750: Part 13 in the UK.) In KADS, we consider that such a standard would be applied to the method via a project management framework (see Section 9.1). ISO 9000–3 covers the following issues:
 – Management responsibility
 – Quality system
 – Internal quality system audits
 – Corrective action
 – Contract review

- Purchaser's requirements specification
- Development planning
- Quality planning
- Design and implementation
- Testing and validation
- Acceptance
- Replication, delivery and installation
- Maintenance
- Configuration management
- Document control
- Quality records
- Measurement
- Rules, practices and conventions
- Tools and techniques
- Purchasing
- Included software product
- Training

Lifecycles – The waterfall and waterfall-based lifecycles (including the 'V' model) are seen as inadequate in describing the process of software development with any degree of realism. There is much research in defining novel lifecycles which can be used with more certainty of accurately modelling a real development. One way to achieve this is by defining a configurable generic lifecycle. Risk-driven models are particularly in favour. In KADS, we see such issues as part of the project management framework (see Section 9.1) – the 'V' model used in this book is for illustration and not suggested as an accurate model of the development process. Various spiral models based on Boehm's original (Boehm, 1988 – see Bibliography, 'Documents about conventional software engineering'), are quite common, and have even been adapted for KADS (see Appendix 4). However, these may be better understood as lifecycle 'generators' or 'generic lifecycles' than as usable models of development in themselves.

Notes

1. The interested reader might like to start researching the topic of lifecycles, with particular reference to KBS versus conventional software development, by reading Wilson *et al.* (1989) – see Bibliography, 'Other relevant KBS topics'.
2. Some object-oriented approaches claim to remove or reduce the amount of creativity required, but perhaps may do this by increasing the level of difficulty in Analysis. (See Appendix 3.)

Appendix 3   Object-oriented development and KADS

This appendix summarizes some issues concerning KADS and KBSs in relation to Object-Oriented Methods (OOMs) – see Graham (1991) in the Bibliography ('Miscellaneous'). These are experiencing a great deal of popularity at the time of writing. One of their key benefits is in re-use, which KADS also shares. OOMs have some of their origins in Artificial Intelligence (AI) research. In addition, Object-Oriented (OO) features are often seen in KBS implementation environments.

A3.1   Definitions

OOMs can refer to a whole raft of different ideas, such as implementation languages, databases, user interfaces, development methods, analysis, design, etc. The essential 'OO' character of these various applications of the term tends to have a fuzzy boundary, but generally, what makes something 'object oriented' is as follows:

Abstraction/Encapsulation – An object is defined by a set of abstract attributes and functions ('methods') to which it can respond; the attributes are hidden from other objects; an object has an internal state.

Class and Inheritance – An object is a member of a class of objects which share common attributes and methods; such an object is called an 'instance'; there is a class *is-a* hierarchy, or more generally a graph, which defines which classes inherit what attributes and methods from which other classes.

Message-passing – Objects communicate by passing messages to each other; a message can be processed by an object if it has a corresponding method; an object that processes a message might change its state.

Polymorphism – Allows different sorts of objects to respond in different ways to the same type of message.

Concepts such as 'object-oriented analysis' and 'object-oriented design' are relatively recent. Major benefits cited for the use of such techniques include: easy re-use of class definitions, better structured implementations (easier to maintain and enhance), and a more 'natural' mapping from real-world to system implementation. However, there is little consensus in OO development methods, with many being available and new ones appearing all the time. It is a very immature technology, despite years of development from diverse fields.

A3.2   Object-oriented ideas and KBSs

The following points summarize some OO ideas with respect to KBSs:

- OO includes the concept of an *is-a* hierarchy built in, which could form the basis of a knowledge structure (in KADS Design, a 'design element').
- The class hierarchy is fixed before run-time in an OO system. In a KBS, an *is-a* hierarchy could be completely dynamic; KBSs may want to add branches, generalize from two existing branches and insert into the middle of an existing tree, etc. Inferences change the 'class attributes (variables)'. Instances may change the class variables of classes other than their own.
- Both OO and KBS systems 'say' they use appropriate representations of real-world concepts. OO takes a minimalist view, however, using a single very general paradigm to implement all objects (but could this result in over-homogeneous systems?). KBS takes a maximalist view, using special representations to represent different knowledge as required (but choosing appropriate representations is non-trivial).
- Both OO and KBS systems are declarative, compared to most conventional software, which is procedural (imperative).
- OO systems are data-dominant, where the emphasis is more on the information that is processed rather than the processing of that information; KBS systems, while being declarative, are not data-dominant, but maintain an equal importance across data and processing.
- OO does not use structures to represent information, it utilizes data stored *within* the structures; KBS tends to use both approaches as required.
- Both OO and KBS systems require greater 'up-front' development effort compared to conventional software – they are 'front-end loaded'.
- Both OO and KBS systems are generally all ultimately based on von

Neumann architecture computers, so they represent merely different perspectives or abstractions over such a machine.

A3.3   Object-oriented ideas and KADS

The following points summarize some OO ideas with respect to KADS:[1]

- Some OO methods and KADS make full use of existing terminology and concepts from conventional software – e.g. Data Flow Diagrams and State Transition Diagrams.
- Some OO methods and KADS are 'modular' in that all the activities and results are not so interdependent that one has to follow the whole method straight through in order to use it. In particular, some OO methods do not assume an OO-based implementation platform.
- One possible mapping from a four-layer KADS Expertise Model to an OO design is to consider an *is-a* hierarchy, with a branch per layer. The class hierarchy of an OO system may be equivalent to a branch of a hierarchical domain structure in the Domain Layer. At each node in the hierarchy would be an object (or class) with attributes and methods. Another branch of the hierarchy would be the inference and/ or task hierarchy. Inference Types would be considered abstract methods (see Section A3.2 for points about what inferences could do to class hierarchies). Domain Roles would be pointers to the class hierarchy branch from the inferences branch. The task hierarchy branch could use the Generic Task Model classification. Methods in the task hierarchy would be associated with goals. Task methods would provide sequence over inference methods.
- One could use this mapping as an analysis framework. It could also be employed as a mapping from KADS Analysis onto an OO design framework.
- Alternatively, Inference and Domain Structures could be seen as static entities; Dynamic behaviour is defined in the Cooperation Model; the latter could map onto the state transition behaviour of objects.
- KADS's application of inference methods and classes via Inference Types and Generic Tasks is polymorphism.
- The Functional, Behavioural, Physical separation in KADS design has its counterpart in OO: Functional (What are the objects?), Behavioural (What is their behaviour?), Physical (How are they related? – in terms of the *is-a* hierarchy and how that hierarchy can be realized in an implementation).

Note

1. These are our own ideas. Another, and very interesting view has been presented in Gardner (1992) – see the Bibliography ('Documents about KADS – non-ESPRIT project 1098 sources').

Appendix 4 ESPRIT KADS and current research

This appendix summarizes three key issues to put KADS, as it is described in this book, in a wider context:

- Where KADS came from
- Where KADS is going
- Where this book fits

The first issue clarifies the origins of KADS, for those who need to know more than is described in the Acknowledgements. The second issue clarifies the on-going related research known about at the time of writing. The third issue clarifies how this book fits into the picture as an attempt to address the practical use of KADS.

A4.1 Where KADS came from

KADS was originally produced by the ESPRIT I Project 1098, which finished in March 1990. It was mainly based on research done at the University of Amsterdam on the modelling of expertise.[1] The result was a 'methodology' (or structured set of activities and their results) for KBS requirements analysis and design, based on a modelling paradigm. The core concept in this 'KADS-I' is Wielinga and Breuker's four-layer model of expertise. A notorious feature of KADS-I is the risk-driven spiral lifecycle model, adapted from Boehm's original. The overview definition of KADS-I is the M1 deliverable – see Bibliography ('Documents about KADS – public documents from ESPRIT Project 1098'). However, KADS-I is also infamous for having produced a large number of highly technical and difficult-to-understand documents attempting to describe the method.

The Acknowledgements section at the beginning of this book lists the organizations involved in the collaborative project. The Bibliography at the end lists the project's public deliverables.

A4.2   Where KADS is going

At the time of writing, KADS is already being used by *many commercial organizations* across Europe, both large and small. Numerous research papers and even some industrial case studies have been published (see Bibliography). Interest has started to be shown elsewhere in the world, especially in the USA. More particularly, BNR is also encouraging its use in Canada and the USA. *User group meetings* have been held in London (organized by Touche Ross Management Consultants and Lloyd's Register), Paris (organized by CAP Gemini Innovation), and Munich (organized by Siemens AG). The UK, French and German groups have planned to meet regularly. In addition, cross-fertilization has been encouraged between the groups, and the first joint meeting was held in Avignon, France, in June 1992. Finally, KADS-based *training courses* are commercially available from at least four organizations in the UK alone.

Where KADS is going is thus easily stated: *it is going into practice*. However, it is also the subject of further research.

The main research is in the form of an ESPRIT II project, number 5248, which started in October 1990 and is scheduled to finish in March 1994. It is based on a new and larger consortium of European academic institutions and companies, some of whom were involved in the previous ESPRIT I project. The key aims of the 'KADS-II' project at the time of writing are:

- To cover the complete KBS development lifecycle beyond analysis and design.
- To define ways of interworking with conventional software methods.
- To include formal techniques and modelling languages.
- To facilitate the production of an industrial-quality software tool (a 'workbench').

The KADS-II vision for the future is a so-called 'Common KADS' which will be a baseline definition of what a method must be to be 'KADS'. KADS as described in this book is expected to be compatible with this standard.

Another important KADS-related research activity is the UK's GEMINI project. This is sponsored by the CCTA and developed within a consortium of industrial partners. It is an attempt to define a 'framework for expert systems development'. Its key features are:

- Compatibility with SSADM (and, ideally, PRINCE).
- Risk-driven spiral lifecycle model.
- Project control guidelines.
- Detailed definitions of deliverables.

At the time of writing, GEMINI has yet to deliver its final results. Its role would seem to be somewhere between a technical development method and a project management framework, as defined in Section 9.1. It may be more important in the UK than in the rest of the world, although it contains some interesting and generally applicable ideas. The spiral lifecycle and some of the deliverables are derived from the ESPRIT I KADS project, among other sources.

Other methods undergoing research and development at the time of writing are also using KADS to a greater or lesser degree. VITAL, another ESPRIT II project, number 5365, is a typical example. They are taking some of the ideas in KADS and, together with other techniques, are developing a less grand, but in their view, more practical method for smaller developments.

The Bibliography cites sources for KADS-II, GEMINI and VITAL ('Other related methods').

A4.3   Where this book fits

This book describes a clarified and refined version of KADS-I. Although KADS has become widely used, the original deliverables from the ESPRIT I project are quite inadequate for practical use of the methodology for all but the most dedicated (or desperate!). This book addresses the deficiencies in the previously available documentation for KADS-I by being written with the following objectives:

- To refine and simplify the development process to be accessible and familiar to those with knowledge of conventional structured methods.
- To use existing, well-established and well-known development techniques and notations wherever possible rather than 're-invent the wheel'.
- To clarify obscure terminology with terms that mean what they say and reduce the amount of jargon.
- To complete the method with respect to the original description, including defining quality assurance checks, full model interrelationships, and step-by-step activities and results for Analysis and Design.
- To describe the method in a practical format – a developer's handbook.

To those readers with previous experience of KADS, the small but important number of terminology changes may be confusing at first. (However, it is interesting and reassuring to note that the KADS-II project has made very similar changes in terminology.) The Glossary provides ESPRIT I equivalent terms where required; in addition, the following list may prove helpful:

ESPRIT I KADS		*KADS in this book*
Modality Framework	→	Process Model + Cooperation Model + Expertise Model.
Conceptual Model	→	(Term not used.)
(Parts of Cooperation Model)	→	User Task Model, System Task Model.
Basic Task Model and Negotiation Space	→	Process Model (augmented dataflow diagrams).
External Requirements	→	Constraints (on the design and project as a whole).
(Parts of External Requirements)	→	System Overview (objectives, structure, functions).
Interpretation Model	→	Generic Task Model (GTM).
Knowledge Source	→	Inference Type.
Metaclass	→	Domain Role.

There are also a few more subtle and perhaps less important changes, such as the use in this book of the Domain Modelling Language in Analysis rather than Design; the clarification of the definitions of the various Inference Types and Domain Roles (in particular, removing the ambiguity between 'match' and 'compare' inferences, clarifying 'specify' by renaming it 'specialize', and avoiding difficult terms such as 'universum of observables'), etc.

Finally, an important point to note is that the improvements we have made to KADS-I for this book have been those we needed to make in order to use KADS in practice *ourselves* – they are based on our real-world experience of developing KBSs to industrial and commercial standards using the methodology. In fact, the book itself has grown out of our own in-house 'software engineer's handbook' for KADS.

Note

1. Wielinga, (1986); although a candidate seminal paper is perhaps Shreiber (1988b) – see Bibliography ('Documents about KADS – non-ESPRIT project 1098 sources').

Summary of notations

The following sections summarize notations one can use to document each KADS Analysis or Design result. This should be useful both as a memory-jogger for the types of result to produce from each activity and as a library of possible notations to choose from. There are three major sections:

- Analysis results and notations
- Design results and notations
- BNF description of the Domain Modelling Language (DML)

The notations presented below should not be taken as prescriptive – they are *suggestions*. The reader should check the full text (Chapters 4 and 7, particularly) for further possible notations and reasoning behind the notations presented here. However, in an attempt to help beginners in KADS and promote standardization, where there is more than one notation for a result below we state the 'preferred' notation first, based on our own experience and preference; alternatives are in parentheses.

The results and notations sections are ordered in the same sequence as KADS activities and results have been described throughout the book. Alternative notations are shown separated by semi-colons; complementary ones are separated by plus signs. Note that many objects can be documented using 'frames', with attributes contained in the slots of such frames.

After the results and notations a final section provides a BNF definition of the Domain Modelling Language (DML), as mentioned in Section 4.3.2. This can be used as a general-purpose knowledge-representation formalism in Analysis, for modelling static domain knowledge where a more specific representation is not available.[1]

Analysis results and notations

Process Model

The Process Model is split into two parts for its development, the Process Decomposition and the Process Distribution, but it is usually based on a single notation – augmented conventional Data Flow Diagrams (DFDs). If markers of ownership are simply added onto the Process Decomposition DFDs, the Process Model is just equivalent to the Process Distribution – shown as augmented DFDs.

KADS Analysis result		Notation
Process Decomposition	→	Conventional DFDs.
Process Distribution	→	Add agent labels to tasks and data/ knowledge stores on the Process Decomposition DFDs, to show 'ownership'.
Process Glossary	→	BNF; (Text; ERDs).

Cooperation Model

The Cooperation Model is split into three basic parts for its development: the User Task Model, the System Task Model and the User Interface Specification. Note that models of the tasks of other agents external to the system can be produced analogously to the User Task Model; likewise, interfaces for such agents can be produced as for the User Interface.

KADS Analysis result		Notation
User Task Model	→	State Transition Diagrams (STDs); (Role-activity diagrams; pseudo-code; JSD).
System Task Model	→	Pseudo-code; (STDs + pseudo-code; Statecharts; Role-activity diagrams; JSD).
User Interface Definition	→	Schematic diagram + *consists-of* hierarchy; (STDs; text).

Expertise Model

The Expertise Model is separated into four layers: Domain, Inference, Task and Strategy.

KADS Analysis result		Notation
Domain Layer	→	Appropriate knowledge structures (domain structures), using: e.g. facts, rules, networks, hierarchies, frames, models.
Inference Layer	→	KADS inference structure notation (see below).
Task Layer	→	Pseudo-code (declarative or procedural); (dependency diagrams; meta-rules).
Strategy Layer	→	Pseudo-code (declarative or procedural); (dependency diagrams; meta-rules).

KADS inference structure notation is similar to DFD notation. Boxes represent Domain Roles, which are analogous to data stores at the inference level; ovals represent Inference Types, which are analogous to tasks at the inference level. Domain Roles and Inference Types are connected in a directed graph, i.e. by arrows. Arrows represent the potential flow of knowledge to and from Inference Types. For each Domain Role and Inference Type, a frame can be used to document their contents:

KADS Analysis result		Notation
Domain Role	→	Box on Inference Structure + Frame, with slots: Name, Description.
Inference Type	→	Oval on Inference Structure + Frame, with slots: Name, Description, Method, Knowledge, Example.

The notation for Generic Task Models is the same as for Expertise Models, ignoring the Domain layer.

Constraints Document

Constraints in KADS are divided into many different categories. In addition, there may be many other types of constraint found in real systems not listed in this book. Most of them are simply best documented in text, although sometimes an appropriate diagrammatic notation can be supplemented.

KADS Analysis result	Notation
Constraints	→ Text + diagrams as required.

System Overview document

The System Overview can be basically described in text, although a central feature will usually be a schematic diagram to show the system concept in a readily comprehensible way.

KADS Analysis result	Notation
System Overview	→ Text + schematic diagram of system concept.

Design results and notations

Global System Architecture

The Global System Architecture is split into two parts: the definition of Sub-Systems and the definition of the Sub-System Interfaces. Sub-systems are distinguished, and may be documented, by *consists-of* relations and input–output relations, i.e. which sub-systems consist of which other sub-systems; and which sub-systems are connected to which other sub-systems (by control or data flows). It is also important at this stage to list the functions within each sub-system. For the definition of sub-system interfaces, one useful format is to separate requests to and from a sub-system; then under both these headings, document each flow according to which sub-system initiates the flow, what the name of the request is, what information is passed by the flow, and what action takes place following the flow. A frame format is particularly useful for the sub-system interfaces.

KADS Design result		Notation
Sub-Systems	→	Schematic diagram showing *consists-of* relations and input/outputs for sub-systems + list of functions per sub-system, cross-referenced back to Analysis results.
Sub-System Interfaces	→	Frame per sub-system, with slots: Initiator, Request, Source, Destination, Information, Recipient, Result; (or pseudo-code).

KBS Design framework

The KBS Design Framework can be basically described in text, although sometimes a more structured format may be appropriate, or a diagram may be useful, etc.

KADS Design result		Notation
KBS Design Framework	→	Text.

Functional Design Model

The KBS Functional Design Model requires the documentation of functional blocks of four basic categories, showing which blocks contain which functions, and which functions consist of which sub-functions, etc. This is best documented using a frame format, in a hierarchical arrangement. Each function should also be specified, using an appropriate DDL (Design Description Language) frame.

KADS Design result		Notation
Breakdown of functions	→	Hierarchical frame per leaf node block, with slots: Name of function, Type (problem-solving (P); domain model (K); data model (D); strategic control (C); support (S)).
Individual functions	→	DDL frame per function (see below) + input/output relation diagram; (or pseudo-code).

The latter ('individual functions') requires further comment. First, the input/output relation diagram simply shows the flow of information between groups of functions. One can use ovals to represent functions, and annotated arrows to show flows, direction and what information is flowing. These diagrams can help to illustrate the processes going on, which are not very visible in the frames. Second, there are DDL frames for each of the five categories of function. (Recall that from the four basic types: Problem-solving-type functions map onto Composite and Inference function frames; Storage type 'functions' map onto Domain/Data Model frames; Strategic Control and Support functions map onto their own frames.) These are summarized below:

KADS Design result		*Notation*
Composite Functions	→	DDL frame per function, with slots: Name, Type (composite), Goal, Input, Output, Activates, Activated by, Supports, Supported by, Control structure, Side effects.
Inference Functions	→	DDL frame per function, with slots: Name, Type (inference), Goal, Input, Output, Activates, Activated by, Supports, Supported by, Control structure, Side effects.
Domain/Data Model	→	DDL frame per item, with slots: Name, Type (domain/data model), Use, Composition, Created by, Used by, Accessed by, Destroyed by.
Strategic Control Functions	→	DDL frame per function, with slots: Name, Type (strategic control), Usage type, Description, Input, Output, Activates, Activated by, Control structure.
Support Functions	→	DDL frame per function, with slots: Name, Type (support), Usage type, Description, Input, Output, Activates, Activated by, Control structure.

Composite and Inference Functions' frames will also have an additional slot: 'Method' or 'Realized-by'; Domain/Data Model frames will have an additional slot: 'Representation'. These are not listed above because the values of these slots will only be filled in during Behavioural Design.

Note that the slots in the frames described above have been optimized for our own use. However, there is nothing inherently special about the choices we have made in their selection. Readers should feel free to choose their own slots but use our suggestions as a starting point.

Behavioural Design Model

There are two main suggested notations used to document the KBS Behavioural Design Model. The first is the Mappings Diagram, showing mappings between inference functions and design elements, via design methods and Domain Model items. (This diagram is optional.) The second is the augmentation of the Composite and Inference function block frames with 'realized-by' slots, showing the methods used to realize those functions; the augmentation of the Domain Model frames with 'representation' slots, showing the proposed knowledge representation or structure for those items. Optionally, one can also document inference methods with their own frames.

KADS Design result	Notation
[Mappings Diagram] →	Largely free-format diagram, showing the relationships between inference functions, domain model items, design methods (computational approaches), design elements[2] and knowledge representations or structures.
Function frame additions →	Add 'Realized-by' slots to Composite and Inference function DDL frames + add 'Representation' slots to Domain/Data Model DDL frames.
[Inference Methods] →	DDL frame per method, with slots: Realizes, Mechanism, Domain relation.

Again, the slots in the frames described above have been optimized for our own use. Readers should feel free to choose their own slots but use our suggestions as a starting point.

Physical Design Model

There are two aspects to the KBS Physical Design Model to document: the KBS Sub-system Architecture and the Module specifications. The former is best documented with a diagram, like the Global System

Architecture. The Module specifications may be documented with frames.

KADS Design result		Notation
KBS Architecture	→	Schematic diagram showing *consists-of* relations and input/outputs for modules; list of functions per module.
Module specifications	→	Frame per module, e.g. with slots: Name, Description, Elements, Called by, Calls, Algorithms, Data.

Again, the slots in the frames described above have been optimized for our own use. Readers should feel free to choose their own slots but use our suggestions as a starting point.

Domain Modelling Language (DML)

Below is a BNF (Backus-Naur Form) definition of the DML, followed by an alternative graphical format. (See Section 4.3.2.)

BNF description of the DML

Key:

< something >	:	The non-terminal denoting *something*.
{ something }	:	A non-empty list containing *something*.
[something]	:	Indicates that *something* is optional.
something	:	The terminal denoting *something*.
::=	:	Separates the antecedent (left-hand side) and the consequent (right-hand side) of a BNF rule.
;	:	Terminates a BNF rule.
|	:	A logical *or* in the consequent of a BNF rule.

< concept def>   ::= **CONCEPT** <concept name>
                    [**sub-type-of**: <concept name>]
                    [**attributes**: { <attribute function> }] ;

<relation def>   ::= **RELATION** <relation name>
                    roles: <role def>
                    [**sub-type-of**: <relation name>]
                    [**attributes**: { <attribute function> }] ;

\<role def\>	::= \<implicit role def\> | \<explicit role def\> ;
\<implicit role def\>	::= { \<construct name\> \<cardinality\> } ;
\<explicit role def\>	::= { \<role name\> = \<construct name\> \<cardinality\> } ;
\<set def\>	::= **SET** \<set name\> **members**: {\<construct name\>} \<cardinality\> [**sub-type-of**: \<set name\>] [**attributes**: { \<attribute function\> }] ;
\<structure def\>	::= **STRUCTURE** \<structure name\> **parts**: \<part def\> [**sub-type-of**: \<structure name\>] [**attributes**: { \<attribute function\> }] ;
\<part def\>	::= {\<part name\> = \<construct name\> \<cardinality\>} ;
\<atom-expr-def\>	::= **ATOMIC EXPRESSION** \<atom-expr-name\> **construct**: \<construct name\> [**attributes**: {\<attribute function\>}] ;
\<attribute function\>	::= \<attribute name\> -> \<value set name\> ;
\<value set name\>	::= boolean | natural number | integer | text | \<enumeration type def\> ;
\<enumeration type def\>	::= **VALUE SET** \<enumeration type def\> **values**: {\<value\>} **ordinal**: \<boolean\> ;
\<construct name\>	::= \<concept name\> | \<relation name\> | \<set name\> | \<structure name\> | \<atom-expr name\> ;

\<concept name\>	::= \<string\> ;
\<set name\>	::= \<string\> ;
\<structure name\>	::= \<string\> ;
\<relation name\>	::= \<string\> ;
\<atom-expr name\>	::= \<string\> ;
\<attribute name\>	::= \<string\> ;
\<value\>	::= \<string\> |
	\<number\> ;
\<cardinality\>	::= \<min\> , \<max\> ;
\<min\>	::= \<natural number\> ;
\<max\>	::= \<natural number\> | infinite ;

A graphical representation for the DML

The following items may be used to document using DML in a graphical form. It can either be used as an alternative to the basic frame notation or as an accessible complementary format.

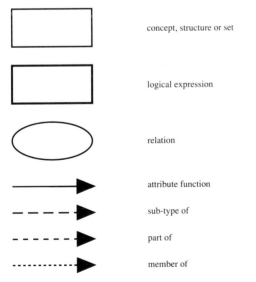

concept, structure or set

logical expression

relation

attribute function

sub-type of

part of

member of

Figure S.N.1 Suggested graphical representation of DML entities

Note

1. In fact, the DML was originally devised as a notation for knowledge representation in Design – see Appendix 4), but this is not its best application.
2. The Mapping Diagram is the only place the design elements are ever recorded, so if no Mapping Diagram is produced it is helpful to produce a specific list of design elements, cross referenced to the functions and stores they map onto.

Glossary

The following glossary of terms presents concise summary descriptions of the key specialized terminology used in this book. Cross-references are denoted by italics. General KBS terms have also been included where there may be ambiguity in the field. Note that certain KADS-specific terms are newly described in this book. KADS's origins in ESPRIT Project 1098 resulted in many difficult terms which have been changed and rationalized for this book. Where this has been done, a special note is made to indicate a change from the older ESPRIT terminology. This is only in order to satisfy those readers with some knowledge of ESPRIT KADS (see also Appendix 4).

Agent An entity which will carry out a task. An agent is usually the 'system' or 'user'. (But one can, in principle, consider other computer sub-systems, other people, or their groupings, as agents.) These are all *external agents*. One can also have *internal agents*.

AI *Artificial Intelligence*.

Analysis The phase of system development that is concerned with defining **what** the system will do. For example, equivalent to the 'Product Definition' phase of the *'V' model* software development lifecycle.

Analyze and Decompose Process The first activity of *Process Analysis*. It is concerned with eliciting and recording the basic problem-solving and cooperative process in the domain, leading to the construction of first parts of the *Process Model*, called the *Process Decomposition* and *Process Glossary*.

Analyze Environmental Constraints See *Environmental Constraints*.

Analyze Policy Constraints See *Policy Constraints*.

Analyze Static Knowledge The part of *Expertise Analysis* which is concerned with eliciting and recording basic facts about the problem-solving domain, eventually leading to the construction of the *Domain Layer* of the *Expertise Model*. Produces *Domain Structures*.

Analyze System Task(s)   The part of *Cooperation Analysis* concerned with identifying and recording the internal system task(s) and the flow of information between the *internal agents*. The output can be viewed as a refined version of the *User Task Model* – the *System Task Model*.

Analyze Technical Constraints   See *Technical Constraints*.

Analyze User Task(s)   The part of *Cooperation Analysis* which is concerned with identifying and recording the activities performed by the user and the information exchanged between user and system. The result is the *User Task Model*.

Artificial Intelligence (AI)   The larger field of which KBS is a specialization (or with which it overlaps). It concerns how one might build systems that exhibit 'intelligent' behaviour – part of that work is investigating what the nature of 'intelligence' is anyway!

Assemble Design Elements   The activity within *KBS Design* that is concerned with assembling the problem-solving design elements into physical code modules, and these modules into a physical KBS subsystem architecture.

Assign Design Methods   During this *KBS Design* activity the methods required to realize the KBS functions are selected and the associated design elements identified.

Assign Tasks and Data Stores to Agents   The second and final activity of *Process Analysis* that is concerned with assigning which *agent* 'owns' (holds, keeps, or is responsible for) which task and data stores, as the system and user interact. Results in the *Process Decomposition* augmented with agent assignments, called the *Process Distribution*. May impact on the *Process Glossary*.

Atomic expression   A construct of the *Domain Modelling Language*.

Attribute function   A construct of the *Domain Modelling Language*.

Backward reasoning   A general type of inference used by KBS, in which the system works backwards from a conclusion to its premises.

Behavioural Design   See *Assemble Design Elements*.

Behavioural Design Model   See *KBS Behavioural Design Model*.

Bespoke Systems   Systems specially developed for a specific client, requiring specific expertise in a specific domain for specific users. Also called 'one-off systems'. Cf. *generic systems*.

BNF   A widely used notation (more precisely, a meta-language) for describing the syntax of other languages or notations. Backus-Naur (or Normal) Form. See Naur (1963) in the Bibliography ('Miscellaneous').

Card Sort   A *multi-dimensional technique* for *knowledge acquisition* similar to, but simpler than, the *Repertory Grid* method. The Card Sort consists of classifying cards representing the domain concepts according to a dimension defined by the expert. The sorting process is repeated until the expert can think of no more dimensions.

CASE tool   Computer-Aided Software Engineering. A conventional software development support tool. One type consists of a general platform upon which specific diagram editors, etc. are run, sharing a common database. Another type consists of a more loosely coupled collection of tools that are able to share data. Finally, there are standalone tools with a specific purpose.

Causal Tracing   A type of diagnostic inference procedure. Typically used in the trouble shooting of mechanical/electrical devices, it works by modelling the device in question in terms of causal relationships – a common area for the application of KBS. See also *Localization*.

Composite Problem-Solving (PS) Function (or Task)   Functions specified in the *Problem-Solving Functional Block* which realize combinations of *Inference Types* specified in the *Expertise Model*. Composite PS Functions realize simple fixed internal control of the problem-solving process.

Concept/Entity/Class   A construct of the *Domain Modelling Language*.

Conceptual modelling framework   A way of viewing KADS Analysis as the construction of a series of three models: *Process Model*, *Cooperation Model* and *Expertise Model*. An old idea from ESPRIT KADS (ESPRIT KADS names: 'Conceptual Modelling Framework', 'Conceptual Model').

Constraints   All external constraints on the future system. Includes quantified and unquantified requirements. KADS categorizes constraints into groups which can be used as a checklist – the *Constraints Documents*.

Constraints Analysis   The part of KADS *Analysis* which is concerned with eliciting and recording *constraints* on the system. KADS provides a checklist of constraint types in the form of the *Constraints Documents*.

Constraints Document   The completed consolidated set of *Constraints Documents*.

Constraints Documents   A checklist of document (or section) titles covering the range of possible external *constraints* on the system and its development. The *Constraints Analysis* activity uses this checklist to ensure that all such constraints are or have been recorded by the end of the Analysis phase. Basic categories of constraints are *Environmental*, *Technical* and *Policy*.

Construct Expertise Model   The part of *Expertise Analysis* which is concerned with building and documenting the *Expertise Model*. New knowledge elicitation is primarily concerned with strategic, task and inference knowledge, eventually leading to the construction of the *Strategy*, *Task* and *Inference Layers* of the *Expertise Model*. The *Domain Layer* is derived from the *Analyze Static Knowledge* activity. Ideally, the model is built by a process of iterative refinement of the *Generic Task Model* selected at the start of *Expertise Analysis*. In practice, the actual construction process will vary.

Conventional Software   Software which is non-*KBS*. Typically built using methods such as Yourdon, SA/SD, JSD, etc. See *DP*.

Cooperation   In KADS, the concept that the user and system (and other *agents*, if present), when taken together, constitute a cooperating overall 'system' that is designed to achieve some problem-solving objective(s) by a process involving *interaction(s)*.

Cooperation Analysis   The part of KADS *Analysis* which is concerned with analyzing the cooperation/interaction between the system and user(s) in performing problem-solving tasks. Split into three sub-activities: *Analyze User Task(s)*, *Analyze System Task(s)* and *Define User Interface(s)*. Results in producing the *Cooperation Model* (ESPRIT KADS name: 'Modality Analysis').

Cooperation Manager   See *Strategic Control (Functional) Block* (ESPRIT KADS name: 'COMA').

Cooperation Model   The final result of *Cooperation Analysis*. It consists of *User Task Model*, *System Task Model* and *User Interface Specification*.

Data (classification of, in Cooperation Analysis)   Three types are distinguished: Information (data exchanged in the context of a specific session), Knowledge (data that are not situation-specific) and Skill (procedural data).

Data Flow Diagram (DFD)   A conventional software diagramming notation, showing a process as a set of tasks and information stores connected by flows of information. Adapted for use by KADS in *Process Analysis*.

DDL (Design Description Language)   A formalism or notation which can be used to record objects produced when following the KADS *Design* process. Based on a series of frames.

Decompose KBS Functions   Part of *KBS Design*, this activity consists of identifying and decomposing the functions that are required in the KBS sub-system. The relations between these functions are defined in terms of input–output.

Define KBS Design Framework   The part of the *KBS Design* which identifies the general technique or design context (often the implementation environment), that will be used to support the KBS sub-system design.

Define User Interface(s)   Part of *Cooperation Analysis*, this activity specifies the user–system interfaces (user interface). The input is the *User Task Model(s)*, and the result is a description of the constituents of the interface (which may be tested/confirmed by mock-ups or prototypes as necessary).

Design The phase of system development that is concerned with defining *how* the system will perform the tasks defined in the *Analysis* phase – down to the code module level of detail. For example, equivalent to the 'System- and Module-level Design' phase of the 'V' model development lifecycle.

Design element A component of a *Design Method*, such as an algorithm or data structure.

Design method In *Behavioural Design*, a computational approach that can be used to realize a *function (block)*. See also *problem-solving method* and *Design Methods Library*.

Design Methods Library Another name for the library of problem-solving methods, presented in Chapter 13.

Design of other Sub-Systems This part of KADS Design is responsible for producing a physical design for all other non-KBS sub-systems; these include user interface design and database system design. This design activity is not addressed in this KADS manual.

Detailed Design In terms of KADS, the final design phase required following the last activity of a KADS design (*Physical Design*). It is concerned with detailing the contents of the code modules. Sometimes called Technical Design; sometimes, perhaps even usually, considered part of coding.

DFD *Data Flow Diagram*.

DML (Domain Modelling Language) A formalism or notation used to represent the concepts and relations of the *Expertise Model's Domain Layer* (i.e. Domain Structures). Suggested as a 'default' knowledge representation when more specific notation is available. Frame-based, but with a graphical alternative. (In ESPRIT KADS, the DML was designed to be used in Behavioural Design.)

Domain An area or field of specialization where human expertise is used, and a KBS application is proposed to be used within it.

Domain Layer The bottom layer of an *Expertise Model*. The result of the *Analyze Static Knowledge* activity during *Expertise Analysis*. It consists of *Domain Structures* and describes basic concepts and their relationships as they occur in the domain, independently of how they may be used during problem solving.

Domain/Data Model An implementation-independent detailed specification of the contents of the *Domain Layer*. Could use the DML as a notation, but it is better to use knowledge representations closer to implementation environments. Part of the *Problem-Solving Functional Block* and produced within *Decompose KBS Functions*, where it can be viewed as the 'storage' equivalent to functions.

Domain Role A Domain Role describes the role(s) a packet of basic static domain knowledge may play in inference. Domain Roles are specified at the *Inference Layer*, and are groupings over knowledge recorded in the *Domain Layer* (ESPRIT KADS name: 'Metaclass').

Domain Structure   Part of the *Domain Layer* of an *Expertise Model* and a result of *Expertise Analysis*. It covers domain concepts and relations, usually expressed in networks like a *consists-of* or similar hierarchies. Domain Structures are simply the constituents of the Domain Layer. Domain Structures represent *Static Domain Knowledge*.

DP (Data Processing)   A commonly used term in computing used to refer to conventional systems and their development, using technologies such as COBOL, 4GLs, database and transaction-processing systems. In this book, contrasted with unconventional systems such as KBS. Sometimes also contrasted with conventional 'technical software', such as is found in embedded real-time systems.

Embedded (KBS) systems   Systems with at least one KBS sub-system or other KBS component, as opposed to a standalone KBS. In practice, the KADS methods may be used in conjunction with other software methodologies to develop such systems.

Environmental Constraints   Part of the *Constraints Documents* checklist which records environmental and other constraints arising from the different contexts the system passes through during development – includes present, development and operational environments. Produced by the *Analyze Environmental Constraints* activity within *Constraints Analysis*.

Evolutionary prototyping   An approach to KBS development where the complete system evolves from a series of usually fast analysis and implementation cycles. While as a system-development technique this approach does not complement the overall KADS modelling approach well, individual models are often usefully refined using evolutionary techniques. Generally, *throwaway prototyping* is found more useful in KADS.

Experimental prototyping   A form of prototyping used primarily to evaluate various options for the system's development, where a specific investigation is required. Often used during the *Design* phase in KADS.

Expert system   An alternative, but increasingly old-fashioned, or more specific term for a *KBS*. Especially covers those systems that mirror the problem-solving and cooperative behaviour of human experts, as opposed to just storing and processing any kind of knowledge.

Expertise   Expert knowledge – knowledge stored by human experts, especially that required to solve problems in some domain.

Expertise Analysis   The part of KADS *Analysis* which aims to produce a model of the problem-solving tasks performed in some domain, e.g. a model of a human expert's problem-solving abilities, produced by analysis of how he or she solves problems. Split into three sub-activities: *Analyze Static Knowledge*, *Select/Construct Initial Generic Task Model*(s), and *Construct Expertise Model*. Results in producing the *Expertise Model*.

Expertise Model   The final result of *Expertise Analysis*. A model of (required) problem-solving behaviour. It is made up of four layers: *Domain*, *Inference*, *Task* and *Strategy* (ESPRIT KADS name: '(4 layer) Model of Expertise').

Exploratory prototyping   A form of prototyping used primarily to gather information about the feasibility of an implementation option. Often used, in the form of mock-ups, in *Cooperation Analysis* and for prototyping the system's user interface.

External agent   An *agent* that is outside the system boundary. (The system itself can be considered equivalent to such an agent in some contexts, although it is not strictly external of course!) Typically the 'user', but one can, in principle, consider other computer sub-systems, other people, or their groupings, as external agents. Cf. *internal agent*.

Fagan inspections (QAC)   QAC techniques which occur at specified times in the development. They take the form of a group of people examining project documents against a checklist of quality checks.

Feasibility study   A *pre-analysis* activity, usually concerned with a shallow but broad study of the domain, with a view to determining the suitability for a (KBS) development. Not directly addressed by KADS, but some KADS techniques and objects can aid it, e.g. the *GTML*.

Focused interview   A knowledge-acquisition technique. The most common and the most akin to normal conversation. The interviewer asks the expert a series of questions which he or she has prepared earlier. The interviewer probes the expert on a number of topics at a high level.

Forward reasoning   A form of inference used by KBS where the system works forwards from its premises to a conclusion.

Four-layer model (Expertise Model)   Another name given to the *Expertise Model*, so called because it has four layers: *Domain*, *Inference*, *Task* and *Strategy*.

Frame   1. A type of knowledge representation, consisting of a named object which contains a set of attribute-value pairs called 'slots'. 2. A general format for describing many KADS entities based on such a format.

Function(al) (block)   A single, well-defined action that will be realized by a piece of software code. Documented in KADS using *Design Description Language (DDL)* frames. Appears in *Global Design* and *Functional Design*.

Functional Design   See *Decompose KBS Functions*.

Functional (Design) Model   See *KBS Functional Design Model*.

General-purpose systems   Systems which operate in a domain common to many (potential) clients' requirements and are therefore relatively domain-independent.

Generic systems   Systems, or libraries of sub-systems, which may be tailored to a specific client's requirements, both in terms of problem-solving and cooperation functionality, and domain.

Generic Task Model (GTM)   Generic Task Models are domain-independent *Expertise Models* – a normal *Four-layer model* minus the *Domain Layer*. They represent generic problem-solving tasks for KBS. The selection of a Generic Task Model is one of the early stages of *Expertise Analysis*, with the model selected being used as a template to drive much of the rest of *Expertise Analysis*. A library of such models is available – see *GTML* (ESPRIT KADS name: 'Interpretation Model').

Global Design   First part of KADS design, Global Design consists of two activities: *Specify Sub-Systems* and *Specify Sub-System Interfaces*. Results in *the Global System Architecture*.

Global System Architecture   Produced during *Specify Sub-Systems*, the Global System Architecture consists of a set of the sub-systems and embedded functions, and a definition of how the information or control flows between the sub-systems.

Global Tasks   The high-level components of the *Process* in some domain.

GTML (Generic Task Model Library)   A library of the Generic Task Models available in KADS at the time of writing is presented in Chapter 12 (ESPRIT KADS name: 'IML').

Heuristic   A form of rule which cannot be derived from first principles; a rule which has been captured on the basis of empirical evidence only.

Hybrid KBS   A KBS (sub-) system working in combination with any other types of system or other KBS (sub-) systems. See also *embedded KBS*.

Inference   In the field of KBS, inference is usually meant to cover any form of knowledge transformation or manipulation, including deduction, searching, classification, matching, etc., as well as the general process of inferring a consequence from antecedents or premises.

Inference Function   Functions specified in the *Problem-Solving Functional Block* which realize *Inference Types* specified in the *Expertise Model*. Inference Functions may realize more than one Inference Type.

Inference Layer   The layer above the *Domain Layer*, and below the *Task Layer* of an *Expertise Model*. One result of the *Construct Expertise Model* activity during *Expertise Analysis*. It consists of one or more *inference structures*. These describe knowledge of what inferences may validly be made using domain concepts and relations. (Not all valid inferences may be used in the actual problem-solving process – the Task

Layer defines these.) It is meta to the Domain Layer, because its structures are not simple pointers to objects in the Domain Layer, but describe their roles in inference, which is a description at a higher level of abstraction.

Inference method   See *Problem-Solving Method*. Also, the *Design Description Language (DDL)* frame that can be used to specify such a method.

Inference Step   An Inference Step describes the action of an *Inference Type* when the latter is executed. It defines the actual processing of the type of inference represented by the Inference Type, in terms of the *Static Domain Knowledge* being processed. Because it uses *Domain Layer* terms, it can be viewed as the 'Domain Layer manifestation' of an Inference Type.

Inference Structure   An Inference Structure is a connected series of *Inference Types* and *Domain Roles*, specifying how Domain Knowledge may be used in inference. There may be many or only one Inference Structure in the Inference Layer. Nesting of inference structures is an unnecessary complication for most domains, but may be found useful.

Inference Type   An Inference Type is a description of the way Static Domain Knowledge may be used to make inferences. It can be more usefully understood as a packet of inference – a basic, potential, 'step of inference'; the smallest piece of an inference process. Cf. *Inference Step* (ESPRIT KADS name: 'Knowledge Source').

Information Flow   In the context of the *Cooperation Analysis*, Information Flow means the transfer of data. There are three basic types of data in Information Flow: information (data used in the context of a specific session), knowledge (not situation-specific) and skill (procedural data) (ESPRIT KADS name: 'Interaction' or 'Ingredient Transfer').

Initiative   An initiative states which agent has the ability to start or instigate a task or process. Three types of information flow are possible: the owner of the initiative may be the sender of the information, or the recipient, or both agents may have the initiative (mixed initiative).

Internal agent   An *agent* that is inside the system boundary. Typically the 'User Interface', 'KBS (sub-system)', 'Database (manager)' and '(Non-KBS sub-) System(s)', but one can imagine many others possible. Cf. *external agent*.

Introspection   A knowledge-acquisition technique where the expert is asked to describe in detail how he or she would solve a problem. There should be very little intervention by the interviewer.

JSD (Jackson Structured Design)   A conventional software development method used in *DP*, some of the notations of which may also be found useful in KADS.

KADS   The set of KBS development methods described by this book. It stands for *KBS Analysis and Design Support* – but it is also conveniently (and less contentiously) used simply as a proper name (ESPRIT KADS name: 'KBS Analysis and Design Structured', among many others).

KBS   *Knowledge Based System* – any computer program which processes *knowledge*, such as human expertise in some domain requiring problem-solving skills, where the knowledge is represented explicitly within the system. First-generation KBS were often called *Expert Systems*, but there are no universally accepted definitions. Different categorizations of KBS have been used in this book: simple general types, types by problem-solving task and types by role played by the system.

KBS Behavioural Design Model   The activity *Assign Design Methods* produces the Behavioural Design Model. The model consists of a detailed description of the methods needed to realize all the KBS sub-system functions, together with a list of design elements required by each method.

KBS Design   The phase of KADS *Design* which aims at producing the design of the problem-solving parts of the system. Here the *Expertise Model* is mapped onto a physical sub-system architecture via *Functional, Behavioural* and *Physical KBS Design*.

KBS Design Framework   This provides a description of the technique, design context, or environment which will be used to implement the KBS system. It can also be loosely described as 'KBS Design guidelines'.

KBS Functional Design Model   This model is the result of the *Decompose KBS Functions*. It provides a graphical representation of the function blocks required to realize the KBS sub-system; the function blocks are arranged in a *consists-of* hierarchy. This model also includes a specification of the functional blocks supported with input–output relations.

KBS Physical Design Model   The Physical Design Model is produced during the final activity of *KBS Design*. The model assembles the design elements which were identified in the previous activity and recorded in the *Behavioural Design Model*. The Physical Design Model comprises the specifications of the KBS modules and a description of the KBS development environment.

Knowledge   Knowledge is a rich form of information, often stored by humans as expertise in some restricted domain, e.g. problem-solving skills such as medical diagnosis or resource scheduling. It is often represented as facts, assumptions, rules, concepts, etc.

Knowledge acquisition   A common KBS term – for this book's purposes it generally covers the activity undertaken by Knowledge Engineers to elicit information from an expert or user for the purpose of KADS modelling. It uses techniques such as interviewing and mock-ups and can also cover the elicitation of domain knowledge from relevant domain documents and other media. In practice, most people treat acquisition as synonymous with *knowledge elicitation*.

Knowledge elicitation   A common KBS term – for this book's purposes, it generally covers the extraction or filtering of relevant domain knowledge, as performed during *Expertise Analysis*. In practice, most people treat elicitation as synonymous with *knowledge acquisition*.

Knowledge engineer(ing)   A common KBS term – for this book's purposes it generally covers the activity of taking raw data (eg. from interview transcripts) and building a formal representation of them (eg. a KADS model). Thus it includes *knowledge acquisition/elicitation*. A 'knowledge engineer' is simply one who practises knowledge engineering.

Knowledge representation   The notation or formalism used for coding the knowledge to be stored in a *KBS*. The characteristics of the problem-solving knowledge determined in *Expertise Analysis* will affect the choice of its representation in the actual system. The four layers of an *Expertise Model* will normally be represented using different knowledge representations, as determined during *Design*.

Lexicon   A list of domain-specific terms and their definitions, i.e. a glossary. Can be built as a specific entry in the *Domain Layer* of an *Expertise Model*. Now largely subsumed by the *Process Glossary*, but the principle is still useful (ESPRIT KADS name: 'Lexicon').

Lifecycle   In the context of methodologies and system or software development, a description of the phases or stages that a system passes through, starting from the original idea to its operation, or even decommissioning. KADS has no specific lifecycle of its own, being a *technical development framework*. But the KADS methods may (and should) be used in practice within the framework of an appropriate product development lifecycle, in conjunction with a *project management framework*. The *'V' model lifecycle* is a simple form of lifecycle used in this book for illustrative purposes.

Localization   A form of troubleshooting inference procedure, where a complex system has components which may be tested independently of others. A common area for the application of *KBS*. See also *Causal Tracing*.

Matrix generation   A *multidimensional technique* used for *knowledge acquisition*. This uses a matrix in which rows and columns represent two dimensions. Pairs of elements are considered and the expert is asked to specify whether a relation between the two elements exists and its strength, and the type of fit. Explanations about the non-existence of relation should be provided as they often give valuable insight into the domain.

Method   1. A technical or non-technical software development technique. *KADS* and *PRINCE* can be considered collections of such methods. See also *methodology*. 2. A computational approach used to realize KBS functions in *Behavioural Design*. See also *problem-solving methods*.

Methodology   Although perhaps rather dubious English usage, now widely accepted as a term to describe a set of technical or non-technical development methods, such as *KADS* or *PRINCE*. In this book, we have succumbed to using 'methodology' as synonymous with 'set of methods'. (Where *method* is sense 1.)

Model   A representation of some non-trivial concept, designed to exhibit some behaviour which matches the behaviour of the real-world manifestation of the concept. For example, in requirements analysis, models are used to represent the required behaviour of the future system. KADS *Analysis* is based around three models; KADS *Design* uses four models.

Module   A logical block containing, or that will contain, software code.

Multidimensional techniques   This category of *knowledge-acquisition* techniques includes *Repertory Grid*, *Card Sorting* and *Matrix Generation*. Multidimensional techniques provide non-verbal information, and they often force the expert to think about the domain in a new way.

Neural networks   An unconventional type of computer architecture based on a connected set of simple computational units analogous to neuron cells found in biological systems. At the time of writing a hot topic of research, these systems have been found useful for performing tasks also suited to KBS approaches, e.g. generalization, classification, correlation, control, recognition and filtering. *Hybrid KBSs* with neural net components are a potent combination for sophisticated applications. KADS can help in identifying the appropriate parts of an application where a neural net approach would be most suitable – e.g. in the realization of an appropriate *Inference Type*.

Ownership   Ownership is a term used during *Process Analysis* and *Cooperation Analysis*. There are two variations: an *agent* may be said to 'own the *initiative* of a task' if it has the ability to start it; and it may be said to 'own the information' if it can supply some object required to complete a task.

Participant Observation   Participant Observation is a similar technique to *Self-report*, used for *knowledge acquisition*. However, with this technique the expert does not provide any verbal report while solving a problem. The knowledge engineer has to infer the meaning of the expert's actions.

Phase   Simply a major portion of a development *lifecycle* – the first level of breaking down a lifecycle is into a set of ordered phases.

Physical Design   See *Assemble Design Elements*.

Physical (Design) Model   See *KBS Physical Design Model*.

Policy Constraints   Part of the *Constraints Documents* checklist which records any miscellaneous policy considerations from the client, developer or sub-contractor, on the system during its development – includes standards, laws, etc. Produced by the *Analyze Policy Constraints* activity within *Constraints Analysis*.

Pre-analysis   The development phase that precedes KADS *Analysis*. Usually will include some sort of *feasibility study*, among other activities. KADS does not have **specific** applicability in this phase, but has some applications nonetheless.

PRINCE   A *project management framework* designed for use with SSADM and other technical development methodologies. Recommended for use with KADS as one possibility.

Problem-Solving (PS) (Task)   In KBS, a general term used to describe the act of seeking to achieve a goal (fixed state) by a process involving *inference*.

Problem-solving (function(al)) block   A group of functions which will provide the problem-solving functionality of the system. It will be part of the *KBS Functional Design Model* and *problem-solving methods* to realize it will be defined within *Assign Design Methods*.

Problem-solving method   In *Behavioural Design*, a computational approach that can be used to realize a *problem-solving (functional) block*.

Process   That collection of *tasks* and information flows between them and data stores, that describes the activities to be carried out in the domain by the user(s) and system (and any other *external agents*).

Process Analysis   The part of KADS *Analysis* which is concerned with analyzing the entire problem-solving process which must be performed by the user(s) and system together (and any other *external agents*). Thus, it includes a high-level analysis of how the system and user will cooperate, as well as an overview of the actual problem-solving tasks themselves. Split into two sub-activities: *Analyse and Decompose Process*, and *Assign Tasks and Data Stores to Agents*. Results in producing the *Process Model*.

Process Decomposition   The first result of *Process Analysis*. It includes a graphical representation of the processes that make up the overall cooperative problem-solving process that the system is designed to support. Usually documented using DFDs (Data Flow Diagrams). Complemented by the *Process Glossary*. It shows what tasks make up the process, and what sub-tasks make up those tasks, etc, and identifies data/

knowledge stores. Produced by the 'Analyze and Decompose Process' activity. The Process Decomposition is constructed using the results of pre-analysis work as a basis. Ideally in the Decomposition, tasks should be decomposed to a level where a unique assignment can be made between (usually) the system or user – for the *Process Distribution*. The analysis of the system should be computer-independent.

Process Distribution   The third and final result of *Process Analysis*. It is a graphical representation of the relationships between *agents* and tasks/ data stores identified in *Analyze and Decompose Process*. Can be documented by annotating the Process Decomposition DFDs. It shows who performs which tasks and who owns which stores. Produced by the *Assign Tasks and Data Stores to Agents* activity. The Process Distribution is constructed using the *Process Decomposition* as a basis. Tasks need to be decomposed to a level where a unique assignment can be made between (usually) the system or user, either when producing the Distribution or in the *Process Decomposition*.

Process Glossary   One of the first results of *Process Analysis*. Complements the *Process Decomposition*. It defines the data/knowledge stored and flowing around the Process Decomposition DFDs. Uses BNF notation. Acts like a data dictionary. Provides one starting point for eliciting static domain knowledge in *Analyze Static Knowledge*. Produced by the 'Analyze and Decompose Process' activity (Subsumes the ESPRIT KADS entity: 'Lexicon').

Process Model   Simply the collective term for the *Process Decomposition*, *Process Glossary* and *Process Distribution*. It is produced by *Process Analysis* activities.

Produce/Update System Overview   See *System Overview*.

Product Definition   In the *'V' model lifecycle*, the phase that matches KADS *Analysis*.

Project management framework   A complementary framework to a *technical development framework* (such as *KADS* or *SSADM*) which is required to structure large software development projects. Supports peripheral project issues to the actual development of the system. An example is *PRINCE*.

Prototype   Any relatively rapid (compared to the development of the complete system) implementation of any part of the target system functionality, or a simulation of the complete system. Contrast 'throwaway' prototypes with *evolutionary* ones. KADS finds use primarily for throwaway prototypes: *exploratory* and *experimental*.

QA (Quality Assurance)   See *QAC*.

QAC (Quality Assessment and Control)   The activity of finding and fixing all sorts of errors during development to ensure the construction of a high-quality system.

Rapid prototyping   Rather than meaning 'building prototypes quickly', usually refers to *evolutionary prototyping*.

Relation   In KADS, the term 'relation' is mainly used to describe the state of affairs which holds between domain concepts, i.e. a relationship between them. They are recorded in the *Domain Structure*. Relations include *is-a*, *consists-of*, *has-attribute*, etc.

Repertory Grid   This is one of the *multidimensional* techniques used in *knowledge acquisition*. With this technique a Repertory Grid describing all the domain elements relevant to the problem is obtained in the following way. The expert is asked to select two elements from a given domain triad and name one attribute which makes them similar and one which describes the third element. These pair of attributes form a bipolar construct. All other elements in the domain are then rated against this construct.

Requirements   See *Constraints*.

Requirements engineering   The capture and documentation of user requirements, design constraints, existing system features, etc. Sometimes includes the tracing of these throughout the development so that a feature in the implemented system can be mapped back onto one or more documented requirements. Equivalent in KADS to *Constraints Analysis*.

Road map diagrams   Diagrams used in this book that give a 'you are here' indication on a pseudo-Gantt chart representation of KADS *Analysis* or *Design*.

Role (in relation to agents in Analysis)   The way an agent (such as the system or user) performs a task it is involved within, in relation to the other agents it cooperates with, i.e. the role will depend on when and if the agent has control of the dialogue; the information it requests, receives and provides, etc.

RPES   Response Point Expert System. A help-desk type KBS. One of the systems we have built using KADS. It has been used in this book as a case study (see Part II).

Rule   A rule is a mapping of a set of conditions (antecedents) onto a set of conclusions (consequences).

SA/SD   Structured Analysis/Structured Design. A well-established form of software development method(ology) for conventional systems. Also known as the Yourdon method. Analogous to KADS.

Select/Construct Initial Generic Task Model   The part of *Expertise Analysis* which is concerned with the initial selection (or building) of the *Generic Task Model* (GTM). This will be used as the seed or template from which the *Expertise Model* will be constructed. The ideal situation is when a suitable GTM is directly found in the library (GTML). However, if necessary, a first GTM can be built up by using pieces of existing GTMs in the library. The aim of this activity is simply to obtain a basis from which the Expertise Model building process can commence (by its process of iterative refinement of the initial GTM – see *Construct Expertise Model*).

Self-report Self-report is one of the observational techniques for *knowledge acquisition*. The expert is asked to think aloud while solving a problem. The role of the knowledge engineer is to listen.

Shelley workbench A research prototype KADS CASE tool, or knowledge engineering 'workbench', i.e. a collection of specialized software tools, small application program modules, specially geared to supporting KADS activities. It was developed as part of the original KADS ESPRIT project. It is named after Mary Shelley, author of *Frankenstein, or The Modern Prometheus*.

Specify Sub-Systems This is the first activity of the *Global Design*. It provides a decomposition of the functions which the system must support into a set of discrete components. It distinguishes the KBS sub-system from the rest of the system.

Specify Sub-System Interfaces This is the second activity of *Global Design*. It defines the information flowing between the sub-systems and the control of these information flows.

SSADM Structured Systems Analysis and Design Method. An industry-standard software development method(ology) for conventional (primarily database-oriented) systems. Notable for its UK government support. Analogous to KADS.

STD *State Transition Diagram*.

State Transition Diagram (STD) A conventional software diagramming notation, showing a dynamic process as a set of states and trigger events that force movements between states. Adapted for use by KADS in *Cooperation Analysis*.

Static Domain Knowledge Knowledge stored in the *Domain Layer* of an *Expertise Model*. It consists of domain entities such as basic concepts, facts, relationships, etc. In KADS, represented by *Domain Structures*. A useful additional representation of such knowledge is a glossary or *lexicon*.

Storage (functional) block This is a group of functions which support knowledge and data storage in the KBS sub-system. It will be part of the *KBS Functional Design Model* and a representation suitable to hold the information stored will be defined within *Assign Design Methods*. (Methods to realize such functions are not an important issue compared with the representation formalism they should use.)

Strategic control (functional) block Also known as the Cooperation Manager, this is a group of functions which control the overall problem-solving/cooperation process at the highest level. Partly it realizes the *Strategy Layer* of the *Expertise Model*. Because of this, it is not required in all systems. When present, it is considered part of the *KBS Functional*

Design Model and a method to realize it will be defined within *Assign Design Methods*.

Strategy Layer   The top layer of an *Expertise Model*. One result of the *Construct Expertise Model* activity during *Expertise Analysis*. It contains strategic knowledge required to decide which Task Structures to use at the Task Layer and when. This is usually represented procedurally. If there is only one Task Structure, a Strategy Layer will be unnecessary. Note that strategic knowledge will often be very domain-specific.

Structured interview   A *knowledge-acquisition* technique used for eliciting detailed information. The interviewer asks the expert questions about his or her area of expertise (domain), continually asking for clarification, justifications, explanations, examples and counter-examples. The knowledge engineer probes the expert on a few topics in depth.

Sub-type relation   A construct of the *Domain Modelling Language*. It is a binary relation used to express sub-types (named smaller groupings) of a more general concept, e.g. 'sub-type(mammal, dog)' tells us that 'dog' is a sub-type grouping of the 'mammal' grouping.

Support (functional) block   This is a group of functions which support the overall problem-solving part of the KBS sub-system. It will be part of the *KBS Functional Design Model* and a method to realize it will be defined within *Assign Design Methods*.

Support knowledge   A type of *Domain Role* (and the knowledge it represents) that provides knowledge to control the way an *Inference Step* is carried out.

System- and Module-level Design   In the *'V' model lifecycle*, the phase that matches KADS Design.

System Overview   A statement of the overall system's objectives and required functionality. It is produced by the 'Produce/Update System Overview' activity in KADS *Analysis*. It takes its input from pre-analysis work, and makes changes if and when required, throughout Analysis. Some form of system overview should be available from the start of Analysis. The System Overview consists of four documents: Objectives of Prospective System, System Functions, Provisional System Structure, and Provisional Information Requirements.

System Overview Document   Another term for the result of *Produce/Update System Overview*.

System Task Analysis   See *Analyze System Tasks*.

System Task Model   Produced by *Analyze System Tasks*, it describes the internal information transfer between tasks within the system itself.

Tasks   Components of a *Process*. Tasks represent a set of functionality. See also *Global Tasks*.

Task Layer   The layer above the *Inference Layer*, and below the *Strategy*

Layer of an *Expertise Model*. One result of the *Construct Expertise Model* activity during *Expertise Analysis*. It consists of one or more *Task Structures*. These describe the order in which the inferences may occur at the Inference Layer. It is meta to the Inference Layer, because its structures are not simple pointers to objects in the Inference Layer, but describe their ordering in problem-solving tasks, which is a description at a higher level of abstraction.

Task Structure   A Task Structure defines the ordering of the inferences at the *Inference Layer* required to execute problem-solving tasks. It is usually expressed in terms of pseudo-code, meta-rules or dependency diagrams.

Technical Constraints   Part of the *Constraints Documents* checklist which records all the technical constraints arising from the different contexts the system passes through during development – includes knowledge base and other storage, database, user interface and hardware requirements. Produced by the *Analyse Technical Constraints* activity within *Constraints Analysis*.

Technical Design   Another name for *Detailed Design*.

Technical development framework   A complementary framework to a *project management framework* (such as *PRINCE*) which is required to structure large software development projects. Supports the actual system details. An example is *KADS* or *SSADM*.

Throwaway prototyping   An approach used in KBS development where prototypes are rapidly built for well-defined specific reasons, and discarded rather than being used as a part of the final system. Includes *exploratory* and *experimental* prototyping.

Tutorial interview   Tutorial interviewing is the simplest technique for knowledge acquisition. The expert is asked to give an introductory talk, or to provide a paper, about the main themes and ideas of the domain.

Types (typology) of information flows   A classification of the different types of *information flows* encountered in *Process Analysis* – includes 'information', 'knowledge' and 'skill'.

Types (typology) of Domain Roles   A classification of the most common *Domain Roles* found in *Inference Structures* to date (see Section 11.1.1).

Types (typology) of Inference Types   A classification of the most common *Inference Types* found in *Inference Structures* to date (see Section 11.2.1).

User-expert dialogue   This is an observational technique for *knowledge acquisition*. The existing expert and a potential user simulate the proposed system, using terminals, Teletypes or a simple screen to separate them. This technique offers a cheaper and less time-consuming alternative to prototypes.

User interface objects   Includes generic interaction devices found in user interfaces such as menus, buttons, dialogue boxes, windows, screens, forms, fields, etc.

User interface requirements In KADS, considered part of the *Technical Constraints.*

User interface specification (Definition) Produced by *Define User Interface(s),* it describes the logical specification of the user interface for the system, including what objects will be required and how they interrelate.

User Model An optional document produced during *Cooperation Analysis* where specific and detailed information is recorded about the classes of users of the future system. This is often useful when there is more than one class of users of the system.

User Task Analysis See *Analyze User Tasks.*

User Task Model Produced by *Analyze User Tasks,* it describes the information transfer between tasks within the Process, from the perspective of the user, i.e. the way the system and user will cooperate.

'V' model lifecycle The *lifecycle* used simply as a convenient framework for showing where KADS fits in terms of the software-development process. KADS is in no way restricted to use this lifecycle model. Pre-implementation phases are shown in waterfall lifecycle fashion; post-implementation phases are shown in reversed-waterfall fashion, forming the 'V'.

Value-set A construct of the *Domain Modelling Language.* A value-set contains members that are one of the types: string, natural number, integer, real or boolean.

Wizard-of-Oz technique A mock-up technique used when analyzing user interface requirements in (Technical) *Constraints Analysis* or *Cooperation Analysis.* With this technique, the expert is placed in one 'room' and the user/developer in another; they communicate via 'terminals', with the expert simulating the finished KBS; the analyst observes the interactions that take place during the expert consultation.

Bibliography

The following are suggested as useful sources of background and further information about KADS, structured KBS development, KBS techniques, and other topics related to the development of knowledge-based cooperative computer systems. The list is not exhaustive! A few of the items listed have been referred to directly earlier in the text; others, namely many of the ESPRIT Project 1098 public documents, have formed the original source material for much of this book. At the end of the Bibliography we have listed two potential sources of further information.

Documents about KADS – public documents from ESPRIT Project 1098

Analysis

op de Hipt, S. (ed.) (1989), *Primer of the Guidelines for Human Factors Engineering in the Development of Knowledge Based Systems*, ESPRIT P1098, part of Deliverable A6 (Task A6), NTE NeuTech, June.

Busche, R. (1988), *User Modelling in the Development of Knowledge Based Systems*, ESPRIT P1098, part of Deliverable A6 (Task A6), NTE NeuTech, May.

Breuker, J., B. Wielinga, M. van Someren, R. de Hoog, G. Schreiber, P. de Greef, B. Bredeweg, J. Wielemaker, J-P Billault, M. Davoodi and S. Hayward (1987), *Model Driven Knowledge Acquisition: Interpretation Models*, ESPRIT P1098, Deliverable D1 (Task A1), University of Amsterdam & STL Ltd., 1987.

Barthélemy, S., G. Edin, E. Toutain and S. Becker (1987), *Requirements Analysis in KBS Development*, ESPRIT P1098, Deliverable D3 (Task A2), Cap Sogeti Innovation.

de Greef, P., J. Breuker and T. de Jong (1988), *Modality: An Analysis of Functions, User Control and Communication in Knowledge-Based Systems*, ESPRIT P1098, Deliverable D6 (Task A4), University of Amsterdam.

Design

Walsh, P., P. Hesketh and T. Barrett (1989), *Integration of Human Factors in KBS Design Using KADS*, ESPRIT P1098, Part of Deliverable B4, STC Technology Ltd, December.

de Greef, P., R. Krickhahn, I. Perrot, T. Mulhall and R. Taylor (1989), *HCI Issues in KBS Design: Volume 2*, ESPRIT P1098, part of Deliverable B4, NTE NeuTech.

Schreiber, G., B. Bredeweg, P. Terpstra, B. Wielinga, E. Brunet and A. Wallyn (eds) (1989), *A KADS Approach to KBS Design*, ESPRIT P1098, Deliverable B6, University of Amsterdam and Cap Sogeti Innovation.

Schreiber, G., B. Wielinga, P. Hesketh and A. Lewis (1989) *A KADS Design Description Language*, ESPRIT P1098, Deliverable B7. University of Amsterdam and STC Technology Ltd, December.

Mulhall, T., G. Edin, M. Readdie and P. Rooke (1986), *A Review of Design Features of KBS and Proposals for Documentation Methods*, ESPRIT P1098, Deliverable D7 (Task B1), KBSC, Polytechnic of the South Bank.

Schreiber, G., B. Bredeweg, M. Davoodi and B. Wielinga (1987), *Towards a Design Methodology for KBS*, ESPRIT P1098, Deliverable D8 (Task B2), University of Amsterdam and STL Ltd.

Organisational issues

Taylor, R.M., D. Porter, F. Hickman, K-H. Streng, D.S.W. Tansley and G. Dorbes (eds) (1989), *System Evolution – Principles and Methods (The Life-Cycle Model)*, ESPRIT P1098, Deliverable G9, Knowledge Based Systems Centre, December.

Readdie M. and K-H. Streng. *Metrication Methods for KBS Development*, ESPRIT P1098, Deliverable G10, SD-Europe Ltd and NTE GmbH, December.

Siedka-Bauer, H.G. (1988), *Prototyping and the LCM*, ESPRIT P1098, Deliverable G13, SCS Organisationsberatung und Informationstechnik GmbH.

Drogemuller, A. and R. Busche (1990), *Operational Systems Issues*, ESPRIT P1098, Deliverable D1, NTE, January.

General and others

Hesketh, P.H. and T. Barrett (eds) (1990), *An Introduction to the KADS Methodology*, ESPRIT P1098, Deliverable M1, STC Technology Ltd, March.

Hayward, S., J. Breuker, R. Lane and J. Killin (1987), *The KADS Methodology: Analysis and Design for Knowledge Based Systems*, ESPRIT P1098, Deliverable Y1, STC Technology Ltd.

Wielinga, B., G. Schreiber and P. de Greef (1989), *Synthesis Report*, ESPRIT P1098, Deliverable Y3, UvA-Y3-PR-001, University of Amsterdam, March.

Anjewierden, A. (ed.) (1990), *Shelley Users Guide – version 1.0*, ESPRIT P1098, Technical Report, University of Amsterdam, January.

Documents about KADS – non-ESPRIT Project 1098 sources

de Alberdi, M. and J. Cheesman (1989), *The KADS Knowledge Based Systems Methodology*, ESPRIT 1989 Conference Proceedings, Kluwer Academic Publishers, pp. 500–10, December.

Anjewierden, A. (1987a), *Knowledge Acquisition Tools*, AI Communications, Volume 0, pp. 29–38.

Anjewierden, A. (1987b), 'The KADS system', in *Proc. First Knowledge Acquisition Workshop*, Reading, UK.

Anjewierden, A and J. Wielemaker (1989), 'An architecture for portable programming environments', in *Proc. NACLP '89 Workshop on Logic Programming Environments*.

Bredeweg, B. and B.J. Wielinga (1988a), 'Integrating qualitative reasoning approaches', in *Proc. ECAI–88*, Munich, West Germany.

Bredeweg, B. and B.J. Wielinga (1988b), 'Reasoning about physical systems: a unifying perspective', in *Proc. IMACS–88*, Paris.

Bredeweg, B. (1989), 'Introducing meta-levels to qualitative reasoning', in *Applied Artificial Intelligence*, **3–2**, New York.

Breuker, J.A. and B.J. Wielinga (1984), *Techniques for Knowledge Elicitation and Analysis*, ESPRIT P12, Deliverable 1.5.

Breuker, J.A. and B.J. Wielinga (1985), 'KADS: structured knowledge acquisition for expert systems', in *Proc. of the Fifth International Workshop on Expert Systems and their Applications*, Avignon.

Breuker, J.A. and B.J. Wielinga (1987), 'Use of models in the interpretation of verbal data', in Kidd, A.L. (ed.), *Knowledge Acquisition for Expert Systems – a practical handbook*, Plenum Press: New York.

Breuker, J.A. and B.J. Wielinga (1989), 'Model driven knowledge acquisition', in Guida, P. and G. Tasso (eds), *Topics in the Design of Expert Systems*, North-Holland: Amsterdam.

Farrell, V.A.M. (1992), 'The Response Point expert system: a mixed initiative user interface', in *Proc. 1st International Workshop on User Interfaces for Expert Systems*, London, 11–12 March.

Gardner, K. (1992), 'KADS OBJECT^{TM}', presented at the second meeting of the UK KADS User Group, Lloyd's Register, Croydon, UK, 29 September.

Georges, M. (1992a), 'Knowledge engineering trends in Europe', in *Current Developments in Knowledge Acquisition, EKAW '92*, Proc. of the 6th European Knowledge Acquisition Workshop, Heidelberg and Kaiserlautern, Germany, May 1992, published as Lecture Notes in *Artificial Intelligence* No.599, Springer-Verlag: Berlin. (Other KADS-related papers also in proceedings.)

Georges, M. (1992b), 'KADS, then and now', presented at the inaugural meeting of the UK KADS User Group, Touche Ross Management Consultants, London, 31 March.

de Greef, P. and J.A. Breuker (1985), 'A case study in structured knowledge acquisition', *Proc.of the 9th IJCAI*, pp. 390–2, Los Angeles.

de Greef, P., G. Schreiber and J. Wielemaker (1988a) 'StatCons een case study in gestructureerde kennisacquisitie', in *Proc. NAIC–88*, University of Amsterdam, Netherlands.

de Greef, P., J. Breuker, G. Schreiber and J. Wielemaker (1988b), 'StatCons: knowledge acquisition in a complex domain', in *Proc. ECAI '88*, Munich, West Germany.

de Greef, H.P. (1989), 'Cooperative statistical problem solving', ESPRIT P1098, Technical Report: B4.1, UvA-B4-W-00l, University of Amsterdam, paper presented at the Second International Workshop on AI and Statistics, February.

Hayball, C.C. (1988), 'Skills support in the ICL Kidsgrove Bonding Shop: a case study in the application of the KADS methodology', in *Proc. Human and Organisational Issues of Expert Systems*, Stratford, UK.

Hayball, C.C. (1990), 'Building expert system applications using the KADS methodology: the synthesis of expertise', in E. Balagwusamy and J.A.M. Howe (eds), *Expert Systems for Management and Engineering*, Ellis Horwood: Chichester.

Hesketh, P.G. and J.C. Cheesman (1990), 'A model for the analysis of planning tasks', in *Proc. 9th UK Planning SIG Workshop*, Nottingham, UK.

Hickman, F., J. Killin, L. Land, T. Mulhall, D. Porter and M. Taylor (1989), *Analysis for Knowledge Based Systems – a practical guide to the KADS methodology*, Ellis Horwood: Chichester.

Land, L. (ed.) (1992), *KADS Bulletin*, published as part of the KADS-II ESPRIT project number 5248, Touche Ross Management Consultants, London, Issue 1, June.

Martil, R. (1992) 'KADS-II and CommonKADS: a progress report', presented at the BCS Specialist Group on Expert Systems KBS Methodologies Interest Group Seminar, Lloyd's Register, Croydon, UK, 20 May.

Mayle, D.T. (1989), *The Application of an Expert System to a New Domain*, MSc Project Dissertation, The Polytechnic of the South Bank, London.

Schreiber, G., J. Breuker, B. Bredeweg and B.J. Wielinga (1988a), 'Modelling in KBS development', in *Proc. 2th European Knowledge Acquisition*, Bonn, West Germany.

Schreiber, G., J. Breuker, B. Bredeweg and B.J. Wielinga (1988b), 'Modelling in KBS development', in *Proc. 8th Expert Systems Workshop*, Avignon, France.

Tansley, D.S.W. and V.A.M. Farrell (1991), 'Requirements analysis for KATE using KADS', in *Proc. 1st International Workshop on Knowledge-Based Systems Methodologies*, London, 3–4 December. (Other KADS-based case studies also in proceedings.)

Taylor, R.M., C. Bright, R. Martil and R. de Hoog (1991), 'The management of knowledge-based systems development and maintenance under KADS-II', in Graham, I. and Milne, R.W. (eds), *Proc. Expert Systems '91, Research and Development in Expert Systems VIII*, London, September. (Other KADS-related papers also in proceedings.)

Wielemaker, J. and A. Anjewierden (1989), 'Separating user interface and functionality using a frame based data model', in *Proc. Second Annual Symposium on User Interface Software and Technology*, ACM Press: Williamsburg, VA.

Wielinga, B.J. and J. Breuker (1984), 'Interpretation of verbal data for knowledge acquisition', in O'Shea, T. (ed.), *Advances in Artificial Intelligence*, Elsevier Science: Amsterdam.

Wielinga, B.J. and J. Breuker (1986), 'Models of expertise', in *Proc. ECAI '86*, Brighton, UK.

Wielinga, B.J. and B. Bredeweg (1988), 'Knowledge and expertise in expert systems', in van der Veer, G.C. and Malder, G. (eds), *Human–Computer Interaction: Psychonomics Aspects*, Springer-Verlag: Berlin.

Wielinga, B.J., B. Bredeweg and J.A. Breuker (1988), 'Knowledge acquisition for expert systems', in Nossum, R.T. (ed.), *Advanced Topics in Artificial Intelligence (ACAI–87)*, Springer-Verlag: Berlin.

Wielinga, B.J., H. Akkermans, G. Schreiber and J. Balder (1989), 'A knowledge acquisition perspective on knowledge-level models', in *Proc. Knowledge Acquisition Workshop KAW '89*, Banff, Canada.

Wielinga, B.J. and G. Schreiber (1989), 'Future directions in knowledge acquisition', in *Proc. Expert Systems '89*, London.

Wielinga, B.J., A.Th. Schreiber and J.A. Breuker (1992), 'KADS: a modelling approach to knowledge engineering', *Knowledge Acquisition*, **4**, March, 5–53. (The whole issue of the journal is dedicated to KADS.)

Documents about KBS technology

Problem-solving methods and knowledge representation

Barr, A. and E.A. Feigenbaum (1981), *The Handbook of Artificial Intelligence* (3 vols), Pitman: London. (This book is especially useful as a support to chapter 13.)

Charniak, E. and D. McDermott (1985), *Introduction to Artificial Intelligence*, Addison-Wesley: Wokingham.

Clancey, W.J. (1985), 'Heuristic classification', *Artificial Intelligence*, **27**, December, 289–350.

Engelmore, R.S and A.J. Morgan (1988), *Blackboard Systems*, Addison-Wesley: Wokingham.

Forbus, K.D. (1988), 'Intelligent computer aided engineering', *AI Magazine*, Fall, 23–36. (See also 'Documents about KADS' above for other sources on qualitative reasoning.)

Newell, A. and H.A. Simon (1972), *Human Problem Solving*, Prentice Hall, Englewood Cliffs, NJ.

Ng, K.-C. and B. Abramson (1990), 'Uncertainty management in expert systems', *IEEE Expert*, April, 29–48.

Rich, E. and K. Knight (1991), *Artificial Intelligence*, McGraw-Hill: New York. (Like Barr and Feigenbaum, 1981, this is especially useful as a support to Chapter 13.)

Ringland, G.A. and D.A. Duce (eds) (1988), *Approaches to Knowledge Representation: An Introduction*, Research Studies Press/John Wiley, Letchworth.

Knowledge acquisition

Cleaves, D.A. (1987), 'Cognitive biases and corrective techniques for knowledge based systems', *International Journal of Man–Machine Studies*, No. 27, 155–66.

Diaper, D. (ed.) (1989), *Knowledge Elicitation: Principles, Techniques and Applications*, Ellis Horwood: Chichester.

Hart, A. (1986), *Knowledge Acquisition for Expert Systems*, Kogan Page: London.

Other relevant KBS topics

Born, G. (1988), *Quality in Expert System Development*, Systems Designers AI Business Centre, Camberley, Surrey, GU15 3XD.

Bratko, I. (1990), *Prolog Programming for Artificial Intelligence*, Addison-Wesley: Wokingham.

Chandrasekaran, B. (1987), 'Towards a functional architecture for intelligence based on generic information processing tasks', in *Proc 10th IJCAI*, Milan.

Hayball, C.C. (1991), 'Dialogue specification for knowledge based systems', in Duce, D.A., M.R. Gomes, F.R.A. Hopgood and J.R. Lee (eds) *User Interface Management and Design*, Springer-Verlag: Berlin.

Jackson, P. (1990), *Introduction to Expert Systems*, 2nd edn, Addison-Wesley: Wokingham.

Laufmann, S.C., D.M. DeVaney and M.A. Whiting (1990), 'A methodology for evaluating potential KBS applications', *IEEE Expert*, December, 43–62.

Sterling, L. and E. Shapiro (1986), *The Art of Prolog: Advanced Programming Techniques*, MIT Press: Cambridge, MA.

Wilson, M., D. Duce and D. Simpson (1989), 'Life cycles in software and knowledge engineering: a comparative review', *The Knowledge Engineering Review*, **4**(3), 189–204.

Waterman, D.A. (1986), *A Guide to Expert Systems*, Addison-Wesley: Wokingham.

Documents about other related methods

Harris-Jones, C. and I. Graham (1991), 'Introduction to Gemini', in *Proc. 1st International Workshop on Knowledge-Based Systems Methodologies*, London, 3–4 December. (Other GEMINI sources are expected to be available in the UK soon.)

The Informatics Resource Centre (1991), *Projects in Controlled Environments – PRINCE*, course notes, The Informatics Resource Centre, 2 The Chapel, Royal Victoria Patriotic Building, Fitzhugh Grove, London, 5 March. (Other PRINCE sources can be obtained from the CCTA in the UK.)

Spee, J.W., M. Koopman, W. Jonker and L. Veld (1991), 'The VITAL conceptual modelling and design approach', in *Proc. 1st International Workshop on Knowledge-Based Systems Methodologies*, London, 3–4 December. (VITAL papers are starting to appear more widely at AI conferences.)

Documents about conventional software engineering

Boehm, B. (1988), 'A spiral model of software development and enhancement', *IEEE Computer*, **21**, May, 61–72.

Checkland, P. (1981), *Systems Thinking, Systems Practice*, John Wiley: Chichester.

Chen, P.P.S. (1976), 'The entity relationship model – toward a unified view of data', *ACM Transactions on Database Systems*, **1**, 9–36.

Gibson, R. (1992), *Managing Computer Projects – Avoiding the Pitfalls*, The BCS Practitioner Series, Prentice Hall, Hemel Hempstead.

Harel, D. (1988), 'On visual formalisms', *Communications of the ACM*, **31**, May, 514–530.

Hares, J.S. (1990), *SSADM for the Advanced Practitioner*, John Wiley: Chichester.

McDermid, J.A. (ed.) (1991), *Software Engineer's Reference Book*, Butterworth-Heinemann: Oxford.

Page-Jones, M. (1988), *The Practical Guide to Structured Systems Design*, 2nd edn, Prentice Hall, Englewood Cliffs, NJ.

Paulk, M.C., B. Curtis and M.B. Chrissis (1991), *Capability Maturity Model for Software*, Technical Report CMU/SEI–91-TR–24, Software Engineering Institute, Carnegie Mellon University, Pittsburgh, PA, August.

Pressman, R. (1987), *Software Engineering: A Practitioner's Approach*, McGraw-Hill: New York.

Sommerville, I. (1989), *Software Engineering*, 3rd edn, Addison-Wesley: Wokingham.

Yourdon, E. (1989) *Modern Structured Analysis*, Prentice Hall, Englewood Cliffs, NJ.

Miscellaneous

Bates, P.E. (1989), 'Prototyping: a motivation', in *Rapid Prototyping for the Software Developer*, part of the Seminar Series on New Directions in Software Development, Wolverhampton Polytechnic, UK, April.

Fagan, M. (1976), 'Design and code inspections to reduce errors in program development', *IBM Systems Journal*, **15**, July, 182–211.

Floyd, C. (1984), 'A systematic look at prototyping' in Budde, R., K. Kuhlerkamp, L. Mathiassen and H. Zullighoven, *Approaches to Prototyping*, Springer-Verlag: Berlin.

Graham, I. (1991), *Object Oriented Methods*, Addison-Wesley: Wokingham.

Helander, M. (1988), *Handbook of Human–Computer Interaction*, North-Holland: Amsterdam.

ISO 9000–3: 1991. Quality Systems – Guide to the application of ISO 9000–1 to the development, supply and maintenance of software. (UK equivalent is BS 5750: Part 13: 1991.)

Naur, P. (ed.) (1963), 'Revised Report on the algorithmic language Algol 60', *Communications of the ACM*, **6**. January, 1–17. (Contains definition of BNF notation.)

Schneiderman, B. (1987), *Designing the User Interface: Strategies for Effective Human–Computer Interaction*, Addison-Wesley: Wokingham.

Further information sources

In its role as project librarian for both KADS ESPRIT projects, the following organization will supply KADS-I and KADS-II public deliverables for a small charge throughout the world, and updates on the progress of the ESPRIT II project:

KADS Information,
Touche Ross Management Consultants,
Peterborough Court,
133 Fleet Street,
London, EC4A 2TR,
UK.
Tel: +44 71 936 3000
Fax: +44 71 583 1198

Alternatively, in case of difficulty, try contacting:

KADS Information,
Software and Systems Engineering Group,
BNR Europe Limited,
London Road,
Harlow,
Essex, CM17 9NA,
UK.
Tel: +44 279 429531
Fax: +44 279 441551

Index